Making Cultural Cities in Asia

T0330642

This book examines the vast and largely uncharted world of cultural/creative city-making in Asia. It explores the establishment of policy models and practices against the backdrop of a globalizing world, and considers the dynamic relationship between powerful actors and resources that impact Asian cities.

Making Cultural Cities in Asia approaches this dynamic process through the lens of assemblage: how the policy models of cultural/creative cities have been extracted from the flow of ideas, and how reinvented versions have been assembled, territorialized, and exported. This approach reveals a spectrum between globally circulating ideals, on the one hand, and place-based contexts and contingencies, on the other. At one end of the spectrum, this book features chapters on policy mobility, in particular the political construction of the 'web' of communication and the restructuring or rescaling of the state. At the other end, chapters examine the increasingly fragmented social forces, their changing roles in the process, and their negotiations, alignments, and resistances.

This book will be of interest to researchers and policy-makers concerned with cultural and urban studies, creative industries, and Asian studies.

June Wang is Assistant Professor of Urban Studies in the Department of Public Policy at City University of Hong Kong.

Tim Oakes is Professor of Geography and Director of the Center for Asian Studies at the University of Colorado, Boulder, USA.

Yang Yang is a PhD candidate at the Department of Geography, University of Colorado, Boulder, USA.

Regions and Cities

Series Editor in Chief:

Susan M. Christopherson, *Cornell University, USA*

Editors:
Maryann Feldman, *University of Georgia, USA*
Gernot Grabher, *HafenCity University Hamburg, Germany*
Ron Martin, *University of Cambridge, UK*
Martin Perry, *Massey University, New Zealand*
Kieran P. Donaghy, *Cornell University, USA*

In today's globalized, knowledge-driven and networked world, regions and cities have assumed heightened significance as the interconnected nodes of economic, social and cultural production, and as sites of new modes of economic and territorial governance and policy experimentation. This book series brings together incisive and critically engaged international and interdisciplinary research on this resurgence of regions and cities, and should be of interest to geographers, economists, sociologists, political scientists and cultural scholars, as well as to policy-makers involved in regional and urban development.

For more information on the Regional Studies Association visit www. regionalstudies.org.

There is a **30% discount** available to RSA members on books in the *Regions and Cities* series, and other subject-related Taylor and Francis books and e-books, including Routledge titles. To order, just email alex.robinson@tandf.co.uk, or phone +44 (0) 20 7017 6924 and declare your RSA membership. You can also visit www.routledge.com and use the discount code: **RSA0901**.

Making Cultural Cities in Asia

Mobility, assemblage, and
the politics of aspirational urbanism

Edited by June Wang,
Tim Oakes, and Yang Yang

Routledge
Taylor & Francis Group

LONDON AND NEW YORK

First published 2016
by Routledge

2 Park Square, Milton Park, Abingdon, Oxfordshire OX14 4RN
711 Third Avenue, New York, NY 10017

Routledge is an imprint of the Taylor & Francis Group, an informa business

First issued in paperback 2018

British Library Cataloguing in Publication Data
A catalogue record for this book is available from the British Library

Library of Congress Cataloging in Publication Data
Making cultural cities in Asia : mobility, assemblage, and the politics of aspirational
urbanism / edited by June Wang, Tim Oakes and Yang Yang. – First Edition.
    pages cm
Includes bibliographical references and index.
1. Urban renewal–Asia.   2. Asia–Cultural policy.   I. Wang, June, 1942 June
4- editor.   II. Oakes, Tim, editor.
HT178.A78M35 2015
307.3'416095–dc23   2015024396

ISBN: 978-1-138-84872-6 (hbk)
ISBN: 978-1-138-36034-1 (pbk)

Typeset in Times New Roman
by Keystroke, Station Road, Codsall, Wolverhampton

Contents

Illustrations

Figures

Tables

Contributors

Jay E. Bowen is a PhD candidate in the Department of Geography at the University of Kentucky, where he maintains interests in critical human geography and political ecology. Focusing on South Korea, he pays particular attention to what the neoliberal turn means for post-developmental states, while considering the 'neoliberalization' of nature in this context. In his dissertation research he studies urban agriculture in Seoul's green belt. Examining the recent promotion and implementation of urban farming initiatives in the region, he explores how these measures restructure local agriculture, and how new agricultural actors add their labour to these initiatives to produce a locally specific, path-dependent iteration of neoliberal urbanization.

T.C. Chang is Associate Professor of Geography at the National University of Singapore. His research focuses on tourism innovations in Singapore and regional tourism in Southeast Asia. His other research interests include gentrification and urban redevelopment, arts, culture, and heritage. He is the co-editor of *Interconnected Worlds:Tourism in Southeast Asia* (2001) and *Asia on Tour: Exploring the Rise of Asian Tourism* (2008).

Dwiparna Chatterjee is a doctoral candidate in Sociology in the Humanities and Social Science Department, Indian Institute of Technology, Bombay. She works on gentrification around the textile mill lands of Mumbai. Her other research interests include everyday life, ethnography of cities, qualitative studies, space and time, and place-making.

Diganta Das is Assistant Professor of Human Geography at the National Institute of Education, Nanyang Technological University, Singapore. His research focuses on the political economy of India, urban processes of South Asia, liveability and sustainability of Asian cities, and city branding and policies. He has been involved in several research projects in relation to urbanizing Asia, including a major project titled Asian Cities: Liveability, Sustainability and Diversity. His work has been published in several journals and also as book chapters.

Xin Gu is a lecturer in the School of Media, Film and Journalism at Monash University. Prior to joining Monash, she was Research Fellow at the University of Melbourne, and Senior Research Associate at Queensland University of Technology. She has published papers in the *International Journal of Cultural Policy*, the *Information Society*, the *International Journal of Cultural Studies*, and *Culture Unbound*, as well as chapters in several edited volumes. She is currently working on a joint-authored book provisionally titled *Culture and Economy in the New Shanghai*.

Agnes Shuk-mei Ku is Associate Professor of Social Science and Associate Dean of the School of Humanities and Social Science at the Hong Kong University of Science and Technology. She is also a faculty associate in the Center for Cultural Sociology, Yale University. Her research interests are cultural sociology, civil society, Hong Kong culture and politics, gender issues, and urban space in Chinese cities. Recent publications include *Hong Kong Mobile: Making a Global Population* (with Helen F. Siu) and *Remaking Citizenship in Hong Kong: Community, Nation, and the Global City* (with Pun Ngai).

Joanne B.Y. Lim is Associate Professor of Communication and Media Studies at Monash University Malaysia. Her teaching and research focus on areas of interculturality, creative industries, new/social media, youth identities and engagement, and participatory culture within the Southeast Asian context. She has authored numerous peer-reviewed journal articles and book chapters, including 'Mobile Media and Youth Engagement in Malaysia' (2014), 'East Asian Trends: Negotiating Youth Identities, Culture and Citizenship in Malaysia' (2014), 'Rhizomatic Behaviours in Social Media: V-logging and the Independent Film Industry in Malaysia' (2013), and 'Videoblogging and Youth Activism in Malaysia' (2013).

Cheng-Yi Lin is Associate Professor of Urban and Regional Planning in the Department of Social and Regional Development at the National Taipei University of Education, Taipei, Taiwan. He is a qualified urban planner and was previously a government officer of the Urban Development Bureau at Taipei City Government. His research focuses on the creative city, the economic geography of cultural creative industries, and culture-led urban regeneration in Asian cities. He has published in *Urban Studies* on culture-led urban regeneration and community mobilization and on the evolution of Taipei's music industry. Recent research projects focus on the innovative practices of the creative industries and the institutional innovation of urban development from the evolutionary perspective.

Jason Luger is a PhD researcher at King's College London and the National University of Singapore (jointly). His research focuses on the relationship between 'creative city' policy and the creative grassroots in Singapore, particularly in regards to cultural activism and resistance, and, more broadly, conceptions of space and place-making in relation to specific cultural policies. His work has been published in the *International Journal of Urban and Regional Research* and he has co-authored work on community-based organizations and city planning and sustainable urban environments.

Margit Mayer was Professor for Comparative and North American Politics at the Freie Universität, Berlin, and, as of 2014, she is an Associate Professor at the Center for Metropolitan Studies at the Technical University, Berlin. Her research focuses on comparative, urban, and social politics as well as social movements. She has published on various aspects of contemporary urban politics, urban theory, (welfare) state restructuring, and social movements. She co-authored *Nonprofits in the Transformation of Employment Policies* (2004) and co-edited *Urban Movements in a Globalising World* (2000), *Cities for People Not for Profit* (2012), and *Neoliberal Urbanism and Its Contestations* (2012). Currently she is writing a monograph on urban social movements and the state.

Tim Oakes is Professor of Geography and Director of the Center for Asian Studies at the University of Colorado, Boulder, USA. His research focuses on China's regional cultural development, culture industries, tourism, heritage, and place-based identities. In addition to writing numerous journal articles and book chapters, he is the author of *Tourism and Modernity in China* (1998) and co-editor of several volumes, including *Translocal China* (2006), *Travels in Paradox* (2006), *Reinventing Tunpu: Cultural Tourism and Social Change in Guizhou* (in Chinese, 2007), *The Cultural Geography Reader* (2008), *Faiths on Display* (2010), and *Real Tourism* (2011).

Justin O'Connor is Professor of Communication and Cultural Economy in the School of Media, Film and Journalism, Monash University, Melbourne, Australia. He has written numerous articles, reports, and books on the cultural and creative industries, creative cities and urban regeneration in Europe, Australia, Russia, and China (especially Shanghai). He has just published *The Routledge Companion to the Cultural Industries* (with Kate Oakley) and is preparing two books, *Culture and Economy in the New Shanghai* (with Xin Gu) and *After Creative Industries*.

Se Hoon Park is a research fellow at the Korea Research Institute for Human Settlements. He earned his PhD in Urban Planning at Seoul National University and studied urban policy and planning at the University of Tokyo. While engaging in numerous national urban projects, he continued to focus on his own interests in culture-led urban regeneration, ethnic districts in Korean cities, and inter-city networks in East Asia. He has authored numerous journal articles, book chapters, and policy reports, including *Cultural Cluster Strategy as a Tool for Urban Revitalization* (2011), *Incheon-Qingdao Intercity Network and Implications for Building a Trans-border Region* (2011), and *Reinventing Urban Policies in Response to Ethnic Diversity* (2009).

Devanathan Parthasarathy is Professor of Sociology at the Department of Humanities and Social Sciences, Indian Institute of Technology, Bombay. He has held visiting positions at the Australian National University, the National University of Singapore, and the Zentrum Moderner Orient. He has authored *Collective Violence in a Provincial City* (1997) and co-edited

Cleavage, Connection and Conflict in Rural, Urban and Contemporary Asia (2013).

Julie Ren is a doctoral researcher in the Department of Geography at Humboldt University, Berlin, Germany, and a former Fulbright fellow. Her research focuses on transnational mobility, cultural perspectives on city-making, and comparative methodology. She has authored articles considering the implications of comparative urbanism for the 'Asian City' and questioning the application of the gentrification lens in China. These articles are published in the *International Journal of Urban and Regional Research* and in a volume edited by Lees *et al.*, respectively.

June Wang is Assistant Professor of Urban Studies in the Department of Public Policy at City University of Hong Kong. Her research interests include gentrification, culture-led urban regeneration, and spectacular urbanism. She has authored several journal papers on cultural cities, such as 'Gentrification and Shanghai's New Middle-Class: Another Reflection on the Cultural Consumption Thesis' (2009) and '"Art in capital": Shaping Distinctiveness in a Culture-led Urban Regeneration Project in Red Town, Shanghai' (2009), and is the co-author of *The Rhetoric and Reality of Culture-led Urban Regeneration: A Comparison of Beijing and Shanghai, China* (2011).

Yang Yang is a PhD candidate in the Department of Geography, University of Colorado, Boulder. Her research interests include urban and ethnic geographies, particularly the visualization of ethnicity and religion in the urban built environment. She obtained her Master of Sciences in Human Geography and Urban Studies from the London School of Economics and Political Science. Her current research concerns visualization of Islam and the Hui nationality as a process of ethno-religious subject-making in inland, second-tier cities in north-western China.

Amy Y. Zhang is a PhD candidate in the Graduate School of Geography at Clark University, Worcester, USA. Her research focuses on China's urban politics and state–society relations. She has done research on China's land politics and land finance, and is currently focusing on the role of art in China's urban development, especially its manifestation within the growing arts districts of Chinese cities. She holds an MPhil from the Department of Geography at the University of Hong Kong.

Introduction

Tim Oakes and June Wang

This book explores the practices and policies of making cultural/creative cities in Asia. Such practices and policies have become widespread, from international film festivals in places like Busan, South Korea, and an urban renaissance driven by the nostalgic invention of imperial culture in Xi'an, China, to the urban promotion of national culture in Malaysia and the competing aspirations of Singapore and Hong Kong to be Asia's cultural hubs. Urban cultural policies in Asia have, in other words, gone far beyond the objective of promoting local culture industries. Culture and creativity are now instruments serving the 'global city' ambitions of Asia. The wave of cultural city-making has become one of the most influential urban developmental strategies worldwide, as cities search for new directions to counteract their decaying Fordist production systems (Castells, 2000; Scott, 2006, 2007). More importantly, these strategies demonstrate an effort to build an 'overall structural competitiveness' (Jessop and Sum, 2000) in the global urban network. The emergence of an urban cultural policy agenda – and the restructuring that often results – is a highly politicized process with often contradictory but very real material impacts. Any study of the politics of cultural-driven urban development must be put within this globalizing context, in which 'elsewhere is right here as much as it is over there' in the policy world (Cochrane, 2011, xi). Innovative ideas, fast policies, and 'best-practice' models have travelled through global networks established by supranational organizations and populated by mayors, consultants, and other key actors.

Taken as a whole, then, the case studies collected here consider Asian cultural/ creative city-making in the context of global policy mobility. The authors – most of whom are Asia-based and represent the fields of geography, sociology, urban planning, communication, cultural studies, media studies, comparative politics, and urban studies – are particularly interested in the political tensions and social dynamics that emerge when Asian cities attempt to become 'cultural' or 'creative' cities. The chapters collected in Part I focus on policy-making practices themselves, while those in Part II explore more of the place-based social implications of these practices. As a whole, the chapters explore the politics of cultural/creative city from the aspect of policy-making. As Margit Mayer points out in the volume's final chapter, the negotiation of creative producers with policy remains a topic about which a great deal of research is still needed. As more and more cultural workers in Asian cities enter the ranks of the precarious, this volume seeks to establish a benchmark from which additional research may dive deeper into the hidden geographies and histories of cultural production in urban Asia as governments and markets strive to promote and brand cities by instrumentalizing artistic and creative production.

Since it is with 'culture' that cultural city policy-making is ostensibly concerned, we begin this introduction with a brief consideration of the disconnect between critical understandings of culture as an everyday human phenomenon, on the one hand, and cultural/creative city policy-making, on the other. We find that putting the latter in conversation with the former requires a recognition of what we might call the postcolonial moment of contemporary urban studies in Asia. Following this, we explore the concepts of policy mobility and, more specifically, assemblage, that help frame the case studies that follow. Finally, we examine the question of urban cultural policy-making in the political context of state authoritarianism that dominates most of the case studies in the volume. This examination compels us to raise questions about how the 'right to the city' might be framed as a struggle over cultural city-making in Asia.

Making cultural cities? Culture and the postcolonial moment of Asian urban studies

What does it mean to make a cultural city? It is important to recognize from the outset that all cities are already cultural. They have their ways of life, their distinctive rhythms, their own practices and rituals, their own tribes and territories. And all cities have their own creativities that emerge from the unique and ever-shifting energies generated by the diversity of their inhabitants. Were he considering the question of cultural cities today, the literary critic and theorist Raymond Williams might have observed that the culture and creativity of the city emerge from the everyday and ordinary struggles of people making a living and making sense of the ever-changing world swirling around them. The urban theorist Henri Lefebvre would have shared in this sentiment, noting the socially transformative and revolutionary potential of creativity embedded in the everyday rhythms of urban dwelling. Neither Williams nor Lefebvre would have recognized as a separate 'class' those whom Richard Florida (2002) has told us, however vaguely, now constitute the creative potential of a city.

What, then, does it mean to *make* something that already exists? At issue here is not the question of cities making culture in an urban 'cultural desert', though this is often the conceit that governments and consultants like Florida concoct to justify their policies. As Wang's chapter in this volume observes (Chapter 8), the city of Shenzhen was often referred to as a 'cultural desert' (*wenhua shamo*) before government initiatives transformed it into a UNESCO-recognized global 'City of Design'. Such arboreal views of culture – a delicate flower to be cultivated in the money-grubbing environment of global production systems – prop up an ideology of culture as 'civilization'. It was precisely this ideology that theorists like Williams and Lefebvre sought to expose and discredit. At issue, then, is the question of culture and creativity as instruments, representations, resources, and articles of faith in the 'worlding' ambitions of powerful urban actors.

Ironically, the more successful cities have been at realizing their worlding ambitions – often resulting in gentrification, real estate speculation, and increased consumption – the more difficult many residents have found it to maintain the ordinary cultural rhythms of their daily lives. The ambitions of powerful actors to make their cities into globally significant centres of culture and creativity have often erased the very conditions within which creativity and cultural production tend to thrive. In his study of the creative economy in Beijing, for example, Chou (2012, 198) argues that 'the construction of cultural space in Beijing is a state-sponsored effort that emphasizes the construction of infrastructure and an institutional framework for the world-city building, but to a great extent neglects the organic construction of the artistic network'. Lin's chapter on Taipei in this volume (Chapter 2) makes a similar observation.

This immediately raises questions, then, about the nature of 'organic' cultural or creative production itself. For many would argue that culture always finds a way of emerging from within the cracks in urban planning and the contradictions of urban life. Culture and creativity also look different in different places, as astutely observed, for example, by Luger, Wang, and Ren in this volume (Chapters 13, 8, and 11). In China, as Visser (2010, 67) has observed, the sometimes absurd fetishisms of urban planning have themselves inspired artistic scrutiny and cultural contestation. 'Artists', she writes, 'have been particularly sensitive to the fact that the frenzied, contingent, and opportunistic development of Chinese cities creates major social and political ruptures rather than a predictable order evolving toward higher degrees of civility.' The result has been cultural production outside and unpredicted by the plans of the state or the market. 'Art', 'culture', and 'creativity' get caught up in the top-down governing of cities, forcing us to think about (hidden) ways the aesthetic might still remain a site of resistance, and bottom-up claims of identity and space. Thus, Carolyn Cartier (2012, 17) has observed that,

> Rancière's understanding of the aesthetic regime ... recognizes diverse cultural projects in the world today whose products and material outcomes are not readily identifiable as 'art' in a public sphere that has been socialized by normative state discourses of 'creative industry', that is, an expectation of 'culture' in saleable forms.

Who, then, *is* a creative producer in the world today and to what extent are they included in (or excluded from) 'creative city' policies? In this volume we consider how cities are trying to make themselves into cultural cities as a way of enhancing their dreams of world city status, their worlding ambitions, their aspirational urbanism. Kong and O'Connor (2009) have argued that creativity tends to be understood by planners and policy-makers as an image or a design attribute. Cho (2010) has similarly noted the South Korean state's instrumental appropriation of 'Hong-dae culture' in its efforts to promote Seoul as a world-class city during the lead-up to the 2002 Football World Cup. But in addition to the appropriation of culture for aspirational urbanism, we consider the city as a cultural space, where people negotiate these worlding ambitions in their everyday lives. There is a precariousness to these cultural spaces and to the everyday production of culture, but there is also resilience, adaptation, and the fact that culture is always being produced in multiple – though often hidden and unacknowledged – ways.

Branding-oriented appropriations of culture and creativity neglect the complex social formations that are productive of actual and emergent creativities. Those social formations do exist all over Asia, but they are more often than not treated as *obstacles* to creative city policy, not as social phenomena to be nurtured. We are therefore interested in this volume in considering cultural/creative city policy-making within the particular social, economic, political, and cultural contexts of the cities where this policy-making occurs. While this interest may, at the outset, appear banal, it bears emphasizing given the extent to which much of the boosterish work, like Florida's, on cultural and creative cities seems to occur as if in a geographical and even (ironically) cultural vacuum. There remains, in other words, a distinct need for research that places urban policy-making firmly in the particular spaces within which it occurs.

Such spaces need not be delimited to the enclosed territory of particular cities, however. Our focus on policy mobility – discussed further below – insists on a networked understanding of space, where practices, actors, ideas, and objects form assemblages of cultural/creative policy-making in particular places and at particular moments. While we highlight the general Asian spaces in which such assemblages occur in our case studies, we reject the notion that there is something called the 'Asian city' characterized by some distinct and essential cultural content. Instead, Asia is important to us as a citational frame, in which mobile policies and ideas about urban planning, 'best practices', and successful models are increasingly being circulated *within* Asia rather than *between* Asia and 'the West'. Acts of citation and inter-referencing among Asia-based policy actors, in other words, are increasingly inter-Asian phenomena themselves.

Making this observation signals a recognition of the postcolonial space that urban studies in Asia has carved out for itself. Our focus on making cultural/creative cities *in* Asia is meant to question a narrative that seeks simply to find the 'Western' origins of Asian urban development. Such a project still haunts many otherwise critical political–economic studies of Asian urbanism. Such narratives, as Edensor and Jayne (2012) have noted, tend to view non-Western cities in terms of their 'problems', making it difficult to understand the ways in which non-Western cities are 'creative' on their own terms. Postcolonial urbanism, Ananya Roy (2011, 310) argues, 'demonstrates how seemingly original templates of modernism, developmentalism, and neoliberalism emerge through global circulations and experiments. They are, in other words, thoroughly hybrid, thoroughly corrupted.' This hybridity and corruption, Roy goes on to argue, suggests an 'unstable' space of inter-Asian *betweenness* where notions of Asia travel, fuelling urban experiments and providing a 'citationary structure' for urban experiments throughout the continent and beyond. But she is also careful to point out that attempts to contain such urban experiments within a framework defined by an essential 'Asian' cultural content would be misguided. Iterations of a cultural 'Asia' in Asian urban policy-making, she writes, 'generate a surplus that cannot be easily contained within familiar frames of urban success and globality' (Roy, 2011, 331).

We hope, therefore, to add our voices to Roy's (2009) 'new geographies of theory' by offering empirical evidence for Castells's (2000, 380) claim that 'the global city phenomenon cannot be reduced to a few urban cores at the top of the hierarchy'. The Asian city, this volume collectively suggests, should be viewed as a (cultural) policy generator, not just (cultural) policy recipient. This is something, of course, that urban studies scholars working in Asia have been observing for some time. As Bunnell and Das (2010, 282) put it in their study of the policy relationship between Kuala Lumpur and Hyderabad: 'Rather than presuming that innovations and models for city development originate in the West, the KL–Hyderabad case unsettles North American-centered or Atlanticist imaginaries.' That said, it is also important to recognize – as Lin's chapter on Taipei, Das's chapter on Hyderabad, and Bowen's chapter on Seoul demonstrate (Chapters 2, 3, and 5) – that 'Western' policy models remain highly influential in the aspirational urbanism of Asian cities. Yet these authors also insist on viewing these cities not as sites of local 'variations' of 'universal' Western models, but as locations where mobile policies are always already remade as they travel within the networked space of global urbanism.

Policy mobility and geographies of assemblage

By now, a significant critical intervention within urban policy studies has established itself as the field of policy mobility. Conventional studies of urban policy transfer have tended to focus on policy as an always already complete package that is transferred from one location to another by the rational and voluntary appropriation of 'best practices' by policy actors who are, for the most part, spatially decontextualized and socio-culturally disembedded. The idea of *policy mobility* seeks to suggest an alternative approach, in which the focus on rational policy actors is replaced by spatially situated institutions with, as Clarke (2012, 27) observes, particular 'path-dependencies, dominant paradigms, powerful interests, and so on'. This institutional situatedness of policy-making is something with which the chapters in Part I of this volume are particularly concerned. Justin O'Connor and Xin Gu (Chapter 1), for example, explore the complex roles of cultural intermediaries in Shanghai's emerging creative industry clusters to point out the unexpected and locally embedded characteristics of creative/cultural city policies. Clarke further argues that, 'notions of static, fully formed, complete policy packages are replaced with notions of learning, translation, and mobility'. This means that policies are in a constant state of transformation, rather than arriving in cities 'as replicas of policies from elsewhere'. They are always being deterritorialized and reterritorialized, making any efforts to find 'global convergence' around successful policy packages (like cultural/creative cities) a fool's errand. Instead of focusing on the package, then, such an approach compels us to focus on the networks of connection, exchange, and circulation within which such 'packages' travel and transform.

That network, as Peck (2011, 43) reminds us, is *inter-urban*. It is one in which officials often engage in what Clarke (2012, 35) calls 'policy tourism' – the practice of policy professionals undertaking 'a brief and guided engagement with a mythologised, exoticised, spectacularised city'. Popular destinations have included London, Bilbao, and Barcelona, while in Asia Dubai and Singapore have emerged as more recent meccas. But mobility also occurs when popular and successful cities become highly mediatized and, as a result, deterritorialized from their spatial contexts. Such cities dominate broadband and broadcast channels, and international print media outlets, and they compel planners and officials to compare their own cities to these deterritorialized ideals. A process of reterritorialization follows in which new policy is produced from an 'original' which does not really exist.

A focus on policy mobility also signals a challenge to the apolitical quality of much of the work conducted on urban policy transfer. There are at least two aspects to this. First, there is the tendency to reduce urban development and planning to a project of technical fixes. This tendency is enhanced when policy is treated as a complete package of best practices that diffuses out and down the urban hierarchy. As Clarke (2012) argues, such fixes are often conveyed as populist 'win–win' scenarios for urban residents, governments, and commercial interests. Second is the way urban policy-making can abolish the political domain and vacate the public sphere. By focusing on spatially situated institutions and how they shape policy practice and implementation, work on policy mobility tends to refocus our attention on the political contests swirling around urban policy-making.

One result of apolitical and aspatial approaches in the study of urban policy-making in Asia has been the tendency to reproduce a long-established dichotomy of innovation versus imitation. Asian states have been repeatedly accused of the latter, from nineteenth-century claims of Japan 'aping' the West in science and technology, to contemporary concerns about China's knock-off *shanzhai* economy and its persistent violation of intellectual property rights (see Chapter 8). The innovation–imitation dichotomy thrives in the study of Asian cultural/creative city policy-making as well, and it tends to result from an unproblematic view of policy transfer. That is, when policy is viewed as a travelling package, it is easy to view new adopters as merely imitating or appropriating some other place's ideas and practices. Indeed, much of urban development in Asia appears, on the surface, to be highly imitative. New cities are being built as if from an off-the-shelf kit, a 'city in a box' (Oosterman, 2012), so that the new towns of Guangzhou, Seoul, and Kuala Lumpur look much the same as those in Astana, Dubai, and Baku.

In viewing such citational urbanism from the perspective of policy mobility, however, such 'generic cities' cannot be taken as merely imitative, but need to be understood as being produced through institutions that are situated spatially within networks and places, and that such situatedness is conditional of particular political, social, and cultural outcomes in different cities. That said, there is clearly a tendency in these citational practices of city planning and policy-making that reduces culture and creativity to an aesthetic image or design attribute, reminding us of Kong and O'Connor's (2009) critique of the 'creative city' idea as culturally repressive. This issue will be discussed further in the next section.

A focus on policy mobility suggests an affinity with the idea of *assemblage*. The recent proliferation of uses of this term in a wide variety of fields and encompassing a wide variety of definitions makes any overview account problematic. We view assemblage as a largely descriptive approach emerging out of loosely related bodies of work, including actor network theory, non-representational thinking, and 'new materialist' geographies. Assemblage has been called on to describe in non-linear and non-hierarchical ways emergent and temporary collectivities of human and non-human elements. An assemblage might then be thought of as the composition of diverse elements into a provisional socio-spatial formation. While little justice can be done to the nuances of assemblage in this brief introduction, it is nevertheless important to point out some elements that resonate with a policy mobility approach to cultural/creative cities. As suggested by McFarlane (2009) and Anderson and McFarlane (2011), these elements include emergence, multiplicity, and indeterminancy. The term 'seeks to blur divisions of social–material, near–far and structure–agency' (Anderson and McFarlane, 2011, 124).

Putting assemblage in conversation with policy mobility might thus view culture/creative cities policy-making as an assemblage of spatial and temporal elements (rather than, say, a linear transfer of a policy package 'down' the global urban hierarchy). McCann and Ward (2011) observe that there is a tension between 'policy as relational and dynamic' and policy as 'fixed and territorial'. Policy both travels and focuses on places. This quality of policy, they suggest, makes assemblage a potentially productive approach. They continue:

> The concept derives from Deleuze and Guattari's work and speaks not to the static arrangement of a set of parts, whether organized under some logic or collected randomly, but to 'the *process* of arranging, organizing, fitting together . . . [where] an assemblage is a whole of some sort that expresses some identity and claims a territory' (Wise 2005, 77; his emphasis). More strongly, 'assemblages create *territories*. Territories are more than just spaces: they have a stake, a claim . . . Territories are not fixed for all time, but are always being made and unmade, reterritorialising and deterritorialising. This constant making and unmaking process is the same with assemblages: they are always coming together and moving apart.'
>
> (McCann and Ward, 2011, xv)

Such an approach compels McCann and Ward (2011, xvii) to argue that the policy-making literature 'needs more empirical accounts of the struggles, practices, and representations that underpin urban–global relations and that assemble or territorialize global flows'.

In considering Ong's (2011) argument that urban theory is dominated by the two dominant and sometimes intransigently incompatible poles of political economy on the one hand and postcolonialism on the other, assemblage approaches appear to suggest an alternative. On the one hand, the political economy approach posits global networks of flows structured by capitalism. The postcolonial approach, on the other hand, tends to argue for a shift from an analytics of structure to an analytics of agency, rejecting the assumption of 'universal laws' established by global capitalism. Ong proposes a shift from the dualistic analytic of structure/agency – which dominates in both political–economic and postcolonial thinking – to the analytic of assemblage, viewing the city not as a fixed locality but as a node in a network of exchange, circulation, mobility. Within this network, she argues, modelling and inter-referencing occur, as well as new associations and solidarities.

The state, democracy, and the right to the city

As suggested earlier, critical scholarship on cultural/creative city policy-making has argued that projects designed to develop cultural and creative economies in cities often produce outcomes that are in fact detrimental to cultural or creative production. Gentrification is the most obvious example, and one discussed at length in Chatterjee's chapter on the postindustrial transformation of Mumbai's chawls (Chapter 14). But the precariousness of cultural and creative production in Asian cities needs to be understood not just in terms of rising rents forcing 'creatives' out of inner-city neighbourhoods. More fundamentally, the implementation of cultural and creative city development projects raises basic questions about the relationship between creativity and democracy, about creativity and access to urban space, about the role of creativity in political movements (such as the recent Occupy Central protests in Hong Kong; see Wong 2015), and about the extent to which cultural/creative city policy-making serves to reproduce state power.

It should not be surprising to observe – as Chou (2012), Chen (2012), and Zhang (2014) have – that cultural/creative city policy-making is sometimes not about promoting creativity at all, despite the sincere desires of planners and officials to incubate the next Silicon Valley in their own city. The creative city is more often about making money, and attracting a certain demographic of young professionals, first as tourists, then as new residents. It is about investment, branding, and creating what Shepherd (2007) called 'happy space'. Lefebvre would have said it is about creating state space, territorializing the city through the aesthetics of display and the rendering visible of the 'arts zone' or the 'arts district'. Creativity, since its 1997 policy debut in the UK (Kong, 2014), is about producing a postindustrial growth engine for building a 'global city'. If it was ever about cultivating and supporting creative producers, that moment in the arc of creative city policy has passed. 'Gone is the emphasis on democratizing culture economies in favor of marginalized social groups,' Peck (2011, 52) argues, 'creativity is now sold as an urban growth strategy, modeled on the achievements and lifestyles of a cosmopolitan elite.' The creative city is now a theme park, modelled on a free trade zone (Easterling, 2014); the creative city is now a 'city in a box' (Oosterman, 2012; de Kloet, 2014).

Thus, as Chen (2013, 283) found in her study of transcultural place-making in Taipei, worlding creative city ambitions have had a suppressing effect on diverse forms of cultural production:

> I have found that all official multicultural activities have disappeared in Taipei since 2008. There appears to have been no space left for multicultural and bottom-up ways of placemaking since then. Aiming to become a World City, Taipei has apparently turned its back on its largest foreign population ... The true multicultural landscapes of Taipei have been sacrificed in the pursuit of aesthetic developmentalism with an ever growing number of consumer-oriented, cosmopolitan places.

Creative city policies, 'smart cities', and other top-down urban planning projects, for Sassen (2013), can be part of the elite and powerful forces that 'deurbanize' cities, smoothing out the chaotic diversity that breeds creative production.

Yet this gloomy outlook may be premature, since it probably gives more credit than deserved to the effectiveness of creative city policy-making to produce significant developmental impacts. Cities all over the world retain their ungovernable spaces of creativity. Recognizing this, Sassen (2013) insists that the city remains the only significant space in which the powerless can still make history. As Julie Ren argues in her chapter in this volume (Chapter 11), creativity can be a powerful political resource for artists precisely because it is so highly valued by planners and officials. And T.C. Chang (Chapter 6) outlines the Singapore state's relatively successful efforts to promote creativity by zoning, districting, and developing new spaces for creative production, even though such spaces seldom end up working in optimal or intended ways. Creativity in cities remains a product of struggle, conflict, negotiation, and resistance, as is made clear in the chapters by Joanne Lim (Malaysia), Agnes Shuk-mei Ku (Hong Kong), and Jason Lugar (Singapore) (Chapters 9, 12, and 13). It is seldom a product of 'good governance' or 'best practice'. At issue, then, is not whether the developmentalist orientation of creative city-making displaces the cultural endeavour, but whether cities are prepared to recognize, and support, creativity where it actually exists.

This is Gyan Prakash's point in his description of Mumbai as a 'kinetic city' where the bottom-up entrepreneurial creativity of the city's slum dwellers challenges the 'slum rehabilitation' gentrification projects emerging out of McKinsey & Company's Vision Mumbai plan. 'The slum rehabilitation projects' of such global consultancy firms, he argues,

> represent attempts to displace the kinetic city, to expunge its existence, and to order Mumbai to the dull discipline of the static city, to the delight of real estate magnates and the middle-class heritage activists. Fortunately, the kinetic city survives in [the massive slum of] Dharavi; Mumbai's legendary

everyday tactic of survival with wit and enterprise stubbornly persists under the looming shadow of the bulldozers of 'development'.

(Prakash, 2010, 339)

This may run the risk of romanticizing poverty, but the point is to recognize the hidden spaces and practices of creativity, and to argue that the making of cultural/ creative cities can just as easily wipe these out as cultivate them.

While cultural/creative city policy-making may sometimes result in the suppression of 'organic' creativity, the 'kinetic city' remains, for some, an irrepressible force in the democratization of creative production. In Asia, where urban governance in some places is carried out in more authoritarian, top-down, and state-centric ways, a similar issue presents itself regarding the relationship between cultural/creative city policy-making and state power. Does the promotion of creative industries merely serve to reproduce state power? And if so, at what scale? These questions points us toward broader issues regarding the significance of the city as a governable space, and of the various components of that space – including the arts and creative production – as technologies of government. Putting the question in these terms suggests a governmentality perspective derived from the late work of Foucault (2004), who argued that in liberal states the control of territorial space for maintaining population security formed the predominant apparatus of state power. As Osborne and Rose (1999) have argued, that territorial space is dominated by cities: that is, liberal government has been territorialized in the urban form. Increasingly, in other words, the city is the experimental zone and model for territorial governance; the state governs its territory as it would govern a city.

In this context, culture would seem to have a role to play in urban government, in the 'conduct of conduct', and in maintaining social and political stability (Barnett, 2001; Bennett, 1998). Yet, the cases collected in this volume, along with much of the broader critical scholarship on Asian cities, suggest a limited role for a notion of governmentalized power in cultural/creative city-making. While many Asian states may aspire to the kind of 'governing at a distance' that Foucault's notion of governmentality describes in relatively wealthy liberal democratic states, they tend to employ a more direct form of rule associated with a notion of disciplinary power. This is most obviously seen in China. In her study of Beijing's Factory 798 and Songzhuan, Zhang (2014) argues that the government is deeply involved in the promotion, and thus the control, of arts and creativity for the purposes of social stabilization. The basic strategy, she points out, is for the government to grant artistic freedom (thus promoting culture and creativity) but retain control of 'the channels through which art is published, exhibited, and circulated' (Zhang, 2014, 841). Nearly every chapter in this volume, and particularly those in Part I, demonstrate such 'state-led creativity' in practice. However, as Se Hoon Park (Chapter 10) demonstrates, such 'state-led creativity' in the service of developmentalism can in fact devolve into genuine 'community-based creativity' under conditions of state decentralization. This and other place-based social implications of cultural development practices are explored throughout Part II.

Perhaps more relevant than Foucault's liberal governmentality in viewing culture as a resource and technology of government, then, is Lefebvre's (2003) notion of urbanism as an ideology that has displaced industrialism as the pivot around which social classes and political contests are formed. Asia seems to have taken the ideology of urbanism to heart. The state, Lefebvre's work suggests, reproduces itself in urbanism, not only through its restructuring and reorganization in the form of urban institutions and partnerships for urban development (for example, with real estate firms or global consultancy groups like McKinsey), but by constructing new urban space itself. In this context, Padawangi (2014) reminds us that the built environment is not an innocent physical structure, but emerges out of the social processes and power relations that shape society. The built environment tends to normalize those power relations by making them part of the infrastructure of people's everyday lives. The space of the city, then, is part of the ideological nature of urbanism, and why Lefebvre (1971) found it so necessary to critique and politicize everyday urban life.

Finally, Lefebvre (2003, 88) also reminds us that the 'space of state control' is largely 'optical and visual': that is, an aesthetic space of representation. This is, in many ways, the space that 'creative cities' policy-making strives to produce – a highly visual, spectacular space of culture rendered as exhibit and object. Here, Lefebvre echoes Debord's (1967/1994) view of image and 'spectacle' as key tools by which powerful class and state actors maintain their positions of authority and control in society. In making cultural cities in Asia, image and spectacle have played significant roles, as this volume's chapters by Lin (Taipei), Zhang (Beijing), Yang (Xi'an), and Wang (Shenzhen) (Chapters 2, 4, 7, and 8) demonstrate.

This volume merely scratches the surface of a vast and largely uncharted world of cultural/creative city-making in Asia. With this brief introduction we have sketched out a few of the key issues touched on by the chapters that follow, and we believe these suggest several productive questions for ongoing research:

- How has cultural/creative city policy-making disrupted established urban hierarchies in Asia and worldwide?
- What is the nature of 'organic' creativity in Asia's vastly diverse and dynamic cities?
- To what extent do cultural/creative city policies prop up authoritarian states, and to what extent do they help produce new struggles for democracy and urban inhabitation?
- What do these struggles even look like in urban Asian contexts?
- How might studies of policy mobility within Asia disrupt existing bodies of work developed in more Euro-American contexts?

These are but a few starting points for what we believe to be a rich and significant area of research in urban and cultural studies.

References

Anderson, B. and C. McFarlane (2011). Assemblage and geography. *Area*, 43(2), 124–127.

Barnett, C. (2001). Culture, geography, and the arts of government. *Environment and Planning D: Society and Space*, 19, 7–24.

Bennett, T. (1998). *Culture: A Reformer's Science*. London: Sage.

Bunnell, T. and D. Das. (2010). Urban pulse – a geography of serial seduction: urban policy transfer from Kuala Lumpur to Hyderabad. *Urban Geography*, 31(3), 277–284.

Cartier, C. (2012). Image, precariousness and the logic of cultural production in Hong Kong. *Portal: Journal of Multidisciplinary International Studies*, 9(3). Retrieved from http://epress.lib.uts.edu.au/journals/index.php/portal/article/view/2554/3343 (accessed 17 August 2015).

Castells, M. (2000). *The Rise of the Network Society*. New York: Blackwell.

Chen, H.-Y. (2013). Placemaking in between urban redevelopment: Little Indonesia in Taipei. In J. Hou (ed.), *Transcultural Cities: Border-crossing and Placemaking* (London and New York: Routledge), 274–284.

Chen, Y. (2012). Making Shanghai a creative city: exploring the creative cluster strategy from a Chinese perspective. In M.V. Geenhuizen and P. Nijkamp (eds), *Creative Knowledge Cities: Myths, Visions, and Realities* (Cheltenham: Edward Elgar), 437–466.

Cho, M. (2010). Envisioning Seoul as a world city: the cultural politics of the Hong-dae Cultural District. *Asian Studies Review*, 34, 329–347.

Chou, T.-L. (2012). Creative space, cultural industry clusters, and participation of the state in Beijing. *Eurasian Geography and Economics*, 53(2), 197–215.

Clarke, N. (2012). Urban policy mobility, anti-politics, and histories of the transnational municipal movement. *Progress in Human Geography*, 36(1), 25–43.

Cochrane, A. (2011). Foreword. In E. McCann and K. Ward (eds), *Mobile Urbanism: Cities and Policymaking in the Global Age* (Minneapolis and London: University of Minnesota Press), ix–xi.

Debord, G. (1967/1994). *The Society of the Spectacle* (trans. D. Nicholson-Smith). New York: Zone.

de Kloet, J. (2014). Imagining a disappearing and reappearing Chinese city. In J. de Kloet and L. Scheen (eds), *Spectacle and the City: Chinese Urbanities in Art and Culture* (Amsterdam: Amsterdam University Press), 77–96.

Easterling, K. (2014). *Extrastatecraft: The Power of Infrastructure Space*. London: Verso.

Edensor, T. and M. Jayne (eds) (2012). *Urban Theory beyond the West: A World of Cities*. London and New York: Routledge.

Florida, R. (2002). *The Rise of the Creative Class, and How It's Transforming Work, Leisure, Community, and Everyday Life*. New York: Basic Books.

Foucault, M. (2004). *Security, Territory, Population: Lectures at the Collège de France, 1977–78* (trans. G. Burchell). New York: Palgrave.

Jessop, B. and N.-L. Sum. (2000). An entrepreneurial city in action: Hong Kong's emerging strategies in and for (inter) urban competition. *Urban Studies*, 37(12), 2287–2313.

Kong, L. (2014). From cultural industries to creative industries and back? Towards clarifying theory and rethinking policy. *Inter-Asia Cultural Studies*, 15(4), 593–607.

Kong, L. and J. O'Connor (eds) (2009). *Creative Economies, Creative Cities: Asian–European Perspectives*. Dordrecht: Springer.

Lefebvre, H. (1971). *Everyday Life in the Modern World* (trans. S. Rabinovitch). New York: Harper Torchbooks.

Lefebvre, H. (2003). *The Urban Revolution* (trans. R. Bononno). Minneapolis: University of Minnesota Press.

McCann, E. and K. Ward (eds) (2011). *Mobile Urbanism: Cities and Policymaking in the Global Age*. Minneapolis: University of Minnesota Press.

McFarlane, C. (2009). Translocal assemblages: space, power, and social movements. *Geoforum*, 40, 561–567.

Ong, A. (2011). Worlding cities, or the art of being global. In A. Roy and A. Ong (eds), *Worlding Cities: Asian Experiments and the Art of Being Global* (Chichester: Wiley-Blackwell), 1–26.

Oosterman, A. (ed.) (2012). City in a box. *Volume*, 34. Amsterdam: Stichting Archis.

Osborne, T. and N. Rose. (1999). Governing cities: notes on the spatialization of virtue. *Environment and Planning D: Society and Space*, 17, 737–760.

Padawangi, R. (2014). Counter-hegemonic spaces of hope? Constructing the public city in Jakarta and Singapore. Asian Research Institute Working Paper Series No. 219. National University of Singapore.

Peck, J. (2011). Geographies of policy: from transfer-diffusion to mobility-mutation. *Progress in Human Geography*, 35(6), 773–797.

Prakash, G. (2010). *Mumbai Fables*. Princeton, NJ: Princeton University Press.

Roy, A. (2009). The 21st-century metropolis: new geographies of theory. *Regional Studies*, 43(6), 819–830.

Roy, A. (2011). Postcolonial urbanism: speed, hysteria, mass dreams. In A. Roy and A. Ong (eds), *Worlding Cities: Asian Experiments and the Art of Being Global* (Chichester: Wiley-Blackwell), 307–335.

Sassen, S. (2013). Does the city have speech? *Public Culture*, 25(2), 209–221.

Scott, A.J. (2006). Creative cities: conceptual issues and policy questions. *Journal of Urban Affairs*, 28(1), 1–17.

Scott, A.J. (2007). Capitalism and urbanization in a new key? The cognitive–cultural dimension. *Social Forces*, 85(4), 1465–1482.

Shepherd, R. (2007). *When Culture Goes to Market: Space, Place, and Identity in an Urban Marketplace*. New York: Peter Lang.

Visser, R. (2010). *Cities Surround the Countryside: Urban Aesthetics in Postsocialist China*. Durham, NC, and London: Duke University Press.

Wise, J.M. (2005). Assemblage. In C.J. Stivale (ed.), *Gilles Deleuze: Key Concepts* (Montreal: McGill and Queen's University Press), 77–87.

Wong, K. (2015). *Art of Protest: Resisting against Absurdity*. Hong Kong: Amelia Johnson Contemporary Gallery.

Zhang, Y. (2014). Governing arts districts: state control and cultural production in contemporary China. *China Quarterly*, 219, 827–848.

Part I

Assembling new models

Global networks and state aspirations

Section introduction

The chapters in Part I investigate the network politics that enable and constrain the flow of ideas, models, and other forms of information. The first three chapters by Justin O'Connor and Xin Gu, Cheng-Yi Lin, and Diganta Das (scholars who themselves have experienced transnational mobility) depict the political construction of global networks constituted by mobile actors, and the institutional frameworks within which these actors operate at various scales, thus providing case studies in the mobile flow of ideas within the broader context of global capitalism. Regarding the worldwide spread of 'cultural city' urban development strategies, one prevailing thesis calls attention to the broad context of neoliberal globalization and, in particular, the surge of competitive-driven city-making resulting from so-called flexible specialization in late capitalism. Attention here is directed to the geography of flows – specifically, policy mobility – which is typically assumed to move from the global north to the global south (Prince, 2012). These chapters pay attention to the 'interplay of forces where a range of actors mobilize, enroll, translate, channel, broker and bridge' (Allen and Cochrane, 2007, p. 1171) the travelling of policies, ideas, and best practices, which, as argued by Marxist scholars, has always been structured by power relations in the broader context of capitalism (Brenner et al., 2011; McCann and Ward, 2011; Merrifield, 2012; Peck and Theodore, 2010).

Fields of power are reconstituted, in other words, through networks connecting places by virtue of the symbolic power carried by such networks in the first place. They create mental maps of 'best cities' for policy that inform future strategies. Cities are thus constituted through their relations with other places and scales (McCann and Ward, 2011). In this light, these chapters respond to questions such as:

- What are the geographic trajectories of mobile cultural/creative city policies?
- How is the cultural/creative city policy network structured by a city's internal characteristics as well as by external linkages among cities?
- What are the institutions that condition how policies are territorialized in specific locations?
- What resources, discursive and material, have been mobilized from wider geographic territories or different scales to establish the infrastructure for formulating and implementing local urban cultural policy?

The next five chapters, by Amy Zhang, Jay Bowen, T.C. Chang, Yang Yang, and June Wang focus more on municipal and national states in Asia and how new policy agendas are assembled through political and socio-economic alignment of various actors, discourses, and materials that have gained prestige in their strategic shift to cultural/creative city development, and the dynamic, contingent and perhaps path-dependent features of this process. Regarding the issue of urban competition, postcolonial scholars reject the idea that Asian cities are merely passively globalized; rather, empirical studies featuring place-based observations frequently uncover 'home-grown' ideas and/or selective adoption of the cultural/creative city package by a calculating local state (Roy and Ong, 2011). Often employing an analytic of assemblage, the postcolonial approach argues for new geographies of theory and deploys alternative ways of thinking that approach cities as *sites of intersection between networked topologies and territorial legacies* (Deleuze and Guattari, 1987; McFarlane, 2011; Ong and Collier, 2005). In this process, various actors deliberately select particular elements and then create and promote them in new packages. The formation of assemblage, which relies on the hard labour of agency to 'draw disparate components together, forge connections between them, and sustain these connections in the face of tension' (Li, 2007, p. 265), is a process of political alignment.

In many Asian cities where the developmentalist model prevails, the state has been one of the most influential actors. Sites such as Singapore, South Korea, and China illustrate how state apparatus draws together disparate ideas and practices to forge new 'worlding' agendas (Roy and Ong, 2011). As such, the situated initiatives of cultural/creative city-making serve the goal of global city status in the midst of inter-city rivalries on the one hand, while shaping new regimes of urban governance that privilege new logics, techniques, and practices in zones of exception on the other. Here, these chapters centre around questions like:

- What are the discursive outcomes of creative/cultural cities productions in Asia?
- How have mobile policy models been re-articulated and re-contextualized in specific spatial and political economic contexts?
- To what extent does the cultural/creative cities model provide a new 'technology of government' for ordering and reshaping state–society relations in Asia?

References

Allen, J., and Cochrane, A. (2007) Beyond the territorial fix: regional assemblages, politics and power. *Regional Studies*, 41(9): 1161–1175.

Brenner, N., Madden, D.J., and Wachsmuth, D. (2011) Assemblage urbanism and the challenges of critical urban theory. *City*, 15(2): 225–240.

Deleuze, G., and Guattari, F. (1987) *A Thousand Plateaus: Capitalism and Schizophrenia* (B. Massumi, Trans.). London and Minneapolis, MN: University of Minnesota Press.

Li, T.M. (2007) Practices of assemblage and community forest management. *Economy and Society*, 36(2): 263–293.

McCann, E., and Ward, K. (eds) (2011) *Mobile Urbanism: Cities and Policymaking in the Global Age*. London and Minneapolis, MN: University of Minnesota Press.

McFarlane, C. (2011) *Learning the City: Knowledge and Translocal Assemblage*. Malden, MA and Oxford: Wiley-Blackwell.

Merrifield, A. (2012) The urban question under planetary urbanization. *International Journal of Urban and Regional Research*, n/a-n/a.

Ong, A., and Collier, S.J. (eds) (2005) *Global Assemblages: Technology, Politics, and Ethics as Anthropological Problems*. Malden, MA, Oxford and Carlton: Blackwell Publishing Ltd.

Peck, J., and Theodore, N. (2010) Mobilizing policy: models, methods, and mutations. *GEOFORUM*, 41(2): 169–174.

Prince, R. (2012) Policy transfer, consultants and the geographies of governance. *Progress in Human Geography*, 36(2): 188–203.

Roy, A., and Ong, A. (eds). (2011) *Worlding Cities: Asian Experiments and the Art of Being Global*. New York: Blackwell Publishing Ltd.

1 Creative clusters in Shanghai

Transnational intermediaries and the creative economy

Justin O'Connor and Xin Gu

Introduction

In 2005 the Shanghai municipal government adopted a 'creative industries' strategy. Explicitly derived, via Hong Kong, from the UK government's rebranding of the 'cultural industries' in 1998, 'creative industries' was not at the time officially recognized as a policy term by the national government in Beijing. This intentionally put Shanghai at the cutting edge of China's next wave of modernization. Shanghai's embrace of the 'creative industries' has to be seen as part of the Chinese national government's new round of economic and symbolic modernization – a shift from the 1980s/90s *gaige kaifang* (reform and opening) to Hu Jintao's emphasis on *gaige chuangxin* (reform and innovation) (Pang, 2012: 8). However, in enthusiastically adopting the term 'creative industries' ahead of Beijing (the capital and national government remained cautious and settled on 'cultural creative industries'), Shanghai asserted its traditional role as the engine of China's cultural and economic modernization.

At the same time, the city officially recognized a number of 'creative industry clusters' (CICs) and promoted their expansion as a key element of this strategy. Over the next five years these official clusters grew to around ninety in number. The active promotion of CICs was also part of Shanghai's aspiration to become a modern, global metropolis. Many of the CICs were high-profile, photogenic destinations attracting media and tourist attention, providing Shanghai with another facet in its accumulation of image capital. Though Shanghai was by no means alone in its promotion of CICs – by 2012 many Chinese cities and towns had built or had plans to build CICs in some shape or form (Yang, 2011; Kern et al., 2011; Keane, 2012) – it was Shanghai that witnessed their most rapid growth and provided some of the emblematic CIC models for other cities and towns to copy. In addition, as we shall see, CICs in Shanghai drew much more explicitly on the urbanistic dimension of clusters (rather than the 'industry base' tradition of socialist planning common in these other cities) with which they were associated in the West.[1]

Shanghai's adoption of both creative industries and CICs thus combined its commitment to economic modernization with its aspirations to become a global city, incorporating high levels of cultural and symbolic capital. It could be seen as an example of 'fast policy' (Peck, 2002), where Chinese cultural and economic policy became further plugged into global policy flows. On the other hand, their adoption/adaptation is deeply marked by the specificity of both China and Shanghai. In this chapter we explore some of the complexities of this adoptive/adaptive process in Shanghai, focusing on the role of intermediaries. In doing so we will draw on the literatures around 'cultural intermediaries' and 'policy mobilities' which have informed recent debates on urban policy transfer, especially around creative economy/creative cities.

Intermediaries and policy mobilities

Cultural intermediaries have figured intermittently in the literature on cultural/creative industries since the 1980s. They were initially associated with the large-scale transformations of the cultural economy, helping to transform the field of cultural consumption, challenging established cultural hierarchies, changing the relation between consumption and identity, and promoting more hedonistic and 'aesthetic' consumer experiences. They also opened up new fields of cultural production by altering attitudes to work, career and life-course among producers while also bringing highly reflective and aesthetic–informational inputs into the production process. Early literature tended to link cultural intermediaries to epochal claims around 'postmodernity' (Featherstone, 1991) and the new 'economies of signs and space' (Lash and Urry, 1994). In the last decade, however, they have been associated more narrowly with constructing markets, mediating between production and consumption in particular circumstances:

> They construct value, by framing how others – end consumers, as well as other market actors including other cultural intermediaries – engage with goods, affecting and effecting others' orientations towards those goods as legitimate – with 'goods' understood to include material products as well as services, ideas and behaviours.
>
> (Maguire and Mathews, 2012: 552)

As these authors acknowledge in passing (Maguire and Mathews, 2012: 551), cultural intermediaries also contribute to the production of symbolic value in urban spaces. This process was first identified by Sharon Zukin in *Loft Living* (1982), an account (still unsurpassed) of the ways in which artists and intermediaries (such as local events magazines, café owners and trendy retailers) began to turn a run-down industrial district into the height of bohemian chic. In a later book she termed this process of culture-led gentrification, in rather binary fashion, the transformation of a working-class vernacular into a gentrified landscape of power (Zukin, 1991). A more positive role was given to 'working-class bohemians' in Manchester in the mid-1990s, who were active in transforming a derelict landscape into one which seemed to promise a different future (O'Connor and Wynne, 1996; O'Connor, 2004; O'Connor and Gu, 2010).

Though these and other accounts emphasized the role of cultural intermediaries in opening up spaces and places for cultural production and consumption in the city, there were intermittent acknowledgements that these were also engaging with the local authorities in some sort of emergent 'creative city' policy coalition. The successful rezoning of New York's SoHo witnessed a new level of contact between artists and City Hall (Zukin, 1982). Manchester's music scene eventually produced an urban cultural adjunct to the existing growth coalition (O'Connor, 2004; O'Connor and Gu, 2010). So too with the musicians of Austin, Texas (Grodach, 2001; Grodach and Silver, 2012). A growing intersection between cultural intermediaries and urban government can also be seen writ large in Currid's (2007) account of New York. Cultural intermediaries not only contributed to the 'relandscaping' of urban areas and created new symbolic values (frequently recouped by developers) but also worked to facilitate a meaningful interaction between these new forms of urban cultural production/consumption and policy-makers.

The rise of this new policy coalition across the 1990s could be seen as an emergent 'epistemic community': 'a network of professionals with recognised expertise and competence in a particular domain and an authoritative claim to policy-relevant knowledge within that domain or issue-area' (Haas, 1992: 3). As initially described, this epistemic community has four features:

1 a shared set of normative and principled beliefs which provide a value-based rationale for the social action of community members;
2 shared causal beliefs which are derived from their analysis of practices leading or contributing to a central set of problems in their domain and which then serve as the basis for elucidating the multiple linkages between possible policy actions and desired outcomes;
3 shared notions of validity, i.e. intersubjective, internally defined criteria for weighing and validating knowledge in the domain of their expertise; and
4 a common policy enterprise, or a set of common practices associated with a set of problems to which their professional competence is directed, presumably out of the conviction that human welfare will be enhanced as a consequence.

(Haas, 1992: 3)

This aptly describes the emergent, transnational policy community of cultural (and later creative) industries and creative cities experts in the 1990s – primarily in Europe, North America and Australia, and increasingly in Latin America, South Africa and East Asia (including Hong Kong and Taiwan but not mainland China). Its members were consultants and consultant–practitioners, local/regional government officers, cultural space managers, academics and representatives of national (British Council, Goethe Institute, etc.) and transnational cultural agencies (UNESCO, Ford Foundation, European Commission, etc.). Their emergent community was extended and consolidated across a series of conferences, networks and projects around cultural/creative industries and creative cities. Its not-quite-recognized field of expertise benefited enormously from the UK government's 'creative industries' brand; and it was this transnational epistemic community that was partly responsible for the unexpected (by the UK govern-ment at least) success of this policy across the globe.[2]

The emergent transnational epistemic community was linked to the local not just through proliferating conference and policy connections but through contact with local cultural 'scenes' (Straw and Marchessault, 2002; Bennett and Peterson, 2004). 'Scenes' can be used here in the sense of informal assemblages, 'fields' or 'art worlds' in which performers/creators, facilities and audiences/consumers come together in a shared investment in a particular activity, such as music scenes, arts scenes, poetry scenes, fashion scenes and so on. Local scenes can be highly mobile and difficult for all but the informed outsider to penetrate. However, one of the tendencies identified in the earlier cultural intermediaries literature (Featherstone, 1991; Lash and Urry, 1994) was for particular areas of the city to become sites for the more public enactment of these scenes. These areas had become linked to cultural or creative 'quarters' that were initially rather ad hoc and informal but increasingly became objects of policy. 'Creative clusters' began to emerge in aesthetically run-down parts of the urban centre, often associated with a venue, gallery or 'creative workspace'. These embodied urban scenes became an informal itinerary for the epistemic community and for 'gurus' such as Charles Landry. By the end of the last decade they had become the subjects of 'creative tourism' literature (Richards and Wilson, 2007). However, their local role should not be underestimated, as they formed a kind of micro-site in which global flows of images, sounds, texts, ideas (and people) were accessed. As such they should be seen in terms of what Saskia Sassen (2002) calls 'micro-sites in a global civil society'.

We might close this section on intermediaries by saying more about 'creative tourists'. As the literature has it (Richards and Wilson, 2007), these sought out not the standard tourist sites (they even resented being called 'tourists'), were often cultural practitioners themselves, and looked for 'experiences' involving inter-action with locals. Along with the epistemic community described above (the keenest creative tourists of all), these creative tourists headed to available sites where a different kind of local (in this case cultural) experience was possible. The 'clusters' or site-based scenes were the ideal destination, providing a more authentic experience and the possibility of glimpsing a new, youthful creative culture hidden from mainstream tourists. In alluding to creative tourists as cultural intermediaries we must note Maguire and Mathews's (2012) warning that 'we are all cultural intermediaries now' can dilute the term into uselessness. However, there is a sense in which these sites could attract flows of consultants, practitioners and cultural consumers in a way that had real impact on the local and carried this local back to the transnational level (often via conference/presentation slides or guest speaker invites extended to managers/owners of these sites).

In the case of Shanghai, on arrival Western visitors frequently reacted with the kind of awestruck disorientation associated with experience of the Kantian sublime – a chaotic challenge to the existing framework of our reason (Hatherley, 2012; Lagerkvist, 2013). Part of this experience was the mixture of memory and futurity associated with the city's recovery of a Western heroic urban modernity and its projection of a new modernity in which China (or Asia) would supplant the West (both exemplified by the Pudong skyline, outdoing both the colonial *bund* and Manhattan itself). This powerful urban imaginary was not just a product of the city's indigenous economic miracle but was produced out of the encounter with (and often 'playing to') a 'West' constituted by mobile intermediaries:

> These mobile elites constitute, through their own bodily movements, parts of the transformations at hand. The production of 'New Shanghai' as a space of memory and futurity is a process enacted by politicians, urban planners, architects, public relations specialists, general tourism promoters, and media workers, but it also occurs . . . through the movements and performances of visitors.
>
> (Lagerkvist, 2013: 20)

As we shall see, 'creative clusters' were a crucial element in this process of creating a 'New Shanghai' out of a relational encounter with the West.

Policy mobilities

'Policy mobilities' involves an extension of the linear account of 'policy transfer' towards one that it more fluid and complex. According to this approach, policy transfer literature, coming out of political science, tended to emphasize how policy is framed as 'best practice' to be rationally selected and copied across space. There is minimal discussion of power relations, and cities are viewed as producers or receivers of policy. Policy mobilities suggests a much more fluid process:

> Once released into the wild, policies will often mutate and hybridize in surprising ways . . . In contrast to the policy transfer tradition, which invokes notions of rational diffusion and best-practice replication, critical approaches to policy mobility tend to explore open ended and politicized processes of networking and mutation across shifting social landscapes.
>
> (Peck and Theodore, 2010: 173)

The transfer process is not one-way but establishes 'dialogic' connections between sites. Policy actors are 'embodied members of epistemic, expert, and practice communities . . . operat[ing] in fields of practice that are heavily intermediated, not least by a range of interests in the policy transfer "business", such as consultants, advocates, evaluators, gurus, and critics'. These mobile policies 'rarely travel as complete "packages", they move in bits and pieces – as selective discourses, inchoate ideas, and synthesized models – and they therefore "arrive" not as replicas but as policies already-in-transformation'. It is not 'emulation and linear replication across policy sites' but 'a complex process of non-linear reproduction'. Thus:

the mobilization of policies is understood to entail the reconstitution of fields of power, as the movement of ideas and techniques remakes the relations between jurisdictions A . . . E, breaching the borders between these policymaking sites, constructing symbiotic networks and circulatory systems across and between them, enabling cosmopolitan communities of practice and validating expert knowledges. Mobile policies, then, are not simply traveling across a landscape – they are remaking this landscape, and they are contributing to the interpenetration of distant policymaking sites.

(Peck and Theodore, 2010: 173)

This account clearly resonates with the proliferation of transnational and local intermediaries, as discussed above.

Creative industry clusters

'Creative cluster' provides an almost paradigmatic case of a policy term 'let loose into the wild'. In Europe and North America the term 'creative cluster' gained profile from Porter's influential papers on industrial clusters (Porter, 1998), where dense interactions, diversity of complementary skills and embedded knowledge allow particular places to achieve a competitive advantage. Porter's notion continues to be invoked by Western and Chinese policy-makers as underpinning creative clusters (see Kern et al., 2011), but it was largely the 'epistemic community' around urban creative economies who specified that the density, diversity and complex environment of city life were essential for cultural or creative clusters. From this perspective, 'creative clusters' were inseparable from creative cities – creativity conceived as a capacity almost co-terminus with the history of the city itself (Hall, 1998). However, though this urban creative milieu was sometimes invoked by the Shanghai government – it made an appearance at the 2010 Expo (see Hatherley, 2012) – this restless urban creativity was downplayed in favour of related but more developer-led aspects of the urban cluster concept (O'Connor and Gu, 2014).

As opposed to those urban clusters which emerged from the 'organic' fabric of the city, this other notion of 'cluster' applied more to specific groups of buildings (or even single ones) that were deliberately created for cultural consumption or production. These clusters could include large-scale subsidized institutions – museums, concert halls, galleries, educational facilities – and were also known as cultural 'precincts' or 'quarters'. From the 1980s in Europe and North America these cultural facilities were linked to the refurbishment of older industrial-era buildings as a way of regenerating run-down parts of the city. From the 1990s and spurred on by the cultural/creative industries agenda (as discussed above) these urban regeneration interventions began to include space for small-scale arts and cultural/creative industry production – though also with strong leisure (cafés, bars, restaurants) and retail (bookstores, design shops) elements. This second aspect was frequently overlaid on to the first, so that the characteristics of an embedded urban 'cognitive-cultural economy' (Scott, 2007) became associated with this more top-down arts facility-, retail- and entertainment-driven model. It resulted in much confusion as to their intended policy outcomes (Mommaas, 2004 and 2009; Evans and Foorde, 2005; Evans, 2009).

In adopting the creative industries agenda Shanghai Municipal Council was keen to interpret creative industries as advanced business services. They were allowed by central government to draw a line between 'safe' creative industries and those cultural industries under the purview of the culture and propaganda bodies; when classed as ideologically safe, creative industries could be given over to the economic committee to drive forward in pure developmental terms (O'Connor and Gu, 2012). Prime office space slightly outside the CBD – such as that being developed along Suzhou Creek – seemed the most apt infrastructure. Shanghai's heroic urban modernity was primarily focused on producing a Manhattan skyline driven by real estate and high-end consumption. The kind of urbanism associated with the broader creative cities agenda – dense interactions, autonomous micro-spaces, affective investment in place, various kinds of artist–bohemian scenes – was not immediately available to use within this model. The return of an older 'urban cultural sensibility' to Shanghai, as evoked by Lee (1999), was quickly reduced to recycled *Shanghai modern* images in film and television, tourist nostalgia (antiques, old posters, colonial-era buildings) and international brand shopping (O'Connor, 2012).

Shanghai's explicit coupling of creative industries with CICs maintained certain elements of the 'industry base' model (they would often be referred to as 'bases' or 'parks' in Chinese) – its directive relocation and integration of an industry value-chain (or section thereof) and FDI within a bounded compound – but increasingly linked to the reuse of an older industrial infrastructure that would previously have been discarded as 'junk'. In this the city adapted a Western culture-led regeneration model, but this was made possible by two other transnational (and dialogical) flows, both of which attempted to reinvent a Shanghainese 'urban cultural sensibility' through its industrial rather than colonial-era past.

First, contemporary art in China emerged on the margins of society in the late 1980s and was barely acknowledged by the authorities until the turn of the century. With most Chinese cities looking to classical music and the traditional performing arts as sources of international cultural capital, the meteoric rise in the profile of the international art world and its accelerated lauding of Chinese artists came as a surprise (O'Connor and Gu, 2012). In the late 1990s Beijing, Shanghai and Guangzhou all witnessed a movement of contemporary artists into old industrial sites, attracted by cheap rents, large spaces and the aesthetic and historical 'feel' of the factories and warehouses. Beijing's famous '798' has its Shanghai equivalent in the warehouses along Suzhou Creek, an old industrial district, where in the late 1990s a number of artists' workshops and one or two gallery/exhibition spaces opened up. These early spaces were subsequently demolished for new development in the face of opposition from artists and academic conservationists.[3] However, one space, first occupied in 1998, survived: an old textile factory, which came to be known as 'M50'. Though its existence was always precarious, it began to attract attention amongst international art brokers, conservationists, cultural policy experts and 'creative' tourists; followed by local academics concerned with the emerging 'creative industries' agenda (for detailed accounts, see: Wang, 2009; Zheng, 2010; Zhong, 2009 and 2011; Gu, 2012).

This was a kind of micro-space, as discussed above, in which transnational visitors and local scenes might encounter each other, and a different imagery of the city might emerge. Yet the reason for M50's rising international profile was not clear for the authorities (who were suspicious) or mainstream developers (who were bemused). It both persisted as a space and was made understandable to the policy world by the intermediation of the M50 manager Jin Wei Dong. He was an employer of an old state-owned enterprise, Shang-Tex, which owned the factory, and was charged with finding industrial tenants to replace the older textile workers. A source of revenue was also required to pay the pensions of the redundant workers. The entry of artists into the empty textile factory and its evolution into M50 was unplanned; the factory management was looking to encourage light-industrial use, but this proved to be more problematic and less profitable than envisaged. The artists paid low industrial rent but it was better than nothing; surprisingly, however, this second group began to outstrip the first, and they made less noise and less mess. It was through this close and increasingly sympathetic interaction with the artists that Jin Wei Dong felt his way towards the specific challenges of managing a 'creative space' that had previously challenged many in the West. It was his assertion of the viability of this kind of model for older factories and his sense of contributing to the wider cultural and urbanistic capacity of Shanghai that began to register with the policy-makers.

Second, overlapping with the emergent connectivity of local and global art worlds was that of architects and designers. Though architectural firms have long been global players, the 'transnational urbanism' they presented to China was directed towards large-scale projects in association with approved local partners (Ren, 2011). It was in fact Hong Kong and Taiwanese architects who had the language skills and connections to begin to move more independently into potential development sites. The iconic manufacturing heartland of Suzhou Creek, with its rich industrial heritage, began to attract small-scale architect-led development at the end of the 1990s, often in association with artist-led spaces. Taiwanese architect Teng Kun Yan began the process in 1998 but others followed (Gu, 2012). Increasingly these newly refurbished spaces – always under threat of demolition to make way for 'real' office development – began to attract not artists but (increasingly international) design and media firms. Similarly, design forms had begun to move into and refurbish old warehouses in the older residential area on Taikang Road, increasingly using the residences themselves as small retail outlets (Zhong, 2012).

Both of these sought to retrieve an urban sensibility based on industrial heritage with the 'distressed' aesthetic common in the West and highly visible (and available) to Hong Kong and Taiwanese architects. It was a different, somewhat vernacular urbanism, and one in which the production of art and design provided a micro-site for a different kind of transnational urbanism. It was of course within these milieu that the 'urban industrial aesthetic' and its application to creative industries became visible to policy-makers.

Indications that the potential of the historical vernacular for real estate development had been recognized came in 2004 with the opening of Xintiandi, an office, retail and bar/dining complex near a major shopping street. It was constructed from the elements of the old *Shikumen* housing blocks, but made fit for modern use and provided with open 'piazzas' in trusted *po-mo* fashion. It was telling that the development company was from Hong Kong, and equally so that the architect, Benjamin Wood, was a protégé of Benjamin Thompson, whose 1979 transformation of Faneuil Hall in Boston represents a foundational moment of heritage-led urban regeneration. The Hong Kong developer was asked to incorporate the old Girls' School which had hosted the first meeting of the Chinese Communist Party. Rather than the burden this would have represented for most Shanghai developers at that time, such historical patina proved to be a godsend, so much so that the developers reconstructed a *Shikumen* house as a period museum over and above the brief (Liang, 2008).

It was some time before local authorities and developers recognized the potential of attracting cultural/creative businesses that were willing to pay commercial-level rents for low-cost industrial space. The big problem was the unofficial nature of these cultural activities in industrial space. The city authorities' attitude to M50 had alternated between benign tolerance and threatening demolition/redevelopment; they had the power to shut down such activities at any time as illegal use of industrial land. It was an uncertain situation. What changed was not an alternative urbanism or even recognition of urban aesthetic–symbolic value but real estate regulation policy.

In this process intermediation took place within the administration, as the option to reuse industrial spaces for creative industries emerged as one clear lesson Chinese official delegations took from their many visits to the UK after 1998. The new lead body for the sector – the Shanghai Creative Industries Association – was a hybrid of Chinese-style industry bodies with the sorts of agencies that had developed in London, Manchester and other pro-creative industry cities. The association was headed by an ex-naval administrator who had been charged with developing industrial design strategies, He Zeng Qiang, who had been an early enthusiast both for creative industries and for the refurbished industrial space in which they seemed to be housed. He Zeng Qiang was a key contributor to the 'business model' that would underpin such a process – the ability to designate what were in fact creative commercial services as industries. That is, not to stress their economic dimension as in the West but more literally as able to occupy industrial spaces without their land use being redesignated as 'commercial'.

The mechanism behind this has been succinctly described by Jane Zheng (2010) and Sheng Zhong (2011). The break-up of the state-owned enterprises (SOEs) in the 1990s had left them with land-use rights over large tracts of land. Given permission to sell on these land-use rights, the SOEs (in the form of the national Danwei, with head offices in Beijing) rapidly became major real estate developers. In 2002 local authorities gained the right to determine land use. Therefore, if an SOE wanted to sell industrial land-use rights for commercial development they had to go through the local state (giving this entity enhanced leverage) and had to pay local tax for redesignation. However, the model that emerged through initiatives such as M50 was that artistic and cultural – soon to be 'creative' – use of old industrial buildings could be effected without a change in land-use designation.

He Zeng Qiang was part of the process of the adoption of the new CIC policy which formalized the occupation of industrial spaces by creative industries. This allowed the owner (of land-use rights) to charge high commercial rent for industrial land without having to seek a formal redesignation or paying the fees associated with such a change and the tax on subsequent commercial land use. More usually, developers (which frequently included the district government's own company) would rent land from the SOEs, invest in minimal refurbishment, and charge high commercial rents to the new tenant. At the same time, the resultant high-density clustering of commercial firms generated great tax returns for local government. This was why ninety appeared in Shanghai within five years. He Zeng Qiang's role was to certify these CICs and provide consultancy services for them.

The re-emergence of old industrial buildings in the form of creative, aesthetically upmarket sites for the contemporary global cultural city was clearly attractive for an ambitious Shanghai. Indeed, only perhaps one or two Chinese cities apart from Shanghai had the capacity to identify such emergent developments as workable within the new CIC policy framework. For many, CICs in Shanghai have been a great success. Their proliferation fed into the burgeoning image of Shanghai as a global cultural city, able to showcase its own refurbished buildings alongside those factories, warehouses, railways stations, tram depots, hospitals, asylums, prisons and so on that had become *de rigueur* in late twentieth-century Europe, North America and ultimately around the world. In Shanghai, as in China generally, the power of the image should not be underestimated (Greenspan, 2011). As the 'new Manhattan' of Pudong helped launch the city's global status, the contribution of the showcase clusters to its global brand was important. The most photogenic CICs rapidly became sites for fashion shoots, launches, events and conferences, regularly appearing in in-flight magazines and ex-pat 'what's-on' guides. Bridge 8 (a media cluster), Red Town (a sculpture park linked to creative office space), 1933 Millfun (a converted abattoir for upmarket design retail) as well as the longer-established 'organic' Tianzi Fang and M50 are all promoted as cutting-edge creative industry initiatives by local and national government officials. They have become well established on the itineraries of the transnational epistemic community of creative city promoters.

Conclusion: a re-imagined creative Shanghai?

In this chapter we have tried to trace a particular aspect of the creative economy project – the 'creative cluster' in refurbished industrial buildings, conceived as a re-imagining of the urban cultural economy. As with the policy mobilities literature we have stressed the fluid, selective and hybridizing aspects of policy transfer, and how it came to be assembled through a series of disjointed packages and dispersed arrival points. Such an assemblage hid many tensions and conflicting interests, and the tensions have only grown in the last decade as different developmental interests have moved into the 'creative cities' agenda and come into conflict with cultural producers and communities (see Indergaard, 2009; Grodach and Silver, 2012; Oakley and O'Connor, 2015). In China artist–intellectuals had been steadily marginalized during the 1990s (Wang, 1996; Kraus, 2004); and cultural producers/entrepreneurs outside the state-owned sector were equally marginalized, especially in Shanghai (Lee et al., 2007). In such a context intermediaries in the creative economy were closely linked to the (local) state. They learned from the models emerging from more autonomous micro-sites such as M50, the Suzhou Creek artist-linked refurbishment and Tian Zi Fan, but this came with an exclusion from control of the cultural intermediaries. This is now a common story in most artists' spaces that have been promoted by government (Pang, 2012).

There are micro-sites in which a re-imagined creative city persists. A small hot-desking creative workspace, Xindanwie, managed to thrive for a while on the edges of the policy world, acting as a test space for a more flexible use of CICs given the current overcapacity (O'Connor and Gu, 2012). Informed visitors (creative tourists, perhaps) to Shanghai can find fast-moving, temporary spaces that are regularly closed down and moved on by the government. Other scenes do not find space in micro-sites, such as the recent 'ant-tribe' phenomenon of low-income, under-employed university graduates who live in poverty in the big cities and move discontentedly around the suburban fringes in the hope of finding a job.

On the other hand, the growing profile of 'culture' as an economic possibility has brought in some big players. As we have seen, CICs became serious real estate machines; De Bi, a huge mining company from far-off (relative to Shanghai) Shanxi Province has recently begun to buy existing CICs and land that could be developed for this sector. The 12th Five Year Plan and the 6th Conference of the 17th CPC Central Committee in 2011 further asserted the role of the cultural/creative industries in China's development. As a consequence a new spurt of CICs has occurred. An estimated 365 existing clusters across China in 2011 will be joined by 950 new ones, with the majority (65 per cent) on land held by county- or district-level local authorities.[4] But this has also been made possible by the national government's freeze on real estate prices in early 2011; developers prevented from selling on property (and servicing their debts) have moved into the cheaper land offered by local authorities for 'cultural/creative industries' development, thereby gaining crucial collateral for further loans.

Given the links between real estate and cultural/creative industries which has taken place in Shanghai and Beijing (Ren, 2011), Joel Andreas (2009) may have been right to suggest that the 'red engineers' (the technically educated cadre which has dominated China since the 1990s) have been joined in their domination by those with large amounts of cultural capital, usually conjoined with real estate interests. Underneath Shanghai's heroic urban modernity, as celebrated by the transnational media, there is increasing disengagement from this imaginary as currently articulated in policy terms. This perhaps is a microcosm of what is facing China's leaders as they attempt not just to catch up with but overtake the West.

Notes

1 This research draws on a three-year research project funded by the Australia Research Council under its linkage programme 'Soft Infrastructure, New Media and Creative Clusters: Building Capacity in China and Australia' (see www.creativeasia.co.uk; accessed 16 November 2012). Partners include Arup, Shanghai Jiaotong University and Creative 100, Qingdao. The authors would like to acknowledge the contributions made to this paper by all three partners, who have provided extensive advice and industry knowledge.
2 This epistemic community was only cautiously welcoming of Richard Florida; his ground was prepared by them though never acknowledged by him. Its statistical work brought in 'non-cultural actors' but also linked to urban developers who recognized aesthetic appeal without buying in to the whole 'creative cities' programme.
3 It was a coalition very similar to that which had successfully resisted development in SoHo, as described in Zukin's (1982) account of culture-led urban regeneration.
4 According to Ma Da at *Creative Times* (www.ccitime.com), a partner on the ARC 'Creative Clusters' project (accessed 16 November 2012).

References

Andreas, J. (2009) *Rise of the Red Engineers: The Cultural Revolution and the Origins of China's New Class*, Stanford, CA: Stanford University Press.
Bennett, A. and Peterson, R.A. (2004) *Music Scenes: Local, Translocal and Virtual*, Nashville, TN: Vanderbilt University Press.
Cochrane, A. and Ward, K. (2012) 'Researching the Geographies of Policy Mobility: Confronting the Methodological Challenges', *Environment and Planning A*, 44(1): 5–12.
Currid, E. (2007) *The Warhol Economy: How Fashion, Art, and Music Drive New York City*, Princeton, NJ: Princeton University Press.
Evans, G (2009) 'Creative Cities, Creative Spaces and Urban Policy', *Urban Studies*, 46(5–6): 1003–1040.
Evans, G. and Foord, J. (2005) *Strategies for Creative Spaces – Phase 1*, report commissioned by the London Development Agency – Creative London, City of Toronto, Ontario Ministry of Economic Development and Trade, and Ministry of Culture.
Featherstone, M. (1991) *Consumer Culture and Postmodernism*, London: Sage.
Florida, R. (2002) *The Rise of the Creative Class*, New York: Basic Books.
Greenspan, A. (2011) 'The Power of Spectacle', *Culture Unbound*, Special Issue: *Shanghai Moderne*, 4: 81–95.
Grodach, C. (2011) 'Before and after the Creative City: The Politics of Urban Cultural Policy in Austin, Texas', *Journal of Urban Affairs*, 34 (1): 81–97.
Grodach, C. and Silver, D. (eds) (2012) *The Politics of Urban Cultural Policy*, London: Routledge.
Gu, X. (2012) 'The Art of Re-Industrialisation in Shanghai', *Culture Unbound*, 4: 193–211.

Haas, P.M. (1992) 'Epistemic Communities and International Policy Coordination', *International Organization*, 46(1): 1–35.

Hall, P. (1998) *Cities in Civilisation*, London: Pantheon.

Harris, A. and Moreno, L. (2012) 'Urban Cultural Economy in a New Era of Austerity', retrieved from www.creativecitylimits.org (accessed 16/11/2012).

Hartley, J. and Montgomery, L. (2009) 'Creative Industries Come to China,' *Chinese Journal of Communication*, 2: 1–12.

Hatherley, O. (2012) 'The Hyperstationary State: Five Walks in Search of the Future in Shanghai', *Culture Unbound*, Special Edition: *Shanghai Modern*, 4: 35–80.

Hollands, R. and Vail, J. (2012) 'The Art of Social Movement: Cultural Opportunity, Mobilisation, and Framing in the Early Formation of the Amber Collective', *Poetics*, 40(1): 22–42.

Hutton, W. (2007) *The Writing on the Wall: China and the West in the 21st Century*, London: Little, Brown.

Indergaard, M (2009) 'What to Make of New York's New Economy? The Politics of the Creative Field', *Urban Studies*, 46(5–6): 1063–1093.

Keane, M. (2007) *The New Great Leap Forward*, London: Routledge.

Keane, M. (2009) 'Creative Industries in China: Four Perspectives on Social Transformation', *International Journal of Cultural Policy*, 15(4): 431–443.

Keane, M. (2010) 'Great Adaptations: China's Creative Clusters and the New Social Contract', *Continuum: Journal of Media and Cultural Studies*, 23(2): 221–230.

Keane, M. (2012) *China's New Creative Clusters: Governance, Human Capital and Regional Investment*, London: Routledge.

Kern, P., Smits, Y. and Wang, D. (2011) *Mapping the Cultural and Creative Sectors in the EU and China: A Working Paper in Support of the Development of an EU–China Cultural and Creative Industries Platform*, Brussels: KEA.

Kong, L., Gibson, C., Khoo, L.M. and Semple, A.L. (2006) 'Knowledges of the Creative Economy: Towards a Relational Geography of Diffusion and Adaptation in Asia', *Asia Pacific Viewpoint*, 47(2): 173–194.

Kraus, R.C. (2004) *The Party and the Arty: The New Politics of Culture*, Oxford: Rowman and Littlefield.

Lagerkvist, A. (2013) *Media and Memory in New Shanghai: Western Performances of Futures Past*, London: Palgrave Macmillan.

Lash, S. and Urry, J. (1994) *Economies of Signs and Space*, London: Sage.

Lee, L.O. (1999) *Shanghai Modern: The Flowering of a New Urban Culture in China, 1930–1945*, Cambridge, MA, and London: Harvard University Press.

Lee, C.-C., He, Z. and Huang, Y. (2007) 'Party–Market Corporatism, Clientelism, and Media in Shanghai', *Harvard International Journal of Press/Politics*, 12(3): 21–42.

Liang, S. (2008) 'Amnesiac Monument, Nostalgic Fashion: Shanghai's New Heaven and Earth', *Wasafiri*, 23(3): 47–55.

Maguire, J. and Mathews, J. (2012) 'Are We All Cultural Intermediaries Now? An Introduction to Cultural Intermediaries in Context', *European Journal of Cultural Studies*, 15(5): 551–562.

Mommaas, H. (2004) 'Cultural Clusters and the Post-industrial City: Towards the Re-mapping of Urban Cultural Policy', *Urban Studies*, 41(3): 507–532.

Mommaas, H. (2009) 'Spaces of Culture and Economy: Mapping the Cultural–Creative Cluster Landscape', in L. Kong and J. O'Connor (eds), *Creative Economies, Creative Cities: Asian–European Perspectives*, Dordrecht: Springer, pp. 45–60.

Oakley, K. and O'Connor, J. (2015) 'Culture and the City', in K. Oakley and J. O'Connor (eds), *The Routledge Companion to the Cultural Industries*, London: Routledge, pp. 201–211.

O'Connor, J. (2004) '"A Special Kind of City Knowledge": Innovative Clusters, Tacit Knowledge and the "Creative City"', *Media International Australia*, 112: 131–149.

O'Connor, J. (2009) 'Shanghai Moderne: Creative Economy in a Creative City?', in in L. Kong and J. O'Connor (eds), *Creative Economies, Creative Cities: Asian–European Perspectives*, Dordrecht: Springer, pp. 175–196.

O'Connor, J. (2011) 'Economic Development, Enlightenment and Creative Transformation: Creative Industries in the New China', *Ekonomiaz*, 78(3): 108–125.

O'Connor, J. (2012) 'Shanghai: Replaying Futures Past', *Culture Unbound*, 4: 15–34.

O'Connor, J. and Gu, X. (2006) 'A New Modernity? The Arrival of "Creative Industries" in China', *International Journal of Cultural Studies*, Special Issue: *China*, 9(3): 271–283.

O'Connor, J. and Gu, X. (2010) 'Developing a Creative Cluster in Post-industrial City: CIDS and Manchester', *Information Society*, 26(2): 124–136.

O'Connor, J. and Gu, X. (2012) 'Shanghai: Images of Modernity', in R. Isar and H. Anheier (eds), *Cultural Policy and Governance in a New Metropolitan Age*, London: Sage, pp. 288–300.

O'Connor, J. and Gu, X. (2014) 'Creative Industry Clusters in Shanghai: A Success Story?', *International Journal of Cultural Policy*, 20(1): 1–20.

O'Connor, J. and Wynne, D. (1996) 'Left Loafing: Cultural Consumption and Production in the Postmodern City', in J. O'Connor and D. Wynne (eds), *From the Margins to the Centre: Cultural Production and Consumption in the Post-Industrial City*, Aldershot: Ashgate, pp. 1–17.

Pang, L. (2012) *Creativity and Its Discontents: China's Creative Industries and Intellectual Property Rights Offences*, Raleigh, NC: Duke University Press.

Peck, J. (2002) 'Political Economies of Scale: Fast Policy, Interscalar Relations, and Neoliberal Workfare', *Economic Geography*, 78: 331–360.

Peck, J. (2005) 'Struggling with the Creative Class', *International Journal of Urban and Regional Research*, 29(4): 740–770.

Peck, J. (2011) 'Creative Moments: Working Culture, through Municipal Socialism and Neoliberal Urbanism', in K. Ward and E. McCann (eds), *Mobile Urbanism: Cities and Policy Making in the Global Age*, Minneapolis: University of Minnesota Press, pp. 41–66.

Peck, J. and Theodore, N. (2010) 'Mobilizing Policy: Models, Methods and Mutations', *Geoforum*, 41: 169–174.

Peck, J. and Theodore, N. (2012) 'Follow the Policy: A Distended Case Approach', *Environment and Planning A*, 44(1): 21–30.

Porter, M.E. (1998) 'Clusters and the New Economics of Competitiveness', *Harvard Business Review*, 76: 77–90.

Ren, X. (2011) *Building Globalization: Transnational Architecture Production in Urban China*, Chicago: University of Chicago Press.

Richards, G. and Wilson, J. (2007) *Tourism, Creativity and Development*, London: Routledge.

Sassen, S. (2002) 'Global Cities and Diasporic Networks: Micro-sites in Global Civil Society', in M. Glasius, M. Kaldor and H. Anheier (eds), *Global Civil Society*, Oxford: Oxford University Press, pp. 217–238.

Scott, A.J. (2007) 'Capitalism and Urbanisation in a New Key? The Cognitive–Cultural Dimension', *Social Forces*, 85(4): 1465–1482.

Straw, W. and Marchessault, J. (eds) (2002) 'Cities/Scenes', *Public*, Special Issue 22/23.

Wang, J. (1996) *High Culture Fever: Politics, Aesthetics and Ideology in Deng's China*, Berkeley: University of California Press.

Wang, J. (2009) '"Art in Capital": Shaping Distinctiveness in a Culture-led Urban Regeneration Project in Red Town, Shanghai', *Cities*, 26: 318–330.

Yang, J. (2011) 'The Chinese Understanding of Cultural Industries', *SANTALKA: Filosofia, Komunikacija*, 19(2): 90–97.

Yeh, W. (2007) *Shanghai Splendor: Economic Sentiments and the Making of Modern China, 1843–1949*, Berkeley and Los Angeles: University of California Press.

Zheng, J. (2010) 'The "Entreprenuerial State" in "Creative Industry Cluster" Development in Shanghai', *Journal of Urban Affairs*, 32(2): 143–170.

Zhong, S (2009) 'From Fabrics to Fine Arts: Urban Restructuring and the Formation of an Art District in Shanghai', *Critical Planning*, 16: 118–137.

Zhong, S (2011) 'Industrial Restructuring and the Formation of Creative Industry Clusters: The Case of Shanghai's Inner City', unpublished PhD thesis, University of British Columbia.

Zhong, S (2012) 'Production, Creative Forms and Urban Spaces in Shanghai', *Culture Unbound*, Special Issue: *Shanghai Moderne*, 4: 169–191.

Zukin, S. (1982) *Loft Living: Culture and Capital in Urban Change*, London: Johns Hopkins Press Ltd.

Zukin, S. (1991) *Landscapes of Power: From Detroit to Disney World*, Berkeley and Los Angeles: University of California Press.

2 Local planning practices and institutional innovation of the creative city

The case of Taipei City

Cheng-Yi Lin

Introduction

The city's institutional responses toward the making of creative cities has become a crucial issue for contemporary urban governance and planning studies (Scott, 2011). Although the exchange of academic knowledge has sped up transference of the normative creative policy from Western cities to East Asian cities over the last decade (Kong et al., 2006; Evans, 2009), less research has focused discussions on the mobility policy of creative city and related planning practices in Asian urban contexts. Particularly, globalising discourses of creative city policy become hegemonic projects that are widely circulated to influence local planning practices; this transnational concept has then been differentiated, adopted, and translated into a new policy panacea by justifying the spatial planning practices for creative industries and individuals (Peck, 2005; Grodach, 2012; Evans, 2009). While the inter-cities network of creative city policy is constantly structured through the mechanism of policy mobility and territorialisation processes (Prince, 2010, 2012), cultural contradictions emerge between global 'best practices' and the territorialisation process of the creative city concept, generating socio-economic and institutional tensions in the implementation process of urban development.

Taipei is no exception to the global practices of creative city policy. While Charles Landry was invited as an international policy consultant to propose strategic suggestions for creative city development in Taipei (Landry, 2012), Taipei City Government (TCG) played a leading role creating an effective environment for the accumulation of creative capital. This was because spatial planning practices and regulations in Taiwan are regarded as an instrument of economic development policy that constantly encourages the spatial accumulation of capital in order to achieve comprehensive economic growth (Wang, 2012). In the developmental state context,[1] TCG presented a strong commitment and intervening power to develop creative cities by launching a series of cultural strategies (Taipei City Government, 2012). These strategies, including mega-projects and bidding campaigns for recognition as a 'World Design Capital', were aimed at constituting what Kong (2007) claimed as the 'cultural icon' of the creative city. Obviously, these planning practices illustrated the less noticed spatial phenomenon that the government's actions are regarded as pivotal interventions in shaping the formation of creative cities through the adoption of international planning practices. However, these 'one-size-fits-all' planning practices not only reflect how neoliberal urban development is dominated by stylised urban governance (Peck, 2005) but illustrate the governance deficits and tensions that limit institutional response to the needs of those creative individuals actually making the creative city (Scott, 2011, 2014). As Scott (2014) indicates, policy elaborations need to cultivate the social mobilisation dynamics of creative communities through the medium of cultural economic planning.[2] While the making of a creative city is by no means the mere transplantation of creative policy from one city, this chapter raises two research questions. First, what kinds of strategies and policy ideas have emerged and been mobilised in the process of Taipei's creative city project? Second, does local government shape institutional innovation for the sustainability of the creative city?

In response, this chapter uses the evolutionary perspective (Boschma and Lambooy, 1999; Boschma, 2004) as an analytic framework to illustrate how Taipei's creative cities policy responds to the internal tensions of urban transformation and the external competitive pressures of economic restructuring. The Taipei case contributes to the policy mobility-mutation dimension of creative city policy by examining planning practices and institutional innovation issues. Three major research strategies were conducted to collect evidence using a discourse analysis, tracing the policy networks of the creative city, and conducting nine semi-structured interviews in Taipei.

The chapter is divided into four sections. First, I critically review the mobility-mutation approach of creative city policy and discuss its limitations and tensions. Next, I draw on the evolutionary perspective to propose an analytic framework for a systematic analysis of the Taipei case. By analysing the evolving discourses and planning practices, I present the divergent and multiple trajectories of policy learning that structure the current version of the creative city project in Taipei. Third, I further explore the emergence of recent tensions during the implementation of creative cities projects in order to understand the importance of institutional innovation in such projects. This empirical study then sheds light on the reflexive relationship between institutions and creative economic development. Finally, I conclude by outlining some lessons from the Taipei case.

Rethinking the making of the creative city

The evolution of the creative city script: from normative policy script to hegemonic idea

The varied concepts of 'creative city', 'creative industry', and 'creative class' have evolved and reassembled into the hegemonic idea of neoliberalism, as a normative policy script aimed at resolving the post-industrial urban development crisis (Kong, 2014; Scott, 2014). As Scott (2007) suggests, the major engine of local economic development is shifting from the Fordist production system to a cognitive-cultural production system. The emergence of cognitive-cultural industry clusters constitutes the spatially 'creative field' of inner cities, which present the recursive linkage between cognitive-cultural capitalism and urbanisation (Scott, 2011, 2014). The urbanisation process explicitly is driven by the enthusiastic consumption pattern of symbolic commodities and flexible production networks with an industry cluster. In order to stabilise the economic ordering of cognitive-cultural capitalism, local governments enthusiastically seek policy innovation strategies through fast policy transfer (Peck, 2002). These include the discovery of innovation synergies in certain cities and cultural production clusters (Hall, 1999, 2000; Scott, 2006; Lin, 2014), constructing heritage as an international tourism attraction (Chang and Teo, 2009), fostering social dynamics of neighbourhood development in culture-led urban regeneration (Sacco and Blessi, 2009; Lin and Hsing, 2009), encouraging urban branding (Okano and Samson, 2010), and mobilising flagship projects and mega-events as the competitive advantage of urban development (Kong, 2007). These planning practices are legitimated as parts of creative city strategies cater to the global business elite and local inhabitants.

However, these place-making initiatives, obviously with different policy rationalities and place-specific contexts, hardly generate a successful creative cities 'script' or policy package that can be easily translated into other cities. This is because creative city policy inevitably generates socio-economic frictions and tensions, and it has varying effects on the spatial ordering of urban development (Peck, 2012). This suggests that planners need to trace the policy mobility-mutation process of the creative city concept in order better to understand the deficits of policy implementation (Prince, 2010; Peck, 2011). As Peck (2011: 170) claims, a social constructivist analysis provides a new angle to explore the dynamic process of creative policy initiatives, suggesting that the policy mobility is 'a more complex process of non-linear reproduction' that is 'shaped by multi-directional forms of cross-scalar and inter-local policy mobility'. In fact, creative city development is by no means a result of the organic growth of the socio-economic activities in the local context. The normative creative city programme, which resulted from the simplistic Floridian formula of the creative class, has only deepened social and economic polarisation (Peck, 2005; Scott, 2006). For example, the emergence of a creative class is relatively accompanied with a new servile class, which in turn is shaping urban social polarisation (Scott, 2012). Meanwhile, the urban poverty problem of the underdeveloped countries might be invisible in a cognitive-cultural urban development (Meagher, 2013). Despite many cities appearing to pursue a similar policy formula that originated from the Western context (Grodach, 2012), international planning practices have mutated according to the different considerations of local politics (Peck, 2012). It is necessary to identify the differences and similarities of the creative city projects and to advance an understanding of policy mutation by acknowledging three embedded tensions in the creative city policy.

First, the plan–project tension describes the fragmented and incoherent nature of the spatial ordering of urban development. While the creative city becomes a fashionable concept in urban governance, local governments seldom propose the kind of long-term masterplan of cultural industry development that is crucial for the cultivation of local networks of knowledge production, sociality, and identity (Sacco and Blessi, 2009). Rather, short-term temporary projects are selectively adapted by urban governments to shape qualities of places by launching mega-events and constructing symbolic buildings. This easily generates a fragmented and uneven effect rather than a continuous intervention in the making of the creative city since politico-social changes happen during the project process. As Lee and Hwang (2012) indicate, Seoul's creative city programme attempts to constitute visible cultural flagship projects, such as the Han River Renaissance Project, that end up generating an increasing crisis of national debt and social resistance. Thus, culture/creativity has been pursued as an instrumentalist rationale in urban governance.

Second, the production–consumption tension describes the contradictions of current spatial planning policy, which overemphasises landscapes of cultural consumption and 'feelgood' factors of place-making through cultural flagship projects (Pratt, 2009), rather than providing spaces for the cultural production of individual artists. This tension shows that creative city-making ought to forge the accumulation of cultural capital by balancing cultural production systems and cultural consumption. Sasaki's (2010) analysis of Kanazawa City is an example.

Third, creative city policy, focusing on the economic rationale, is creating an exclusion–inclusion tension through the branding of symbolic districts or quarters. As Catungal and Leslie (2009) indicate, while government emphasises the economic potential of gentrification through cultural projects, it neglects to balance the social inclusion–exclusion relationship that results from the trans-lation of a narrow definition of the creative class into planning policy. Nakagawa (2010) used the city of Osaka to illustrate community participation in art cultural activities that encouraged forging social inclusion as the progressive form of the creative city. Three tensions created opportunities for path-breaking in the creative city evolution process. Since they impacted the spatial ordering of creative city development, it was necessary to integrate these three tensions into creative city policy-making by considering the issue of institutional response.

Conceptualising institutional innovation in creative city-making: the evolutionary perspective

The evolutionary perspective is used to inscribe the interactive relationship between global 'best practice' and the process of territorialising the creative city concept. While institutional responses are crucial elaborations of the collective actions of creative city policy practices (Scott, 2014), the evolutionary perspective provides a dynamic and contextualised angle to explore the mobility-mutation process and the institutional dimension of the creative city policy. Although this perspective has been widely applied to the evolution of economic landscapes (Boschma and Lambooy, 1999; Boschma, 2004), it has seldom been applied to discussions of institutional changes in Taipei's creative city development. Inspired by Martin and Sunley (2006), the evolutionary perspective emphasises two advantages of explaining policy mutation. First, previous experience of policy-making will shape the varieties of future policy-making while policy actors face an uncertain environment. Second, the role of selection environment, whether intra-government or inter-cities dimension, is a structural condition enabling or constraining policy actors' actions that led to the situation in which policy is changed or stabilised. Thus, the perspective is a dynamic angle that explores an ongoing process for variation, selection, and retention of innovation in planning practices. Applying the evolutionary concept into an analytic framework of this chapter, institutional innovation is defined as the ongoing socio-political interactions among policy actors as they propose new institutional forms of planning practices and strategic arrangements to govern the tensions of creative city projects. Institutional innovation lies in the recursive process between path-dependent and path-creation effects of creative city policy intervention.

First, path-dependent effects of creative cities programmes in East Asian countries have displayed state interventionism patterns that are deeply influenced by the context of state-driven policy initiatives. On paper, the planning routines of Taipei's creative city projects fail to match the spatial-organisational dynamics of creative industry clusters since they rely on pre-existing experiences of planning practices, such as industrial districts or science parks. Local planning practices were obviously triggered by the institutional inertia of the spatial planning regime (Wang, 2012), leading to a self-enforcement and regressive model of policy interventions, rather than stimulating the potential opportunities of path-creation effects. Thus, the path-dependent effect is conceptualised as the context of previous policy actions structurally enabled and constricted by future planning practices. This axis analyses how the historical context shapes the geographical trajectory of Taipei's creative policy evolution.

Second, path-creation effects of creative city policy depend on the cultivation of the reflexive rationalities and capacities of policy communities that overcome the existing institutional inertia of the planning regime and display new planning practices in order to foster institutional change and progressive actions of local grassroots groups. As Amin (1999) argues, recursive rationalities tend to generate creative actor-networks with capacities actively to reconfigure the context of environment. The mobilisation capacities and active agencies of creative individuals respond to and resist path-dependence configurations. Path-creation effects therefore require the agencies of reflexive policy actors to launch new institutional arrangements. Thus, policy-makers' agencies and rationalities are conceptualised as crucial factors for the adaptation of creative policy to local institutional contexts. During the mobilisation process, creative city planning knowledge is influenced by trans-local policy networks (Prince, 2012). The opportunity for institutional innovation depends on the agencies of policy actors who initiate new planning processes and projects to respond to the emerging tensions of the creative city. Drawing on the evolutionary perspective, this chapter argues that the evolution of creative-led urban development policy has been an interactive relationship between different contexts and different actors' rationalities that co-determine the geographical trajectories of creative policy transfer.

The evolution of Taipei's creative city initiatives

Global discourses and the evolution of local planning practices

Taipei's creative city policy has developed rapidly since 1991. International discourses and experiences were constantly translated and emulated by the Taipei City Government through a spatial-relational understanding of policy learning sites. Despite Taipei having hosted several conferences on creative city policy since 2005, creative cities policies remained influenced by historical contexts and this generated the three stages of policy evolution within the developmental state context.

In the first stage, the creative city concept was not really mentioned by local government during the late 1990s. Local and national government officers developed a community-based cultural development initiative as an integrative cultural strategy in order to reform bureaucracy-oriented urban planning. Apparently, the Japanese colonial context shaped the geographical sourcing of policy transfer. Through studying Japanese cities, the Taipei City Government transplanted the concept of *machizukuri*[3] in order to enhance social participation and community involvement in Taipei's environmental improvement between 1996 and 2000 (Lin and Hsing, 2009). This stage, however, displayed dual meanings of cultural industries as, on the one hand, the means to revitalise local identities through planning empowerment for local inhabitants and, on the other hand, releasing public spaces from strict state regulation (Huang, 2005). Meanwhile, local government used *machizukuri* as the embryonic cultural industry strategy to awaken the senses of place and to promote a variety of place-specific cultural heritage sites, such as the Taipei Bao-an Festival (Lin and Hsing, 2009). Thus, the cultural industry idea was borrowed to echo the political democratisation and transformation trends of urban Taipei.

Second, the rhetoric of creative cities was first introduced in Taipei through academic knowledge transfer during between 2000 and 2008. The concepts of 'creative class' (Florida, 2002) and 'creative city' (Hall, 2000) were increasingly translated into creative industry policy by outsourcing to academic researchers or inviting policy consultants to join the cabinet. Taipei's embedded policy actors rearticulated the cultural industries concept with the UK government's creative industry (DCMS, 2004, 2008) to propose a new concept: cultural creative industries (CCIs). The normative policy of CCIs was an integrative rhetoric that was meant to maintain urban economic regeneration. However, Taipei's discourses were strongly influenced by neoliberalism, emphasising the transplantation of trans-local experience that fostered creative industries clusters by building cultural flagship projects. For example, the innovation synergies of Taipei's music industry are recognised as a competitive creative industry sector in Taiwan (Lin, 2014); the path-dependent effect of planning practices resulted in a plan to build a visible building project, the Pop Music Centre, which obviously emulated the antecedent experience of Sheffield's National Pop Music Centre (Banks et al., 2000). Echoing Kong's (2007) global cultural city argument, turning to the symbolic role of a music production centre in Taipei is not an accidental policy action but an intentional move reflecting the state's ambitions to become a creative city. Meanwhile, the Wanshan Cultural Creative District and Songyan Cultural Creative District provide examples to legitimise creative-led, consumption-oriented urban development, rather than foster community-based initiatives. This stage illustrated the finding that the transformative role of the developmental state was fostering a competitive urban entrepreneurialism in the creative economy, rather than encouraging social democracy and community activism.

The third stage of the creative city discourse emerged as part of Taipei's urban regeneration during 2008–2012. Taipei's policy discourse was not to celebrate as a creative city through joining UNESCO's 'Creative Cities Network'. Rather, the city attempted to develop a localised developmental model of the creative city by integrating trans-local experience with local planning practices. As an urban renewal officer explained, Taipei's mayor, Hou Long-Bing, visited Yokohama, Barcelona, and Amsterdam, viewing them as successful models of mega-event-driven urban regeneration. Despite these cities that exported the policy experience of culture-led urban regeneration (see Peck (2012) for the Amsterdam case), the policy-making contexts that are shaped by the colonial past and developmentalist mind explicitly enabled selecting these antecedent (Japanese and European) cities for creative policy-learning. These first-mover cities then become inspirational sites for creative policy-making even though their experiences are hardly transplanted into latecomer cities. Here, Taipei, with beta-city status in the global city hierarchy, performed an ambition of catch-up growth through trans-local policy-learning; the best-practice creative policy scripts were especially regarded as a panacea that was mobilised through policy-learning network mechanisms.

Figure 2.1 presents the major policy actors and their strategic roles during the policy-making stage, including international consultants, academic researchers, the mayor of Taipei, and local political elites. This network mobilised various international reference frames (e.g., Charles Landry and Richard Florida) and the experiences of antecedent cities (e.g., Yokohama) to translate trans-local best practices into creative city-making. In this network, Landry was the most important consultant. He was directly involved in policy-making of the creative city through intensive meetings, workshops, and conferences in Taipei from 2005 to 2014. Eventually, the academic consultants and local partnerships, which were embedded in the policy-making process, successfully conveyed to government officers and the mayor the importance of being a creative city. Although the creative policy knowledge-sharing activities were then conducted through study tours, policy outsourcing, and embedded policy translation, academic researchers played a role as crucial policy translators who brought fashionable concepts into the policy-making process and directly framed the three kinds of strategic intervention: mega-event cultural flagship projects, Urban Regeneration Stations, and social mobilisation initiatives for creative clusters. Obviously, Taipei's policy network was embedded in the related meetings, conferences, overseas study tours,

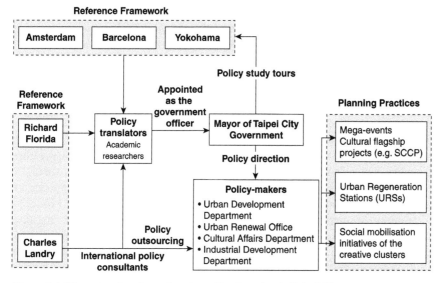

Figure 2.1 The networks of creative city policy-learning in Taipei City
Source: the author.

and academic workshops that were spatially constituted as the relational space of the creative city policy (see Prince, 2010).

However, Taipei not only reassembled and translated various versions of creative city scripts but also stimulated the territorialisation of creative city-making by pursuing mega-events and a bidding campaign for the World Design Capital. Local government particularly referred to the global centres of policy knowledge, such as Seoul, Helsinki, and Cape Town, reshaping itself as a significant cultural industry centre. Meanwhile, the Taipei City Government launched a series of sport and cultural mega-events to spur urban regeneration, such as the 21st Summer Deaflympics (2009), the Taipei International Flora Exposition (2010), the Taipei World Design Expo (2011), the World Design Capital (2016), and the Summer Universiade (2017). As Scott (2014: 10) indicates, mega-events are 'continually intensifying pressure on cities to assert their global presence and ambitions by means of vibrant visual images and branding campaigns'.

Despite these pretentious strategies to display the dominance of global economic rationales over local discourse, local transformative capacity is still underdeveloped. First, transformative capacity needs bottom-up community mobilisation. While local policy was influenced by inter-referencing effects (Bunnell, 2013), soft infrastructure that underpins the needs of creative individuals and local creative industries is relatively less cultivated, even though the social mobilisation capacity is a prerequisite for cultivation of the creative city. As one local officer stated:

Taipei's creative city planning is just the emulation [of global creative city policy]. The public officers often use [imitation] to find out the key concept, or keyword [creative city], or to find the global gurus to teach us. But this learning process is on the surface. We do want to figure out the way. However, the political–economic structure of the city [planning] is a rigid barrier that obstructs the emergence of creativity.

(Representative of the Urban Renewal Office)

This statement demonstrates the absence of social vitality in Taipei's mobilisation of creative city policy. The city's policy-learning is inclined to copy the prototype creative policy as the frame of planning practices without elaborating on intangible socio-cultural assets, such as cultivating a community network.

Second, urban transformation needs to identify the contextual influence of implementing the creative city concept. While the contextual difference produced differences in planning practices, policy-makers must identify the existing governing deficits and the potential crises when mobilising the creative city concept into urban development. In Taipei, the prescriptive state-intervention strategies are structurally constituted by the path-dependent planning system (Wang, 2012). This path dependency could weaken the autonomy of cultural development and narrow social participation in the policy-making process. Without concern for different developmental contexts, the state-driven planning system cannot cope with the multifaceted location preferences and precarious organisational networks of the CCIs (Lin, 2014).

The evolution of Taipei's creative city policy is involved with different politico-economic rationalities that respond ambiguously to different stages of urban developmental goals. The developmental process of creative city-making means that the historical context is constantly shaping the formation of urban transformative capacity (see Scott, 2006), which implies place-specific geographical trajectories of creative policy-learning. The selection and adaptation of the creative city discourse is situated in a place-specific spatial–temporal context. Despite the idea coming from various cities (Prince, 2012), planning practices were still restricted by the institutional inertia of the government. Therefore, previous policy action displayed different rationalities of state interventions, politically or economically, on the recursive relationship between the cultural industry clusters and urban (re)development.

Creativity platform: the new urbanism in Taipei

Taipei has generated a series of institutional innovations that display creative city initiatives in the promotion of local creative synergies. The Taipei City Government invited the international professional consultant Charles Landry to visit the city eight times between 2008 and 2014. He suggested the concept of a 'creativity platform' as the innovative solution to foster the bottom-up dynamics of the creative city. Compared to hard-branding city strategies, this creativity platform was proposed as the major pivot of the creative-led institutional innovation that encouraged collaborative partnerships within creative quarters, or clusters, in Taipei (Landry, 2014). According to Landry, the creativity platform is a 'public interest entity' that is driven by private sectors to create a temporal–spatial environment for multiple goals: the gathering of interdisciplinary creative workers, supporting culture of creative entrepreneurship, facilitating training and education, and promoting creative quarters. However, the creativity platform idea needs a new form of urbanism in order to integrate civic creativity with urban regeneration policy effectively. As the director of the Urban Renewal Office Lin Chung-Cheih (2013: 88) noted, Taipei's new urbanism 'aims to create the environmental stimulation and opportunities to assist individuals in re-exploring spatial planning and taking action'. This implies that institutional innovation needs to be incubated by encouraging the self-organisation of creative communities in response to overlapping socio-economic and institutional tensions. As Scott (2014: 10) indicated, the institutional framework needs to 'manage the common-pool resources that abound within the cognitive–cultural economy'. The institutional framework has to include the reduction of uneven socio-economic development, securing the democratisation of urban space and the revitalisation of communal life.

However, collaborative relationship-building between the Taipei City Government and the local community is an overly optimistic solution to encouraging intensive interactions between local inhabitants and government. To put it simply, this platform is conceptualised as an invisible hand of local government that fosters the collaborative linkages between local government, NGOs, and local communities. But the participation of small-scale privileged communities in the creative city projects is explicitly mobilised through interpersonal networks of policy actors rather than through their self-mobilisation. This is because of the hierarchical policy-making process and the uneven power relationships from structural obstacles constraining the possibility of the creativity platform in Taipei. As one officer stated,

> Landry emphasised that Taipei has to build the creativity platform as the mechanism in order to foster the building of collective consequence and decision-making. However, the problem is that the government does not empower communities even though local inhabitants do not know how to participate in real creativity platforms.
>
> (Representative of the Urban Renewal Office)

This statement reveals that the global best practices of the institutional innovation encountered the socio-institutional barriers of urban governance. Despite the existing institutional frame being situated in a developmental state context, planning practices still need to elucidate a progressive movement and innovation in the institutional setting. Compared to the institutional framework-building process in Western cities, Taipei relies on the reflexive agencies of political elites rather than on the collective consciousness of the community, which tries to translate creative city ideas into the local context. Regarding contextual differences, socio-cultural sustainability is obviously not a priority of the Taipei creative city project. Rather, the modernisation and transformation process of urban development led the path-dependent effects of planning practices, which constitute the visible cultural infrastructures to attract the mobile creative class. While a creativity platform was proposed as one crucial conception of the creative city, the policy-makers should have more understanding of the tensions of Taipei's creative city development in order to decentralise planning practices and reduce over-reliance on mega-projects.

Tensions and institutional innovation of Taipei's creative city development

Taipei's creative city programmes, such as the idea of a creativity platform, are related to the institutional innovation of promoting creative clusters. Here, it is important to identify the tensions that are crucial to understanding the practices of creative city policy in Taipei. These current planning practices of the creative city and the hidden tensions are illustrated through the institutional innovation models of creative cluster planning initiatives, including the Urban Regeneration Stations (URSs), the Songshen Cultural Creative Park (SCCP), and the social mobilisation initiatives of the creative clusters. Three tensions of the creative cities initiatives are explored below.

The plan–project tension: URS as the temporary form of urban redevelopment showcase

The Taipei City Government launched the Urban Regeneration Station (URS) projects as an institutional innovation in response to existing bureaucracy-oriented planning practices. This path-creation initiative was used to reuse six state properties as regeneration frontiers. It attempted to stimulate the physical–social outcome of urban regeneration by reusing historical buildings and explicitly fostering various organic cultural activities. However, the URS projects were mostly located in the historical districts of the inner city, and due to the short-term contracts they served only as temporary forms of urban redevelopment. This could hardly generate the long-term effect of spatial clustering of the creative industries. As one local officer stated in 2014:

> URS is obviously the other innovation mechanism that could create a positive effect. But, this project actually is related to the intentions and agency of the government. The project will be abandoned and not prolonged if the mayor decides to replace it.
> (Representative of the Urban Development Department)

This statement shows that the sustainability of creative city policy cannot be maintained through temporary spatial projects. A similar situation was evident in another example. The National Property Agency (NPA) released a historical

Figure 2.2 A temporary site for designers' studios
Source: the author.

building for low-rent designers' studios through the URS#21 project. Although this project functioned as a magnet for the clustering of creative designers in the inner city, it was cancelled in 2014 due to the financial constraints of the NPA. Obviously, these visible short-term projects were influenced by Taipei's political context, and periodic elections politicised the goal of the creative city. As the creative producers claim, the URSs are spatial projects; they do not indicate an institutionalisation of the creative industry cluster. Clearly, then, there is tension between long-term plans and short-term projects, generating 'a disruptive energy around an initiative positioned on the edge of existing institutions' (Peck, 2012: 6). Even if the micro-agencies of the policy-makers could create temporary spatial projects, prioritising local political interest remains part of the creative city-making process.

The production–consumption tension: the financialisation of Songshen Cultural Creative Park

The global best practices of the creative city script argue that urban entrepreneurial governance calls for market-oriented planning intervention. Taipei is no exception. The Songshen Cultural Creative Park (SCCP) was launched as a spatial project fostering the clustering of cultural creative industries. This project, including a sports stadium (especially for baseball), heritage sites, a shopping mall, and a cultural production studio, created a cultural production–consumption complex in the inner city. Due to the financialisation mechanism, local government tended to dominate the development pathway of the SCCP through the use of new financial instruments, known as Building Operation Transfers (BOTs). These financial instruments, based on the principles of urban entrepreneurialism (Harvey, 1989), were used to minimise government spending risk in the development process of the SCCP. However, the SCCP reflected the uneven cultural production–consumption tension that prioritised cultural consumption landscapes over cultural production spaces. Although the SCCP is designed for the promotion of Taipei's creative industries, the controversy is that the consumption landscapes and facilities, such as hotel, shopping area, and sports stadium, occupy the largest percentage of land use in the SCCP. Even if some cultural production studios were also created, the average rent for a creative industry studio would be higher in the SCCP than in the surrounding area. The governance of the SCCP is thus dominated by consumption-oriented activities and the economic rationalities of the real estate industry, rather than prioritising a cultural-centred production cluster. However, this planning practice as a form of institutional innovation hints at the weakening role of state intervention, which is no longer in dominant control over the SCCP. Eventually, the financialisation of the cultural creative industries district will exacerbate uneven preferences and unintentional outcomes that hardly attract creative industries.

Figure 2.3 The modern architecture of cultural creative industries in SCCP
Source: the author.

The exclusion–inclusion tension: social mobilisation initiatives of the creative clusters

The Taipei creative city project also proposed a series of initiatives to encourage social mobilisation and interactions among creative individuals or local communities in order to foster 'organic' creative clusters. Compared to self-organisation in the project-led creative industry (Grabher, 2002), the state-led mobilisation strategies, including creative partnerships, sharing space platform, innovation laboratory, and creative districts initiatives, sought to enhance social inclusion, social innovation, and micro-level social enterprises. Compared to the heavy-handed interventions of the developmental state (Lee and Hwang, 2012), the Taipei City Government was not regarded as a regulator but rather as a collaborator facilitating bottom-up synergies and community mobilisation (Lin and Hsing, 2009). By providing subsidies, releasing state-owned spaces, and strategic actions of collective marketing, it attempted to foster the new state–society relationship in the process of making a creative city.

However, the social mobilisation initiatives met social resistance. Despite local officers' attempts to use these community-level initiatives to achieve ideals of social inclusion, such initiatives may generate social exclusion as well. For instance, the environmental preferences of creative individuals often run counter to the liveability requirements of local inhabitants. So a music festival might generate a 'buzz' that encourages intensive interactions between creative individuals while stimulating innovation and creativity in cultural production, but it would also likely encounter neighbourhood resistance against the disruptive creative activities. Therefore, the social participation dimension of the creative city project was too narrow to include various interest groups, leading to tension and increasing scepticism toward social mobilisation initiatives.

Conclusion

This chapter has argued that if Taipei wants to advance creative city-making, policy-makers should not apply borrowed normative strategies, but should instead foster social and institutional innovation. The geographical trajectories of Taipei's creative city policy are historically structured through the trans-local policy learning networks that (re)assembled the overlapping experiences of diverse cities. Compared to existing Euro-American research (Scott, 2006, 2014), the crucial tasks of becoming creative cities focus neither on fostering the clusters of cultural creative industries nor on retaining the creative class. Rather, policy actors need to foster effective institutional responses, and even institutional innovation, to solve the emerging multi-tensions and potential contradictions of creative individuals who are situated in the Taipei city context. This suggests that the making of the creative city relies on institutional innovation beyond the imaginings of prescriptive creative policy-learning. By responding to the increasing socio-economic transformation of urban development, the Taipei City Government presented an active public–private partnership, which is the crucial institutional basis for dealing with the negotiation of emerging tensions. This is because market-oriented creative city planning only exacerbated uneven socio-economic tensions of urban development; it fails to stimulate social democracy and inclusion.

This chapter has three conclusions. First, the case of one East Asian city, Taipei, shows that local governments have selectively adopted the normative and prescriptive creative city concept and adapted it according to local context. However, the Taipei City Government does not clearly understand the geniuses of the creative city, which originated within the contextual differences among cities. Therefore, the evolution process of the Taipei creative city programme as a whole could be described as a *bricolage*[4] style of planning practice that is involved with emerging contradictions and tensions. Second, planning practices for creative clusters are highly path dependent and influenced by the planning knowledge of the industry cluster idea without understanding the spatial-organisational dynamics of cultural creative industries. Despite the wide promotion of global best practices of the creative city script, it is clear that there is no single successful route to a future creative city or creative cluster. Similar creative city policy transplantation must create the institutional innovation that resolves overlapping tensions. In the Taipei context, policy elaborations toward socio-cultural sustainability remain weak. Finally, Taipei's creative city projects ideologically reflect how local government attempted to use mega-events and cultural flagship projects as leverage to promote the visibility of Taipei's creative industries, as well as to brand the city as a Chinese cultural production centre.

Acknowledgements

The author acknowledges the book's editors, who invested a lot of time and effort to provide excellent comments on this chapter. These efforts and comments were greatly appreciated. The author also thanks the interviewees who provided valuable information and data. This chapter was funded by the Ministry of Science and Technology (MOST 102-2410-H-152-019).

Notes

1 The concept of developmental state is developed to explain the characters of state interventions on economic development in East Asia.
2 The cultural economy planning practices referred to the agencies of local government intervening where certain creative places develop.
3 *Machizukuri* is a Japanese community-building initiative that stresses civic participation in neighbourhood planning.
4 The concept of *bricolage*, which was first proposed by French anthropologist Claude Lévi-Strauss, is used in this chapter to explain the contemporary character of urban governance in Taipei. A range of planning routines of urban development in Taipei relies on the combinations of the existing spatial resources to create new opportunities for creative city development.

References

Amin, A. (1999) 'An institutional perspective on regional development', *International Journal of Urban and Regional Development*, 23(2): 365–378.

Banks, M., Lovatt, A., O'Connor, J. and Raffo, C. (2000) 'Risk and trust in the cultural industries', *Geoforum*, 31(3): 453–464.

Boschma, R. (2004) 'Competitiveness of regions from an evolutionary perspective', *Regional Studies*, 38(9): 1001–1014.

Boschma, R. and Lambooy, J. (1999) 'Evolutionary economics and economic geography', *Journal of Evolutionary Economics*, 9(4): 411–429.

Bunnell, T. (2013) 'Antecedent cities and inter-referencing effects: learning from and extending beyond critiques of neoliberalisation', *Urban Studies.* Retrieved from http://usj.sagepub.com/content/early/2013/10/14/0042098013505882.full.pdf+html (accessed 22/7/15).

Catungal, J.P. and Leslie, D. (2009) 'Placing power in the creative city: governmentalities and subjectivities in Liberty Village, Toronto', *Environment and Planning A*, 41(11): 2576–2594.

Chang, T.C. and Teo, P. (2009) 'The shophouse hotel: vernacular heritage in a creative city', *Urban Studies*, 46(2): 341–367.

DCMS (2004) *Culture at the Heart of Regeneration*, London: DCMS.

DCMS (2008) *Creative Britain: New Talents for the New Economy*, London: DCMS.

Evans, G. (2009) 'Creative cities, creative spaces and urban policy', *Urban Studies*, 46(5–6): 1003–1040.

Florida, R. (2002) *The Rise of the Creative Class*, New York: Basic Books.

Grabher, G. (2002) 'Cool projects, boring institutions: temporary collaboration in a social context', *Regional Studiesi* 36(3): 205–214.

Grodach, C. (2012) 'Before and after the creative city: the politics of urban cultural policy in Austin, Texas', *Journal of Urban Affairs*, 34(1): 81–97.

Hall, P. (1999) 'The future of cities', *Computers, Environment and Urban System*, 23(3): 173–185.

Hall, P. (2000) 'Creative cities and economic development', *Urban Studies*, 37(4): 639–649.

Harvey, D. (1989) 'From managerialism to entrepreneurialism: the transformation in urban governance in late capitalism', *Geografiska Annaler: Series B, Human Geography*, 71(1): 3–17.

Huang, L. (2005) 'Urban politics and spatial development: the emergence of participatory planning in Taipei', in R. Kwok (eds), *Globalizing Taipei: The Political Economy of Spatial Development*, London: Routledge, pp. 78–98.

Kong, L. (2007) 'Cultural icons and urban development in Asia: economic imperative, national identity, and global city status', *Political Geography*, 26(4): 383–404.

Kong, L. (2014) 'From cultural industries to creative industries and back? Towards clarifying theory and rethinking policy', *Inter-Asia Cultural Studies*, 15(4): 593–607.

Kong, L., Gibson, C., Khoo, L.-M. and Semple, A.-L. (2006) 'Knowledges of the creative economy: towards a relational geography of diffusion and adaptation in Asia', *Asia Pacific Viewpoint*, 47(2): 173–194.

Landry, C. (2012) *Talented Taipei and the Creative Imperative*, Taipei: Urban Regeneration Office.

Landry, C. (2014) *A Creativity Platform: Harnessinng the Collective Imagination of Taipei*, Taipei: Urban Regeneration Office.

Lee, Y.-S. and Hwang, E.-J. (2012) 'Global urban frontiers through policy transfer? Unpacking Seoul's creative city programmes', *Urban Studies*, 49(13): 2817–2837.

Lin, C.-C. (2013) 'Practice of soft urbanism in Taipei's urban newal', *Journal of Taiwan Architecture*, 9: 988–993 (in Chinese).

Lin, C.-Y. (2014) 'The evolution of Taipei's music industry: cluster and network dynamics in innovation practices of music industry', *Urban Studies*, 51(2): 335–354.

Lin, C.-Y. and Hsing, W.-C. (2009) 'Culture-led urban regeneration and community mobilization: the case of the Taipei Bao-an Temple area, Taiwan', *Urban Studies*, 49(7): 1317–1342.

Martin, R. and Sunley, P. (2006) 'Path dependence and regional economic evolution', *Journal of Economic Geography*, 6(4): 395–437.

Meagher, S.M. (2013) 'The darker underside of Scott's third wave', *City: Analysis of Urban Trends, Culture, Theory, Policy, Action*, 17(3): 395–398.

Nakagawa, S. (2010) 'Socially inclusive cultural policy and arts-based urban community regeneration', *Cities*, 27(S1): S16–S24.

Okano, H. and Samson, D. (2010) 'Cultural urban branding and creative cities: a theoretical framework for promoting creativity in the public spaces', *Cities*, 27(S1): S10–S15.

Peck, J. (2002) 'Political economies of scale: fast policy, interscalar relations, and neo-liberal workfare', *Economic Geography*, 78(3): 331–360.

Peck, J. (2005) 'Struggling with the creative class', *International Journal of Urban and Regional Research*, 29(4): 740–770.

Peck, J. (2011) 'Geographies of policy: from transfer-diffusion to mobility-mutation', *Progress in Human Geography*, 35(6): 773–797.

Peck, J. (2012) 'Recreative city: Amsterdam, vehicular ideas and the adaptive spaces of creativity policy', *International Journal of Urban and Regional Research*, 36(3): 462–485.

Pratt, A.C. (2009) 'Urban regeneration: from the arts "feel good"' factor to the cultural economy: a case study of Hoxton, London', *Urban Studies*, 46(5–6): 1041–1061.

Prince, R. (2010) 'Policy transfer as policy assemblage: making policy for the creative industries in New Zealand', *Environment and Planning A*, 42(1): 169–186.

Prince, R. (2012) 'Metaphors of policy mobility: fluid spaces of "creativity" policy', *Geografiska Annaler: Series B, Human Geography*, 94(4): 317–331.

Sacco, P. and Blessi, G.T. (2009) 'The social viability of culture-led urban transformation processes: evidence from the Bicocca district, Milan', *Urban Studies*, 46(5–6): 1115–1135.

Sasaki, M. (2010) 'Urban regeneration through cultural creativity and social inclusion: rethinking creative city theory through a Japanese case study', *Cities*, 27(S1): S3–S9.

Scott, A.J. (2006) 'Creative cities: conceptual issues and policy questions', *Journal of Urban Affairs*, 28(1): 1–17.

Scott, A.J. (2007) 'Capitalism and urbanization in a new key? The cognitive-cultural dimension', *Social Forces*, 85(4): 1465–1482.

Scott, A.J. (2011) 'Emerging cities of the third wave', *City*, 15(3–4): 289–321.

Scott, A.J. (2012) *A World In Emergence: Cities and Regions in the 21st Century*, Northampton, MA: Edward Elgar.

Scott, A.J. (2014) 'Beyond the creative city: cognitive-cultural capitalism and the new urbanism', *Regional Studies*, 48(4): 565–578.

Taipei City Government (2012) *Annual Report of Urban Development*, Taipei: Taipei City Government.

Wang, C.-H. (2012) 'Moving toward neoliberalization? The restructuring of the developmental state and spatial planning in Taiwan', in B. Park, R. Child and A. Saito (eds), *Locating Neoliberalism in East Asia: Neoliberalized Spaces in Asian Developmental States*, Oxford: Blackwell, pp. 168–195.

3 Sub-national neoliberalism through city restructuring and policy boosterism

The case of Hyderabad, India

Diganta Das

Introduction

Today, half of the world's population lives in cities. Cities today present humanity with enormous challenges and opportunities. While they are sometimes seen as dystopian, they are also the places where utopian ideas are reflected and implemented (see Bunnell 2004). Cities today are at the centre of the world's economy. They are the motors of regional, national and global economies (Scott 2001). While global cities have been accorded the command and control centres of global finance and services (see Sassen 1994), major cities around the world have been rescaled due to the contemporary processes of globalization (Brenner 1998, 1999a, 1999b), but such rescaling need not be always at the cost of nation-states (Bunnell 2002). While scholars such as Kenichi Ohmae (1995) argue that rescaled city-regions have emerged with a significant reduction in the role of national government, Brenner (1998) advocates this as a strategy adopted by national governments to encourage the rescaling of cities and city-regions. Cities are thus becoming central to the *project of globalization* (see Massey 2000).

Governments around the world are increasingly projecting their cities as engines and 'real and symbolic nodes' of globalization through investments in 'high-tech' infrastructure and through place-marketing and policy boosterism (see Brooker 2013; McCann 2011; Bunnell and Das 2010). While cities are being marketed as possessing unique qualities and characteristics, often they have been subjected to and influenced by visioning policies and projects attempted elsewhere. Transfers of city-making ideas are not new. For instance, since the 1990s many Asia-Pacific nations have attempted to replicate the skyline of New York City (King 1996). With intense processes of globalization in Asia, the travel of city-making ideas is becoming more common. Geographers have been paying increasing attention to urban experts and 'starchitects' involved in multiple projects across nations and their practices (McNeill 2009). Jamie Peck (Peck and Tickell 2002) has considered the role played by neoliberal consultants in 'fast policy transfer'. Increasingly, it is the elite politicians and bureaucrats in Asia who are travelling around the globe, seeking best practices and best models for developing their own cities. They are invited by technology industries promising 'smart' ideas for their cities, provided with glossy reports of success stories, presented with magnificent slide shows and promises of skylines of cities of tomorrow. Aggressive marketing and seductive presentations are becoming the mantra for (urban) policy boosterism. As Doreen Massey points out, 'the contemporary urbanization is being produced through application of the (mobile) policies which are themselves part and parcel of the production of neoliberal globalization' (Massey 2000: 137). City competitiveness has brought to the fore the idea of being entrepreneurial, and local governments are increasingly being roped in as actors to contribute towards making their cities prolific, competitive and market-friendly.

Undoubtedly, cities are rising in prominence under processes of globalization. Yet, such prominence at urban and regional levels is not new. Scholars have documented the trend of urban rescaling, especially in European and American contexts where local and/or provincial governments are seen to have gained enhanced roles and special privileges in promoting transnational linkages (see MacLeod and Goodwin 1999; Brenner 1997). Jessop (1997) called this a 'denationalization of the state'. Beyond denationalization, MacLeod and Goodwin (1999: 505–506) add two more processes into the rescaling debate: destatization of political systems and internationalization of policy regimes. Destatization is leading to minimal state responsibilities and increasing engagement of non-state actors. Internationalization of policy regimes is leading to the increasing role for networked policy communities and international policy transfers to provide competitiveness. As Brenner argued, these processes operating at different levels in the current round of globalization have significantly reconfigured the state and 'produced both sub-national and supra-national geographical scales' and they do coexist (Brenner 1999a: 41; 2004). Brenner further points out that this re-scaling 'does not entail the state's erosion but rather its *reterritorialization* onto both sub- and supra-national scales' (Brenner 1999a: 53; original emphasis).

Increasingly, with contemporary processes of globalization, similar state restructuring is becoming evident in Asia. As the continent is urbanizing rapidly, major urban centres are rising in prominence (Bunnell 2002; Das 2015b). Cities are being projected as technopoles (Brooker 2013), high-tech and smart (Das 2015a) to attract investments. In Malaysia, for example, the federal government initiated a national project to make Kuala Lumpur (KL) a global city by adopting visioning policies prescribed by the international consultancy policy-maker McKinsey & Company. Massive resources were sourced to develop the KL Twin Towers and to develop Putrajaya and Cyberjaya – the new administrative capital of Malaysia and a high-tech industrial space, respectively (Bunnell 1999; Moser 2010). While Malaysia was successful, albeit partially, in projecting KL as a global city, unevenness increased (Bunnell 2004). In other corners of Asia, supra-national organizations are playing prominent roles in the proliferation of neoliberal policies, often by connecting sub-national governments and bypassing the national. Kirk (2005, 2011) provided an interesting account of the World Bank (WB) and its strategy to connect to sub-national (state) governments in India, bypassing the federal government structure in New Delhi. Through sub-national neoliberalism, the WB attempted to create new routes and thereby strengthen and deepen their roots in India. One of the beneficiary states of the WB's sub-national project was Andhra Pradesh (AP).

Following MacLeod and Goodwin's (1999) discussion on rescaling, this chapter will give more emphasis, first, to destatization, through which I will detail the ways in which the state government minimized government responsibilities and became the facilitator/manager for neoliberal proliferation. Second, I will focus on internalization of policy regimes, through which city-centric policies were being transferred, emulated and implemented to make Hyderabad a globally connected high-tech urban centre. Further, this chapter will discuss recent issues where urban-centric politics became the central argument in deciding to bifurcate the state of AP, validating the sub-national rescaling argument. Sub-national neoliberalism in India was very much facilitated by a more relaxed federal–state relationship after the economic liberalization process of 1991. The next section details the economic liberalization process since 1991, resultant rescaling of state governments and the ways in which the political elites of AP exploited the opportunity to brand Hyderabad as a high-tech destination.

Going sub-national: the AP story

After independence from British colonial ruler was achieved in 1947, India followed a mixed-economy model featuring characteristics of both capitalism and socialism. While India followed a federal governance model, the decision-making process was largely hierarchical, with major decisions pertaining to economic planning, industrialization and defence taken at the federal level. The Indian economy followed a five-year planning model with a major focus on heavy industrialization during the earlier phase. However, the GDP growth rate was below 4 per cent from 1950 to 1980. More than 65 per cent of population was dependent on agriculture, but productivity was weak, leading to higher poverty incidence. With substantial bureaucratic inefficiency, public sector industries were not performing well, leading to low industrial output. By 1985, the federal government was slowly moving towards liberalizing the Indian economy and opening it up for private investors. Taxes were relaxed, administrative red tape was cut, and licence restrictions on various sectors were reduced (see McCartney 2009; Panagariya 2004). The new administration in Delhi also prioritized the development of modern infrastructure and an investment in technology.

Around this time, India's telecommunication revolution began as the technology was laid to create a countrywide telephone network, with emphasis on adequate rural telecommunications. However, the liberalization process of the mid-1980s was ultimately derailed. James Manor (1987) noted that the attempt at liberalization launched in 1985 failed due to extensive political opposition to the process. While greater economic liberalization was welcomed by the middle classes and private investors, there was enormous opposition from the trade unions and left-wing parties within India. However, from the 1990s onwards, with an increasing fiscal deficit, the Indian economy faced a severe balance of payments crisis. As early as

1991 India had to negotiate Structural Adjustment Programme (SAP) loans from the WB and the International Monetary Fund (IMF). As Gurucharan Das (2000: 215) noted, 'part of the nation's gold reserves had been flown out to London to provide collateral against the $2.2 billion loan'. The SAP loan conditions stipulated that India's government had to reform the economy. As Jason Kirk (2011: xiii) observed, in the post-1991 period, the WB transformed itself from being 'a lender to becoming a partner in policy making both at federal and state government level'.

Initially, the economic reform process was used to stabilize the Indian economy during the crisis. Once the stabilization had been achieved, the actual economic restructuring could begin. Nayar (2001) noted that in the post-1991 liberal economic regime, top political leaders embraced globalization and lobbied for integration of the Indian economy into the world economy. However, Prime Minister P.V. Narasimha Rao, whose ministry announced the liberalization policy in 1991, 'realized that people were ahead of politicians in wanting the reform' (Das 2000: 219). Efforts were made to attract foreign direct investment (FDI), significantly reduce red tape around Licence Raj,[1] reform capital markets, and increase privatization and competition. Das (2000: 216) noted that while it took nearly forty years to build the extremely complex rule book of trade policies under Licence Raj, the new government had to dismantle it within a few hours.

Along with intense economic reforms, changes were introduced to the relationship between the federal and state governments. In the aftermath of the reforms, the state government enjoyed more decision-making power on issues relating to state investment and industrialization. While defence and issues of national importance remained with the federal government, state issues were transferred from New Delhi to the regional state capitals. As coalition politics dawned in India in the mid-1990s, regional parties gained more influence over various policy decisions. The parliamentary (federal) election of 1996 resulted in no majority for any single party, thus a coalition government had to be formed in New Delhi. Several regional parties became significant stakeholders in this new ministry, including the Telugu Desam Party (TDP) of AP (Das 2010). A new shared sovereignty between the federal government and the states emerged in the background of the evolving market economy (Rudolph and Rudolph 2001; see also Kirk 2011). The states' chief ministers began to play important roles at the federal level (Burki et al. 1999).

Chandrababu Naidu, the leader of the TDP, became the chief minister of AP in 1994 and he was soon influencing the federal government in several economic and other decisions in relation to his state (Naidu and Ninan 2000). In the introduction to his biography, Naidu wrote: 'players at the state level have come to count much more than before . . . state governments were much more active in attracting foreign investments to finance their development projects' (Naidu and Ninan 2000: xxiv). As the states became influential actors, the WB and IMF began focusing on sub-national (state) scale beyond the national (federal) government since it made more sense for the WB to contribute to policy-making, consultation for various state agencies and the creation of a network between transnational agencies and state policy-makers. While at a micro-level this helped in understanding the efficacies of various programmes for which loans were sought, at a macro-level it ensured better penetration of the WB-initiated neoliberal programmes. Kirk (2005, 2011) called the sub-national strategy of the WB a 'focus-state' approach.

In 1994, Naidu inherited a strained state economy and he desperately needed financial assistance. He met former WB chief James Wolfensohn and explained his intentions in relation to economic reform and his vision for AP. Very impressed with Naidu, Wolfensohn asked the WB's India chief Edwin Lim to go to AP and examine possibilities for WB involvement. Lim reported that the WB should seize the opportunity through its focus-state strategy, given Naidu's enthusiasm for reform and the TDP's strong showing in the federal coalition (see Kirk 2005: 297).

The WB moved quickly in AP and subsequently prepared a report for the state, suggesting restructuring of the power sector, attracting private investments in infrastructure, education and primary health, increasing user charges for public utilities, and abolishing all social subsidy programmes (Das 2010: 124). Naidu's ministry duly introduced a bill to reform the state power sector and later reduced government subsidies to various social programmes. Entrepreneurial chief ministers such as Naidu became the WB's 'poster boys' for neoliberal proliferation at the sub-national scale (Sainath 2004). In 1998, the WB provided AP with a much-needed loan of US$543 million under the auspices of the AP Economic Restructuring Project (Kirk 2011). Naidu shifted the state's role from traditional welfare-oriented governance to entrepreneurial governance, reducing subsidies and extending a red-carpet welcome to private investors. As a member of the new generation of political elites, Naidu saw the liberalization policy as a golden opportunity for his state. Given his political party's crucial role in the federal government and his increasing ease when doing business with the WB, he began to promote his state as a prime investment destination. He participated in various business forums both within and outside India, and issued invitations to private investors and country ambassadors to visit the state (see Bunnell and Das 2010). Naidu projected himself as a smart and practical politician and reiterated his support for a market-led development process in AP, ideologically distancing himself from his party's earlier ideas. Kevin Ward (2007) has argued that business forums, CEO meetings, seminars and summits are the sites of neoliberal ideas and their exchange. Through well-managed public relations, Naidu attended such meetings and marketed his state. These marketing efforts brought significant results. By 1999, AP was the third most popular investment destination among India-based CEOs (Kirk 2005).

Naidu wanted to build a technology-driven, smart AP. He much admired the growth trajectory taken by Malaysia under Mahathir Mohamed through the 'Malaysia Vision 2020' policy and that country's determination to develop a knowledge economy. Leveraging AP's local engineering graduates, and the ongoing reform process, Naidu decided to follow a similar technology-driven

Figure 3.1 Cyber Towers: Hyderabad's first and iconic high-tech building
Source: the author.

trajectory in order to leapfrog towards a knowledge-based economy. He initiated construction of a 'knowledge corridor' in the western periphery of Hyderabad, the state capital. In 1998, the 'Cyber Towers', a ten-storey 'intelligent' building was inaugurated as part of this knowledge corridor development (Figure 3.1). Shrewd (neoliberal) marketing with hard-developmental demonstration helped to attract businesses to the state. For instance, Bill Gates decided to establish Microsoft's non-US developmental centre in Hyderabad. This was followed by many other software companies locating their business operations there. The visit by US President Bill Clinton provided worldwide publicity showcasing Naidu's economic reform initiatives (see Manor 1998). The sub-national strategy of the WB and Naidu's neoliberal efforts helped launch Hyderabad into the global league of high-tech destinations and allowed it to become a serious contender to Bangalore.

Scholars such as MacKinnon and Phelps (2001), Peck and Tickell (2002) and Phelps and Parsons (2003) have documented inter-urban competition in relation to cities undergoing neoliberal processes, and such competition became increasingly evident in India from the mid-1990s. The next section details Naidu's travels to Southeast Asia, his learning from and emulation of their city-centric policies, and the subsequent construction of Cyberabad, Hyderabad's high-tech space aimed at achieving the state's desired neoliberal growth trajectory.

Production of (high-tech) space

Naidu sincerely believed that AP's desired developmental trajectory would be possible only through the adoption of a competitive economy, inviting in private investors and leapfrogging towards a high-tech knowledge economy. Therefore, he followed the WB's neoliberal prescriptions, restructured the state's public infrastructure agencies, reduced public subsidies, and initiated several other structural changes to attract private investors to the state. He also attended World Economic Forum at Davos to market his state and attract private investment. Naidu said,

> an Indian chief minister in today's global economy has to be a salesman . . .
> [Y]ou have to go back again and again to a place like Davos, have face-to-face sessions with CEOs, make your sales pitch to them in their own countries, in short – market yourself.
>
> (Naidu and Ninan 2000: 9, 148)

Perhaps through one of those meetings, Naidu learned from the former head of McKinsey & Company in India, Rajat Gupta, that the CEOs of Fortune 500 companies did not have a very positive attitude towards investing in India (Naidu and Ninan 2000). AP was far off potential investors' radar. Therefore, Naidu was 'convinced' that economic reform and restructuring alone were not enough to develop his state. AP needed to have a plan to achieve its developmental goals and a 'road map' (Das 2010: 126).

In 1997, with an entourage of ministers, bureaucrats and businessmen, Naidu visited a number of Southeast Asian countries, including Malaysia and Singapore, to witness the trajectories of the 'tiger economies' at first hand and learn their 'best practices'. He was very impressed by the development of the Malaysia Multimedia Super Corridor (MSC), outside KL, and was full of praise for both Singapore and Malaysia, expressing personal admiration for the Malaysian Prime Minister Mahathir Mohamed, his Vision 2020 policy and the way it had positioned Malaysia (or, more precisely, KL, with Cyberjaya) as the knowledge hub of Southeast Asia (Sen and Frankel 2005). Naidu was fascinated with technological utopian ideas of leapfrogging from an agricultural economy to an advanced services economy with the help of information technology (IT) (Kirk 2005; Sen and Frankel 2005). Seduced by the glossy utopian dream of modern Malaysia (Bunnell and Das 2010), it was in KL – nearly 2000 miles from Hyderabad – that Naidu found his state's future road map. Returning from his Southeast Asian tour, he and the rest of the state leadership began working on a framework to make AP a premier hub for modern technological industries, with special emphasis on IT, biotechnology and pharmaceuticals. However, to attract private investment into the state, Naidu needed a demonstration effect.

AP's leadership moved fast to construct the first high-tech building in Hyderabad, later known as 'Cyber Towers'. The inauguration of the iconic building by the Indian prime minister generated a great deal of publicity, both domestically and internationally. Soon, US President Clinton and British Prime Minister Tony Blair visited. Naidu also managed to arrange a ten-minute meeting with Bill Gates when the head of Microsoft visited India in 1997. With the help of a PowerPoint presentation, Naidu persuaded Gates to bring his company to Hyderabad and found only the second software development centre outside the United States (Karmali 1998; Rao 2002). These high-profile visits by heads of states and heads of software companies – along with the emergence of a number of local entrepreneurial leaders – helped to generate even more international publicity about Hyderabad, with the city increasingly presented as a serious competitor to Bangalore. *Time*, the *New York Times*, the *Financial Times* and many other internationally renowned publications printed articles about Hyderabad and cast it as the new IT destination in India. *Time* went as far as to name Naidu 'South Asian of the Year' in 1999, while the *Wall Street Journal* said he was a model for other state leaders (Sainath 2004). The demonstration effect worked well, and the related media boosterism undoubtedly helped in the state's rescaling and turning Hyderabad into an engine of growth, as previously envisaged by the WB and the state leadership.

After the initial success of Cyber Towers, Naidu invited McKinsey & Company to draft a road map for AP, similar to Malaysia's growth trajectory. The resulting document, titled *Andhra Pradesh Vision 2020*, included similar technological leapfrogging ideas and economic buzzwords as had appeared in *Malaysia Vision 2020*, also prepared by McKinsey. It projected a developed AP by 2020 – with almost a ninefold increase in per capita income compared with 1995 (GoAP 1999: 4). Although the document mentioned agriculture as one of the key growth areas, the clear focus was on making AP a services-led economy, with IT as the principal growth engine. While the document itself was at the centre of policy mobility, travelling from Southeast Asia to India, it mentioned best practices from other corners of the world as well, including China, Korea and Chile. *AP Vision 2020* can be seen as one of the main (state-led) neoliberal policy transfer activities that led to viewing Indian cities as engines of growth and to develop cities for nations (and sub-national states).

The document emphasized three strategies to achieve the targeted goals for AP:

1   attracting investments;
2   creating growth engines; and
3   maintaining a market-friendly government.

It suggested that the state must be attractive for private investors in areas such as infrastructure, healthcare, and higher and technical education. It also suggested restructuring and/or privatizing state government infrastructure agencies. Interestingly, the document advocated trajectories that were similar to earlier WB prescriptions. Examples of successful practices elsewhere (Malaysia, Argentina and the Philippines) were cited in order to argue for privatizing public services. Examples and best practices from Singapore, the Netherlands, New Zealand, Australia and USA were provided to showcase the growth engine strategy. Building on the foundation of AP's existing benefits of large numbers of engineering graduates and Naidu's Cyber Towers, the document suggested developing a full-fledged 'knowledge corridor' in Hyderabad – a designated region equipped with high-tech labs for offices and research in IT, biotechnology, medicines and pharmaceuticals (GoAP 1999: 282). With the development of IT and other knowledge-based industries, it predicted that the knowledge corridor would be similar to North Carolina's Research Triangle Park, Taiwan's Hsinchu Industrial Park (GoAP 1999: 286), or indeed Malaysia's Multimedia Super Corridor, suggested by McKinsey in its vision document for that country. Finally, it was suggested that AP should transform into a managerial rather than welfare-oriented state. A managerial/entrepreneurial state, the vision document argued, should be able to facilitate and attract more private investment, and persuade the federal government to introduce more reforms and allocate more resources to AP (GoAP 1999: 46).

So McKinsey's vision document gave AP the road map that its political elites desired. However, it was not long before scholars (Bandhyopadhyay 2001; Venkatramaiah and Burange 2003) started to criticize it for an alleged over-reliance on private investment in social sectors such as healthcare, education and agriculture. There was also scepticism about the projected industrial growth. Meanwhile, other scholars, such as Subrahmanyam and Chakravarty (2002), pointed out that leapfrogging straight from an agricultural to a services economy, skipping the industrial economy phase, might lead to a majority of the semi-skilled population remaining unemployed, and hence to greater social inequality (see Das 2015b). Disregarding all such doubts and concerns, the state government accepted the document in full and began restructuring several sectors.

Accordingly, the state's leaders earmarked a large area for the development of the Andhra Pradesh Knowledge Corridor (APKC) and major spatial engineering projects were launched, especially around Hyderabad's Cyber Towers region. Naidu's government purchased land from seventeen villages in the western periphery of Hyderabad, around the Cyber Towers, and created a new 52-square-kilometre high-tech enclave, later named Cyberabad (see Figure 3.2). The Cyberabad Development Authority (CDA) was formed to administer this new knowledge region. In this context, Graham and Marvin (2001) noted that the processes of city restructuring and creating authorities/agencies are prerequisites of (urban) splintering practices.

The CDA's masterplan highlighted the goal of becoming an exemplary centre and 'model' for other urban areas in the country (GoAP 2001: 1). It emphasized land use zone regulations with a particular focus on locating software-related industries. An expressway was constructed specifically to connect Cyberabad directly with the international airport. The state increasingly viewed the laying of fibre optics all around Cyberabad and the construction of

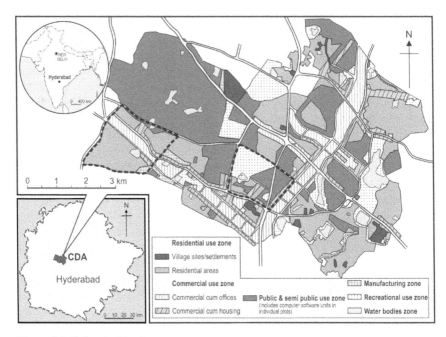

Figure 3.2 Cyberabad land-use map

Source: the author (adapted from Cyberabad Development Authority land-use map, redrawn by Lee Li Kheng).

wider roads, tolled expressways and a 'world-class' international airport as necessities if Cyberabad were to connect to other global cities. Once this state-of-the-art infrastructure was in place, the CDA successfully placed Hyderabad on the world IT map. Moreover, with world-renowned political and business leaders witnessing the growth of Cyberabad, AP's reputation as a business-friendly location was enhanced. However, Hyderabad's increasing affluence has meant poor families have been evicted and moved to the peripheries, a process that David Harvey (2003, 2008) has termed 'accumulation by dispossession'.

City-centric developments in AP were accompanied by increasing socio-spatial inequalities in Hyderabad – where elite 'digeratis' were able to connect to the wider world through premium modes of connection, while poor residents continued to struggle for everyday livelihood opportunities (Das 2012). With the creation of the new state of Telangana in 2014, with Hyderabad as its capital, it is interesting to consider whether the city-centric initiatives of earlier governments will continue, or if the focus will shift towards a more equitable development of the new state. The next section elaborates on this new state's recent policy trajectories.

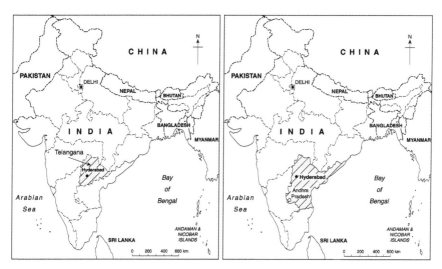

Figure 3.3 Hyderabad City in the newly formed state of Telangana and in erstwhile AP
Source: the author.

New state, old (policy) trajectory

The original unified AP state had three distinct regions – Telangana, coastal Andhra and Rayalaseema. Hyderabad, situated in the Telangana region, was the capital. Although this city became the engine of growth for the whole state, Telangana was the poorest of the three regions, while coastal Andhra was the richest. The people of Telangana demanded secession for many years, largely on the basis of politico-historical tradition but also to address their socio-economic problems. However, they were opposed by the political leaders (and people) of coastal Andhra and Rayalaseema, largely because the political leaders of Telangana insisted that Hyderabad should remain their new state's capital. Coastal Andhra's and Rayalaseema's leaders were either against the bifurcation altogether or demanded spatial autonomy for the city so that business interests and the interests of Hyderabad residents originally from their regions remained secure.

The conflict between Telangana and the other AP regions can be traced back largely to the political and economic upscaling of Hyderabad itself, beginning with Naidu's neoliberal initiatives in the mid-1990s and then carried forward by successive state governments. Hyderabad had always been the principal city of the state (see Ramachandraiah and Bawa 2000), but it had never previously achieved such rapid economic growth and such a degree of regional political prominence. With the success of the neoliberal city-centric strategies, it became an economic centre not only of AP but of the whole of southern India and a platform for middle-class Indians to fulfil their aspirations. All of AP's political parties therefore felt the need to route their regional political aspirations through Hyderabad.

Telangana Rashtra Samiti (TRS), which led the secessionist struggle for decades, viewed Hyderabad as an integral part of Telangana, given its historical background as well as the city's more recent rise to economic prominence, which meant it was generating the majority of the state's GDP.[2] On the other hand, political leaders from the other regions wanted Hyderabad to remain as their state capital, and pointed out that the city had joined the network of global cities largely through the efforts and vision of Naidu, who hailed from the coastal Andhra region.

Telangana officially became the twenty-ninth state of India, with Hyderabad as its capital, in June 2014. However, Hyderabad will also remain AP's administrative capital until coastal Andhra and Rayalaseema decide on a new capital for the residual state over the next ten years.[3] The new chief minister of Telangana, K. Chandrasekhar Rao (KCR), has already signalled his intention to make Hyderabad a world-class city with a city-wide internet network and significant development of infrastructure. Phrases like 'world-class city', 'global' and 'smart' have been employed by political leaders for quite some time in relation to Hyderabad's development. While KCR had earlier protested against several of Naidu's policies, when it came to Hyderabad's development as an engine of growth for the new state, clearly he intends to maintain the city-centric trajectory. Political rivalries of yesteryear have now shifted more towards competition between the two neighbouring state governments to attract city-specific investments.

In an echo of Naidu's 1997 visit to Southeast Asia, KCR visited Singapore and Malaysia during August 2014 (Special Correspondent 2014). Impressed with Singapore's development, he wanted to arrange training for his ministers and legislators within the city-state. He also attended meetings with potential investors and invited them to invest in Hyderabad, while also briefing them about the new state's industrial policy, which focused on IT and pharmaceuticals. KCR specifically informed the potential investors about the wide availability of land for the development of industrial parks and promised all possible government assistance (TNews 2014). The very next month, Singapore sent a team of officials led by former Prime Minister Goh Chok Tong to Hyderabad, where they discussed future collaboration. KCR did not only look to international 'models' for ideas about how to restructure and develop Hyderabad. He also initiated domestic linkages with other Indian states and asked his ministers to visit Gujarat and Orissa to understand their development strategies.

It is important to note that while KCR was visiting familiar neoliberal networks, Naidu invited the Singaporean delegation to invest in his new state, too. Similarly, Goh Chok Tong encouraged Naidu to visit Singapore to learn about its 'best practices' and connect with potential investors. Accordingly, Naidu travelled to Singapore once again to promote brand AP. However, this time he went further, going on to China, Japan and Korea in order to market his state (Nagaraju 2014).

Back in Hyderabad, KCR has welcomed business delegates, policy-makers and planners from around the world, and he has been tireless in promoting Hyderabad as a 'global smart city' (Press Trust of India 2014). These visits and revisits, learning and re-learning through best practices, have further strengthened policy boosterism at the sub-national level. It is noteworthy that while both Telangana and the residual AP are (re)connecting to Southeast Asian models of best practice, this time the sub-national effort has also been connecting to East Asian models from China, Japan and Korea. At the same time, they have learned from domestic models by connecting to other sub-national regions within India. While both new states have largely followed old policy trajectories, new additions and adaptations to learning from best practice have been made, too.

Conclusion

The WB's sub-national strategy through the focus-states initiative was perhaps one of the most innovative strategies in relation to India, and the amount of financing disbursed through this strategy to several Indian states (including AP) was surely among the largest at sub-national level anywhere in the world (Kirk 2011: 44). With the coalition *dharma*, where the federal government had to rely on support from its state allies, state governments enjoyed more decision-making power at federal level. Furthermore, with the increasing role of the WB at sub-national levels, many argued about the rescaling of states and (selected) state leaderships in liberalized India, at least in investment-related decisions (see Saez 2002, cited in Kirk 2011). Cities such as Hyderabad have been accepted and adapted as engines of growth, with the result that Hyderabad has been promoted by subsequent governments, often with ever more zeal and vigour. While the development of high-tech and smart Hyderabad has had complex socio-spatial grounded realities (see Das 2012), it has also provided the state government with a sustained neoliberal network that bypasses the nation-state. Naidu's entrepreneurial style of governance was applauded and criticized in almost equal measure, but subsequent government leaders have followed a very similar trajectory.

Beyond AP and Telangana, sub-national neoliberalism has continued, and it is becoming a dominant trend in India. While the federal government retains strong control over the state governments, it has supported sub-national neoliberalism as this doctrine coincides with larger economic liberalization processes that began in 1991. Through the Hyderabad case, what we see today are locally specific assemblages such as sub-national agencies and (sub-national) political elites as neoliberal agents, extending broader global agendas. Cities are pushed to prominence, increasingly projected and branded as smart sites of the future, through which neoliberal projects are now rooted, routed, experimented with and driven towards a global agenda of building creative/high-tech cities.

Notes

1 'Licence Raj' is widely used to describe the heavy regulation of the private sector in India between 1947 and the 1990s. Licences were issued after strict scrutiny by government departments in order to control private-industry production.

2 Before India achieved independence in 1947, Hyderabad was a separate state governed by the Nizam. In 1948, it was incorporated into a union with India; eight years later, the state of Andhra Pradesh was formed by integrating Telugu-speaking districts of the Nizam's Hyderabad. The city of Hyderabad became the state capital of AP.
3 Chandrababu Naidu, the new chief minister of the residual AP, recently stated that the new capital will be located in Amaravathi, near Vijayawada.

References

Bandhyopadhyay, D. (2001) 'Andhra Pradesh: looking beyond "Vision 2020"', *Economic and Political Weekly*, 36(11): 900–903.
Brenner, N. (1997) 'State territorial restructuring and the production of spatial scale', *Political Geography*, 16: 273–306.
Brenner, N. (1998) 'Global cities, glocal state: global city formation and state territorial restructuring in contemporary Europe', *Review of International Political Economy*, 5(1): 1–37.
Brenner, N. (1999) 'Beyond state-centrisim? Space, territoriality, and geographical scale in globalization studies', *Theory and Society*, 28(1): 39–78.
Brenner, N. (1999) 'Globalisation as reterritorialisation: the re-scaling of urban governance in the Europoean Union', *Urban Studies*, 36(3), 431–451.
Brenner, N. (2004) *New State Spaces: Urban Governance and the Rescaling of Statehood*, New York: Oxford University Press.
Brooker, D. (2013) 'From "wannabe" Silicon Valley to global back office? Examining the socio-spatial consequences of technopole planning practices in Malaysia', *Asia Pacific Viewpoint*, 54(1): 1–14.
Bunnell, T. (1999) 'Views from above and below: the Petronas Twin Towers and/in contesting visions of development in contemporary Malaysia', *Singapore Journal of Tropical Geography*, 20(1): 1–23.
Bunnell, T. (2002) 'Cities for nations? Examining the city–nation-state relation in Information Age Malaysia', *International Journal of Urban and Regional Research*, 26(2): 284–298.
Bunnell, T. (2004) *Malaysia, Modernity and the Multimedia Super Corridor*, London: Routledge.
Bunnell, T., and Das, D. (2010) 'A geography of serial seduction: urban policy transfer from Kuala Lumpur to Hyderabad', *Urban Geography*, 31(3): 1–7.
Burki, J. S., Guillermo, E. P., and Dillinger, W. R. (1999) *Beyond the Center: Decentralizing the State*, Washington, DC: The World Bank.
Das, D. (2010) 'Splintering urbanism in high-tech Hyderabad', unpublished PhD thesis, National University of Singapore.
Das, D. (2012) 'Ordinary lives in extraordinary Cyberabad', in N. Perera and W. S. Tang (eds), *The Transforming Asian Cities: People's Practices, Innovative Planning, Emergent Spaces* (pp. 112–122), London: Routledge.
Das, D. (2015a) 'Hyderabad: visioning, restructuring and making of a high-tech city', *Cities*, 43: 48–58.
Das, D. (2015b) 'Making of high-tech Hyderabad: mapping neoliberal networks and ground realities', *Singapore Journal of Tropical Geography*, 36(2): 231–248.
Das, G. (2000) *India Unbound: From Independence to the Global Information Age*, New Delhi: Penguin.

Government of Andhra Pradesh (GoAP) (1999) *Andhra Pradesh Vision 2020*, Hyderabad: Government of Andhra Pradesh.

Government of Andhra Pradesh (GoAP) (2001) *Master Plan for Cyberabad Development Authority Area*, Hyderabad: Government of Andhra Pradesh.

Graham, S., and Marvin, S. (2001) *Splintering Urbanism: Networked Infrastructures, Technological Mobilities and the Urban Condition*, London and New York: Routledge.

Harvey, D. (2003) *The New Imperialism*, Oxford: Oxford University Press.

Harvey, D. (2008) 'The right to the city', *New Left Review*, 53: 23–40.

Jessop, B. (1997) 'The entrepreneurial city: re-imaging localities, redesigning economic governance', in N. Jewson and S. MacGregor (eds), *Realizing Cities: New Spatial Divisions and Social Transformation* (pp. 28–41), London: Routledge.

Jessop, B., and Sum, N.L. (2000) 'An entrepreneurial city in action: Hong Kong's emerging strategies in and for (inter) urban competition', *Urban Studies*, 37(12): 2287–2313.

Karmali, N. (1998) 'Microsoft's passage to India'. Retrieved from www.forbes.com/global/1998/0727/0108030a.html (accessed 27/10/14).

King, A. (1996) 'Worlds in the city: Manhattan transfer and the ascendance of spectacular space', *Planning Perspectives*, 11: 97–114.

Kirk, J.A. (2005) 'Banking on India's states: the politics of World Bank reform programs in Andhra Pradesh', *India Review*, 4(3–4): 287–325.

Kirk, J.A. (2011) *India and the World Bank: The Politics of Aid and Influence*, London: Anthem Press.

MacKinnon, D., and Phelps, N.A. (2001) 'Devolution and the territorial politics of foreign direct investment', *Political Geography*, 20: 353–379.

MacLeod, G., and Goodwin, M. (1999) 'Space, scale and state strategy: rethinking urban and regional governance', *Progress in Human Geography*, 23(4): 503–527.

Manor, J. (1987) 'Tried, then qbandoned: economic liberalization in India', *IDS Bulletin*, 18(4): 39–44.

Manor, J. (1998) 'A coming Asian Tiger in India?', *International Herald Tribune*, January 7.

Massey, D. (2000) 'Understanding cities', *City*, 4(1): 135–144.

McCann, E. (2011) 'Urban policy mobilities and global circuits of knowledge: toward a research agenda', *Annals of the Association of American Geographers*, 101(1): 107–130.

McCartney, M. (2009) '"Episodes" or "evolution": the genesis of liberalization in India', *Journal of South Asian Development*, 4(2): 203–228.

McNeill, D. (2009) *The Global Architect: Firms, Fame, and Urban Form*, New York and Abingdon: Routledge.

Moser, S. (2010) 'Putrajaya: Malaysia's new federal administrative capital', *Cities*, 27: 285–297.

Nagaraju, J. (2014) 'Naidu eyes Far East to fetch investments for AP', *Times of India*. Retrieved from http://timesofindia.indiatimes.com/city/hyderabad/Naidu-eyes-Far-East-to-fetch-investments-for-AP/articleshow/44165721.cms (accessed 21/7/15).

Naidu, N.C., and Ninan, S. (2000) *Plain Speaking*, New Delhi: Viking.

Nayar, B.R. (2001) *Globalization and Nationalism: The Changing Balance in India's Economic Policy, 1950–2000*, New Delhi: Sage.

Ohmae, K. (1995) *The End of the Nation State: The Rise of Regional Economies*, London: HarperCollins.

Panagariya, A. (2004) *India: The Emerging Giant*, New York: Oxford University Press.

Peck, J., and Tickell, A. (2002) 'Neoliberalizing pace', *Antipode*, 34(3): 380–404.

Phelps, N.A., and Parsons, N. (2003) 'Edge urban geographies: notes from the margins of Europe's capital cities', *Urban Studies*, 40(9):1725–1749.

Press Trust of India (2014) 'Telangana government working towards making Hyderabad global smart city: minister', *Economic Times*. Retrieved from http://articles. economictimes.indiatimes.com/2014-10-08/news/54785061_1_telangana-government-state-minister-intensive-household-survey (accessed 22/7/15).

Ramachandraiah, C., and Bawa, V.K. (2000) 'Hyderabad in the changing political economy', *Journal of Contemporary Asia*, 30(4): 562–574.

Rao, K.S. (2002) 'Bill Gates to meet Naidu today', *Times of India*. Retrieved from http:// timesofindia.indiatimes.com/city/hyderabad/Bill-Gates-to-meet-Naidu-today/article show/28202897.cms (accessed 22/7/15).

Rudolph, L.I., and Rudolph, S.H. (2001) 'Iconisation of Chandrababu: sharing sovereignty in India's federal market economy', *Economic and Political Weekly*, 36(18): 1541–1550.

Saez, L. (2002) *Federalism without a Centre: The Impact of Political and Economic Reform on India's Federal System*, New Delhi: Sage Publications.

Sainath, P. (2004) 'Chandrababu: image and reality', *The Hindu*, 5 July. Retrieved from www.thehindu.com/2004/07/05/stories/2004070503400800.htms (accessed 22/7/15).

Sassen, S. (1994) *Cities in the World Economy*, Thousand Oaks, CA: Pine Forge.

Scott, A.J. (ed.) (2001) *Global City-Regions: Trends, Theory, Policy*, London: Oxford University Press.

Sen, S., and Frankel, F. (2005) 'Andhra Pradesh's long march towards 2020: electoral detours in a developmentalist state', in *Doing Business in India: Political Social and Cultural Overview* (n.p.), Philadelphia: Centre for the Advanced Study of India, University of Pennsylvania.

Special Correspondent (2014) 'KCR comes away impressed after Singapore visit', *The Hindu*, 25 August. Retrieved from www.thehindu.com/news/cities/Hyderabad/ kcr-comes-away-impressed-after-singapore-visit/article6350814.ece?css=print (accessed 22/7/15).

Subrahmanyam, S., and Chakravarty, D. (2002) 'Regional disparities in industrial development', in Y.V.K. Rao and S. Subrahmanyam (eds), *Development of Andhra Pradesh: 1956–2001: A Study of Regional Disparities* (n.p.), Hyderabad: N.R.R. Research Centre.

TNews (2014) 'Telangana CM KCR speech in Singapore – invites entrepreneurs to invest in Telangana'. Retrieved from www.youtube.com/watch?v=sJ7VVlNCsYo (accessed 22/7/15).

Venkatramaiah, P., and Burange, L.G. (2003) 'Structure and growth of industry', in C.H.H. Rao and S.M. Dev (eds), *Andhra Pradesh Development: Economic Reforms and Challenges Ahead* (n.p.), Hyderabad: Centre for Economic and Social Studies.

Ward, K. (2007) 'Business improvement districts: policy origins, mobile policies and urban liveability', *Geography Compass*, 1(3): 657–672.

4 Arts districts or art-themed parks

Arts districts repurposed by/for Chinese governments

Amy Y. Zhang

Introduction

> Chinese cities face a new, urgent issue: how to move away from the mass production of fabricated space and nurture the rise of healthy, diverse, and creative urban centres. To this end, creative clusters are a pivotal planning tool. Creative districts around the world have been able to assimilate into existing urban fabrics and effectively reinvent themselves as unique and profitable destinations. However, 798, the first district to complete this cycle of gentrification in China, has become a victim of its own success. The area now has the resources to develop and densify, but it has lost the involvement of the artistic community that can inspire new buildings and generate creative content.
>
> (Ullens Center for Contemporary Art 2014)

The above quote is extracted from the introduction to a forum held during 'Beijing Design Week' in 2014, a week-long event featuring exhibitions, design award ceremonies, forums, and design fairs, which took place in several commercial and arts districts, including the neighbouring 798 arts district and 751 design park, and overlapped with the National Day 'golden week' for three days – the time when Beijing usually attracts the largest number of tourists. The 798 Art Festival and the Beijing People Beneficial Cultural Consumption Season were also held around the same time. In 2013, during the first Cultural Consumption Season, the 798 arts district was the venue of the Creative Consumption Carnival, one of the ten key events of the season. In 2014, the carnival moved to Beijing's Olympic Park, but 798 was still involved in the Cultural Consumption Season, as the 798 Art Festival was designated as one of the special events organised by Chaoyang District for the season.[1] This connection between art and consumption was evident on the banner that promoted the 798 Art Festival, where the slogan of the Cultural Consumption Season – 'Consuming Culture, Tasting Life' – was displayed along with the theme of the festival – 'Art, Time, Space'.

This intersection of art, design, tourism, festivals and consumption is where the 798 arts district stands now. As one of the most famous arts districts in China, it has gone through a process of grassroots initiation and conflicts over preservation, and has been institutionalised as an official 'cultural and creative industry cluster', resulting in commercialisation and displacement of artists and art-related uses. The forum for which the quote at the beginning of this chapter sets the tone was said to address the 'creative cluster conundrum' that 798 was facing – mainly the displacement of artists from the arts district – and was endorsed by the manager of the district, with the head of Seven Star Group (the landlord and de facto manager of the 798 arts district) sitting on the panel along with people from several consulting firms and think-tanks. However, the symbolic presence of the manager did not necessarily indicate that he was willing to make a U-turn on the future of 798. While defining gentrification as the main achievement of 798, the quote makes it explicit that the purpose of developing arts districts like 798 in China is essentially more about revalorisation of land than about art per se. 'Artistic communities' are viewed merely as effective tools for turning obsolete industrial compounds into urban destinations or, in the case of the 798 arts district, for regentrification.

Although it resembles classic art-led gentrification (Deutsche 1996; Zukin 1989; Ley 2003; Mathews 2010), I argue that the transformation of arts districts in China is not simply a Chinese manifestation of 'loft living' (Zukin 1989), but rather part and parcel of intensifying depoliticisation and growing consumerism in Chinese society. Arts districts in China are (re)produced as 'art-themed parks', which are spectacular places for play and consumption (Hannigan 1998) geared towards China's consumption-oriented middle class (Dickson 2010; Zhou and Chen 2010). Viewing from an assemblage perspective, this chapter examines how arts districts in Beijing, and the 798 arts district in particular, are subject to aestheticising and depoliticising processes that are directed by the municipal government. It demonstrates that, by drawing attention to the expressive role of the built environment of arts districts – the aesthetics of arts districts – the municipal government of Beijing is able to displace the potential political challenges that arts districts may posit while engaging urban consumer-citizens (Davis 2006) in the scheme of depriving the art community of their space.

Interpreting China's arts districts

Focusing on the role of local government, existing scholarship has suggested two main theoretical frameworks for interpreting arts districts and creative industry clusters (CICs) in Chinese cities. On one hand, arts districts are studied through the lenses of state–society relations and governance in China. Some studies argue that the success of artists in convincing local governments to maintain the artistic use of derelict industrial compounds demonstrates China's growing social forces vis-à-vis the strong presence of the state, and may indicate a new kind of state–society dynamic (Zhong 2009; Currier 2012). Other studies, however, are less optimistic (Ren and Sun 2012; Zhang 2014). They point out that although, on the surface, the involvement of government in developing arts districts seems to show the increasing tolerance of the state towards the art community, in fact it is a new way of controlling the location, production, exhibition, and circulation of art, as 'art districts provide the censors with convenient access to monitor the artists and their works' (Zhang 2014: 842).

On the other hand, some studies situate arts districts and CICs in the context of the entrepreneurial state, and emphasise the role of CICs as local revenue generators (Zheng 2010; O'Connor and Gu 2014). Research argues that CICs are now developed through a real estate model (see also Chapter 1, this volume) through which local governments are able to turn obsolete industrial land into land for commercial use that can generate taxes and jobs at very low cost (Zheng 2010). Developers are attracted by the obvious difference in cost between renting originally allocated industrial land and acquiring 'commercial use' land on the land market, and by the relatively high prospective return in developing CICs, which often turn into commercial and entertainment complexes that can yield profitable rents under the loose regulation of land use (Keane 2009; Zheng 2010; O'Connor and Gu 2014). Local governments not only benefit from tax incomes and job opportunities generated through CICs but also enjoy a certain rate of rental income, for some of the developers are companies established by them (Zheng 2010: 151; O'Connor and Gu 2014: 7).

Arts districts and CICs are thus recognised as mechanisms mobilised by local governments for their own political and economic gains, whether for social control (Zhang 2014), fiscal benefits (Zheng 2010), or both (Ren and Sun 2012). This study intends to enrich these findings by integrating assemblage thinking into the existing discussion, namely viewing arts districts as urban assemblages and examining their transformation through the main dimensions that characterise assemblages.

Assemblage is both a particular object and an orientation to the world (McFarlane 2011a). Viewing arts districts as sociomaterial ensembles (Farías 2010) emphasises that arts districts are historical and ongoing constructions, and each arts district is a result of the co-evolution of heterogeneous elements that are drawn together at a particular conjuncture through contingently obligatory relations (DeLanda 2006; Bender 2010; McFarlane 2011a). Elements of one arts district assemblage can be aligned with other elements in making another assemblage, and these elements are also assemblages themselves, which are continuously emerging and evolving. Arts districts thus consist of a series of overlapping assemblages, and are part of the overlapping assemblages that compose the urban world (McFarlane 2011c).

This study builds upon the idea, proposed by DeLanda (2006: 18), that assemblages are characterised by three dimensions:

1 the dimension along which elements move between playing material and expressive roles;
2 the dimension characterised by the processes of stabilising (territorialisation) and destabilising (deterritorialisation) the assemblage; and
3 the dimension of those processes that consolidate the identity of the assemblage (coding) and that grant more flexibility to the assemblage (decoding), through the intervention of specialised expressive media.

'Arts district', whether referring to a collective phenomenon or a specific case, therefore represents a series of historical assemblages that have gone through several territorialisation and deterritorialisation processes, accompanied by constantly competing processes of coding and decoding.

Using the theoretical infrastructures provided by assemblage thinking does not deny the importance of focusing on the role of the (local) state to interpret China's arts districts, for assemblage studies also emphasise that 'assemblages are structured' (McFarlane 2011c: 381) and that they are subject to unequal relations of power (McCann and Ward 2011; McFarlane 2011b;). Moreover, the three dimensions of assemblages all suggest approaches through which the politics and power relations around arts district assemblages can be examined, and I argue that existing research on China's arts districts has paid inadequate attention to some of these approaches. This chapter therefore intends to explore some of these potential approaches and to provide some suggestions for future research. I will focus on two of the three dimensions that characterise assemblages – the dimension of coding/decoding and the dimension of the material/expressive role of elements – to examine all of Beijing's arts districts and the 798 arts district in particular.

Beijing Municipal Government and the arts districts

Coding arts districts

According to DeLanda (2006), the processes of coding consolidate the identity of a relatively stable assemblage, thus coinciding with the processes of territorialisation. For the purposes of this chapter, I will focus on the processes of coding arts district assemblages in the period when arts districts have been institutionalised and officially recognised. In the case of Beijing, this period is from 2006 until now. Saying that arts district assemblages in this period are relatively stable does not imply that there have been few changes in these places or that every case in Beijing is in the same condition. However, as the following discussion will show, the coding of arts districts since 2006 has been continuously reinforcing the notion (identity) of arts districts along the same line. While the situations of individual cases may vary, the identity of the arts district as a particular kind of place has been relatively stable.

One way to examine the coding processes is to review how arts districts are defined in policies. In centrally issued policies, an arts district is defined as one type of cultural industry park (CIP, *wenhua chanye yuanqu*). Few specific policies are made on CIPs. One exception is a notice issued by the Ministry of Culture (MoC) on enhancing the administration of CIPs (MoC 2010). Aimed at resolving the problem that many CIPs were developed as real estate projects with very little (if any) culture-related elements, this notice mandated that local governments, mainly culture departments at local levels, should be more strict when approving proposals of new CIPs. While emphasising that CIPs should have 'clear cultural elements and orientation', this document also reveals that cultural theme parks are officially recognised as CIPs, which indicates that both places of production (of cultural products) and places of consumption (of cultural elements) can become CIPs, and the transformation from the former to the latter, such as through the commercialisation of arts districts, is justifiable. While commercialisation of arts districts is often associated with a displacement of an arts community without displacing the aesthetic 'feel' and 'look' of the district itself, one recent document issued by the MoC provides the condition for making the aesthetic 'feel' and 'look' the defining characteristics of arts districts (MoC 2014). This document on supporting 'cultural creative and design industry' (CCDI)[2] asserts that arts districts should contribute to beautifying the urban residential environment and aestheticising urban space, rather than merely being sites for the production and circulation of art.

This latest stance of the central government on arts districts grants local governments the permission they need to push through further commercialisation and 'theme-park-isation' of arts districts, namely recoding those districts from places of art production and circulation to places of consumption and play with an aestheticised built environment. For example, in Beijing, arts districts have been characterised as tourism attractions and art-themed places for fashion consumption, entertainment, and 'experience' as a result of policies issued in recent years (BMG 2007, 2008, 2011; BMBIA 2008; BMCEIT 2011; BMCTD 2011). While the assumed commercial nature of these places was expressed in a quite subtle way in previous policy documents, it is stated more explicitly by the municipal government in its latest plan, which is backed by the central government's 2014 policies on CCDI (BMG 2014; MoC 2014; SCPRC 2014). In this new policy, the municipal government indicates that Beijing's cultural and creative industry clusters (CCICs, *wenhua chuangyi chanye jijuqu*) are expected to become cultural commercial complexes that can turn surrounding areas into 'creative communities', and specifically identifies arts districts as 'areas for fashion and creative functions' (BMG 2014). As a result, the association of art with arts districts is further diluted, whereas the arts districts become infrastructures that provide an aestheticised built environment for entertainment and commercial activities, as the label 'fashion and creative functions' is so ambiguous that 'all traditional entertainment and commercial businesses' can fall under it:

> Restaurants offer creative food (*chuangyi canyin*), bars serve creative desserts (*chuangyi xiaochi*), and retail shops sell creative products (*chuangyi xiaofei*). Under the same logic, a shopping mall may similarly be called a creative industry cluster as all their activities may be attributed to fashion and consumption creativity.
>
> (Zheng 2010: 159)

Coding arts districts in the above ways not only provides justifications for the municipal government and multiple landlords to turn arts districts into more profitable real estate projects, but also creates opportunities for the municipal government to reap political benefits. By keeping the 'arts district' identifier, Beijing Municipal Government is able to build an image for itself and the city as 'supporting art', which furthermore implies a series of labels with which it would like to be associated, such as 'diverse', 'open', 'tolerant', and 'international'. But by coding arts districts as places of consumption and play with an aestheticised built environment, it is then possible and convenient for the government to depoliticise these districts, dissolve the potential political challenges posited by publicly displayed art, and remove artists from public attention.

The built environment of arts districts

The role each element plays in an assemblage moves along an axis from purely material to purely expressive (DeLanda 2006). The changing roles an element is assigned to can also provide an entry point for examining how the assemblage is subject to different power relations. Taking the 798 arts district as an example, the factory compound and the factory buildings were important material factors that drew artists to the place in the first instance. These elements, however, served more than a material role: in the efforts to preserve the 798 arts district when there was contention over the use of the land, artists particularly emphasised the significance of conserving the factory buildings, arguing that those buildings represented the Bauhaus architectural style and should be preserved as industrial heritage.[3] Such a strategic move assigned an expressive role to the factory buildings: they represented certain aesthetics, which soon became the aesthetics of the arts district itself. This expressive role of the factory buildings was then subsequently captured in the coding processes through which the 798 arts district was redefined by the municipal government as an urban attraction that provides a particular type of themed space, namely an aestheticised post-industrial built environment (BMG 2007; BMBIA 2008; BMCEIT 2011; BMCTD 2011).

Although the factory buildings are in fact playing a mixture of material and expressive roles, the material role they play – as suitable and affordable spaces for producing and displaying art – is increasingly marginalised in the discourses about arts districts, whereas the expressive role has been reinforced and depicted as the focal function the buildings serve. On one hand, disputes between 'tenants' (artists and galleries) and the landlord (the Seven Star Group) over rising rents have rarely been addressed by policies on arts districts or even perceived as an issue that needs (or can even be subject to) intervention by government agencies.[4] And, on the other hand, regarding to the maintenance of the buildings, the landlord is mainly concerned with maintaining the 'features of industrial heritage' rather than improving the conditions of the facilities. While the winter (from November to March) heating, for which artists and galleries pay more than $1600, hardly works and needs a thorough overhaul, the property management office of Seven Star Group pays more attention to whether its tenants are able to protect and maintain all the 'industrial features' that are attached to the buildings.[5] Moreover, after realising the attractiveness of graffiti, murals, and sculptures to visitors, the management office deliberately encouraged the addition of more of these artistic features to the built environment of the arts district,[6] which turned 798 into a place of consumption *and* a place to be consumed: an art-themed park. The morphology of the compound – with clear boundaries to separate the arts district from surrounding areas – further enhanced the 'theme-park' atmosphere.

The overemphasis on the expressive role of the built environment has had two consequences. First, it has resulted in the displacement of artists and art-related uses from the arts district. Second, it has made the aesthetics of the 798 arts district the signified of the signifier 'arts district', which renders the displacement of artists insignificant and the presence or absence of art-related uses in the arts district irrelevant, thus justifying the first consequence. Also, similar to gentrification, where the 'feel' and look of gentrified neighbourhoods have become commodities that can be packaged and mass produced and are employed in new constructions to attract middle-class consumers (Jager 1986; Mills 1988; Davidson and Lees 2005), the aesthetics of arts districts are now commodities that can be produced and displayed to draw consumers. The mass production of the aesthetics of arts districts in Beijing has been facilitated through a series of policies on conservation of industrial heritage, which specifically encourage turning industrial buildings and compounds into arts districts or CCICs in general (BMBIA 2007, 2008, 2009; BMG 2008, 2013, 2014; BMCUP 2011). The potential result then is the proliferation of art- or culture-themed spectacular places for play and consumption, where 'art' exists as commodities sold in boutique stores and, at best, as sculptures on the streets.

Moving forward

The processes of coding arts districts and the movements of the role of the factory buildings along the material/expressive axis are intertwined, and connected with a broader context of intensifying depoliticisation and growing consumerism in Chinese society. By focusing on these two dimensions, this chapter demonstrates that arts districts are reproduced as aesthetic and apolitical places. Mobilising the expressive role of the built environment for coding arts districts not only eliminates potential political controversies but also enlists middle-class consumer-citizens as advocates of commercialising and 'theme-park-ising' arts districts. While arts districts as such are positioned as catering to the needs of the people, 'the people' mainly refers only to urban middle-class consumer-citizens. The absence of members of the art community in arts districts, just like their absence on the panel of the forum mentioned at the beginning of this chapter, is now accepted and even viewed as normal.

This chapter explores how assemblage thinking can contribute to research on China's arts districts and provide new dimensions for discussing the politics of arts districts. The potential contributions of assemblage thinking, however, are not limited to this end. Engaging with assemblage thinking also means regarding arts districts as always emerging and remaining open to new possibilities, which, I argue, is a perspective that has been relatively lacking in existing research on China's arts districts. Viewing arts districts as urban assemblages emphasises that processes of stabilising the identity of arts districts (territorialisation and coding) are always accompanied by processes of destabilising the identity (deterritorialisation and decoding). While current studies (including this one) have focused on how arts districts are turned into mechanisms that Chinese governments utilise for their own interests, it is also important to pay attention to possible approaches and practices that may challenge and change this situation. These practices may already exist but are too subtle to draw attention; by taking an assemblage perspective researchers could be more attuned to such small changes towards deterritorialisation. Moreover, as DeLanda (2006: 12) points out, 'one and the same component may participate in both processes by exercising different sets of capacities'.

A starting point for identifying actions that counter the dominant coding processes, then, could be locating the multiple roles that a certain element plays for different purposes. For example, while the built environment of arts districts is now assigned an expressive role and serves for the coding processes that consolidate the identity of arts districts, it can also play a role in decoding and thus deterritorialisation processes by performing its material role, and practices that focus on bringing the material role of the built environment into the discourses around arts districts can be viewed as attempts aiming to challenge the existing situations. More academic effort needs to be devoted to studying such practices, which would potentially inform more strategies that challenge the status quo.

Acknowledgements

This study is supported by the Foundation for Urban and Regional Studies (FURS) studentship within the field of urban and regional studies. I would like to thank the editors for their constructive feedback and the work they have put into this volume, and Deborah G. Martin for support as I developed this chapter. Additionally, I greatly appreciate the help and contributions from my interviewees in this research.

Notes

1 Information obtained from http://zhengwu.beijing.gov.cn/zwzt/hmhwxf/qxhd/t1367258. htm (in Chinese) (accessed 2 October 2014).
2 Scholars often argue that 'cultural industry' (*wenhua chanye*) is the preferred term of central government as it implies continuity from the previous state-owned sector (public cultural institution) and the persistent state power over cultural production, while 'creative industry' (*chuangyi chanye*) is favoured by local governments because its ambiguity helps to justify commercial and consumption practices in the cultural realm (O'Connor and Gu 2006; Shan 2014). However, when reviewing policies for this study, I found that the term 'cultural creative industry', which is defined as one kind of cultural industry, has appeared in central government documents since 2006 (GOCPCCC 2006), and its function in promoting consumption has even been highlighted (SCPRC 2014), which runs contrary to the prevailing opinion of existing scholarship.
3 Interviews with two artists, Beijing, 2 December 2014 and 11 February 2015.
4 Interviews with two managers, Beijing, 18 December 2014 and 26 January 2015.

5 Interviews with four artists, Beijing, 22 November, 11 December, 21 December and 28 December 2014.
6 Interview with artist, Beijing, 13 January 2015.

References

Beijing Municipal Bureau of Industry Advancement (BMBIA) (2007) 'Guiding Opinions of Beijing Municipality on Protecting and Using Industrial Resources, Developing Cultural and Creative Industry', Beijing: Beijing Municipal Bureau of Industry Advancement. Online. Available at www.chycci.gov.cn/news.aspx?id=5826 (accessed 12 September 2014).

Beijing Municipal Bureau of Industry Advancement (BMBIA) (2008) 'Guiding Opinions of Beijing Municipality on Advancing the Development of Industrial Tourism', Beijing: Beijing Municipal Bureau of Industry Advancement. Online. Available at www.creativeindustry.org.cn/policies/bj11.htm (accessed 21 September 2014).

Beijing Municipal Bureau of Industry Advancement (BMBIA) (2009) 'Work Guidance of Beijing Municipality on Preserving and Reusing Industrial Heritage', Beijing: Beijing Municipal Bureau of Industry Advancement. Online. Available at www.pkulaw.cn/CLI.12.360135 (accessed 18 September 2014).

Beijing Municipal Commission of Economy and Information Technology (BMCEIT) (2011) 'Plan of Beijing Municipality on the Development of Urban Industries during the Era of the Twelfth Five-Year Plan', Beijing: Beijing Municipal Commission of Economy and Information Technology. Online. Available at http://zhengwu.beijing.gov.cn/ghxx/sewgh/t1202278.htm (accessed 18 September 2014).

Beijing Municipal Commission of Tourism Development (BMCTD) (2011) 'Plan of Beijing Municipality on the Development of the Tourism Industry during the Era of the Twelfth Five-Year Plan', Beijing: Beijing Municipal Commission of Tourism Development. Online. Available at http://zhengwu.beijing.gov.cn/ghxx/sewgh/t1204036.htm (accessed 18 September 2014).

Beijing Municipal Commission of Urban Planning (BMCUP) (2011) 'Plan of Beijing Municipality on Protecting and Constructing Historical and Cultural Renowned City during the Era of the Twelfth Five-Year Plan', Beijing: Beijing Municipal Commission of Urban Planning. Online. Available at www.bjghw.gov.cn/web/bjghw_125.html (accessed 18 September 2014).

Beijing Municipal Government (BMG) (2007) 'Plan of Beijing Municipality on the Development of Cultural and Creative Industry during the Era of the Eleventh Five-Year Plan', Beijing: Beijing Municipal Government. Online. Available at http://zhengwu.beijing.gov.cn/ghxx/sywgh/t833175.htm (accessed 9 January 2014).

Beijing Municipal Government (BMG) (2008) 'Opinions of the Beijing Municipal Government on Fully Advancing the Development of Tourism Industry of Beijing Municipality', Beijing: Beijing Municipal Government. Online. Available at www.pkulaw.cn/CLI.12.267543 (accessed 9 January 2014).

Beijing Municipal Government (BMG) (2011) 'Plan of Beijing Municipality on the Development of Social Public Service during the Era of the Twelfth Five-year Plan', Beijing: Beijing Municipal Government. Online. Available at www.pkulaw.cn/CLI.12.575327 (accessed 18 September 2014).

Beijing Municipal Government (BMG) (2013) 'Outline of the Plan of Constructing and Developing Beijing into a "Capital of Design"', Beijing: Beijing Municipal Government.

Online. Available at http://zhengwu.beijing.gov.cn/ghxx/qtgh/t1328939.htm (accessed 18 September 2014).

Beijing Municipal Government (BMG) (2014) 'Notice of the Beijing Municipal Government on Issuing Plan of Beijing Municipality on Constructing and Developing Cultural and Creative Industry Function Areas (2014–2020) and Plan of Beijing Municipality on Improving Cultural and Creative Industry (2014–2020), Beijing: Beijing Municipal Government. Online. Available at www.pkulaw.cn/CLI.12.872265 (accessed 2 October 2014).

Bender, T. (2010) 'Reassembling the City: Networks and Urban Imaginaries', in I. Farías and T. Bender (eds), *Urban Assemblages: How Actor-Network Theory Changes Urban Studies*, London: Routledge, pp. 303–323.

Currier, J. (2012) 'Selling Place through Art: The Creation and Establishment of Beijing's 798 Art District', in P.W. Daniels, K.C. Ho, and T.A. Hutton (eds), *New Economic Spaces in Asian Cities: From Industrial Restructuring to the Cultural Turn*, London: Routledge, pp. 184–201.

Davidson, M., and Lees, L. (2005) 'New-build "Gentrification" and London's Riverside Renaissance', *Environment and Planning A*, 37: 1165–1190.

Davis, D.S. (2006) 'Urban Chinese Homeowners as Citizen-consumers', in S. Garon and P.L. Maclachlan (eds), *The Ambivalent Consumer: Questioning Consumption in East Asia and the West*, Ithaca, NY: Cornell University Press, pp. 281–300.

DeLanda, M. (2006) *A New Philosophy of Society: Assemblage Theory and Social Complexity*, London: Continuum.

Deutsche, R. (1996) *Eviction: Art and Spatial Politics*, Cambridge, MA: MIT Press.

Dickson, B.J. (2010) 'China's Cooperative Capitalists: The Business End of the Middle Class', in C. Li (ed.), *China's Emerging Middle Class: Beyond Economic Transformation*, Washington, DC: Brookings Institution Press, pp. 291–309.

Farías, I. (2010) 'Introduction: Decentring The Object of Urban Studies', in I. Farías and T. Bender (eds), *Urban Assemblages: How Actor-Network Theory Changes Urban Studies*, London: Routledge, pp. 1–24.

General Office of CPC Central Committee (GOCPCCC) (2006) 'Outline of the Plan of National Development of Culture during the Era of the Eleventh Five-Year Plan', Beijing: General Office of CPC Central Committee. Online. Available at www.pkulaw. cn/CLI.2.79531 (accessed 9 January 2014).

Hannigan, J. (1998) *Fantasy City: Pleasure and Profit in the Postmodern Metropolis*, New York: Routledge.

Jager, M. (1986) 'Class Definition and the Aesthetics of Gentrification: Victoriana in Melbourne', in N. Smith and P. Williams (eds), *Gentrification of the City*, London: Unwin Hyman, pp. 78–91.

Keane, M. (2009) 'The Capital Complex: Beijing's New Creative Clusters', in L. Kong and J. O'Connor (eds), *Creative Economies, Creative Cities: Asian–European Perspectives*, New York: Springer, pp. 77–95.

Ley, D. (2003) 'Artists, Aestheticisation and the Field of Gentrification', *Urban Studies*, 40(12): 2527–2544.

Mathews, V. (2010) 'Aestheticizing Space: Art, Gentrification and the City', *Geography Compass*, 4(6): 660–675.

McCann, E., and Ward, K. (2011) 'Urban Assemblages: Territories, Relations, Practices, and Power', in E. McCann and K. Ward (eds), *Mobile Urbanism: Cities and Policymaking in the Global Age*, Minneapolis: University of Minnesota Press, pp. xiii–xxxv.

McFarlane, C. (2011a) 'Assemblage and Critical Urbanism', *City*, 15(2): 204–224.

McFarlane, C. (2011b) *Learning the City: Knowledge and Translocal Assemblage*, Oxford: Wiley-Blackwell.

McFarlane, C. (2011c) 'On context', *City*, 15(3–4): 375–388.

Mills, C. (1988) 'Life on the Upslope: The Postmodern Landscape of Gentrification', *Environment and Planning D: Society and Space*, 6: 169–189.

Ministry of Culture (MoC) (2010) 'Notice of the Ministry of Culture on Strengthening the Administration of Cultural Industry Parks and Bases, Facilitating the Healthy Development of Cultural Industry', Beijing: Ministry of Culture. Online. Available at www.pkulaw.cn/CLI.4.134977 (accessed 9 January 2014).

Ministry of Culture (MoC) (2014) 'Opinions of the Ministry of Culture on Implementing Several Opinions of the State Council on Promoting the Fusion of Cultural Creative Design Service and Relevant Industry and Its Development', Beijing: Ministry of Culture. Online. Available at www.pkulaw.cn/CLI.4.221744 (accessed 23 September 2014).

O'Connor, J., and Gu, X. (2006) 'A New Modernity? The Arrival of "creative industries" in China', *International Journal of Cultural Studies*, 9(3): 271–283.

O'Connor, J., and Gu, X. (2014) 'Creative Industry Clusters in Shanghai: A Success Story?', *International Journal of Cultural Policy*, 20(1): 1–20.

Ren, X., and Sun, M. (2012) 'Artistic Urbanization: Creative Industries and Creative Control in Beijing', *International Journal of Urban and Regional Research*, 36(3): 504–521.

Shan, S.-L. (2014) 'Chinese Cultural Policy and the Cultural Industries', *City, Culture and Society*, 5(3): 115–121.

State Council of the PRC (SCPRC) (2014) 'Several Opinions of the State Council on Promoting the Fusion of Cultural Creative Design Service and Relevant Industry and Its Development', Beijing: State Council of the PRC. Online. Available at www.chycci.gov.cn/news.aspx?id=5801 (accessed 12 September 2014).

Ullens Center for Contemporary Art (2014) 'City—useum: 798 and the Creative Cluster Conundrum'. Online. Available at http://ucca.org.cn/en/program/citymuseum-798-creative-cluster-conundrum/ (accessed 23 July 2015).

Zhang, Y. (2014) 'Governing Art Districts: State Control and Cultural Production in Contemporary China', *China Quarterly*, 219: 827–848.

Zheng, J. (2010) 'The "Entrepreneurial State" in "Creative Industry Cluster" Development in Shanghai', *Journal of Urban Affairs*, 32(2): 143–170.

Zhong, S. (2009) 'From Fabrics to Fine Arts: Urban Restructuring and the Formation of an Art District in Shanghai', *Critical Planning*, 16: 119–137.

Zhou, X., and Chen, Q. (2010) 'Globalization, Social Transformation, and the Construction of China's Middle Class', in C. Li (ed.), *China's Emerging Middle Class: Beyond Economic Transformation*, Washington, DC: Brookings Institution Press, pp. 84–103.

Zukin, S. (1989) *Loft Living: Culture and Capital in Urban Change*, New York: Rutgers University Press.

5 Spaces of restriction and leisure

Seoul's vision of the creative city

Jay E. Bowen

Introduction: Cheonggyecheon as a 'test-bed' for the South Korean ubiquitous-eco-city

Cheonggyecheon, a recently restored stream and greenway, cuts 5.8 kilometres across central Seoul and links the Dongdaemun History and Culture Park, Dongdaemun Market, the central business district, and Sejong Boulevard, facing Gyeongbok Palace. Cheonggyecheon is the centrepiece of urban development initiatives that aim to increase Seoul's global competitiveness, encourage business investment and tourism, and increase quality of life and accessibility for a new generation of young urban professionals.

Such projects are impressive pieces of a new amenities infrastructure, representing a site-specific, path-dependent manifestation of the Floridian logic of urban growth and the creative class (Florida 2003). Cities like Seoul are sites of emergence, 'where intense experiments with city-making are inflected by strategic global influences and investments, but are also inevitably "homegrown", defying the plotted coordinates of "planetary capitalism"' (Roy 2011: 310). Mindful of recent work on 'developmental neoliberalism' in East Asia by Choi (2012a) and Park and Lepawsky (2012), this chapter examines the Seoul Capital Area (SCA) as an authoritarian developmental state cityscape moulded by subsequent entrepreneurial neoliberal urbanization and socio-political struggle.

While Cheonggyecheon and the city greenbelt reflect Seoul's developmental state urbanization under the Park Chung Hee dictatorship, the city and national governments have begun translating fragments of these sites into the amenity spaces of the creative city. Here, the Floridian strategies that entrepreneurial cities employ to retain competitiveness often find a spatial fix in Seoul's obsolete authoritarian infrastructure. This evinces a distinctive expression of the creative city that emerges through costly, strong-state, redevelopment initiatives amidst an authoritarian urban landscape. The city and national governments categorize many of the resulting projects as components of the 'ubiquitous-eco-city'.

In 2006, South Korea's Ministry of Information and Communication and the Prime Minister's Office approved the U-Korea Master Plan, initiating ubiquitous, or 'u-City', 'test-bed' construction projects nationwide with hopes of becoming 'the ultimate "u-City republic"' (National Information Society Agency 2007: 15;

Figure 5.1 'Cheonggyecheon Stream': Cheonggyecheon in Seoul, October 2005, shortly
    after reopening
Source: riNux, licensed under CC BY-SA 2.0.

Oh and Larson 2011: 113). From the beginning, these projects promoted sustainability, seeking to produce liveability through healthy urban environments and
abundant leisure and amenity spaces. While the strategies remain unchanged,
Yigitcanlar and Lee (in press) write, 'All u-cities are now rebranded as u-eco-
cities.' They are cities 'in which urban information and services are provided to
residents through high-tech ubiquitous computing, with sensors and communication resources embedded in urban elements, to increase the quality of life while
minimizing environmental impacts' (Yigitcanlar and Lee in press). Moreover,
these strategies seek economic growth and consumer satisfaction, while granting
the feeling of democratic participation and environmentalism to a busy citizenry
without the hassle that previously defined these engagements.

Cheonggyecheon, refurbished, opened to the public in 2005, after four decades
under an elevated expressway (Cho 2010; Kang and Cervero 2009; Seoul
Metropolitan Government 2009). In 2007, the city presented the stream as a
showcase of the u-City movement, dubbing it '"U-Cheonggyecheon"', and touting
the deployment of high-tech assemblies to "monitor its purity and water and pollution levels"'. Here, ecological responsibility becomes a chic, stress-free activity,
as participatory environmental surveillance and management emerge as 'techno-
logically-enhanced leisure' (Choi and Greenfield 2009: 6). Thus, the National
Information Society Agency's (2007: 20) publication on u-City planning promotes Cheonggyecheon as a 'ubiquitous stream', adding high-tech ubiquitous

technologies to a site establishing Seoul as a 'cultural city promoting the harmony of tradition and modernism'. As the city government and Samsung unveiled the augmented Cheonggyecheon, they invited visitors to monitor stream ecology through a video image system and receive area history tours on their cell phones (National Information Society Agency 2007: 20; Oh and Larson 2011: 124–125). Moreover, onsite touchscreen services and downloadable cell-phone applications help visitors locate nearby stores and cultural sites. Through the project, the city government demonstrates an interest in rebranding Seoul as an ecologically resilient cultural city, with low entry barriers to Florida's (2003) 'creative class' and ample support for selected commercial and economic activities.

While the ubiquitous-eco-city's 'ubiquity' connotes an incorporation of everything and everyone within a seamless high-tech infrastructure, it has marginalized many people, businesses, and land uses. Furthermore, one can trace the underpinnings of the ubiquitous-eco-city through past examples of developmental dictatorship and authoritarianism, as well as within the government's recent push to increase competitiveness through fashionable creative city and sustainability initiatives. Nevertheless, urban development in the SCA both produces and remains a product of the people who inhabit and struggle over its spaces. Diverse coalitions of state and civilian actors contest, construct, and embrace or reject new public spaces such as Cheonggyecheon.

Authoritarianism and the physical infrastructure and form of modern Seoul

The SCA's urban form bears the imprint of decades of developmental dictatorship (Cho 2010; Lee 2004). Although South Korea initiated democratic reforms just before the 1988 Seoul Olympics, new urban development initiatives continue to reflect aspects of authoritarianism. Seoul's urbanization pattern mirrors the nation's division and the concomitant securitization of the South's capitalist metropole from Northern invasion. Both city and national governments use extensive and displacing renewal projects to furnish trendy 'creative city' amenity spaces within authoritarian-era cityscapes, such as Cheonggyecheon and Seoul's greenbelt.

Elsewhere, greenbelts often connote benign notions of ecological stewardship. However, President Park Chung Hee envisioned Seoul's greenbelt as a military security space wherein the South Korean Army could drill, engage in mock combat, and operate checkpoints. Although Park (1979: 104) emphasized protecting 'the beauty of nature', preservation was largely a proxy for expanded political securitization and militarization. Demarcating the greenbelt in 1971, Park further wished to prevent northward growth towards the Demilitarized Zone, locate army facilities near Seoul, and neutralize potential North Korean incursions without disruption to the built environment and urban economy (Bengston and Youn 2006; Ha and Cho 2009: 193; Jung 2011: 214). Consequently, residents' feelings towards the greenbelt and its regulations carry a site-specific complexity reflecting contradictory opinions about the Park dictatorship, its military and developmental legacy, and the greenbelt's urban amenity potential.

With the greenbelt, the national government used the rhetoric of ecological stewardship to help legitimize its interventions into peri-urban land uses. In its first iteration, the greenbelt was a defence against communist threats to Seoul's political and economic security, such as the 1968 Blue House Raid that was meant to culminate in President Park's assassination. Underscoring this interrelationship between geopolitical security and ecological management in Asia, Peluso and Vandergeest (2011: 604) argue, 'It is difficult to understand the ecological and political lives of contemporary forests without understanding their connections to Cold War-era insurgencies and counterinsurgencies.' Since the Korean War ended in stalemate, the South Korean government has responded to cross-border military incursions and pre-emptively dealt with perceived internal communist threats. Seoul's greenbelt has played a role in both of these arenas. It provided a physical space for military training, security, and potential conflict, and created a new regulatory space to facilitate the removal of heavy industry and factory workers to remote, government-planned, satellite cities. In its new role as an amenity space where urbanites can enjoy Seoul's proximity to gardens, farms, and forests, the greenbelt represents both neoliberal urban entrepreneurialism and Cold War antagonism. In Seoul's mountain parks and greenbelt, one still encounters trenches and bunkers where soldiers train for confrontation with the North.

Foucault (2003: 47–48), speaking on the emergence of national sovereignty and the production of the national subject, intuits that war is 'the nucleus of political institutions' and politics is 'a continuation of war by other means'. In the Cold War construction of Seoul, war, state violence, and the generation of threat and vulnerability pervade 'peacetime' politics and produce anti-communist subjects who legitimize and defend South Korea. This process is further internalized through state structures that marginalize and discipline specific groups of people within the nation's territory and disseminate guidelines for proper citizenship. Thus, the centre and periphery established by the constant politics of state violence are social as much as geographical. Because of South and North Korea's continuing political, ideological, and military hostility, the production of sovereignty and subjecthood through state structures is readily apparent in Seoul.

Militarization permeates life and landscape. Periodically, city residents must evacuate the streets in response to facsimile broadcasts and sirens warning of a North Korean air raid, as South Korean fighter jets scream across the sky. Likewise, greenbelt residents still feel the oppression of undemocratic and militarized arrangements. For many, the greenbelt is a 'weapon' that facilitated the 'invasion' of their communities and dispossessed them (Jung 2011: 224).

These civil rights issues assert a problematizing counterpoint to manifold bipartisan arguments, which increasingly promote the greenbelt in terms of ecological securitization and sustainability, rather than geopolitical security. Moreover, President Park's strategic buffer split communities, severely restricted land use, facilitated clearances of peripheral informal settlements, and caused urban land prices to skyrocket, as Seoul became one of the world's densest cities.

Within the city, Seoul's premier consumption space and residential district, Gangnam, developed through a matrix of authoritarian state guidance, domestic conglomerates, and finance responding to Cold War paranoia. Gangnam, meaning 'south of the river', long remained undeveloped. However, the 1968 North Korean commando assault on the presidential palace spurred plans to move Seoul's population centre south of the Han River (Lee 2004: 120). More than a mere strategic manoeuvre, this move epitomized the bond between iron-fisted government urban policy directives and the facilitation of capital reinvestment.

Moreover, Park enforced control over regional planning through large-scale slum clearances and the relocation of poor residents and industries in a vast satellite city project (Seoul Metropolitan Government 2009: 83). Arguably, given Park's distrust of rural Koreans, whom he described as indolent and easily misled (Moore 1984: 580, 588; Park 1979: 43, 70), and who filled the slums, factories, and sweatshops of Seoul after the Korean War (Kim and Han 2012; Koo 2001), the government resettled the industrial working class in southern satellite cities to secure the capital politically, as much as to remove polluting industries from the city. In 1970, the government relocated many of Seoul's poor to the new satellite city of Gwangju (Gyeonggi-do), promising loans and property for housing construction. However, the government's failure to provide sewage and water services, paved roads, factories, and schools resulted in demonstrations involving thirty thousand settlers, known as the Gwangju Grand Housing Complex Incident (or the Gwangju Settlers' Riot), of 1971 (Lee 2007: 33–34). Such large-scale attempts at relocating Seoul's urban poor south of the Han River, and away from foci of urban and national security, presaged both recent 'new-town' renewal

Figure 5.2 Gwangju Grand Housing Complex Incident (Gwangju Settlers' Riot), 1971

Source: Seoul Metropolitan Government, licensed under CC BY 3.0 and KOGL.

projects and cultural, creative, and green ubiquitous-eco-city developments, like Cheonggyecheon and the Songdo International Business District.

Cheonggyecheon, like the greenbelt, also emerged from the authoritarian groundwork of Park's regime as an integral part of modern Seoul's green infrastructure of ecological security. In 1961, when Park seized power, the stream was an open-air sewer amidst a large informal neighbourhood. In building the Cheonggye Expressway over the stream, Park combined economic development, geopolitical securitization and legitimization, anti-communism, and the forced relocation of the indigent.

In 1967, Park's military government, assisted by his ally, 'bulldozer' Mayor Kim Hyun Ok, began construction of the Cheonggye Expressway together with the Gyeongbu Expressway, connecting Seoul to the south-eastern port of Busan (Cho 2010: 149; Choi 2012b: 191; Podoler 2010: 127). At this time, only Seoul's wealthiest residents owned cars, and the construction of a nationwide system of

Figure 5.3 The demolition of unlicensed buildings during the construction of the Cheonggye Expressway

Source: Seoul Metropolitan Government, licensed under CC BY 3.0 and KOGL.

expressways signified more than a transportation infrastructure. As Choi (2012b: 186) asserts, the Gyeongbu Expressway symbolized a '"modernization of father-land", presupposing a speed war and anti-communism within the project'. Through expressway construction, Park desired to grow the economy through a more efficient circulation of goods, consolidate his political power, and develop military superiority over the North through territorial integration (Choi 2012b: 191). The Cheonggye Expressway was an expression of these principles at the urban scale, and demonstrated, like the Cheonggyecheon restoration, Seoul's accommodation of modernization. Establishing an upwardly mobile national and civic identity, the government overlooked human rights in the displacement of numerous streamside squatter communities. Many ended up in southern satellite communities, like Gwangju, due to Park's security-driven push to move population growth away from North Korea and industrial development out of the city proper.

An overview of creative and cultural city policies in Seoul

Since Park's assassination in 1979, potential air-based attacks and long-range artillery and missile strikes have obviated the security aspects of the greenbelt and southward growth. Due to increasing density, changing security dynamics, and a 'rent gap' between actual and potential ground rents (Smith 1984/1990), the city government, urban planners, and investors are bringing Gangnam-style develop-ment north of the river (Kim and Choe 2011: 51). In the process, enormous 'new town' apartment blocks have displaced many communities. Furthermore, spec-tacular mixed-use nodes, rearticulating culture, amenities, commerce, consumption, and everyday life within the Floridian discourse of the creative city, are replacing older neighbourhoods.

Several urban policy and development studies promote the strong community ties defining Seoul's older neighbourhoods (Ha 2010; Han et al. 2012). However, new theories about urban growth, aimed at constructing the creative city, have emerged to contest social processes that generate strong bonds among long-term residents. Florida (2003: 5, 6) states, 'Social structures that were important in earlier years now work against prosperity ... [social capital] can just as easily shut out newcomers, raise barriers to entry, and retard innovation.' Florida claims that the weakening of traditional bonds lowers entry barriers to the creative class, composed of the young urban professionals, wealthy bohemians, immigrants, and gay people, who supposedly attract the engineers, intellectuals, and business majors through whom urban economic growth occurs.

Creative city policies, reframing culture as bohemian consumption, entertain-ment, experience, and amenity (Florida 2003: 13, 16), have become popular in the upper chambers of the Seoul Metropolitan Government. Mayor Oh Se Hoon was quick to adopt Florida's recommendations, declaring 2008 as 'the year in which the city of Seoul would be reborn as the "City of Creative Culture"' (Lee and Hwang 2012: 2821). That same year, Oh visited eight global cities to promote his 'culturenomics' strategy (Lee and Hwang 2012: 2823). By 2007, Seoul had begun to designate and promote certain 'creative' and 'cultural' industries with increasing expenditures. The government identified 'tourism; design and fashion; digital content; conventions; research and development (R&D) in information technology (IT), nanotechnology (NT), and biotechnology (BT); and financial and business services' as the six new growth engines of the urban economy. In 2008, the city added cultural industries to this development strategy, including the performance arts, the visual arts, film, and animation, and also promoted community centres, museums, galleries, festivals, heritage, and the restoration of historical sites through its Cultural Affairs Bureau. In 2009, Seoul spent US895 million on its creative culture programmes and urban remodelling (Lee and Hwang 2012: 2824). The transformation of the city's downtown is vast and includes Gwanghwamun Square, special tourism zones in Myeongdong, Insadong, and Cheonggyecheon, the Dongdaemun Design Plaza, and a planned greenway to connect Jongmyo Shrine and Namsan Mountain (Kriznik 2011: 298–299).

While the Seoul Metropolitan Government produces the creative city at great expense, the enthusiastic embrace of such endeavours is not universal. Evans notes that Floridian strategies seem to suppress cultural production and traditions, since they have value only if they attract 'knowledge workers'. He further criticizes Florida's creative cities approach as a universal capitalist measure that fosters openness to trade by encouraging global creative industries instead of the production of local heterogeneity (Evans 2009: 1008, 1009). Seeking survival, cities must reframe cultural practices within the logic of competing creative global cities. As a universal capitalist measure that attempts to make social spaces and practices legible to capitalist markets, the creative city inspires urban development and policy strategies that reorder the space of everyday practice, constituting a landscape traversed by struggle, adjustment, accommodation, and the formation of new notions of citizenship. Within this logic there is no endpoint or successful completion.

Devising strategic planning for the regeneration of Seoul, Lee et al. (2013) echo the ideas of Roach and Lam (2010) of Morgan Stanley, who claim that 'inefficient 'mom and pop' proprietors' limit the growth of the South Korean economy. Thus, Lee et al. (2013) promote large-scale, mixed-use nodes of commerce and culture in place of the traditional local differentiation of Seoul's consumption spaces. Seoul remains a city of distinct neighbourhoods, dedicated to selling distinct goods, linked to localized sources of production and supply: Chungmuro for film and camera supplies; Dongdaemun for clothing; and Cheongnyangni for fruits and vegetables. For many developers, these distinctions present barriers to the creation of a new culture of efficient mass consumption that is more legible to global capitalism and trade. Thus, Lee et al. (2013: 5) point to the new I-Park Mall in Yongsan as 'a cultural living space representing "Malling culture" as a major strategy of spatial marketing'. These enthusiastic endorsements of the 'culture' of the new creative city overlook the five tenants and police officer who died in a burst of flames on a Yongsan rooftop in 2009, as the tenants resisted their forced relocation for the mall's construction (Park 2012).

However, Seoul's spaces of difference do not face an inevitable defeat to globally mobile urban growth strategies. Lefebvre (1974/1991: 55) characterizes the city as a site of constant struggle, which prevents the abstract space of capitalism 'from taking over the whole planet and papering over all differences', and Seoul has witnessed many struggles over its spaces of difference. However, Korea also has a tradition of accommodating difference in social space amidst a pursuit of greater order. Pimatgol, or 'avoiding horses alley', has a history spanning more than 600 years, and arose as a place where commoners could avoid the processions of dignitaries, to whom they were obliged to kneel (Kwon 2009). A convenient refuge from the burdens of a strict social order, it hosted boisterous restaurants and bars just a few hundred feet from the processional avenue. Such spatial struggles and practical accommodations of difference continue to this day, and they are features of an urban landscape contrarily marked by a hierarchical urban planning and policy process, which continues to connote authoritarianism (Lee 2015: 3–4).

Creative authoritarianism: forcing participatory planning by confronting the state

Im (1987: 239) identifies the emergence of South Korean bureaucratic authoritarianism in Park's Yushin Constitution of October 1972. South Korea's bureaucratic authoritarian regimes were similar to those of South America, involving the political exclusion of the popular sector with the banning of elections, the curtailing of labour organization, and the suppression of basic human rights (O'Donnell 1979). Furthermore, government policy excluded the majority from the benefits of economic growth and depoliticized social issues, justifying the suppression of democracy through social stability, rationality, and efficiency. Unlike the bureaucratic authoritarian regimes of South America, however, South Korea's bureaucratic authoritarianism did not respond to economic crises of import-substitution industrialization, but was justified 'on the pretext of preserving . . . economic development and the continuation of a high rate of economic growth' (Im 1987: 240).

While South Korea's government has emerged from military dictatorship, the Park regime still courts a cult of personality, with many justifying its severity in these same terms. Such sentiments continue to legitimize strong centralized leadership and economic development projects. One can find examples in the recent 'bulldozer' mayorship and presidency of Lee Myung Bak, or new assaults on the Korean Railway Workers' Union and the Korean Teachers' and Education Workers' Union (Kwak 2014). In December 2014, the South Korean Constitutional Court ruled to dissolve the leftist Unified Progressive Party for undermining national security and democracy (Hong 2015). Ultimately, many extant elements of authoritarian leadership and development appear to facilitate Seoul's current creative city policies, which are tempered by the rhetoric of the smart and sustainable ubiquitous-eco-city.

Prominent features of Seoul's urban landscape, like the greenbelt, the Han River, abandoned railroad beds, and dismantled expressways, have morphed from an infrastructure of authoritarian security into one of amenity spaces in the creative cultural metropolis. Greenbelt residents, with restricted land use rights, often contest city residents, who value the greenbelt's recreational, cultural, and environmental assets (Jung 2011). Meanwhile, others weigh these amenity values against social costs, such as rising rents, land speculation, and congestion resulting from the greenbelt (Bengston and Youn 2006; Yoo 2009). But which practices and land uses in Seoul's repackaged amenity spaces get to be reformulated as amenity values, and which are restricted and marginalized?

In Seoul's 'test-bed' urbanism, planners and policy-makers imagine the city as a model for new, exportable, forms of urban development. Experimentation in model subject-making also occurs through the people and practices that these projects value and exclude. Citing Hoffman (2011), Roy (2011: 312–313) writes,

> Modelling is a 'mode of governing the urban', 'tied to the fostering of civilized and quality citizens who have a sense of national obligation and social responsibility, as well as the skills desirable for the global knowledge economy' ... The making of the world-class city is also a worlding of subjects, of the taking up of the world-class aesthetic by urban residents desiring a new future.

Such processes of subject-making through 'test-bed' urban modelling materialize in the Lee mayorship's refashioning of the Cheonggye Expressway into a stream and greenway. By 1992, the expressway had become structurally unsound (Kim et al. 2011: 32). At the millennium's end, what had once symbolized modernity and helped solidify President Park's military power and political legitimacy had become an eyesore. Furthermore, the area was host to a teeming informal economy: 'a place of bustling wholesale markets, small workshops and stores, street restaurants and bars, stretching along the expressway to the narrow alleys of nearby neighbourhoods' (Kriznik 2011: 302). Much of the trade constituted a quasi-legal shadow economy, deemed antithetical to a modern economy. Thus, the Lee mayorship identified the crumbling remnants of authoritarian develop-mentalism as an opportunity to revitalize surrounding neighbourhoods and elimi-nate undesirable commerce competing with the regulated market. Echoing Park's slum clearances during the expressway's construction, the Seoul Metropolitan Government relocated poor residents and merchants, resulting in confrontations between police, shopkeepers, and street vendors before their ultimate removal (Lee 2015: 4).

The Hwanghak-dong neighbourhood around Cheonggye Street contained over '60,000 shops, employing 800,000 workers, and a large number of illegal street vendors', who, fearing for their livelihoods, opposed the stream's renovation (Cho 2010: 154). Their resistance jeopardized the restoration project, leading to their emergence as citizens from whom the mayor needed to seek a degree of consent. Eventually, the city won over some vendors with the offer of more compensation, leaving a smaller opposition group.

In November 2003, riot squads and construction company hands forced out the remaining vendors (Biggs 2010). The city corralled the vendors into Dongdaemun

Stadium, where they operated a 'flea market' from January 2004 to April 2008 (Hwang 2014). The city then demolished the stadium to build the Dongdaemun Design Plaza – a component of the larger Dongdaemun History and Culture Park, which is a linchpin of Seoul's new tourism-oriented creative cultural infrastructure. Again, the city relocated the market. However, in a strange twist, the vendors were granted a permanent site on the grounds of an old school and their market was rechristened the 'Seoul Folk Flea Market' within the matrix of the same creative city development project that sought to exclude them. Today, the Korea Tourism Organization's (n.d.) English website boasts that the flea market plays a role in 'preserving the culture of the traditional Korean marketplace and drawing in visitors with a range of folk items that embody the unique charm of Korea'. The reality is more complex, as even the website hints when it explains that the market originated on Seoul's streets before being 'modernized'.

From the Cheonggyecheon street vendors' struggles against the urban renewal projects of Mayors Lee and Oh to their reconstitution in the legalized brick-and-mortar Seoul Folk Flea Market, unpredictably contingent outcomes occur even within Seoul's relatively authoritarian creative city overhaul. As Scott (1998: 348) theorizes, 'Human resistance to the more severe forms of social straitjacketing prevents monotonic schemes of centralized rationality from ever being realized.' Centralized high-modernist development schemes can never prepare for the many variables confronting often well-intended civic plans envisioning abstract

Figure 5.4 Seoul Folk Flea Market, April 2013

Source: Republic of Korea, licensed under CC BY-SA 2.0.

subjects. Through the Seoul Folk Flea Market, Seoul produced and recognized new subjects, as previously resistant street vendors consented to state power through negotiation with the city government.

Scott's critique of high-modernist centralized development planning applies to creative-city-influenced growth projects in Seoul. Strangely, the societal arrangement Scott (1998: 349) poses as an alternative to such rigid central planning – a 'resilient, flexible, adept population' within 'complex, diverse, animated environments', as advocated by Jane Jacobs – sounds like a prototype for Florida's creative class and city. Whereas Florida (2003: 3) claims to espouse Jacobs's 'cauldrons of diversity and difference', Seoul pursues a creative city policy that attempts to produce vibrancy, culture, and dynamism in frequent opposition to that which existed. While US cities employ Floridian approaches as low-cost alternatives to expensive urban renewal, in Seoul the Floridian logic accompanies extravagant centrally planned renewal projects, which often attempt to steamroller opposition and difference with unintended consequences.

In 2008, when Lee became Korea's president, he parlayed his successes with the Cheonggyecheon restoration into a nationwide project to dam, dredge, beautify, and reintroduce the nation's four major rivers as an infrastructure of amenities and trade. Thus, the controversial Sadaegang (Four Major Rivers) Project began. Reminiscent of the political–economic reasoning behind President Park's grand expressway plan in the 1960s, President Lee 'promised that the waterway would take heavy trucks off roads, draw tourists to artificial lakes, and reinvigorate rural communities' (Normile 2010: 1569). Seemingly, Lee hoped this would strengthen his political support, design out backward land uses, and foster economic expansion.

Within the SCA, the Sadaegang Project had major implications for riverside farming operations in the greenbelt near Namyangju, Yangpyeong, and Paldang. These villages host some of South Korea's oldest organic farming operations, as the government eased local agricultural land use restrictions in 1994, but applied strict regulations to prevent water contamination (Lydon 2011). Farmers thus exploited a niche by catering to both government regulations on greenbelt land and emerging consumer concern for food safety and interest in organic local produce. Nevertheless, through Lee's Sadaegang Project, nationwide riverside eviction and gentrification were components of a plan that espoused environmental restoration, but resulted in degradation.

Supporting the government's plan, reports promoted the restorative and sustainable elements of Lee's vision to remove apparently unsightly contaminating farmlands (Shin and Chung 2011: 23). Chung et al. (2010: 422) explained the need for riparian buffer systems to filter agricultural pollution in the Paldang watershed and supported the project, since it appeared to encourage these buffers. However, artistic renderings of the government's plans contained little visible emphasis on riparian ecosystem recovery. Instead, they foregrounded amenities like bicycle paths, athletic facilities, grass lawns, marinas, and mid-river swimming pools. It became questionable whether the planned amenities would solve the environmental contamination Lee blamed on riverside farmers. Furthermore, a vast network of resort-like amenities was not the riparian buffer system that Chung et al. (2010) described.

Local organic farmers opposed the partisan politics redefining their land uses as unsustainable. Originally, this group numbered about eighty farming families, who contested the unilateral annihilation of their farmlands and government assertions that they were the primary cause of regional water contamination (Park 2013). Eventually, many families accepted some government compensation and relocation packages, and the struggle narrowed to a tiny triangle of land, called Dumulmeori, where the North and South Han rivers meet. Only four farmers remained, but others joined them and began growing their own vegetable gardens to protest against the government's plans to replace the farms with performance stages, picnic sites, exhibition areas, gardens, and grass lawns (Lydon 2011; Park 2013). Similar to the Cheonggyecheon restoration, where the government ignored initial attempts at participatory planning and democratic involvement, the farmers and their supporters forced a participatory result.

In August 2012, the remaining farmers negotiated with the government to reserve the greenbelt land at Dumulmeori, which they had rented from the government for many years, as an 'ecology–education–experience village'. The farmers finally agreed to relocate after the government promised assistance in resettlement and gave them rights to manage the ecology village (Won and Hong 2012). Thus, the farmers reached a satisfactory solution with the government and modified the more egregious and environmentally harmful government plans into something that could promote public support for their livelihoods. Like the Seoul Folk Flea Market, the people victimized by authoritarian creative development strategies became citizens participating in, and ultimately legitimizing, the creative and cultural economy.

The following year, however, the government still had not fulfilled its promise to provide resettlement assistance, and the farmers were unable to plant in the spring (Kim 2013; Park 2013). Furthermore, these projects often fail to achieve many of their planners' stated objectives. While policy-makers promote the sustainability and resilience of 'green, creative, and cultural' development projects, the outcomes of both the Sadaegang Project and the Cheonggyecheon renewal are largely the opposite. Ultimately, the Sadaegang Project, beyond increasing eutrophication, has destroyed sandbanks and wetlands, fish and bird habitats, and ancient cultural heritage sites (Chang et al. 2012; Nam 2012). Meanwhile, the restored Cheonggyecheon cannot flow without pumping water through its concrete channel (Cho 2010). As planning regimes merely append new rhetorical components, the contradictions become more manifest and numerous.

Conclusions: the ubiquitous-eco-city re-examined

As an assemblage of planning prescriptions, combined with centralized execution at massive scales, and exacted upon a landscape traversed by the infrastructure of authoritarianism, Seoul presents a local iteration of globalized trends. Here, planners have laboured to demonstrate the seamless connectivity between chic notions of sustainability and 'ubiquitous' infrastructure. While ubiquitous-eco-city projects pay lip service to the popularity of sustainability, the environmentalist rhetoric embellishes conventional economic growth promotion.

Through the ubiquitous-eco-city, government-planned development at the urban and national scales reframes sustainability in terms of responsible consumption, expanding South Korea's market for high-tech products, fuelling 'creative' industries in R&D and IT, and growing the domestic economy. Seemingly green practices, like greenbelt organic farming, or apparently creative and cultural urban milieus, like the Cheonggyecheon street markets, are less legible to this vision and only reincorporated through political struggle.

Songdo, a massive public–private development in the SCA, seeks to be the first entirely ubiquitous-eco-city. However, constructed over dredged tidal flats in a rich coastal ecosystem, Songdo is anything but ecologically conscious. Furthermore, the ecologically conscious citizenship its planners envision is not ubiquitous, since only a wealthy minority with the capacity to consume the new, high-tech, green lifestyle of instant gratification is able to enjoy it.

Emphasizing the intersection between its ubiquitous infrastructure and the ecologically conscious citizens it serves and constructs, Songdo touts automatized trash sorting, recycling, and disposal, its unique water-cooled air-conditioning system, and its central home-network system, which allows residents to control their home-energy consumption remotely (Tanaka 2012). Its ubiquitous technology helps curb expensive waste and responds to consumers' desires for ecological responsibility while freeing them from the burden of worrying about how to be 'green'. In the ubiquitous-eco-city, the old environmentalism of political practices of social responsibility and civic activism is repackaged as consumable notions of ease and convenience.

The passivity of the consumption-oriented, ecologically conscious citizenship that the ubiquitous-eco-city encourages leads some observers to unsettling conclusions about the future. Halpern et al. (2013: 279–280) see Songdo as indicating emerging dystopian, machine-governed, data-driven metropolises in which 'strategic planners envision a totalizing sensory environment in which human actions and reactions, from eye movements to body movements, can be traced, tracked, and responded to in the name of consumer satisfaction and work efficiency'. While some worry about the implications for civil liberties and democratic participation, Kim (2010: 17), like Scott (1998), avoids 'technological determinism' when analysing these abstracting plans, emphasising that people's lives are not shaped merely by their physical and technological surroundings.

Confronting predictions of socio-political disintegration through the ubiquitous-eco-city, Kim (2010: 17) stresses that the 'e-topian space supporting the lifestyles of the mobile young professional workers and residents who live there' is a marketing myth. Spaces will always be constructed as much through the desires and practices of their inhabitants as by the people who govern and plan them. Novel socio-political organizations and practices always exist, and emerge, independent of government plans and developmental goals rushing to implement

94   *Jay E. Bowen*

the ubiquitous-eco-city's infrastructure. Too many people and practices are pushed out, or unintentionally left out, in these sweeping hierarchically applied policies and plans, and the inhabitants always seek to renegotiate the outcomes.

References

Bengston, D.N. and Youn, Y. (2006) 'Urban containment policies and the protection of natural areas: The case of Seoul's greenbelt', *Ecology and Society*, 11(1). Online. Available at www.ecologyandsociety.org/vol11/iss1/art3/ (accessed 10 December 2013).

Biggs, A. (2010) 'Seoul gets image of soft city with Cheonggyecheon', *Korea Times*, 28 June. Online. Available at www.koreatimes.co.kr/www/news/biz/2012/04/291_68399.html (accessed 8 March 2014).

Chang, Y.B., Han, J.K., and Kim, H.W. (2012) 'Green growth and Green New Deal policies in the Republic of Korea: Are they creating decent green jobs?', *International Journal of Labour Research*, 4(2): 151–171.

Cho, M.R. (2010) 'The politics of urban nature restoration: The case of Cheonggyecheon restoration in Seoul, Korea', *International Development Planning Review*, 32(2): 145–165.

Choi, B.D. (2012a) 'Developmental neoliberalism and the hybridity of the urban policy of South Korea', in B.G. Park, R.C. Hill, and A. Saito (eds), *Locating neoliberalism in East Asia: Neoliberalizing spaces in developmental states*, West Sussex: Blackwell, pp. 86–113.

Choi, B.D. (2012b) 'Gyeongbu Expressway: Political economic geography of mobility and demarcation', *Korean Social Sciences Review*, 2(2): 181–218.

Choi, J. H., and Greenfield, A. (2009) 'To connect and flow in Seoul: Ubiquitous technologies, urban infrastructure and everyday life in the contemporary Korean city', in M. Foth (ed.), *Handbook of research on urban informatics: The practice and promise of the real-time city*, pp. 21–36. Online. Available at http://eprints.qut.edu.au/14105/ (accessed 10 December 2013).

Chung, S.J., Ahn, H.K., Oh, J.M., Choi, I.S., Chun, S.H., Choung, Y.K., Song, I.S., and Hyun, K.H. (2010) 'Comparative analysis on reduction of agricultural non-point pollution by riparian buffer strips in the Paldang watershed, Korea', *Desalinization and Water Treatment*, 16(1–3): 411–426.

Evans, G. (2009) 'Creative cities, creative spaces and urban policy', *Urban Studies*, 46(5–6): 1003–1040.

Florida, R. (2003) 'Cities and the creative class', *City and Community*, 2(1): 3–19.

Foucault, M. (2003) *Society must be defended: Lectures at the Collège de France, 1975–76*, M. Bertrani, A. Fontana, and F. Ewald (eds), D. Macey (trans.), New York: Picador.

Ha, S.K. (2010) 'Housing, social capital and community development in Seoul', *Cities*, 27(1): 535–542.

Ha, S.K. and Cho, S.C. (2009) 'Suburban development and public housing provision on greenbelt zones in the Seoul Metropolitan Region', *Journal of the Korean Urban Administration Association*, 22(1): 183–207.

Halpern, O., LeCavalier, J., Calvillo, N., and Pietsch, W. (2013) 'Test-bed urbanism', *Public Culture*, 25(2): 272–206.

Han, S., Kim, H., and Lee, H.S. (2012) 'A multilevel analysis of social capital and self-reported health: Evidence from Seoul, South Korea', *International Journal for Equity in Health*, 11(3): 1–12.

Hoffman, L. (2011) 'Urban modeling and contemporary technologies of city-building in China: The production of regimes of green urbanisms', in A. Roy and A. Ong (eds), *Worlding cities: Asian experiments and the art of being global*, Oxford: Wiley-Blackwell, pp. 55–76.

Hong, S. (2015) 'Court dissolution of left-wing party in South Korea raises alarm', *Al Jazeera America*, 15 January. Online. Available at http://america.aljazeera.com/articles/2015/1/15/korea-left-troubles.html (accessed 23 February 2015).

Hwang, J.T. (2014) 'Territorialized urban mega-projects beyond global convergence: The case of Dongdaemun Design Plaza & Park Project, Seoul', *Cities*, 40(A): 82–89.

Im, H.B. (1987) 'The rise of bureaucratic authoritarianism in South Korea', *World Politics*, 39(2): 231–257.

Jung, H. (2011) 'Contested space, contested imaginations: Deconstructing the greenbelt controversy in South Korea', *Horizons*, 2(2): 205–236.

Kang, C.D. and Cervero, R. (2009) 'From elevated freeway to urban greenway: Land value impacts of the CGC project in Seoul, Korea', *Urban Studies*, 46(13): 2771–2794.

Kim, C. (2010) 'Place promotion and symbolic characterization of New Songdo City, South Korea', *Cities*, 27(1): 13–19.

Kim, K.J. and Choe, S.C. (2011) 'In search of sustainable urban form for Seoul', in A. Sorensen and J. Okata (eds), *Megacities: Urban form, governance, and sustainability*, Tokyo: Springer Japan, pp. 43–65.

Kim, H.M. and Han, S.S. (2012) 'Seoul', *Cities*, 29(2): 142–154.

Kim, J.S. (2013) 'Four Major Rivers Project victims gather to air their grievances', *The Hankyoreh*, 21 May. Online. Available at http://english.hani.co.kr/arti/english_edition/e_national/588352.html (accessed 8 March 2014).

Kim, S.H., Jung, S.H., and Rowe, P.G. (2011) *A city and its stream: An appraisal of the Cheonggyecheon Restoration Project and its environs in Seoul, South Korea*, Hollis, NH: Puritan Press.

Koo, H. (2001) *Korean workers: The culture and politics of class formation*, Ithaca, NY: Cornell University Press.

Korea Tourism Organization (n.d.) 'Seoul Folk Flea Market'. Online. Available at http://english.visitkorea.or.kr/enu/SI/SI_EN_3_1_1_1.jsp?cid=999775 (accessed 8 March 2014).

Kriznik, B. (2011) 'Selling global Seoul: Competitive urban policy and symbolic reconstruction of cities', *Revija za sociologiju*, 41(3): 291–313.

Kwak, B.C. (2014) 'Retrospective on Pres. Park's first year in office', *The Hankyoreh*, 28 February. Online. Available at http://english.hani.co.kr/arti/english_edition/e_editorial/626262.html (accessed 8 March 2014).

Kwon, M. (2009) 'The memories of Pimatgol disappearing', *Korea Times*, 26 March. Online. Available at www.koreatimes.co.kr/www/news/culture/2013/07/320_42052.html (accessed 8 March 2014).

Lee, D.Y. (2004) 'Consuming spaces in the global era: Distinctions between consumer spaces in Seoul', *Korea Journal*, 44(3): 108–137.

Lee, H. (2015) 'Branding the design city: Cultural policy and creative events in Seoul', *International Journal of Cultural Policy*, 21(1): 1–19.

Lee, J.H., Mak, Y.M., and Sher, W.D. (2013) 'Strategic planning indicators for urban regeneration: A case study on mixed-use development in Seoul', paper presented at the 19th Annual Pacific-Rim Real Estate Society Conference, Melbourne, Australia, January.

Lee, N. (2007) *The making of minjung: Democracy and the politics of representation in South Korea*, Ithaca, NY: Cornell University Press.

Lee, Y.S. and Hwang, E.J. (2012) 'Global urban frontiers through policy transfer? Unpacking Seoul's creative city programmes', *Urban Studies*, 49(13): 2817–2837.

Lefebvre, H. (1974/1991) *The production of space*. Oxford and Cambridge, MA: Basil Blackwell.

Lydon, P. (2011) 'South Korea's Four Rivers Project', *Sociecity*, 5 September. Online. Available at http://sociecity.com/rethink/south-koreas-four-rivers-project (accessed 8 March 2014).

Moore, M. (1984) 'Mobilization and disillusion in rural Korea: The Saemaul Movement in retrospect', *Pacific Affairs*, 57(4): 577–598.

Nam, J.Y. (2012) 'Four Rivers project damaging water quality', *The Hankyoreh*, 17 January. Online. Available at http://english.hani.co.kr/arti/ENGISSUE/76/515109.html (accessed 8 March 2014).

National Information Society Agency (2007) *u-City*. Online. Available at http://eng.nia. or.kr/english/bbs/board_view.asp?BoardID=201112221611231975&id=9261&nowpage= 2&Order=303&search_target=&keyword=&Flag=&objpage=0 (accessed 8 March 2014).

Normile, D. (2010) 'Restoration or devastation?', *Science*, 327: 1568–1570.

O'Donnell, G. (1979) 'Tensions in the bureaucratic–authoritarian state and the question of democracy', in D. Collier (ed.), *The new authoritarianism in Latin America*, Princeton, NJ: Princeton University Press, pp. 285–318.

Oh, M. and Larson, J. (2011) *Digital development in Korea: Building an information society*, New York: Routledge.

Park, B.G. and Lepawsky, J. (2012) 'Spatially selective liberalization in South Korea and Malaysia: Neoliberalization in Asian developmental states', in B.G. Park, R.C. Hill, and A. Saito (eds), *Locating neoliberalism in East Asia: Neoliberalizing spaces in developmental states*, West Sussex: Blackwell, pp. 114–147.

Park, C.H. (1979) *Korea reborn: A model for development*, Englewood Cliffs, NJ: Prentice-Hall.

Park, K.M. (2013) 'Documentary tells story of farmers who fought the Four Major Rivers Project', *The Hankyoreh*, 4 September. Online. Available at www.hani.co.kr/arti/ english_edition/e_national/602109.html (accessed 8 March 2014).

Park, T.W. (2012) 'Couple torn apart by Yongsan tragedy still hanging on', *The Hankyoreh*, 17 January. Online. Available at http://english.hani.co.kr/arti/english_ edition/e_national/515083.html (accessed 8 March 2014).

Peluso, N. and Vandergeest, P. (2011) 'Political ecologies of war and forests: Counterinsur- gencies and the making of national natures', *Annals of the Association of American Geographers*, 101(3): 587–608.

Podoler, G. (2010) 'Seoul: City, identity, and the construction of the past', in T. Fenster and H. Yacobi (eds), *Remembering, forgetting and city builders*, Farnham and Burlington, VT: Ashgate, pp. 121–140.

Roach, S.S. and Lam, S. (2010) *The resilient economy*. Online. Available at www.mckinsey. com/insights/winning_in_emerging_markets/south_korea_finding_its_place_on_the_ world_stage (accessed 8 March 2014).

Roy, A. (2011) 'Postcolonial urbanism: Speed, hysteria, mass dreams', in A. Roy and A. Ong (eds), *Worlding cities: Asian experiments and the art of being global*, Oxford: Wiley-Blackwell, pp. 307–335.

Scott, J.C. (1998) *Seeing like a state: How certain schemes to improve the human condition have failed*, New Haven, CT: Yale University Press.

Seoul Metropolitan Government (Department of Urban Planning) (2009) *Urban planning of Seoul*. Online. Available at http://lib.seoul.go.kr/search/detail/CATLAZ000000061763 (accessed 8 March 2014).

Shin, J.H. and Chung, J.Y. (2011) 'The Four Major Rivers Restoration Project in South Korea', *Proceedings of the ICE – Civil Engineering*, 164(1): 19–26.

Smith, N. (1984/1990) *Uneven development: Nature, capital, and the production of space*, Cambridge, MA: Basil Blackwell.

Tanaka, W. [producer] (2012) *Cities of the future: Songdo, South Korea – Energy*. Online. Available at http://newsroom.cisco.com/feature-content?type=webcontent&articleId= 677558 (accessed 10 December 2013).

Won, J. and Hong, S. (2012) 'Land dispute ends in compromise', *Catholic News Asia*, 17 August. Online. Available at www.ucanews.com/news/land-dispute-ends-in-compromise/58514 (accessed 8 March 2014).

Yigitcanlar, T. and Lee, S.H. (in press) 'Korean ubiquitous-eco-city: A smart-sustainable urban form or a branding hoax?' *Technological Forecasting and Social Change*.

Yoo, C. (2009) 'Social cost of green-belt in Seoul Metropolitan Area with an optimal location model for new-Ttowns', *Journal of the Korea Planners Association*, 44(5): 27–43.

6 Housing the arts in a developmental state

Renaissance City Singapore

T.C. Chang

Introduction

Singapore's Renaissance City Plan is an overarching twelve-year policy statement aimed at developing a 'Global City for the Arts'. Spanning three phases of 2000–2004, 2005–2007, and 2008–2012, the plans were formulated by what was then known as the Ministry of Information and the Arts (today the Ministry of Culture, Community and Youth (MCCY)) 'to position Singapore as a key city in the Asian renaissance of the 21st century and a cultural centre in the globalised world' (MITA 2000: 4). Socio-political and economic agendas undergird the Renaissance City policies, and Singapore offers a compelling case of arts and cultural planning under a developmental state. Sometimes also referred to as a 'corporatist state', 'interventionist state', 'paternalistic state' or simply a 'strong state' (Chong 2005: 554), the Singapore government plays a central role in cultural policy formulation aimed at maximising economic growth, securing nation-building, and ultimately steering a path towards global city-making.

This chapter presents a threefold discussion on the *institutional* visions, *infrastructural* provisions and socio-spatial *implications* of state-led cultural planning. In Singapore, the role of the state has been well documented in broad overviews on the arts and nation-building (Chong 2005, 2010; Kong 2012) as well as in more specific studies on state planning of 'arts festivals' (Purushothaman 2007; Lim 2012) and 'precarious labour' in creative economies (Kong 2011). Rather than rehearse well-trodden terrain, the case of arts housing is presented here. In land-constrained Singapore (currently 711 square-kilometres), spaces that serve as offices, studios, rehearsal and informal meeting sites are extremely important to artists and cultural organisations. How these spaces are made available to artists and how artists have responded to these provisions under the Arts Housing Scheme (1985–2010) and Framework for Arts Spaces (from 2011 onwards) will be examined. The process of arts gentrification – through which the National Arts Council (NAC) identifies and converts old buildings for artists – is also critically explored, making use of fieldwork findings from the Little India Arts Belt (an outcome of the first housing scheme) and the Goodman Arts Centre (the pilot centre under the new framework). The discussion reveals what artists feel about these 'housing' spaces, the socio-spatial constraints of working within state-managed enclaves as well as opportunities for personal growth, community development and global connections. In the conclusion, two key questions are posed: whether the state can ever plan for creativity and how government-led gentrification differs from market-oriented gentrification in developing the arts in a city.

Institutional visions: globalising agendas of cultural policies

Arts and cultural policies exemplify the state's vision of developing Singapore as a global cultural hub. The notion of a cultural economy may be traced back to 1989, when a high-level government committee was established to develop the country's arts and cultural potential. The main role of the Advisory Council on Culture and the Arts (ACCA) was to nurture a culturally vibrant centre through arts infrastructure, education, publicity and administrative organisation (ACCA 1989). In addition to socio-political goals, the ACCA plan outlined economic recommendations to ensure that the arts would contribute to the tourism and entertainment sectors. Alongside the ACCA, an Economic Committee was also convened in the aftermath of 1985's recession. This committee recommended the development of a creative sector which would include art galleries, museums, performing arts, film production, entertainment centres and theme parks aimed at 'enhancing Singapore as a tourist destination; improving the quality of life and helping Singaporeans become more productive; and creating a vibrant cultural scene to attract foreign professionals to work and develop their careers here' (*Report of the Sub-Committee on the Service Sector* (1985), cited in Kong 2012: 282).

While the ACCA report of 1989 set the foundation with world-class standards in infrastructure (namely, performing venues and museums) and institutions (arts administration and governance), the Renaissance City Plans of the 2000s introduced into common parlance the term 'Global City for the Arts'. The vision was spelled out as follows:

> We want to position Singapore as a key city in the Asian renaissance of the 21st century and a cultural centre in the globalised world. The idea is to be one of the top cities in the world to live, work and play in, where there is an environment conducive to creative and knowledge-based industries and talent.
>
> (MITA 2000: 4)

Two global city-making strategies should be noted, the first being for Singapore to leverage on Asia's economic and cultural ascendance to serve as a cosmopolitan hub for the region. As an English-speaking country in a region of multiple languages, Singapore hopes to function as a connecting point between Asia and the Western world by serving as a performance venue for blockbuster arts and cultural events, as well as a business centre for international companies hoping to invest in and expand within Asia.

Second, the arts are to serve as an essential element in the development of a holistic global city meeting the needs of a cosmopolitan populace. By the 2000s, it was no longer enough to measure urban liveability by quantitative economic criteria alone; qualitative factors, such as the availability of arts events, cultural venues and entertainment options, had to be included, too. The 'softer' aspects of urban life are also expected to serve instrumentalist global city needs. Arts, entertainment and lifestyle benefits are marketed to foreign talent in a bid to persuade them to work and live in Singapore; international organisations are also more likely to invest in a country that is attractive to expatriate workers. A vibrant cultural scene also entices arts and media tourists, an increasingly important market segment in tourist destinations around the world (Wang 2012). The government also notes that, with 'increased mobility of Singaporeans . . . travel[ling] overseas and the ability to access information online', there will be domestic 'higher-order needs' that Singapore's cultural industry must strive to meet (MICA 2011, cited in Kong 2012: 290).

In what Aihwa Ong (2011: 4) calls 'urban worlding practices', she notices the 'seemingly unavoidable practices of inter-city comparison, referencing or modelling', particularly among Asian cities. The Renaissance City plans exemplify this worlding stance in at least two ways, with the first being the identification of top-tier 'world cities', such as London, New York and Tokyo, as well as 'second-tier' cities like Sydney, Edinburgh and Hong Kong, against which Singapore may be benchmarked (Chong 2005: 556). Infrastructural standards, attendance at cultural events and the annual number of arts-related activities were some criteria identified to compare Singapore with other cultural capitals. The benchmarking impulse derives from then Prime Minister Goh Chok Tong's quest for a 'world-class city'; he declared that the 'government would study and match the distinctive features of the best cities in the world, adapting them to suit Singapore's needs' (*Straits Times*, 19 January 1998). Osaka's airport-style travellators in shopping malls, New York and London's entertainment and cultural precincts, and new business districts such as London's Docklands were all identified as aspirant projects. Even scenic waterfront views are to be emulated: in the Prime Minister's words, 'Vistas will be created to rival the panoramic views of San Francisco Bay and Sydney Harbour. Besides the Singapore River, the Government will look at ways to make other waterfront areas such as Kallang Basin, Marina Bay and the coastline more attractive' (*Straits Times*, 19 January 1998).

Second, while worldly cultural hubs can serve as motivations to Singapore, the inverse is also true when cautionary lessons are drawn from around the world. In the Renaissance City plans, the NAC (2008) noted that cultural centres like New York City and Cologne faced problems of overcrowding and competition for space in the 1990s. When this happened, artists, arts organisations and performing venues moved to suburban sites (for example, Brooklyn in New York's case) or even neighbouring cities (explaining why Berlin soon overtook Cologne as Germany's cultural capital). The difference between these cultural cities and Singapore is the availability of and access to a hinterland within national borders. Geography does not afford Singapore this luxury; without adequate sub- and trans-urban spaces to access, alternative uses of *existing* spaces must be sought locally. Affordable, appropriate and accessible environments are needed for the arts to thrive, and this is best achieved through adapting old and dysfunctional buildings (not a novel phenomenon, as exemplified by Manhattan's SoHo in the 1980s and subsequently in other US and European cities in the 1990s). Therefore, instead of creating 'new' spaces, Singapore's arts housing is the result of the conversion of 'old' sites into new uses.

Perhaps more novel are the two state-initiated/funded arts housing programmes, the first of which was the Arts Housing Scheme (initiated in 1985 under the auspices of the Ministry of Community Development but subsequently transferred to the NAC's auspices) and the second of which is the Framework for Arts Spaces (since 2011, administered by the NAC). Both schemes identify and convert old buildings into suitable housing, to be leased to select artists at highly subsidised rates for use as offices, studios, administrative, rehearsal and performance spaces. According to Chong (2005: 556), the 'international trend' of infusing rust-belt sites with the arts, and converting derelict buildings into new cultural uses, in the West is a lesson that the Singapore government has learned well. The NAC worked with the Urban Redevelopment Authority (URA) to identify suitable buildings for arts housing, explaining that old buildings provide 'an important impetus for artistic creativity' and, in turn, the arts help to 'revitalise and give added value to new developments in forgotten areas' (NAC 2013). It is no surprise that the earliest arts belts were set up in the historic neighbourhoods of Waterloo Street, Chinatown, Little India and the Singapore River. A total of 64 arts organisations and 30 artists have been housed in 38 properties under the Arts Housing Scheme.

While adaptive reuse and gentrification are lessons from the West, the specifics of how artists are to be selected and the housing schemes administered are based on home-grown ideas grounded in local contingencies. The Little India Arts Belt comprises pre-Second World War shophouses on Kerbau Road that were redeveloped in the mid-1990s by the Housing Development Board at a cost of S$3.8 million (around US$2.8 million in 2015; Kong 2011; see Figure 6.1). In 2001, the NAC acquired ten units for arts housing. Tenants were selected based on track record, managerial strength, artistic standard, level of activity, growth potential, need for housing, merit of planned activities and commitment to artistic development. Existing tenants in Little India include a mix of traditional ethnic arts groups, dance and music groups and contemporary theatre outfits. This eclectic mix is meant to provide a 'good opportunity for exchange of ideas and learning from each other', while the location in a residential and commercial neighborhood is supposed to add to the 'vibrancy of the place' (NAC 2013). Artists pay only 10 per cent of the market rate in rent, with the balance underwritten by the NAC (payments are made to the Singapore Land Authority, the government landowner).

While we talk about policy mobility across countries, it is worthwhile to note that intra-national policy transitions also take place as one programme supersedes another. For instance, the Arts Housing Scheme was reviewed in 2010 and the

Figure 6.1 Historic shophouses in Little India
Source: the author.

new Framework for Arts Spaces was introduced in December of that year after a number of problems were identified with the old scheme. First, the housing scheme was meant to provide short-term leases of one to three years; however, in 2010, 44 per cent of artists/organisations had occupied their space for between ten and twenty years, while 13 per cent had been in the same place for more than twenty years (NAC 2010: 4). This stagnancy prevented emerging artists from securing any housing space. Second, artistic interactions under the old scheme were deemed insufficient. The NAC (2010: 7) explained: 'While the Scheme has brought the arts closer to our neighbourhoods, there is scope for arts housing to facilitate more meaningful engagements with the public as well as greater collaborations amongst the arts community.' The original goal of engaging the residential community and each other thus remained largely unfulfilled.

The new framework addresses the above issues by strictly enforcing three-year tenancy conditions and overseeing artistic engagements. Rather than leave artists to collaborate on their own, a dedicated 'place manager' was appointed to oversee each centre, facilitate collaborations and promote activities involving artists and the wider community. The new arts spaces are also meant to be self-sufficient, with shared amenities such as a multi-purpose hall, exhibition spaces, theatre, dance studio and black box gallery, as well as dining options to attract the public. The arts spaces are also located in suburban sites to expose 'heartland'

Singaporeans to the arts, thereby expanding their world-views and cultural sensitivity. As a meeting place for different artists, it is hoped that new partnerships may be forged, leading to novel artistic products that will put Singapore on the cultural world map. Unlike older arts spaces that function mainly as office sites, new arts spaces are to serve as 'connector[s] bringing the arts into the lives of the wider community as well as enabling artists and arts groups to interact and dialogue with the public' (NAC 2010: 8). The worlding principles discussed by Ong (2011) thus apply not only to *cities* learning from/emulating each other but also to *people*. Through arts spaces, local communities are exposed to worldly art forms in the hope that these will expand their cultural sensibilities; by sharing and working in the same space, artists are also encouraged to collaborate and learn from each other, thereby broadening their knowledge and repertoires.

Two arts spaces have emerged under the new framework – the Goodman Arts Centre (which opened in early 2011; Figure 6.2) and the Aliwal Arts Centre (which opened in mid-2013). The Goodman compound, which will be the focus of this study, was adapted from its former use as an education establishment (between 1962 and 2009, the compound was occupied by three different schools). Today, over forty artists/organisations call the centre home, enjoying access to various shared amenities, two eateries and the corporate office of the NAC. The

Figure 6.2 The old-school aesthetics and verdant environment of the Goodman Arts
         Centre

Source: the author.

three-year leases are renewable up to a maximum of nine years, and rental subsidies cover 80 per cent of the market value of the properties (although tenants are required to pay a service charge to the place manager for general maintenance, security and routine repairs).

Infrastructural provisions: old spaces and worldly dreams

Much of Singapore's arts housing is the product of adaptive reuse. As activities outgrow structures, buildings are decanted of their former uses/users, then restored and adapted for new activities. In some cases, the buildings are sold by the state but in most cases the government retains the lease and rents it to select businesses and activities which often include hotels, retail or food/beverage outlets, offices and arts/cultural organisations (Chang and Teo 2009). The NAC argues that, rather than leaving these spaces to market forces, a deliberate infusion of the arts will add non-commercial activities to retail/residential environments, bringing about land use diversity and stronger place identity and introducing the arts to the community. The spaces are also promoted as arts venues for tourists who prefer alternative sites to museums and other venues in the urban core. This section explores the notion of old spaces adapted for new arts and worlding purposes.

Field work undertaken in the Little India Arts Belt (between 2010 and 2011) and the Goodman Arts Centre (in 2013) involved a total of seventeen artists, organisations and arts managers/administrators. It was discovered that most of the artists appreciated the historic space of Little India, expressing particular delight to be working in pre-war shophouses with their quaint architecture and ambience. Over at Goodman Road, the surrounding greenery and 1960s buildings were described as inspirational by some. As one artist reflected, the verdant, low-rise Goodman compound exudes an 'arty feel'. More than just aesthetic reasons, the artists also felt that space is essential in legitimising their work and providing some degree of permanence. Dance and music academies, for example, conduct classes for students on-site, and it is essential for them to have semi-permanent spaces for their activities. Interestingly, the owner of a gamelan music group remarked that her Little India shophouse space contributes to Singapore's global educational agenda:

> it [space] gives a lot of companies stability. There is a place for everybody to come, gather and talk [whereas,] in the past, we had to find space everywhere. So, I can now offer to schools this alternative to come; the Ministry of Education [has a] new global aim to encourage local artists, to get schools to go 'outside', teach less learn more, so schools are encouraged to go out and explore. They like the idea of coming here [to Little India]. Dunman High and Nanyang Girls' School ... have taken workshops here. Now they are willing to come and that is good. With this space, we can give an ambience; we create that ambience for them.
>
> (Interview, 12 May 2010)

Figure 6.3 Inside an artists' studio at the Goodman Arts Centre
Source: the author.

At the Goodman Arts Centre, spatial 'ambience' also plays an important role in giving artists a sense of purpose and respectability. As renewal of tenancy is contingent on achievement, all of the artists spoke of the importance of fulfilling their community outreach responsibilities. Before they were granted space at Goodman Road, almost all of the artists were either working from home or meeting clients at fast-food joints or other public spaces. The Goodman Centre provided them with 'a sense of our own space', 'healthy space' and a 'home'. These descriptions not only suggest a sense of ownership but underscore the importance of place/space in artistic production (Figure 6.3).

This is not to say that working in adaptive reuse buildings has been problem-free, as is evinced by the on-site challenges faced by several artists. Unlike other adapted sites, such as Beijing's 798 zone or Shanghai's 50 Moganshan Road, Little India and the Goodman Arts Centre fall far below the standards set by world-reputed arts amenities and tourist attractions. Many artists dismiss the possibility of Singapore's suburban arts spaces ever becoming viable tourist lures. Unlike the factory sites or industrial lofts in other cultural hubs, Singapore's spaces are far too small to allow for a full range of artistic uses, possibilities and collaborations. One tenant in Little India, for example, bemoaned the lack of space to collaborate with dancers and theatre practitioners. She also spoke of the hygiene problems that came with working in old buildings:

Architecturally it is not easy. For us who have to rehearse, just the music instruments, once we spread them out, the whole floor is occupied. So if we want to collaborate with, say, a dance group, how to get them to dance? Maybe one individual or two dancers is possible, very stylistically they try to weave between us, but it is not conducive. Second, if you want to do a theatre show, it is even worse. Design wise, whilst a nice space, and it has given us stability, to get to the next level of creating something or producing something out of the box, we are constrained by the space . . . So the thing is, if you want to continue long term, something has to be done. The other problem I face is with roaches. You know the 'no entry' [sign] on my door there? It's not for humans; it's pest control.

(Interview, 12 May 2010)

Artists at Goodman Road similarly question the suitability of the centre, observing that the old school buildings have not been entirely refurbished and retrofitted for their new purpose. Some interviewees mentioned the lack of en-suite bathrooms in artists' studios, that the school hall lacks theatre-style seating, and that the black box gallery has not been adequately sound-proofed. Others complained about the narrow stairways and doors, the lack of loading/unloading bays and the inadequate waste disposal, all of which serve to limit artistic work. Despite the ACCA's vision of establishing a world-class administration, a dance practitioner also noted that arts administrators do not understand the basic amenity needs of dancers:

When the NAC want to provide space for artists, they will ask for advice. Internally, not all of them know what they are supposed to be in charge of. For example, those who are in charge of the venue might not know exactly what dancers need . . . Sometimes it's hard for them to train officers. I don't know how often they have changed officers, but we need someone who knows what artists need. A simple example would be the sprung floors. There are different levels of sprung floors, and Indian dance groups do not need them that much. [But] for contemporary dance and ballet, we need good sprung floors. Chinese dancers might also need it, whereas the Malay dancers might accept semi-sprung floors. So this is a really simple thing for us. It is almost like 'You should know this!' When we spoke to some officers from the NAC, due to their lack of knowledge, we needed to spend a lot of time explaining that this is important.

(Interview, 25 March 2013)

More than just bricks and mortar, therefore, a worldly cultural capital needs expertise and enlightened administrative knowledge.

The Singapore government is very strict with respect to how historic buildings are to be conserved, maintained and used. As the shophouse units in the Little India Arts Belt fall within the 'core' conservation area, architectural façades, exterior window fixtures, awnings, signage, wall colours and roof tiles must adhere to strict guidelines. The shophouse units cannot be converted into residential use and lofts cannot be used as working/living/sleeping spaces. The Goodman Arts Centre, while technically not a state-gazetted conservation site, has maintained its charm through careful preservation of its 1960s modernist architecture. However, it lacks the colour, vibrancy and stylistic individuality of privately owned cultural spaces in cities like Berlin, Beijing and Toronto (see Bain (2003) and Heebels and van Aalst (2010) for examples from Toronto and Berlin, respectively). The resident artists suggest that there are too few alfresco events and performances within the Goodman compound (a reason being that the centre is located in a residential neighbourhood), and insufficient public art works and 'prominent' signage to announce the centre as an arts enclave. If the Goodman is ever to become a world-class arts centre that is attractive to international visitors, it must first achieve the architectural and ambient qualities of a worldly cultural venue.

Implications of arts housing: global connections and cosmopolitan citizens

This section explores the socio-spatial implications of worldly arts spaces, and how artists have tried to embody the worlding principles as outlined in the first section of this chapter. The NAC hopes that a vibrant and cohesive community will emerge through artists sharing a common space. Spontaneous networks and artistic collaborations, along with community involvement in the arts, are expected to animate the arts spaces and then the city as a whole. As we shall see, this has not happened in Little India, and it is only beginning to occur at Goodman Road. As one interviewee from Little India remarked: 'How many of us know our neighbours in the HDB [Housing Development Board] block? Just because we stay next to each other, it doesn't mean we know them. There is no idea of coming together, and there is no space for us to converge' (interview, 12 May 2010).

Geographic proximity within Little India has not led to interactions between artists because each organisation has its own activities and priorities. Hence, while the Bhasker Academy and Sri Warisan focus on training students in Indian and Malay cultural arts, companies like Wild Rice and iTheatre are more concerned with staging plays and performances. While the training takes place on-site in Little India, the performances/plays are often staged in downtown venues. There is therefore no reason or opportunity to collaborate. Another interviewee attributed the lack of collaboration to work pressure. Every artist is participating in a 'rat race' to retain space leased by the government, meaning they have no time to meet with each other. Spatial agglomeration in Little India has generated a large volume of individual work, but few collaborative or cross-cultural events, as these are far more difficult to organize. Community engagement with Little India's residents is also minimal, attributed to the lack of space in shophouses to entertain large crowds and the logistical challenge of organizing events involving multiple artists and audiences.

In contrast to Little India, a nascent sense of community is beginning to emerge at the Goodman Arts Centre. With a critical mass of over forty artists and organisations at the centre (as opposed to only seven in Little India) and the presence of the place manager, the possibilities for partnerships are much higher. Indeed, many artists spoke about serendipitous meetings and collaborations between neighbours. A visual artist, for example, spoke of an unexpected collaboration when an adjacent dance company performed in his studio and used his paintings as backdrops. Similarly, a Chinese musical group explained that a chance meeting with the same artist led to their decision to digitize his works for use as backdrops in their performances. On these collaborations, the artist said: 'This is something refreshing and new to me. These [collaborations] only happened after coming here' (interview, 13 March 2013). Chance encounters, sharing clients, visiting one another's studios and participating in each other's activities are all common activities in the Goodman Centre. One actress revealed that collaborations with musicians and dance academies are now possible because various parties have met through sharing the same compound:

> Yes, it [collaboration] is possible of course. I've been taking dance classes and I might talk to them [the dance group] in the future. There's always the possibility because it depends on whether you want to work with a fellow artist. Like with Justin [a visual artist]; if we have projects, we can give them to him. We can help each other out; it's my personal interest. My work is also performance art and I want to understand better from a dance perspective. It takes time. The Observatory [a dance company] is here and they are quite open to working with other people.
>
> (Interview, 12 March 2013)

While neighbourhood ties reflect fledgling solidarity at the Goodman Centre, a sense of community in Little India cannot be entirely discounted. While formal interactions may not exist, there is a dense network between Little India's artists and counterparts *beyond* Singapore. Indeed, international outreach is something that artists take very seriously, and several artists have performed at events such as the Edinburgh Festival and other events in Australia, England, India, Korea and Malaysia. International collaborations are regular features in many artists' portfolios. Spell 7, for example, collaborated with a UK company on a project called 'Dreamwork & Dreamhome', while Sri Warisan enjoys strong partnerships with dance groups in Brunei that have seen regular exchanges between the two countries. Interviews revealed that all seven of the arts organisations that are based in Little India have performed in overseas venues, and four enjoy ongoing relationships with foreign partners. One artist even noted the importance of 'introducing' her Little India neighbours to foreign partners:

> To establish Singapore as a global city, that was [our] first [goal]. Let's take Singapore beyond and establish it because once we have done it, it is easier for others to come on. So when we perform [overseas] and people ask us if there are others [like us], I always take [the publicity material] of other groups with me . . . We take it to the festivals. So once we are finished, when the

organisers ask who they can invite next year, we give them the contacts and say, 'Liaise with them directly.'

(Interview, 12 May 2010)

Trans-national collaborations and connections such as those described above are essential in boosting Singapore's reputation as a global arts hub.

While this chapter has focused so far on artistic collaborations and international networks, we must not forget local community engagement as a necessary component in Singapore's worlding agenda. Part of the Global City for the Arts vision entails cultivating an enlightened populace that is culturally engaged. These 'Renaissance Singaporeans' are also essential in advancing the country's creative and knowledge economy:

> Renaissance Singapore will be creative, vibrant and imbued with a keen sense of aesthetics. Our industries are supported with a creative culture that keeps them competitive in the global economy. The Renaissance Singaporean has an adventurous spirit, an inquiring and creative mind and a strong passion for life.
>
> (MITA 2000, cited in Tan 2007: 2–3)

Cultural spaces have a role to play in socialising Singaporeans to the arts. The Little India Arts Belt is sited in the heart of Little India, surrounded by three blocks of HDB flats (government-subsidised residential units), while the Goodman Arts Centre is adjacent to private housing along the Goodman and Branksome roads as well as the HDB flats of the Mountbatten area. Such arts spaces provide an 'opportunity for the public to enjoy and participate in the arts within their neighbourhoods' so that 'a stronger connection between arts and the community' may be established (NAC 2010: 3). However, these goals are not always met, and artists encounter various challenges in their outreach efforts.

In Little India, for instance, the lack of appropriate infrastructure prevents artists from engaging effectively with the surrounding neighbourhood. The historic shophouses are extremely narrow and performances can hardly take place on-site. There are also no outdoor spaces to organize alfresco events, and no place manager to coordinate events. While Little India is popular with South Asian migrant workers, especially over the weekends, none of the artists has considered staging cultural activities for them. It is generally felt that the workers prefer to shop, eat or relax rather than engage in organized activities. At the Goodman Arts Centre, the place manager has identified neighbourhood schools and resident committees as well as senior citizens, youths at risk and needy families in the Mountbatten area as potential patrons. Customised outreach arts programmes are thus tailored specifically to cater to these groups. Goodman Open Studios is one example of an outreach event. Essentially an 'open day', the public are invited to try their hand free of charge at clay-sculpting, puppet-making and batik-painting, among other activities (Chia 2011).

It should be noted, however, that the Mountbatten neighbourhood is one of the oldest residential areas in Singapore, and the Goodman Arts Centre was established only in 2011. Consequently, its 'intrusion' into an entrenched environment has not always been warmly received by the residents. One tenant musician noted that the upper-middle-class neighbourhoods along the Goodman and Branksome roads have not been particularly receptive to the arts, with regular complaints to the NAC regarding road congestion caused by festivals and noise from alfresco music events. As she noted, even individual musicians rehearsing along the corridors of the arts centre have met with complaints from an intolerant neighbourhood:

> The recent complaint was that someone was rehearsing in one of the rooms in the curved block [of the Goodman Arts Centre]. Because one of the trumpeters wanted to come out [to the open], maybe he was happy and he played a few horn lines. The resident went ape and complained to both the police and the NEA [National Environment Agency]. This was well before 10.30 [p.m.]. For some reason, they entertained [the complaint] . . . Any day of the week, it's supposed to be an arts centre! I think it's really strange, the public perception of artists and art. They don't see it as something that adds to the environment. They see it as a liability.
>
> (Interview, 5 March 2013)

Such local, ground-level hostilities ultimately serve to frustrate Singapore's worldly ambitions.

The cold reception towards the arts suggests that, while arts centres have emerged in suburban Singapore, the heartland community is not quite ready to accept them as aspects of their everyday life. The disconnect between local residential needs and worldly cultural ambition is a greater challenge than the infrastructural problem Singapore faced in the 1990s when it first embarked on cultural development. While arts infrastructure, buildings and amenities ('hardware') can be created and upgraded over a relatively short period of time, changing people's mindsets and behaviours ('software') will take far longer and demands more effort. Generally, many people still view the arts as a dispensable (or even unaffordable) luxury rather than a necessary and enriching feature in Singaporean life. Many Singaporean schoolchildren's parents, for example, still demand excellence in mathematics and science, rather than the social sciences and certainly the performing arts. While there are currently over 170 secondary schools offering science, mathematics and humanities lessons, only one secondary-level school (the School of the Arts) teaches the performing arts, and it was established as recently as 2008. This limited socialisation of the arts among Singaporeans arguably remains the greatest challenge in the country's quest to become a global cultural hub.

Conclusion

Expanding on Aihwa Ong's (2011) original notion of urban worlding as the practice of inter-city comparison and modelling, Singapore's aspiration to become a 'Global City for the Arts' is manifested in four cultural-worlding principles: developing world-class institutions and administrative frameworks; creating international-standard infrastructure and spaces; nurturing globally connected artists and organisations; and socialising the arts within the community. Imported models and best practices, namely adaptive reuse/gentrification of old buildings, and benchmarking Singapore against top-tier and secondary cultural cities have also guided the country's cultural policies.

This chapter has focused on a particular aspect of cultural city-making – state provision of arts housing through adaptive reuse. While the practice of arts gentrification is not new, with antecedents in Manhattan in the 1980s and other Western cities throughout the 1990s (see Zukin 1982; Ley 2003; Matthews 2010), what distinguishes Singapore is the dominant role of the state and its clear ideological intent. As we have seen, the state wields considerable influence through the Ministry of Culture, Community and Youth, the NAC and the URA. Over the years, cultural policies have closely charted Singapore's cultural development in the form of the twelve-year Renaissance City plans and arts housing programmes, such as the Arts Housing Scheme (1985–2010) and the Framework for Arts Spaces (since 2011).

To conclude this study, two questions are posed on the role of government in developing the arts. The first is whether creativity can ever be planned for and managed by the state. Space is a perennial concern in land-strapped Singapore and as the country's largest landowner, the government's role in opening up new spaces and legislating cultural uses is instrumental. However, the state must be careful not to overreach this role. In a recent account on arts clusters in Singapore, an artist was quoted as saying that the government should help artists by making 'space available and then get[ting] out of the way' (cited in Ho 2015: B7). The two arts housing schemes discussed in this chapter are clear examples of the government 'making space available', but with contrasting outcomes. In Little India enforced clustering has not led to collaborative work among artists because of the different agendas and interests of the artists themselves, whereas in the Goodman Centre creative networks have emerged because of the efforts of the place manager and the artists' genuine interest in working together. The state's role in fostering artistic creativity therefore remains critical in three ways: by providing space in which artists may work; by offering welcome rental subsidies; and by introducing a place manager to foster collective action. However, it is impossible to *force* artists to collaborate. Likewise, it is difficult to deepen public acceptance and patronage of the arts unless socialisation and education policies inculcate an appreciation for them within a structured school system.

A related question concerns the differences between state-led and market-oriented gentrification. It should be noted that most of Singapore's arts spaces have been created through state support (in addition to the two case studies, state-funded arts gentrification has taken place in Chinatown, Waterloo, the Aliwal Arts Centre and elsewhere). While market-oriented gentrification is less common, there have been a few examples in Little India: art studios along Perumal Road and at least two independently run museums on Rowell Road (the Post Museum and the Museum of Shanghai Toys). Unlike the working conditions in the Little India Arts Belt, which tend to be stable and predictable, work in non-state-funded sites is frequently precarious and unpredictable (see Kong 2011). Indeed, while many artists in the Little India Arts Belt have remained in the neighbourhood for up to nine years, the museums along Rowell Road have folded (the toy museum closed in June 2010, and the Post Museum was wound up in August 2011, citing poor patronage and unsustainable operating costs). While it is difficult to generalise, state-led gentrification in Little India does seem to have provided artists with levels of support that independent artists and organisations often lack. Further research should be undertaken to verify this hypothesis so that comparisons can be made between artists/organisations with and without government aid.

In the quest to 'go global' cultural cities should not forget the local. In the case of Singapore, the social connections between artists, the outreach efforts by artists towards the community, and the socialisation of the arts among heartland Singaporeans remain critical 'ground-level' goals that demand policy attention. Far more challenging than any infrastructural development or institutional reform is the cultivation of social capital, community appreciation and artistic engagement. Only then will the lofty rhetoric of a 'Global City for the Arts' and 'Renaissance Society' come to fruition in the form of grounded, tangible realities.

Acknowledgements

The author acknowledges the National University of Singapore grants R-109-000-105-101 and R-109-000-140-101, and the assistance of Aloysius Chua in the completion of this chapter.

References

Advisory Council on Culture and the Arts (ACCA) (1989) *Report of the Advisory Council on Culture and the Arts*, Singapore: Advisory Council on Culture and the Arts.

Bain, A. (2003) 'Constructing contemporary artistic identities in Toronto neighbourhoods', *Canadian Geographer*, 47(3): 303–317.

Chang, T.C. and Teo, P. (2009) 'The shophouse hotel: vernacular heritage in creative Singapore', *Urban Studies*, 46(2): 341–367.

Chia, A. (2011) 'A new Goodman', *Straits Times*, 15 September: C4.

Chong, T. (2005) 'From global to local: Singapore's cultural policy and its consequences', *Critical Asian Studies*, 37(4): 553–568.

Chong, T. (2010) 'The state and the new society: the role of the arts in Singapore nation-building', *Asian Studies Review*, 34(2): 131–149.

Heebels, B. and van Aalst, I. (2010) 'Creative clusters in Berlin: entrepreneurship and the quality of place in Prenzlauer Berg and Kreuzberg', *Geografiska Annaler: Series B*, 92(4): 346–363.

Ho, O. (2015) 'Kudos for Esplanade in book on culture', *Straits Times*, 26 February: B7.

Kong, L. (2011) 'From precarious labor to precarious economy? Planning for precarity in Singapore's creative economy', *City, Culture and Society*, 2(2): 55–64.

Kong, L. (2012) 'Ambitions of a global city: arts, culture and creative economy in "post-crisis" Singapore', *International Journal of Cultural Policy*, 18(3): 279–294.

Ley, D. (2003) 'Artists, aestheticisation, and the field of gentrification', *Urban Studies*, 40(12): 2525–2542.

Lim, L. (2012). 'Constructing habitus: promoting an international arts trend at the Singapore Arts Festival', *International Journal of Cultural Policy*, 18(3): 308–322.

Ministry of Information and the Arts (MITA) (2000) *Renaissance City Report: Culture and the Arts in Renaissance Singapore*. Online. Available at www.acsr.sg/renaissance_city. aspx (accessed 1 June 2013).

Ministry of Information, Communication and the Arts (MICA) (2011) *Arts and Culture Strategic Review Public Consultation*, Singapore: Ministry of Information, Communication and the Arts.

Matthews, V. (2010) 'Aestheticizing space: art, gentrification and the city', *Geography Compass*, 4(6): 660–675

National Arts Council (NAC) (2010) *Review of National Arts Council's Arts Housing Scheme*. Online. Available at http://nac.gov.sg/docs (accessed 1 June 2013).

National Arts Council (NAC) (2013) *Arts Spaces in Singapore*. Online. Available at www. nas.gov.sg/arts-spaces/overview (accessed 1 April 2014).

Ong, A. (2011) 'Introduction: Worlding cities, or the art of being global', in A. Roy and A. Ong (eds), *Worlding Cities: Asian Experiments and the Art of Being Global*, Malden, MA: Wiley-Blackwell, pp. 1–25.

Purushothaman, V. (2007) *Making Visible the Invisible: Three Decades of the Singapore Arts Festival*, Singapore: National Arts Council.

Tan, K.P. (2007) 'In renaissance Singapore', in K.P. Tan (ed.), *Renaissance City? Economy, Culture, and Politics*, Singapore: NUS Press, pp. 1–14.

Wang, J. (2012) 'Flying for concerts and chasing after stars: insights into the conceptualisation of concert tourism sensation', unpublished Honours thesis, Department of Geography, National University of Singapore.

Zukin, S. (1982) *Loft Living: Culture and Capital in Urban Change*, Baltimore, MD: Johns Hopkins University Press.

7 Displaying Han–Tang culture in urban development projects in Xi'an, China

Yang Yang

> Xi'an, or Chang'an as it was called in ancient times, is known as the city of 'everlasting peace'. It was one of the most important cradles of Chinese civilization. It marked the start of the famous 'Silk Road' that linked China with Central Asia and the Roman Empire. And it served as the first capital of a unified China and capital of thirteen dynasties periodically from the eleventh century BC to the early tenth century AD.
>
> (Municipal Tourism Bureau of Xi'an 2008; my translation)

Introduction

The quote above, while outlining the history of Xi'an, reflects a dilemma encountered by many Chinese cities that cannot rival first-tier coastal cities such as Shanghai. Aspiring to become parts of the global urban skyline, cities like Xi'an lack the first-tier cities' access to financial resources. They cannot achieve their global dreams simply by replicating successful models like Shanghai's. So, in order to gain national status in inter-urban competitions such as the National Civilized City and the National Hygienic City, Xi'an has opted to build a cultural city by reinventing its history as an imperial capital. Similar to other cities that use heritage and cultural theming to boost their urban images, Xi'an aims to build an imagined Han–Tang imperial capital (*Hanyuan Tangcheng*) based on Chang'an, the city's imperial precedent. As a result, a quaint-looking ancient city has emerged in Xi'an to mark its progress in urbanization. The key theme of this imagined imperial capital is 'Han–Tang culture' (*Hantang wenhua*), namely the cultures of the Han and Tang dynasties (see Figure 7.1). The theme encompasses various plans and objectives of urban development in Xi'an, and echoes the initiative of positioning Xi'an as the terminus of a new Silk Road. Similar to the national strategy adopted by the Chinese state to expand its geopolitical influence (Agnew 2012), looking back to the past becomes a way of moving forward and producing a cultural city in Xi'an.

In this chapter, I examine how culture is used as a convenient resource for urban governance by looking at cultural heritage-based urban projects in Xi'an. Specifically, I investigate two questions to address the above issues. How is the imagined imperial capital, Chang'an, excavated, repackaged, and modelled as an

Figure 7.1 Tang-themed pavilions in the Qujiang District, Xi'an
Source: the author.

expedient resource for implementing cultural policies in Xi'an? And how is Han–Tang culture, the main theme of this imaginary, assembled by different actors to realize myriad objectives relating to Xi'an's global city aspirations?

These questions are closely linked to transferring 'cultural cities' policies from elsewhere to local contexts and outcomes (McCann and Ward 2011; Peck 2011). Specifically, cultural strategies are contextualized to accommodate local agendas of urban development, and have become a new technique for engineering state–society relations. The process of making a cultural imaginary also resonates with the inextricable links between cities and culture (Zukin 1995). Culture lends itself to the production of urban space through its involvement in the 'symbolic economy'. Cultural symbols and references are associated with commercial exchange in urban creative and cultural industries. Culture marks certain cities as magnets that attract a class of 'creative' workers (Florida 2002, 2005). Culture also contributes to generating consuming citizens in postsocialist urban China (Wang 2001a, 2001b). The state effort to redirect culture to consumption and leisure reflects its changing governance. Scholarship has extensively discussed the relationships between culture and cities, but there has been less focus on cultural cities' role in the state's project of displaying China's global influence. This chapter intends to address these issues.

I draw upon Yúdice's (2003) notion of the 'expediency of culture' to analyse culture as a convenient resource for urban governance. In so doing, I explore the role of the Chinese state at both central and local scales in rendering the cultural imaginary applicable to cultural city policy-making. Furthermore, I utilize the assemblage approach (McCann and Ward 2011; McFarlane 2011a, 2011b) to trace how different actors and practices contribute to assembling an imagined imperial capital with Han–Tang culture and the different possibilities of this cultural ensemble. Assemblage is viewed here as a process of arranging, organizing, and combining different actors, resources, and procedures. This process reveals how different actors and cities are related to each other in the network of cities. Different locations become references for each other in implementing policies that travel from elsewhere in local contexts (Collier and Ong 2005; McFarlane 2011a, 2011b; Anderson and McFarlane 2011). Different assembling possibilities also show different outcomes and effects of arranging networks of actors and resources (McCann and Ward 2011). Emphases on how certain assemblages emerge rather than solely on results help to reveal how different actors and practices contribute to making a cultural city. Assemblage thus allows a relational approach to understand how making cultural cities in China is an ongoing process of putting different elements together in contingent ways (Anderson and McFarlane 2011). Emphases on uncertainty and contingency also show that making cultural cities and implementing cultural policy are not simply premised on a central governing power. Rather, specificities in local political and economic conditions make a generic model of cultural cities difficult to formulate due to the participation of local actors, practices, and processes.

By analysing these processes, I argue that cultural city policies in Xi'an are premised upon an imaginary of past cultural references. The visual presence of Han–Tang culture contributes to making this imaginary applicable as a resource to urban development projects. This Han–Tang imaginary is assembled by multiple overlapping projects to rebuild the Silk Road and by actors who intend to use the cultural imaginary and the Silk Road to make their own interest claims.

Making a cultural city in Xi'an

Given that it served as the imperial capital of thirteen dynasties, Xi'an is endowed with rich historical resources for its cultural development. Among these dynasties, the Han (206 BC–AD 220) and Tang (AD 618–907) are the two main themes to be referenced in current urban development plans in Xi'an. Yet, despite being two disparate dynasties, the Han and the Tang are often combined into a single adjective to modify the term 'culture'. As a result, a new formation known as Han–Tang culture (*Hantang wenhua*) has been coined.

Culture has always been central to urban development in Xi'an. Local history, as a cultural resource, has long been used in branding the city for tourism development. Yet, culture was not prioritized on the agenda of urban development until the establishment of the Qujiang cultural development district in the early 2000s. The district of Qujiang features tourism, real estate development, museums, music halls, galleries, and art studios. In this cultural industrial district, art, tourism, and cultural heritage projects seek to restore the landscape of the Tang era (Qujiang Management Committee 2011). For instance, the Qujiang media group invested significantly to make a movie titled 'The Daming Palace' (*Daming Gong*), featuring the love story of the Tang Emperor Li Shimin and Lady Yang, his most famous concubine on account of her beauty and tragic execution. In the meantime, a heritage park was built on the site of the original Tang-era Daming Palace (Suo 2011). These efforts to promote the image of a Tang imperial city were designed to turn the rich histories and cultures in Xi'an into usable resources for economic development and other aspects of making Xi'an a global city. Moreover, at the city level, the municipal government added building a new terminus for the Silk Road to its agenda of urban development. In relation to cultural development, the new terminus is designed to feature 'the aesthetics and style of the Han dynasty' (*Hanfeng Guyun*), especially in heritage tourism and urban planning. For instance, a Silk Road Museum and a tourism street were built at the Great Tang West Market (*Datang Xishi*), featuring images of merchants riding camels across deserts to Chang'an and exotic female dancers in taverns. In this way, the built environment itself comes to represent Han–Tang culture. Museums, tourism streets, the Han wall lake (*Hancheng Hu*), and UNESCO-recognized heritage sites such as the Weiyang Palace of the Han dynasty visually present an imperial capital of the Han era. Prior to the Silk Road initiatives, the municipal government had already introduced a plan to restore the imperial capital (*Huangcheng fuxing jihua*), in which the cultural heritage of the Tang dynasty was primarily emphasized as an asset to turn Xi'an into a cultural city (*renwenzhidu*) (Xi'an Municipal Government 2005). One of the major foci is the city wall, which was built in the Tang era but rebuilt and restored in the Ming, the Qing, and the Republican eras. Gate opening and greeting ceremonies, which are said to date to the Tang era, are performed every day at the south gate of the city wall to showcase Tang traditions. Residential buildings near the city wall have been removed to make the surrounding area less cluttered. Several urban development projects in Xi'an intersect in the overall restoration of Chang'an in the Han and Tang dynasties, and have provided the basis for producing an imagined Han–Tang culture.

Han–Tang culture: modelling after an imaginary

Han–Tang culture has received much attention from Chinese scholars due to its applicability to contemporary cultural politics in the People's Republic. Within Chinese-language scholarship (Xiong 1987; Yan 2008; Huang 2010; Gao 2013; Pan 2015), it is considered a synergy of unifying different practices, traditions, and ideas that are associated with religions and cultures originating outside imperial China into a new collection of Chinese ideas and practices. While different thoughts and practices originating from non-Chinese cultures have conflicting interests between one another and with their counterparts in China, Han–Tang culture allows these differences to coexist. Diversity in ideas and practices in

Han–Tang culture offers a cultural premise for developing an inclusive metropolis where individuals from many different backgrounds dwell (Xiong 1987). Han–Tang culture is inclusive because different ideas, originating from either within or outside China, can develop without being excluded or marginalized by Chinese culture. While Han–Tang culture primarily addresses prosperity in past cultural, political, and economic exchange, it is also applicable to contemporary policies of the People's Republic. Scholarship in Chinese, especially work that focuses on policy-making, suggests that Han–Tang culture has profound implications for the Chinese Communist Party to present a cosmopolitan image in its cultural development agenda (Huang 2010; Yan 2008). Despite constantly referencing it in academic and policy publications, however, scholars, government officials, and policy practitioners have been unable to provide a clear definition of Han–Tang culture. Nevertheless, this ambiguity has not constrained their ability to invoke it when drafting new policies, attempting to attract investment, or appealing for government funding for research. Indeed, the ambiguity itself makes Han–Tang culture especially useful for policy-makers.

Thus, while academic references define Han–Tang culture as the result of continuous cultural exchange between the feudal Chinese empire and other centres along the Silk Road, policy-makers and practitioners have extended this definition. For instance, in a handbook for prospective investors published by the Qujiang District Government in Xi'an (Qujiang Management Committee 2011), the term 'Han–Tang', and specifically its 'Tang' component, is presented as a backdrop for new commercial districts, including the 'Great Tang Nightless Business District' (*Datang Buyecheng*). Here, 'the magnificent culture of the Tang era' echoes the necessity of using a vibrant commercial district to energize cultural development. Thus, the Hang-Tang model fulfils the mission of rehabilitating Chang'an by integrating 'cultural ideas' with local economic development projects. This approach can be seen in naming a recently opened shopping mall the 'Qin–Han–Tang Plaza of International Business and Culture' (*Qin Han Tang Guoji Wenhua Shangye Guangchang*), in which global brands and chains such as Costa reflect the prosperous commercial culture of these three historic eras.

Using the ambiguous Han–Tang culture to globalize Xi'an reflects a cultural strategy to produce a 'world-class' city. Specifically, cultural references are circulated as a resource for objectives in economic development and urban governance (Yúdice 2003). When culture is employed in strategies of economic development and local boosterism, its meanings are less important. Rather, culture is instrumentalized to fulfil objectives in economic development and governance. Thus, culture works as a field of governance, and is 'hollowed out' as it is applied to political agendas. Han–Tang culture is read differently as scholars, officials, and entrepreneurs invest resources in it to serve their own interests. Thus, similar to the process of 'making an empty show' (Oakes 2012), a hollowed-out cultural imaginary is palpable in the practices and narratives that insert cultural content into projects that are immaterial to cultural development. Culture is thus a convenient concept to use whenever local governments seek to stimulate the local housing market (Suo 2011).

In addition to local government officials, individuals who consume particular versions of Han–Tang contribute to the process of assembling cultural imaginaries of Chang'an. Interestingly, many visitors and locals seem able to identify Han–Tang culture, especially its presence in the built environment as specific symbols. As the targeted audience of Han–Tang culture, they often associate the Han dynasty with grey roof tiles inscribed with tigers and dragons. Meanwhile, red cylindrical supporting columns in buildings are often perceived as an archetype of the Tang era. In addition to these architectural designs, Han–Tang culture is understood in terms of the prominent historical figures of the two eras. Some people, for example, refer to emperors with good reputations for managing their regimes effectively and for increasing imperial China's prosperity. Two that figure prominently are Emperor Wu of Han (*Han Wudi*) and Emperor Taizong of Tang (*Tang Taizong*). Another historical figure is the Buddhist monk Xuanzang, who made a pilgrimage to India during the Tang era. These figures are often presented in urban public spaces, with statues and quotations from their work inscribed on walls and lampposts. Finally, Han–Tang culture is also seen as a lifestyle of leisure, aesthetics, and the upper class. The Tang often suggests women who wear vividly coloured, loose silk dresses with a high waists (see Figure 7.2). These women, as depicted in artworks, attend upper-class activities such as royal banquets and polo matches. For the Han image, a standing tall male figure in a black loose-sleeved ceremonial robe often comes to mind. However, while these images

Figure 7.2 Sculptures of women in Tang-style costumes in the Tang Paradise Park
Source: the author.

effectively convey Han–Tang culture visually, they do nothing to clarify what constitutes this cultural formation.

Another important process in assembling Han–Tang culture is the visible rendering of a cultural imaginary. Consumers of the imagined Han–Tang culture, alongside real estate developers and government officials, project their understandings of Han–Tang culture by looking, designing, and financing the construction of cultural icons in cities. In this, visual representations of Han–Tang culture play a significant role. Representing this ambiguous culture through symbols and visual practices echoes the visual aspect of governing practices. Dean's (2010: 41) 'forms of visibility' suggest specific ways of making objects seen and unseen. Each of these 'characterizes a regime of government, by what kind of light it illuminates and defines certain objects and with what shadows and darkness it obscures and hides others'. Visible fields of government 'make it possible to "picture" who and what is to be governed, how relations of authority and obedience are constituted in space, how different locales and agents are to be connected with one another, what problems are to be solved and what objectives are to be sought' (Dean 2010: 41). In visualizing Han–Tang culture, urban planners, architects, and government officials pick symbols to feature the future of Xi'an as a global city. This is realized through showing how Chang'an attracted foreign traders and diplomats and how the powerful emperors of the Han and Tang dynasties governed the city to make it prosperous. Specifically, the Xi'an Municipal Government makes full use of the shadow of Chang'an, a global hub of cultural and economic exchange in its time, to draw global attention to Xi'an today. If Xi'an's global ambitions are to be realized, the municipal government has decided that it must reference and revitalize the city's own history through visual representation. Thus, representations of Tang and Han poetry, dance, music, and leisure activities are carefully chosen to fit with the imagined global city.

Yet, while an imagined vibrant and enjoyable urban life is now visible in public spaces such as squares, plazas and parks, the residents who live within these cultural development projects have become increasingly invisible in the landscape of the Han–Tang city. This is because government officials, real estate speculators, and consumers of Han–Tang culture all view dilapidated houses, migrant workers, and chaotic street markets as eyesores. Such scenes are incompatible with the desired clean and orderly, well-managed city with architectural designs that reflect Han and Tang cultures. Thus, the Han–Tang city renders visible only cultural icons and their possibilities of attracting investment. Potential obstacles to economic development and local boosterism are removed to make way for the desired images in the urban space.

In addition to locals and tourists who consume products and services associated with Han–Tang culture, artists contribute to making the cultural imaginary tangible by tailoring their works towards the government's agenda. Local artists and intellectuals, especially writers, often criticize the commercialization of local histories and cultures. However, these vanguards of 'authentic Chang'an culture' have been ambivalent towards the 'authenticity' of Han–Tang culture. This is largely because of the potential benefits of tailoring their opinions and works to that culture. For instance, in the cultural district of Qujiang, a Tang theme park named 'Tang Paradise' has been criticized for building a sham 'historic' site for tourists and branding it as cultural heritage (Kangfu 2006). Yet, Jia Pingwa, a Shaanxi novelist who is almost always critical of local cultural development projects, has been surprisingly tolerant towards Tang Paradise. He often associates changing daily lives in the countryside with his perception of culture in Xi'an. In his works, cultural urban development is frequently portrayed as the enemy of a fading rural life once industrialization and urbanization have become dominant (see Jia 2010b). Yet, somehow, Tang Paradise escapes such criticism. This is especially evident in one short poetic piece that Jia dedicated to the theme park:

> [the Tang Paradise] materializes the most representative components of the grand Tang dynasty into the detailed ornament of this contemporary royal garden. [These components include] the emperors, poetry, music and dance, market places, Buddhism, food, women, intellectuals, tea and alcohol ceremonies, technologies, and so forth.
>
> (Jia 2010a; my translation)

Jia's uncharacteristic tolerance in this instance may be explained by the fact that the Qujiang district built a museum in which his novels are on prominent display right next to the theme park. His explanation of why a 'fake' copy of Han–Tang culture matters to the urban future of Xi'an echoes the official definition of the Qujiang cultural flagship projects. The debates on the authenticity of Han–Tang culture remain meaningless since today's 'fakes' will become true heritage in the future. As the head of Qujiang district asserts, 'what we have built is not cultural heritage, but cultural property [*Wenhua caichan*]. A site of cultural property will become a cultural heritage site in the future' (*People's Daily* 2010). That said, while the local government is well aware that Han–Tang culture is fake – or *shanzhai*, as some critical voices might term it (see Chapter 8, this volume) – the invention of Han and Tang histories still needs to be supported through scholarship and artworks if it is to be useful. It is precisely because Han–Tang culture is an invention that local governments, intellectuals, artists, and real estate speculators can employ it to meet their various needs.

The use of contemporary aesthetics of imagining a 'fake' historical past sheds light on the concept of *shanzhai* applied in the analysis of transnational architecture (de Kloet and Scheen 2013; Chapter 8, this volume). *Shanzhai*, in the context of producing a cultural imaginary for urban development shares a similar logic. Many Chinese cities reference Western models in their urban development plans, but produce 'original copies' of the Western originals by making them work for local agendas of development (Bosker 2013). Thus, instead of questioning the authenticity of the replicas, it is more important to ask what *shanzhai* does to realize the vision of the local government in urban public spaces. As de Kloet and Scheen (2013: 16) suggest, *shanzhai* is more of 'a unique copy of an original that has ceased to exist as a univocal entity'. The process of copying a hollowed-out image from elsewhere allows local state and non-state actors to fill in the content of the copy with their own interpretations of the original based on local contexts. This offers a different approach to considering the process of assembling the cultural imaginary of the Han and Tang dynasties. Newly built Han- and Tang-themed flagship projects are not made to recover the landscape of Chang'an in the past. Rather, they offer a stage to display the agendas of local governments in local urban development. The invented Han–Tang culture reflects local municipal governments' goal of achieving the status of 'world-class city'. While heritage preservation has been widely used in other cultural cities, such as Rome and Cairo, the Xi'an Municipal Government has decided that preservationist strategies do not offer enough room for exploring new possibilities of developing cultural industry (Xi'an Municipal Bureau of Planning and Construction 2015). Thus, the Han–Tang culture is invented to make room for new interpretations of Chang'an. This is exemplified in new architectural styles, such as 'New Tang style' (*Xintangfeng*) and 'New Han style' (*Xinhanfeng*). In other words, inventing a 'fake' culture does not limit Xi'an merely to restoring an old city by producing a *shanzhai* version. Rather, a *shanzhai* version allows Xi'an to create a completely new cultural city. This is because a *shanzhai* version of Chang'an does not need to adhere to historic evidence.

Han–Tang culture as a one-man show

Individual political authorities, as well as scholars and real estate speculators, play an important role in making Han–Tang culture applicable to cultural city policy-making in Xi'an. Political figures, especially those at the local level, contribute to developing this cultural imaginary by linking cultural-based urban development projects to their own achievements. Officials use various cultural imaginaries as themes for their own governing strategies. In Xi'an, one former vice-mayor, Duan Xiannian, is a case in point. Duan is known for successfully developing the Qujiang cultural district between 2004 and 2012. He was recognized as a successful leader of the municipal government because he used Han–Tang culture to energize the development of the local real estate market (Wang 2011). Often called 'an entrepreneur in a red hat' (*hongding shangren*), Duan was previously employed as the chief manager of a local real estate tycoon. He combined his entrepreneurial insight with cultural resources for real-estate-led urban development, arguing that this strategy allowed culture to 'set the stage for the play of economic development [*wenhua datai, jingji changxi*]' (CNWest 2010). A similar strategy has been used by many cultural-oriented projects throughout China over the past two decades. For instance, in the early 1990s, it was used to develop ethnic tourism in Guizhou (*Guizhou Daily* 2013). Several successful local experiments in the district of Qujiang have subsequently been turned into a national, or even international, model for developing cultural cities (Huashang 2012). In other words, Qujiang has been transformed from a sub-district administered by the Xi'an Municipal Government into a multi-scalar model whose influence is not restricted by its narrow administrative boundaries.

This cultural mode of urban development has won Duan a reputation as a humble culturalist with an ambitious political plan. Han–Tang culture has thus become an emblem of his political achievements. For example, in his speech at the awards ceremony for 'Chinese cultural figure of the year' (*niandu zhonghua wenhua renwu*), he claimed, 'I am not a cultural expert, just a facilitator to the development of cultural industry' (*People's Daily* 2010). Yet, this modesty does not undermine his pervasive influence in shaping Han–Tang culture in certain ways over the entire Qujiang project. The ultimate determinant of success in Qujiang, as Duan suggests, is a differentiated approach to cultural heritage. Cultural heritage, specifically the theming of local real estate with Han–Tang culture, is the very technique employed by reformers. Furthermore, Duan underscores the significance of turning culture from something distant and intangible into 'consumable, tangible, and experiential products to satisfy individual needs of consumption and to make the locals feel proud of the city' (*People's Daily* 2010). In other words, Han–Tang culture needs to be presented as something visible and comprehensible to contemporary urban citizens. Aesthetics, a crucial aspect that determines the visibility of Han–Tang culture, needs to be closely associated with the contemporary fashion of consumption. Duan's specific understanding of the contemporary aesthetics of Han–Tang culture involves fitting real estate speculation into the newly constructed Han–Tang imaginary. As Hu Chang, a scholar of religious studies, suggested in an online commentary:

> Here is what they [the Qujiang Management Committee] do. They make up a grand and mysterious story as a premise for the construction of theme parks. Then, as a result, tourists and money flow into the city. Finally, the value of the land in surrounding areas escalates. The first story of Qujiang centred on the Wild Goose Pagoda and the Tang monk Xuanzang. This story was well received as it could be seen in the sales of the shops on the Tang-themed business street on the two sides of the Wild Goose Pagoda Square. On 31 December 2002, the Wild Goose Pagoda Square was officially opened to the public. A year later, the land value of the Qujiang district was three times higher than it used to be.
>
> (CNWest 2010; my translation)

Hu's critique suggests that culture is a convenient strategy used by officials like Duan as an emblem to boost their achievements during their administrations. Duan's approach in stimulating the local real estate market to develop the local economy is not much different from other common strategies in developing urban economies. Yet, his emphasis on using culture as a stage to serve the needs of economic development allows him to play the role of a culturalist who hopes to revivify the historic Chang'an city.

The story of Duan's vision shows the role than can be played by individual political figures in assembling a cultural imaginary that is central to the making of cultural cities. This is especially critical when considering the Han–Tang city as a manifestation of authoritarian visions, particularly the vision of post-socialist urban governance in China. The centrality of aesthetics in the post-socialist setting reveals a nuanced technique of using neoliberal economic rationales to maintain state authority. Socialist symbols in the built environment are transformed from signs of modernity and progress into indicators of failure and backwardness (Pusca 2008; Schwenkel 2012). Yet socialist rule is maintained by encouraging new practices of cultural consumption in the market economy. By the same token, Han–Tang culture is seen as Duan's creative strategy for maintaining the local government's authority in managing the real estate market. While Qujiang has been designed as a development zone of cultural industry, the district of Qujiang uses the cultural industries only as assets to turn this area into a new hotspot on the local real estate market. Using culture to boost the local real estate market addresses the need of individual political figures to prove their success to higher-level supervisors in order to gain promotion. That said, while culture and creativity have been emphasized as the main foci of cultural cities, they have become assets in attracting real estate investment to generate more revenue for local governments. Local governments' interest in real estate development and individual political figures' visions are combined to create a strong stimulus to keep Han–Tang culture relevant to urban plans, yet it remains less relevant to the creative industries and the individuals who are involved. These two seemingly irrelevant strategies are fused to make the assemblage of Han–Tang culture an expedient resource, as Yúdice (2003) suggests. Han–Tang culture in this case, similar to other culture-led governing strategies, is assembled to benefit individual political careers.

Making Han–Tang culture as national and global projects

Two other important actors in the assembling of Han–Tang culture are the current regime of President Xi Jinping and UNESCO. They contribute to making Han–Tang culture by positioning it as a crucial resource for building a new Silk Road. From the perspective of the Xi regime, Han–Tang lends itself to the state agenda of expanding China's influence through the new Silk Road. Rebuilding the historic trans-Asian trade routes contributes to formulating potential financial and political alliances between China and other countries along the route (Ye 2014). As the 'new terminus of the Silk Road', Xi'an often represents the image of a powerful Chinese state by identifying itself as an 'ancient Chinese capital'. It is often designated as the first stop when foreign leaders, such as Prime Minister Narendra Modi of India, visit China (BBC 2015). Xi also frequently calls Xi'an as his home town, giving the city a politically significant status within the regime he leads. The rise of Xi'an as a host city of international prominence reflects the new national initiative to expand China's influence in Central Asia and the Middle East. Thus, the seemingly unconventional decision to use Xi'an as a host city for state visits is no coincidence. Rather, Han–Tang culture makes Xi'an an inclusive historic capital that suits Xi's plan to build a strategic alliance along and beyond the maritime and terrestrial Silk Roads. The Silk Road Economic Belt turns Xi'an into a crucial site for projecting Chinese state aspirations of global political and economic power, while Han–Tang culture offers a cultural narrative to present China as a benevolent cultural ambassador. The Silk Road Economic Belt, as the domestic part of the new Silk Road, is premised on China's explicit interest in procuring natural resources. However, positioning a cultural city as its eastern terminus has fulfilled the Xi regime's expectation of competing globally with the soft power of the Chinese state (Ye 2014).

UNESCO, on the other hand, provides a strategic tool to make heritage relevant to Han–Tang culture, especially the UNESCO Chang'an–Tianshan Heritage Belt. The Silk Road holds crucial significance because of its vast geographical distribution over western China and Central Asia and the long time span of its original existence, between the second century BC and the sixteenth century AD (UNESCO 2013). A collaborative project between China, Kazakhstan, and Kyrgyzstan, the UNESCO project is titled 'Silk Roads: Initial Section of the Silk Roads, the Routes Network of the Tian-shan Corridor'. It highlights Xi'an as a crucial site along the heritage corridor during the Han and Tang dynasties. Specifically, four Buddhist heritage sites, archaeological sites of the Weiyang Palace in the Han era and the Daming Palace of the Tang era, and the tomb of Zhang Qian are included in the application report filed with UNESCO. These sites represent Han–Tang culture because they are compatible with UNESCO's expectation of heritage sites that accurately convey 'Chinese civilization'. On the basis of the rules relating to the selection of cultural heritage sites (UNESCO 2005), the Municipal Bureau of Historical and Archaeological Preservation in Xi'an chose the seven sites as representative of the two most prosperous dynasties in Chang'an's long history. Han–Tang culture is therefore measured by the evaluation criteria stipulated by UNESCO for its value in representing cultural traditions, architecture, and technological development in the Chinese empire. UNESCO recognition allows the municipal government to make maximum use of Han–Tang culture in its bid to make Xi'an a world-class city.

Assembling Han–Tang culture is simultaneously involved in making a global cultural city and building the state along the new Silk Road. The overlaps between these two processes address the relationship between urban assemblages and the broader flows of relations. Assemblages do not only emerge from these flows; they also impact the broader flows of social relations by selectively grouping certain actors into new combinations (McCann and Ward 2011). Han–Tang culture, while organized as a result of a national initiative and the international heritage project of the Silk Road, has impacted decision-making at the central government level. The local representation of Han–Tang culture as a resource to energize economic development has offered the central government a convenient concept through which it may explain why a rebuilt Silk Road will link other countries with China to their common strategic advantage in security and the exploitation of resources. Furthermore, while using UNESCO-recognized heritage sites in cultural city-making is a common strategy (Chapter 9, this volume), its impacts vary according to local levels of urban development.

Specific outcomes of implementing cultural policies in urban development address another aspect of urban assemblages (Olds and Thrift 2005). This is because the specific outcomes and effects of implementing urban policies constitute the assemblages. Han–Tang culture and the UNESCO heritage project in this light are combined in line with the interests of policy-makers in Xi'an and Beijing. At the municipal level, recognition by UNESCO becomes an emblem of the success of using Han–Tang culture for urban development. At the national level, UNESCO's recognition of Han–Tang heritage supports the national narrative of using the Silk Road to make China a peaceful power to formulate a global strategic alliance.

Conclusion

In this chapter, I have examined the process of assembling a cultural imaginary as a basis of building a globalized cultural city in Xi'an, China. Based on my analysis, I summarize the case study with the following conclusions. First, assembling a cultural imaginary for cultural city policy-making involves a wide range of actors and strategies. Rather than being defined by a central governing figure, meanings of Han–Tang culture are produced by government officials, international organizations, scholars, and cultural consumers. Specifically, various interpretations of the visual presentation of Han–Tang culture allow this imaginary to be highly malleable for fitting various projects. This is made possible largely by the will of individual political authorities to present their achievements to their supervisors. In order to meet their own interests, other actors collaborate with the political authorities to support their visions of engaging culture in economic development. Thus, assembling a cultural imaginary to implement urban cultural policies does not simply rely on top-down projects. Rather, it is made possible by combining the interests of various participants in specific contexts.

This assemblage links cultural policy-making and urban assemblages to different possibilities in implementing cultural policies in relation to local political agendas. This approach allows the production of cultural cities to move beyond the dichotomy of global/local (McCann and Ward 2011). Since cultural policies from elsewhere constitute only parts of urban assemblages, a cultural city, specifically the Han–Tang city of Xi'an, constitutes broader processes of nation-building and economic development. Second, policies of cultural urban development are assembled under an invented cultural narrative. Culture, in this case, as Yúdice (2003) and Oakes (2012) suggest, matters less in terms of content than in how it is applied to policy-making and local boosterism. Han–Tang culture is hollowed out to stimulate the local housing market because cultural flagship projects increase land values. In relation to the expediency of culture, an imagined culture, similar to *shanzhai* (de Kloet and Scheen 2013; Chapter 8, this volume), should not be viewed as an inauthentic copy. Rather, it is a different invention and cannot be compared with examples of cultural cities elsewhere. Specific outcomes of developing a Han–Tang city thus work as manifestations of assembling different actors and resources into the overarching imaginary of Chang'an during Han, Tang, and other dynasties.

References

Agnew, J. (2012) 'Looking back to look forward: Chinese geopolitical narratives and China's past', *Eurasian Geography and Economics*, 53(3): 301–314.

Anderson, B. and McFarlane, C. (2011) 'Assemblage and geography', *Area* 43(2): 124–127.

BBC (2015) 'Indian Prime Minister Narendra Modi begins key China visit', www.bbc.com/news/world-asia-china-32730803 (accessed 14 May 2015).

Bosker, B. (2013) *Original Copies: Architectural Mimicry in Contemporary China*, Hawaii: University of Hawaii Press.

CNWest (2010) 'Qujiang Moshi Yin Zhengyi, Zhuanjia Zhiyi Wenhua Datai Dichan Changxi [Scholars suspect the validity of using culture as the basis for real estate speculation in the Qingjiang mode]', http://finance.cnwest.com/content/2010-09/03/content_3446612_2.htm (accessed 10 March 2014).

Collier, S.J. and Ong, A. (2005) 'Global assemblages, anthropological problems', in A. Ong and S. Collier (eds), *Global Assemblages: Technology, Politics, and Ethics as Anthropological Problems*, Malden, MA: Blackwell, pp. 3–21.

de Kloet, J. and Scheen, L. (2013) 'Pudong: the i global city', *European Journal of Cultural Studies*, 16(6): 692–709.

Dean, M. (2010) *Governmentality: Power and Rule in Modern Society*, London: Sage.

Florida, R. (2002) *The Rise of the Creative Class and How It's Transforming Work, Leisure, Community, and Everyday Life*, New York: Basic Books.

Florida, R. (2005) *Cities and the Creative Class*, London and New York: Routledge.

Gao, W. (2013) *Xi'an Hantang Wenhua* [Han-Tang Culture in Xi'an], Beijing: Jingji Kexue Chubanshe.

Guizhou Daily (2013) 'Cong wenhua datai dao wenhua changxi [From using culture as a backdrop to letting culture play a leading role]', http://gzrb.gog.com.cn/system/2013/09/13/012677127.shtml (accessed 20 May 2015).

Huang, L. (2010) 'Guanyu Hantang wenhua de jige wenti [Questions on Han-Tang culture]', *Journal of Chang'an University*, 12(2): 8–24.

Huashang (2012) 'Feizhou meituan lai Xi'an Qujing "Qujiang fazhan moshi" [African media groups visit Xi'an to learn the Qujiang model]', http://news.hsw.cn/system/2012/09/12/051458213.shtml (accessed 10 May 2015).

Jia, P. (2010a) 'Datang Furongyuan [The Tang Paradise]', http://blog.sina.com.cn/s/blog_7aaf04d001017890.html (accessed 10 May 2015).

Jia, P. (2010b) *Tumen* [The Dust Gate], Anhui: Anhui Art Press.

Kangfu (2006) 'Datang Furongyuan, ni rang renmen kan shenme? [The Tang Paradise, what do your expect people to see in it?]' http://kangfu.blog.sohu.com/2008207.html (accessed 10 May 2015).

McCann, E. and Ward, K. (eds) (2011) *Mobile Urbanism: Cities and Policymaking in the Global Era*, Minnesota: University of Minnesota Press.

McFarlane, C. (2011a) 'Assemblage and critical urbanism', *City*, 15(2): 204–224.

McFarlane, C. (2011b) *Learning the City: Translocal Assemblages and Urban Policies*, Oxford: Wiley-Blackwell.

Municipal Bureau of Planning and Construction (2015) *Xi'an Lishi Wenhua Mingcheng Gailan* (Overview of Building the Historic Cultural City in Xi'an), Xi'an: Municipal Bureau of Planning and Construction Press.

Municipal Tourism Bureau of Xi'an (2008) 'Xi'an jianjie [A brief introduction to the city of Xi'an]', www.xian-tourism.com/static/?type=detail&id=9 (accessed 10 March 2014).

Oakes, T. (2012) 'Making an empty show of strength: media and the politics of discernment in China's place branding projects', in W. Sun and J. Chio (eds), *Mapping Media in China: Region, Province, Locality*, London and New York: Routledge, pp. 161–175.

Olds, K. and Thrift, N. (2005) 'Cultures on the brink: reengineering the soul of capitalism – on a global scale', in A. Ong and S. Collier (eds), *Global Assemblages: Technology, Politics, and Ethics as Anthropological Problems*, Malden, MA: Blackwell, pp. 270–290.

Pan, P. (2015) 'Hantang sichou wenhua he fushi yishu yu zhongxi wenhua hudong jiaoliu [Cultural exchanges between China and the West in the art of silk costume in Han and Tang dynasties]', *Northwestern Art Studies*, 1: 83–86.

Peck, J. (2011) 'Creative movements: working culture, through municipal socialism and neoliberal urbanism', in E. McCann and K. Ward (eds), *Mobile Urbanism: Cities and Policymaking in the Global Era*, Minneapolis: University of Minnesota Press.

People's Daily (2010) 'Xi'an Qujiang: wenhua chanye, wenhua minsheng, wenhua chengshi de xin fanshi [Qujiang in Xi'an: a new model of developing cultural industry and cultural cities]', http://culture.people.com.cn/GB/106905/15111668.html (accessed 10 May 2015).

Qujiang Management Committee (2011) *Qujiangqu shi'er-wu guihua* [The 12th five-year plan of the Qujiang district]', Xi'an: Qujiang Management Committee.

Pusca, A. (2008) 'The aesthetics of change: exploring post-communist spaces', *Global Society*, 22(3): 369–386.

Schwenkel, C (2012) 'Civilizing the city: socialist ruins and urban renewal in central Vietnam', *Positions: Asia Critique*, 20(2): 437–470.

Suo, Y. (2011) *Xi'an Qujiang moshi* [The Qujiang Model of Xi'an], Beijing: Central School of the Chinese Communist Party Press.

UNESCO (2005) 'The criteria for selection', http://whc.unesco.org/en/criteria/ (accessed 10 May 2015).

UNESCO (2013) 'Silk Roads: the Routes Network of Chang'an-Tianshan Corridor', http://whc.unesco.org/en/list/1442 (accessed 10 May 2015).

Wang, H. (2011) *Qinli Qujiang* [Experiencing Qujiang], Xi'an: Shaanxi Normal University Press.

Wang, J. (2001a) 'Culture as leisure and culture as capital', *Positions*, 9(1): 69–104.

Wang, J. (2001b) 'The state question in Chinese popular cultural studies', *Inter-Asia Cultural Studies*, 2(1): 35–52.

Xi'an Municipal Government (2005). 'Xi'an shi 2005 zhengfu gongzuo baogao [The annual report of the municipal government of Xi'an]', www.xa.gov.cn/websac/cat/107/10745.html (accessed 10 May 2015).

Xiong, T. (1987) 'Han–Tang wenhua fazhan tezheng [Characteristics of the development of the Han–Tang culture]', *Journal of Huazhong Normal University*, 4: 10–16.

Yan, X. (2008) 'Han-Tang wenhua dui Shaanxi jianshe wenhua qiangsheng de zuoyong [Impacts of the Han–Tang culture on cultural development in the province of Shaanxi]', *Xi'an Social Science*, 26(4): 61–63.

Ye, M. (2014) 'China's Silk Road strategy', http://foreignpolicy.com/2014/11/10/chinas-silk-road-strategy/ (accessed 15 March 2015).

Yúdice, G. (2003) *The Expediency of Culture: Uses of Culture in the Global Era*, Durham, NC, and London: Duke University Press.

Zukin, S. (1995) *The Cultures of Cities*, Oxford: Blackwell.

8 Worlding through *shanzhai*

The evolving art cluster of Dafen in Shenzhen, China

June Wang

Introduction

For many Chinese cities, urban initiatives of negotiating a position in the global landscape of power are frequently caught in two entangled circulations: the low vector of global intersections involving migrant labourers, petty traders, trivial commodities (Mathews, 2011); and high-profile citational practices that borrow symbolic images from established brands and/or advanced cities (Ong, 2011b). Perhaps it is the two happening in tandem that leads to the emergence of so-called *shanzhai* industries and *shanzhai* global cities. *Shanzhai*, the Chinese term for 'fake', has triggered heated debates since 2008. Scholars have revealed that *shanzhai* entails multiple layers, from resemblance to subversion (Chubb, 2015; Wu, 2010; Zhang and Fung, 2013), while the *shanzhai* global city may be a valuable field to reveal the situated urbanisation of Chinese cities (de Kloet and Scheen, 2013), where all cities are treated as ordinary (Robinson, 2006).

The city of Shenzhen appears to be located in the centre of such investigations. While it is commonly recognised as a hotbed of *shanzhai* industry (Chubb, 2015; Zhou, 2008), the emergence of the city, being one pilot site to try new experimentations in China's market transition, started from the citational practices inspired by Deng Xiaoping's exhortation to create 'a few Hong Kongs' (Cartier, 2002). Dafen Art Village has been one key pilot scheme and strategic site in Shenzhen's experimental quest for a cultural turn. Indeed, the village might be a valuable field site to explore situated urbanisation in terms of two entangled circulations: those of people and commodities at the low end and those of symbolic images from the so-called higher tiers. On the one hand, Dafen is a node of the trade painting industry, where low-skilled migrant painter–workers and low-budget art dealers assemble for production and sale of decorative paintings, a sizeable number of which are copies of masterpieces. On the other hand, the village has also witnessed multiple rounds of image branding through citational practices, from the 'home-grown' image of the innovative masses to the borrowed image of Hollywood with rearticualted intellectual property rights (IPR) at its core.

This study attempts to interrogate these two intertwining and conflicting circulations with the transformation of Dafen Village. I attempt to illustrate a distinct form of cultural city production, which establishes and justifies its own new economy, and seeks world recognition, through *shanzhai*. In using this term, I refer to a metonymy of presence (Bhabha, 1994) in the circulation of both products and images, which are carried out by different actors: low-end painters and art dealers for the first circulation, and the contingent coalitions constituted by the state, elites and the local industry association for the second circulation. I use the term *shanzhai* on account of its relative flexibility in methodology: first, to include a wide range of actors, from individuals to coalitions; second, to explore the political and economic power struggles of these actors, not just domestic against overseas, through resemblance and subversion. The two circulations harness symbolic values and particular modes of production, and also bring about new power struggles with new instruments of subject-making and norm-shaping. Whereas a home-grown reference is deployed to depict the cultural turn as a mass dream of entrepreneurial migrant workers, paving the way for the host city to step into the global cultural market, an overseas reference is appropriated to discipline the same innovative mass with a rearticualtion of IPR.

I have been following the transformation of Dafen with an ethnographic approach since March 2011. A questionnaire survey, participant observation and semi-structured interviews have been the main data-collection methods. In addition, I have maintained contact with the interviewees through social media, such as Weibo and Wechat. In the following discussion, I will first introduce debates in the literature, then elaborate on the two circulations: low-end globalisation and high-profile citational branding. Finally, I shall discuss and offer some conclusions on power struggles through resemblance and subversion.

Worlding through *shanzhai*

Globalisation as circulation of people, goods and ideas

Globalisation has reshaped scholarship on cities. If we take globalisation to mean the circulations of capital, goods, ideas and people (McCann and Ward, 2011; Roy and Ong, 2011), examining cities through 'the lens of high-profile vectors of global intersection' like high finance and transnational companies, we will likely gain only a partial understanding of the world (Knowles, 2014, p. 188). Digging into Chungking Mansion, Mathews (2011) introduces the term 'low-end globalization' to illustrate how transnationally mobile people, not professionals but those at the bottom of society (usually asylum-seekers, illegal migrants and low-budget traders from sub-Saharan Africa, South Asia and elsewhere), have converted the building into budget guesthouses, food stands, and shops selling cheap household items at the heart of Hong Kong's commercial centre. Knowles (2014) likewise traces the trail of plastic flip-flop production to reveal 'globalisation's backroads', which link cities and villages scattered in a wide range of countries, from Egypt to South Korea and China. It is through this low-end globalisation process that the roles of many unexpected actors such as farmers, (illegal) migrant workers, petty merchants and village heads unfold. These minor players encounter and exchange ideas, knowledge, skills, stories and rumours that they have learned on the journey, and in turn these shape the network at the low end of globalisation.

The cases of Chungking Masion and the flip-flop trail have revealed multiple processes with different valences and trajectories that are seriously challenging our understanding of globalisation as a process with 'a unified logic, set of agents, and target of world transformation' (Ong, 2011b). Increasingly, scholars are rejecting the idea that Asian cities are merely passively globalised by transnational capital, and are suggesting that they may be more proactive in experimenting with ways of being global in the midst of inter-city rivalries. Worlding city practices, or the art of being global, entails an assemblage of urban initiatives that harness disparate ideas, logics and techniques from various places. Worlding, drawing upon Spivak (1999, p. 11), is about how subjects 'tend towards centering' and asks about the development of subject-power (Roy and Ong, 2011).

Knowledge, be it an image, slogan or model of development, flows from one place to another. The geography of knowledge maps out the unequal relationship between the two terminals of the flow of knowledge, which, for Peck (2011), reflects transnational capital's constant search for a new spatial fix, consequently figuring a clear directional flow from the Global North to the Global South. However, empirical studies reveal alternative patterns, suggesting alternative driving forces. Roy and Ong (2011) point out that place-based observations frequently uncover 'home-grown' ideas or selective adoption of the package. The green urban regime, illustrated by the 'Garden City' of Singapore, advocates the capability of the state to transform a developing world city into a world-class one. The modelling effort of the Singaporean government, which obviously serves political ends, reinterprets state intervention as 'non-political technical solutions to a host of social problematizations' (Ong, 2011b, p. 21). In light of this, it is not surprising to see its popularity among many other Asian cities, from Dalian to Manila (Hoffman, 2011; Shatkin, 2012). The wave of hyper-building fever, in Asia and beyond, has accelerated the inter-city rivalry to hard-sell world status through monumental skylines (Ong, 2011a). Likewise, experimentations in the cultural turn in Chinese cities must be put within the context of the national state's political desire for world recognition, which emphasises developing China's soft power. As argued by Pang (2012), the development of creative industries aims to encourage the consumption of Chinese cultural products, therefore establishing a world status of cultural products 'created in China' (Keane, 2006), and eventually foster the reciprocity of cultural, economic and political development.

Shanzhai *amidst the geography of knowledge and subject-power negotiation*

Shanzhai space may be the node where low-end globalisation encounters high-profile image branding through citational initiatives, in particular when the circulation of knowledge entails mostly discursive components like name, logo or advertising campaigns. This leads to a blossoming of places like 'a few Hong Kongs' in southern China (Cartier, 2002) and 'little Manhattan' in Shanghai (de Kloet and Scheen, 2013). Looming large are parallel discourses like 'fake global cities' in China (Huang, 2004). Shanghai is frequently cited when describing the often obvious gap between the copied image and the actual physical infrastructure and modes of production: whereas the skyline of Pudong resembles that of Manhattan, in other respects the city can scarcely be classed a global city. This account views many emerging Chinese cities as 'fake', noting the unequal endeavours of copying a landscape versus those of copying an infrastructural or developmental model. However, the idea of copying itself needs to be explored. Initiatives of copying the image frequently stimulate and tweak 'world-class' values, and consequently discipline the behaviour of citizens (Ghertner, 2010). Learning particular models of urbanism, which is observed in many places, hardly aims to bring modern and desired life to the local society as a whole, but simply introduces a new means of capital accumulation (Cox, 2013; Peck and Theodore, 2010). I argue that it is through the 'not quite' part of mimicking projects (Bhabha, 1994) – that is, the gap between the copied knowledge and the situated model of urbanism – that we may better understand how the circulation of knowledge is 'grabbed' and appropriated to legitimise local practices and achieve local agendas.

Worlding practices, especially when they are carried out by the state, serve local political intentions to claim the emergence of the local on the global landscape and perhaps reshape the geography of power. For Bhabha (1994, p. 130), 'mimicry . . . is a part-object that radically re-values the normative knowledge of the priority of race, writing, history. For the fetish mimes the forms of authority at the point at which it de-authorises them.' Therefore, mimicry is 'at once resemblance and menace' (p. 123). The Chinese term *shanzhai* appears to be more open and flexible in exploring the overlaps of these different layers (Zhou, 2008).[1] Literally meaning 'mountain fortress', the term first appeared in the folk novel 'Outlaws of the Marsh' (*Shui Hu Zhuan*), and refers to an enclave established by 108 warriors who were either persecuted or marginalised by the royal court during the Song dynasty. Therefore, it implies resistance to and rebellion against authority and perhaps even depicts a utopian dream of the subordinated. Nevertheless, the *shanzhai* regime itself established a hierarchy for its warriors that resembled existing court systems in many ways and perhaps indicated an aspiration to join the ranks of authority. Therefore, two parallel meanings have long accompanied the term: low-quality replication with a rogue spirit; and a self-demarcated area with self-created rules that openly flout official authority and its institutions. Some studies on *shanzhai* (Chubb, 2015; Zhou, 2008) argue for another interpretation of 'grabism' (*nalai zhuyi*), which refers to the active reappropriation of economic and cultural authority for diverse local purposes.

Shanzhai, in this light, well serves studies on activities carried out by a wide spectrum of actors from individual subjects to coalitions. Despite its often elusive political subversions, the core of *shanzhai* rests on the initiative to emerge and participate in official political, economic, social or cultural spheres (Chubb, 2015; de Kloet and Scheen, 2013; Zhang and Fung, 2013). In order to achieve that goal, '*shanzhai*-ing' frequently leads to relentless interactions, negotiations and struggles between the ruler and the subordinated, the powerful and the powerless, the mainstream and the subcultural (Zhang and Fung, 2013), including, but not confined to, a spatial dichotomy of coloniser and colonised, Global North and Global South.

Using *shanzhai*, I intend to examine two concurrent practices in Shenzhen: the assemblage of the low-end *shanzhai* art industry, and the branding of *shanzhai* art space through a collaboration between the state, elite artists and the industry association. Through this examination, I attempt to answer two questions. First, is it always a one-direction flow of ideas or models from advanced to the less developed regions? Second, how does subject-power change in this process – that is, how are particular forms of subject-power articulated and consolidated, while other forms are disavowed?

Shanzhai art in low-end globalisation

The emergence of trade painting clusters in Shenzhen must be understood in the context of the network built up for Chinese trade and 'China as world factory', both of which are historical phenomena (Siu, 2011). The trade painting industry is not a contemporary phenomenon either, but a continuation of the Chinese export painting industry that flourished in Guangzhou during the late Qing dynasty. The geographic shift of the industry, from Guangzhou to Shenzhen, reflects painters' willingness to relocate in response to shifts in Chinese trade, 'centering on Guangzhou and later tied to Hong Kong' (Siu, 2011, p. 132).

The Chinese export painting sector emerged in the late Qing dynasty with the opening of Guangzhou as a trading port (Crossman, 1991; Hong Kong Museum of Art, 1982; Wong, 2013). Goods and people thus assembled in the city, including Chinese returnees who introduced Western oil painting. Several Chinese painters, such as Spoilum, Lamqua, Fatqua and Youqua, were among the pioneers of Chinese export painting. The fusion of Chinese and Western painting techniques and styles, coupled with comparatively low prices based on cheap labour, resulted in high demand for their works in overseas decorative painting markets. During the heyday of Chinese export painting (1830s–1860s), painting workshops occupied almost every shop on Tongwen Street in Shisanhang (at the time the busiest commercial street in Guangzhou). However, before China closed its doors to the outside world in 1949, the remnants of the industry moved to Hong Kong (Crossman, 1991). Former painter–workers either shifted to wallpaper painting in the booming property market or moved into different industrial sectors (Hong Kong Museum of Art, 1982). In the early 1980s, China resumed contact with the outside world, and the painting industry started to shift back.

Since then, the trade painting sector has attempted to survive by riding on the coat-tails of, although remaining outside, the official economic order of Chinese trade. After the establishment of Special Economic Zones (SEZs) in southern China, numerous Hong Kong entrepreneurs moved their factories to the SEZs, attracted by preferential policies that applied to the '*sanlai yibu*' sector. Painting masters in the trade painting sector also flocked to these cities. In the early stages they headed mostly to Xiamen, before moving on to Shenzhen, where they tried to establish themselves at Huangbeiling, a village within the city's SEZ. However, only a few managed to survive there, where they remain an incongruous presence amidst numerous electronic appliance assembly factories. Constant rent hikes pushed most of the trade painting studios to more marginal areas. Thus, Dafen Village, which lies outside of the SEZ, came to the attention of Huang Jiang, a trade painting master searching for a cheaper place to relocate his workshop. Dafen Village was something of a last resort for the trade painting sector but it had two distinct advantages: proximity to the Hong Kong checkpoint, and a constant supply of flexible migrant labour (Wang and Li, in press). In this trade painting production chain, individual painters assemble closely around several masters and art dealers, with the latter playing 'godfather' roles. Given the industry's heavy dependence on the market, it is not surprising to observe the dominating role of those who are able to place large-volume orders, namely the well-connected masters and professional art dealers. This resembles the earlier case of Chinese export painting. In the late Qing dynasty, George Chinnery, an art dealer who bridged the supply of decorative paintings in Guangzhou and the demand from overseas markets, became so popular that the term 'Chinnery School' was coined to refer to the paintings he exported (Crossman, 1991). In Dafen Village, today's equivalent figure was Huang Jiang, a master who migrated to Hong Kong at an early age and established connections with trade agents through his wife. More recently, Wu Ruiqiu, a former apprentice of Huang, tried his luck at the Canton Fair and secured a huge contract with Wal-Mart. Consequently his influence among painter–workers grew and he eventually supplanted Huang as director of the Art Industry Association of Dafen (AIAD) (Li, 2006; Wen, 2006).

Like their predecessors, contemporary masters run their workshops as master–apprentice studios, recruiting teenagers from their home towns. Proximity to established masters-cum-art dealers is crucial for painters to learn the ever-changing preferences of overseas consumers. In the early years, most orders were confined to replicating a few classic masterpieces, such as Da Vinci's *Mona Lisa*, Van Gogh's *Sunflowers* and Vermeer's *Girl with a Pearl Earring*. However, with the rise of contemporary Chinese art in the global art market, the painter–workers have recently turned their hands to producing more avant-garde pieces, such as copies of works by Fang Lijun and Yue Mingjun. Meanwhile, ever more painters are learning and practising Chinese traditional arts, from painting and calligraphy to embroidery and thangka (painting on cotton or silk), to meet demand from the emerging niche market for Chinese culture. Likewise, staying close to a master makes it possible for painters to exchange adaptive skills they have accumulated through years of practice and quickly shift from one genre to another. Knowledge-sharing even extends beyond the domain of work to of the painters' private lives. Junior painters are advised when they should plan vacations, home-town visits or even when to start a family, because of the strong seasonal pattern of their work. For many years, Christmas has been 'the golden season' for Dafen's painters, who work day and night for several months to produce numerous snow-covered landscapes. By contrast, the summer is far less busy, so this is the time to take care of private matters. Painters and their masters, who generally gather together on the basis of their original home towns, form a multitude of clusters that resemble clans in the host city.

Constructing the mass dream imaginary

Whereas inter-referencing practices are widely viewed as one strategy for economic development in the making of a *shanzhai* global city (de Kloet and Scheen, 2013), a reverse pattern is observed in Dafen Village. An art cluster was first discovered in the village in 1988 during a national 'Civilisation Construction' (*jingshen wenming chuangjian*) campaign. Shen, an official in the Propaganda Division of Buji's town government, immediately recognised Dafen's great potential for political propaganda (Wen, 2006). Thereafter, a series of measures built up, enhanced and broadcast the image of the art village. Two of these initiatives stand out: the iconic architecture of Dafen Museum; and the Shenzhen Pavilion in Shanghai's Expo 2010.

Shanzhai *as a mass dream of cultural production*

The idea of constructing a museum was inspired by the development of Hu County in Shanxi Province, to which the State Ministry of Culture awarded the official title of 'Cradle of Contemporary Chinese Folk Art' in 1988.[2] Contemporary folk art refers to 'peasants' painting', a hybridisation of traditional folk art practices such as paper-cuts, new-year painting and embroidery. The 'simple and naive rustic style'[3] gives these paintings a strong flavour of 'Chineseness'. In the 1970s, peasants' paintings were highly visible in a wide variety of media, from official posters to newspapers, textbooks and comic books, disseminated to every corner of the country. More importantly, folk art was designated as the official representative of Chinese art in many state-curated overseas exhibitions. In her attempt to convince the district head to approve her plan for a grand museum, one former official of the Longgang Planning Department ascribed Hu County's success to the Hu County Peasants' Painting Exhibition Hall, which has remained the largest centre for Chinese folk art since its construction in 1976. The commission for the Dafen Museum project was then granted to Meng Yan, a Chinese returnee architect who brought back with him the cutting-edge concept of 'public architecture' from the United States. The project's website declares:

> Our concept focuses on reinterpreting the urban and cultural implications of Dafen Village, which has long been considered as a strange mix of pop art, bad taste, and commercialism . . . The question is whether or not it can be a breeding ground for contemporary art.[4]

Likewise, the museum has been designed to express the official attitude towards trade painting: it is not just tolerated but actively encouraged. One of most visually striking features of the museum is its façade, on which huge blank painting frames await input from Dafen's painters, implying that 'the architecture – an

Figure 8.1 Dafen Art Museum, Shenzhen
Source: the author.

elite-designed avant-garde art – [will host] . . . trade painting – the vulgar art'
(Lai, 2011, pp. 102–103; see Figure 8.1).

In Expo 2010, the idea of the innovative masses was further fine-tuned from
peasants to migrant peasant workers, with the imported element of Western oil
painting. The Shenzhen Pavilion was composed of two contrasting images: a
gigantic image of the *Mona Lisa* representing the achievement of migrant workers
on the front façade; and, inside, an installation that recreated the daily working
and living environment of the painters themselves (see Figure 8.2). The interior
scenes conjured a narrative of painters exerting themselves to accomplish their
personal transformation, including the tiny, dimly lit and often messy rooms
where they work and live, their tireless experiments in front of rows of paintings,
a number of containers – finished artworks awaiting export – indicating their
achievement in actualising the convergence of art and commerce, and eventually
their prospects for becoming 'authentic' artists through a collection of genuine
artworks. At the end of this series of scenes, there was a ramp on which were
several stones, together with video stories of painters projected on to the side wall,
to evoke the message of 'crossing the river by feeling the stones'. Dafen Village,
and more broadly Shenzhen City, provided a considerate, tolerant and encouraging environment, and was therefore named a 'Dream-Field', after the Hollywood
animation studio 'Dream Works'.

Figure 8.2 The Shenzhen Pavilion at Shanghai Expo 2010
Source: Urbanus, authorized for reuse.

Constructing the mass dream

> It must be downplayed in a locally inclusive 'we' who can be imagined as
> sharing the wealth in a place local and global inequalities are covered up, yet
> they must conjure a transnational 'we' to amplify this small cause with
> enough volume to speak.
>
> (Tsing, 2005, p. 211)

Situated in a national climate of enhancing cultural, economic and political
sovereignty, domestic initiatives are promoted to counter the intrusions of other
cultures in policy-making. Likewise, the new policy that favours 'independent
innovation' (*zizhu chuangxin*), introduced in 2004,[5] clearly signals a new direction
for China's development projects. In the image-citing initiatives mentioned above,
'home-grown ideas' distilled from the rural soil of China ascribe the emergence
of an art village to the bottom-up, innovative endeavours of (former) farmers.
Participation, an idea advocated by 'public architecture', shows a benevolent state
guiding the masses in 'trade painting'. 'The Renaissance of an Urban Village' –
theme of the Shenzhen Pavilion in Expo 2010 – claims that the turn towards
'culture as capital' is in fact the mass dream of Chinese farmers. As addressed in
the preceding paragraphs, the assemblage of the trade painting industry in Dafen
draws on multiple actors: the painting masters-cum-dealers, the art dealers and
the painter–workers. The story told by the Shenzhen Pavilion, however, singles
out migrant painter–workers and places them in the spotlight. The role of
the 'godfathers' (art dealers or wholesale merchants, such as Wal-Mart) has
disappeared from this narrative. Detached from the global chain of the ornamental
art market, trade painting production is reinterpreted as the 'fruitful struggle' of
individual migrant workers.

Nevertheless, the home-grown image is narrated in a way that is appealing to
the 'Western' neoliberal discourse. In both the branding events of the museum's
construction and Expo 2010, the principal role played by the architect, a recent
Chinese returnee, implies the citational attempt to participate in the symbolic
imaging of the Global North. The official citational behaviour might be influenced
by the fact that *Time* magazine had named 'the Chinese Worker', and specifically
Shenzhen's migrant peasant workers, as one of four runners-up in its 'Person of
the Year' award in 2009.[6] Deploying the image of peasants for place branding is
nothing new for Dafen Village, but *Time* certainly gave the local state the confi-
dence to broadcast that image on a global scale. Nevertheless, such a presentation
has proved appealing to overseas audiences because of the strategy of 'metonymy
of presence', which renders Chinese migrant workers as the self-motivating entrepreneurial individuals that have been championed by neoliberal discourse in the
Global North. The presentation of a home-soil distilled image perhaps illustrates
how mimicry is camouflage, with its effect, 'against a mottled background, of
becoming mottled' (Bhabha, 1994, p. 172). The narrative of the Shenzhen Pavilion
invented the 'self-exploration' and 'self-improvement' endeavours of the diligent
migrant workers who bravely embraced the market. The image of entrepreneurial

individuals that is so strongly promoted in Western neoliberal discourse, in return, demonstrates the validity of the Chinese slogan 'crossing the river by feeling the stones' – a principle established by Deng Xiaoping.

The image that the state has created lends low-end globalisation the camouflage of the neoliberalised Chinese masses. Citing the aspirations and endeavours of the grassroots, the state orchestrates an image that celebrates the democratic potential of *shanzhai*, claiming a collective innovation booming at home. The deployment of the home-grown image of the migrant worker serves the development of China's soft power. Moreover, such citational practices are not simply top-down actions from the central state, or intruding ideas from overseas, but rather are constructed by an ensemble of actors from various scales.

Discipline the mass dream

Shanzhai *for mass consumption – populist in tone*

Abbas (2008, p. 254) views the fake as a temporary phenomenon that 'would come to an end' upon a city's mature integration with the global standard. The turning point for the *shanzhai* painting industry of Dafen, and perhaps for the *shanzhai* design industry in general, appears to be the global financial crisis of 2008. The weakening of overseas markets and the consequent drainage of foreign capital slowed the pace of development in Dafen, forcing the local economy to search for a new market niche. The technique of citational practices was deployed again, but this time by the local trade painting community, in particular the elite masters who have gradually distinguished themselves from the mass of painter–workers and have enjoyed ever-higher relative incomes as a result.

In 2011, Luan, the CEO of the Shenzhen Silver Wave Art Company, become head of AIAD on the back of his campaign for a 'derivative art industry'. According to Luan, derivative artwork reproduces original masterpieces in an innovative way, such as reproducing them on different media, including porcelain, silk and paper, extracting sections from the original work or making smaller versions, merging two or more original pieces, and so on. Innovation, for Luan, involves 'introducing abstract art to the populist life of daily consumption'.[7] During his election campaign, Luan cited Hollywood and framed the new image of the 'Hollywood of Oil Painting' for Dafen Village. To explain the derivative art industry, the secretary of AIAD commented, 'Hollywood animation film is the derivative of Hollywood [traditional] film' (interview, 2014). This explanation obviously simplifies the development of the Hollywood film industry. As such, a more detailed elaboration on the correlation between Hollywood and derivative art scarcely appears in any exhibition catalogues or newspaper articles. Instead, the task of framing the discourse of derivative art has been taken up by the *People's Daily* to legitimise the industry through cases of elite artists around the world (Li, 2014). In a special forum debating the issue of derivative art, the *People's Daily* commented that the practices of the industry are so widespread that almost every museum in the world has a commercial section, selling copies of masterpieces. Moreover, modern renowned artists have profited from derivative production, with Andy Warhol the most obvious example. The *People's Daily* cited the collaboration between Warhol and Absolut vodka as a classic example, which gave birth to the 'Andy Warhol edition' – a series of bottles designed by Warhol and three contemporary artists. This derivative art on a bottle not only let 'Absolut reimagine nightlife through the power of creativity'[8] but also 'let Warhol transcend different disciplines and continue his search for an expanded space of artistic production' (Li, 2014). Boosting the domestic consumer market needed cultural support, expressed in foreign language and foreign culture, where value is cultivated as the 'discreet charm of the bourgeoisie' (Abbas, 2008, p. 256).

Built upon the legitimised image of derivative art, the local campaign in the village shifts to distil one feature from the historic trajectory of Hollywood: the long history of fighting against counterfeiting. The AIAD has organised a growing number of workshops and exhibitions that have presented the history of Hollywood. The emphasis has frequently been on the relentless disputes and lawsuits over counterfeiting and the subsequent IPR legislation, which eventually helped Hollywood to survive and thrive. Now the AIAD is emphasising the importance of IPR for the sustainable development of Dafen Village.

The IPR-defined hierarchy of labour

In the campaign to establish a 'derivative art industry', the hierarchy of the Hollywood film industry lends moral support to Dafen Village, where painting masters and painter–workers coexist. While it is beyond the scope of this chapter to discuss the contested issue of IPR, I argue that the seemingly bottom-up 'salutation and trivialization' of IPR (Pang, 2013) in Dafen Village must be considered within the context of the ever-widening inequalities within the community.

If it is to maximise profits, trade painting production must rely on cheap and insecure human hands, and, more importantly, on a stratified, hierarchical labour force. In a traditional master–apprentice workshop, apprentices offer free labour in return for training from the master. The mode of production thus naturalises masters' claims of authorship. However, the naturalisation of master authorship ceases to work after the graduation and subsequent autonomy of his apprentices. The tension between former master and former apprentice, who are now rivals, is heightened by the increasingly fierce competition within the market place.

Disputes between masters and workers have become increasingly common, with complaints from big workshop masters against their former apprentices now a major issue of daily work at the AIAD (interviews, 2013, 2014). In one interview, the secretary of the AIAD reiterated the importance of establishing a patent system to prevent the departure of elite masters. For instance, the owner of one workshop who employed over a hundred apprentices wished to ban a former apprentice from producing the same images he had worked on during his apprenticeship. Although it is difficult to judge whether the master of over a hundred apprentices can provide anything like substantial training to each apprentice, or contribute enough to a painting to claim authorship, this master was fully supported by the AIAD. Thereafter, the case was frequently cited as an example of how the patent system operates to keep the 'talent' within the village while punishing 'theft' by painter–workers. In 2013, the Unitrust Time Step Authority (TSA) was introduced to Dafen Village, allowing painters to register their work online via computers or smartphones.[9] The TSA, as indicated by its slogan 'Let Time Testify for You', issues digital certificates for products based on the mere indicator of time.[10] The 'salutation and trivialization of IPR' (Pang, 2012), at least in the context of Dafen Village, seems to revolve around large, established workshops limiting the working scope of young, struggling painters.

Vaidhyanathan (2001, p. 5) argues that the shift in the United States from copyright law, which was justified in terms of the health of the public sphere, to IPR reveals the shift to 'legal thoughts to protect "property" at all costs and see nothing good about "public good"'. The property-oriented thinking that serves commercialisation and marketisation has been appropriated in Shenzhen by an emerging elite group through the introduction of TSA – perhaps a *shanzhai* version of IPR in Dafen Village – to regulate *shanzhai* behaviour among the struggling masses. Framed in property-oriented law, the IPR legislation is meant to safeguard the local haves: the established painters and the big workshops. This citational practice serves the needs arising from the fracturing of the cultural community and the polarised interests of various social forces in its late stage of commercialisation. While Abbas (2008) worries that *shanzhai* might merely confirm and enhance the global division of labour, the case of Dafen raises a new issue of the local division of labour when a local *shanzhai* economy nurtures its own neoliberal model.

Conclusion

Image citing in the *shanzhai* global city of Shenzhen does not constrain itself to any particular geography for references; nor does it adopt any particular model as a whole package. Instead, this is a deliberate action of rearticulation that combines fragmented pieces appropriated from multiple origins. The government deploys a citational strategy – namely, articulating the city as the breeding ground for the innovative masses – to legitimise an already-formed node of low-end circulation and eventually establish the economic presence of a new cultural city in the global landscape. The local coalition formed by elites and elite-dominated industrial organisations deploys citation to participate in the symbolic value of an overseas industry – Hollywood – which has been widely promoted as one of the few thriving sectors since 2008's global financial crisis. Twin circulations of images and goods establish a reciprocal relationship, serving each other in a material sense.

Nevertheless, neither delivers the promise of the branded image to the massive workforce in the trade painting industry. The first image of the innovative masses covers up the stratification within the community and the income inequality among art dealers, painting masters, painter–workers and apprentices, which, at a later stage, is legitimised by the image of Hollywood. The generous praise bestowed on migrant workers must be viewed in terms of the dual dimension of neoliberal morality with self-motivated entrepreneurialism and self-responsibility. The glory is always bound by responsibility. Bauman (2011, p. 12) suggests: 'the responsibility for the choice and its consequences remain where it has been placed by the liquid modern human condition – on the shoulders of the individual, now appointed to the position of chief manager of life politics and its sole executive'. In Dafen, migrant workers are now responsible for their own well-being through self-improvement (Dean, 2007). The trouble taken by the state to put peasants (and later migrant peasant workers) under the spotlight hardly reveals any intention to empower these labourers; rather, it signals an intention to discipline them. The innovative mass of migrant workers, whose image has made appealing the 'art as capital' transformation of Shenzhen, have sunk to the bottom of the community and, more importantly, have been left to bear the brunt of criticism over the inauthenticity of their products.

Acknowledgement

This research was supported by two grants awarded by the Research Grants Council of the Hong Kong Special Administrative Region, China [CityU 247713] and the City University of Hong Kong [Seed Grant 7003046].

Notes

1 See also D. Zhu (2009) *Shanzhai* culture is a social deconstruction movement, *Shidai Zhoubao*, 24 July, www.time-weekly.com/2009/0724/xMMDAwMDAwMjIxMg.html (accessed July 2015).
2 Shanxi Association of Fine Art (n.d.) Peasants' painting: the village of painting in China, www.sxgongmei.cn/html/newslist_1039.html (accessed September 2012).
3 China Huxian Farmer Painting Exhibition Hall (2005) The origin of farmer's painting, www.farmerpainting.net/hzqy.asp (accessed 12 February 2014).
4 For an introduction to the project, see: www.urbanus.com.cn/public_class.php?action=projectandnum=1andaid=1andsaction=sclass# (accessed July 2014).
5 Jiabao Wen (2007) Report to the 10th People's Congress, 5 March, www.sipo.gov.cn/yw/2007/201310/t20131024_851184.html (accessed March 2012).
6 Austin Ramzy (2009) Person of the Year: the Chinese worker, *Time*, 16 December, http://content.time.com/time/specials/packages/article/0,28804,1946375_1947252_19 47256,00.html (accessed July 2014).
7 *Art China* (2012) Dafen: the Hollywood that brings oil painting to households worldwide, 2 July, www.artx.cn/artx/huihua/209449.html (accessed July 2014).
8 See www.absolut.com/en/warholspirit/ (accessed January 2015).
9 Hairuo Li (2013) Dafen's anti-plagiarism measure, 8 May, www.chinanews.com/cul/2013/05-08/4797136.shtml (accessed January 2015).
10 See www.tsa.cn/ (accessed January 2015).

References

Abbas, A. (2008). Faking globalization. In H. Andreas (ed.), *Other Cities, Other Worlds: Urban Imaginaries in a Globalizing Age* (pp. 243–264). Durham, NC: Duke University Press.

Bauman, Z. (2011). *Culture in a Liquid Modern World.* Cambrige and Malden, MA: Polity Press.

Bhabha, H.K. (1994). *The Location of Culture.* London and New York: Routledge.

Cartier, C. (2002). Transnational urbanism in the reform-era Chinese city: landscapes from Shenzhen. *Urban Studies*, 39(9), 1513–1532.

Chubb, A. (2015). China's *shanzhai* culture: 'grabism' and the politics of hybridity. *Journal of Contemporary China*, 24(92), 260–279.

Cox, K.R. (2013). Territory, scale, and why capitalism matters. *Territory, Politics, Governance,* 1(1), 46–61.

Crossman, C.L. (1991). *The Decorative Arts of the China Trade: Paintings, Furnishings and Exotic Curiosities.* Woodbridge: Antique Collectors' Club.

Dean, M. (2007). *Governing Societies: Political Perspectives on Domestic and International Rule.* Maidenhead: Open University Press.

de Kloet, J. and Scheen, L. (2013). Pudong: the *shanzhai* global city. *European Journal of Cultural Studies*, 16(6), 692–709.

Ghertner, D.A. (2010). Calculating without numbers: aesthetic governmentality in Delhi's slums. *Economy and Society*, 39(2), 185–217.

Hoffman, L. (2011). Urban modeling and contemporary technologies of city-building in China: the production of regimes of green urbanisms. In A. Roy and A. Ong (eds), *Worlding Cities: Asian Experiments and the Art of Being Global* (pp. 30–54). New York: Blackwell.

Hong Kong Museum of Art (1982). *Late Qing China Trade Paintings.* Hong Kong: Urban Council.

Huang, T.-Y.M. (2004). *Walking between Slums and Skyscrapers: Illusions of Open Space in Hong Kong, Tokyo and Shanghai.* Hong Kong: Hong Kong University Press.

Keane, M. (2006). From made in China to created in China. *International Journal of Cultural Studies*, 9(3), 285–296.

Knowles, C. (2014). *Flip-flop: A Journey through Globalisation's Backroads.* London: Pluto Press.

Lai, D. (2011). Wall, public sphere and China architecture: a journey starting from the Dafen Museum, Shenzhen. *21st Century*, 123(2), 90–104.

Li, L. (2006). *Legend of Dafen (in Chinese).* Hong Kong: Asia Publishing House.

Li, T. (2014). Art derivatives: dilemma faced by the sun-rise industry. 'People Vision' section, *People's Daily*, 6 November, 40.

Mathews, G. (2011). *Ghetto at the Center of the World: Chungking Mansions, Hong Kong.* Chicago: University of Chicago Press.

McCann, E. and Ward, K. (eds) (2011). *Mobile Urbanism: Cities and Policymaking in the Global Age.* Minneapolis and London: University of Minnesota Press.

Ong, A. (2011a). Hyperbuilding: spectacle, speculation, and the hyperspace of sovereignty. In A. Roy and A. Ong (eds), *Worlding Cities: Asian Experiments and the Art of Being Global* (pp. 205–225). New York: Blackwell.

Ong, A. (2011b). Introduction: World cities, or the art of being global. In A. Roy and A. Ong (eds), *Worlding Cities: Asian Experiments and the Art of Being Global* (pp. 1–29). New York: Blackwell.

Pang, L. (2012). *Creativity and Its Discontents: China's Creative Industries and Intellectual Property Rights Offenses.* Durham, NC, and London: Duke University Press.

Pang, L. (2013). Depoliticization through cultural policy and intellectual property rights: the case of Lijiang. *Positions*, 21(4), 885–919.

Peck, J. (2011). Geographies of policy: from transfer-diffusion to mobility-mutation. *Progress in Human Geography*, 35(6), 773–797.

Peck, J. and Theodore, N. (2010). Mobilizing policy: models, methods, and mutations. *Geoforum*, 41(2), 169–174.

Robinson, J. (2006). *Ordinary Cities: Between Modernity and Development*. London and New York: Routledge.

Roy, A. and Ong, A. (eds) (2011). *Worlding Cities: Asian Experiments and the Art of Being Global*. New York: Blackwell.

Shatkin, G. (2012). *Collective Action and Urban Poverty Alleviation: Community Organizations and the Struggle for Shelter in Manila*. Aldershot: Ashgate.

Siu, H.F. (2011). Retuning a provincialized middle class in Asia's urban postmodern: the case of Hong Kong. In A. Roy and A. Ong (eds), *Worlding Cities: Asian Experiments and the Art of Being Global* (pp. 129–159). New York: Blackwell Publishing Ltd.

Spivak, G.C. (1999). *A Critique of Postcolonial Reason: Toward a History of the Vanishing Present*. Cambridge, MA: Harvard University Press.

Tsing, A.L. (2005). *Friction: An Ethnography of Global Connection*. Princeton, NJ, and Oxford: Princeton University Press.

Vaidhyanathan, S. (2001). *Copyrights and Copywrongs*. New York: New York University Press.

Wang, J. and Li, S.-m. (in press). Re-territorialization, counter-territorialization, and the remaking of Dafen oil painting villages in Shenzhen, China. *Urban Geography*.

Wen, Y. (2006). *The Rise of Dafen*. Shenzhen: Haitian Publishing House (in Chinese).

Wong, W.W.Y. (2013). *Van Gogh on Demand: China and the Readymade*. Ed. C.A. Jones. Chicago: University of Chicago Press.

Wu, J. (2010). *Shanzhai* economy and new media creativity: a discussion of the formation of post-modernist public sphere. *China Media Report*, 1, n.p. (in Chinese).

Zhang, L. and Fung, A. (2013). The myth of '*shanzhai*' culture and the paradox of digital democracy in China. *Inter-Asia Cultural Studies*, 14(3), 401–416.

Zhou, Z. (2008). '*Shanzhai* wenhua' zhong de xiaofei xiangxiang. *Renmin Luntan*, 238(22), n.p.

Part II

Encountering the cultural/creative city

Negotiation, resistance, and community aspirations

Section introduction

We argue that any analysis of the mobilities inherent in cultural/creative city policy formation and implementation is fundamentally incomplete without an accounting for the roles communities play in this process. These communities include art and cultural groups, relevant industrial organizations that compete for power and resources, and ordinary citizens participating in the public good of cultural services or pursuing lifestyles based on cultural consumption. The advent of a 'creative turn' in the economic and public aspirations of Asian cities has been marked by fragmentation and contradiction. As argued by Joanne Lim's chapter on Malaysia, such fragmented conditions pertaining to the construction of cultural cities allow for negotiations to take place, resulting in new ways of thinking, as well as the production of new urban spatial orders. Julie Ren's chapter on Beijing and Berlin details how art groups have organized strong networks with political machines like foreign embassies to protest controversial issues, such as the demolition of organically formed cultural clusters. Se Hoon Park's chapter on Busan details how local state developmentalism is negotiated, contested, and ultimately reinvented by local actors as it articulates with cultural/creative city policy formation and implementation. Questions asked in the chapters by Lim, Ren, and Park include:

- Who are the diverse urban actors behind cities' cultural/creative city agendas?
- What are the new community coalitions and alignments fostered through negotiation and contestation?
- How have the various elements of the cultural city agenda been materialized through negotiations?

The final three chapters by Agnes Ku, Jason Luger, and Dwiparna Chatterjee and Devanathan Parthasarathy focus our attention on the community resistances and negotiations occurring in the unstable and fragmented spatial constellations of power generated through cultural/creative city policy. Peck (2005) has argued that Florida's creative class theory travels well because of its resonance with an already established neoliberal discourse of urban entrepreneurialism. The emergence and restructuring of an urban cultural policy agenda privileges particular economies, particular places, and particular social forces. Politics emerges in this new round of dynamic and contingent (re)alignment of actors, opening another chapter of state–society relations. Art-led gentrification is reported in many cities, nevertheless, there also emerges the 'creative resistance', in which independent creative workers, or artists, are becoming 'a strong voice in contestation of the present-day urban order' (Novy and Colomb, 2012, p. 1819), although always in a contradictory or ambiguous manner. These chapters assemble studies of Hong Kong, Singapore, and Mumbai, responding to questions like:

- What are the social resistances that arise in Asian cities, where the legacy of an authoritarian state is still evident?
- How do we explain the hybrid, paradoxical social resistance against the cultural/creative city idea and/or policies?

The volume concludes with an Afterword by Margit Mayer, offering a round-up of the chapters and putting them in conversation with global trends of neoliberal urban restructuring and the role of the 'cultural/creative city' as a global practice of neoliberal governing. Mayer's chapter focuses on linking neoliberal urban restructuring with social resistance movements and asking about the connections among these movements across Asia and between Asian and other parts of the globe.

References

Novy, J., and Colomb, C. (2012) Struggling for the right to the (creative) city in Berlin and Hamburg: new urban social movements, new 'spaces of hope'? *International Journal of Urban and Regional Research*, 37(5): 1816–1838.

Peck, J. (2005) Struggling with the creative class. *International Journal of Urban and Regional Research*, 29(4): 740–770.

9 Accessing spaces, negotiating boundaries

The struggle between cultural policies and creative practices in Malaysia

Joanne B.Y. Lim

Introduction

I have great respect for how a piece of street art has turned a negative perception of JB into something people admire, pose for photos and talk about.

(Roslani, 2013)

The wall painting reflects the desire of the people, and should therefore be preserved. No one should attempt to modify or whitewash the painting just because they want to paint a rosy picture of the city . . . a city that does not accommodate dissident voices will never be one that deserves the respect of people.

(Kubo, 2013)

Figure 9.1 Controversial painting by Ernest Zacharevic in Johor Bahru
Source: the author.

In November 2013, Lithuanian artist Ernest Zacharevic painted the walls of buildings in Jalan Molek, Johor Bahru (JB), with the Lego-like image of a robber and a lady carrying a Chanel handbag to symbolize the city's rising crime rates, much to the alarm of authorities who took immediate action to whitewash the painting, labelling it 'contentious' and a form of 'vandalism'.[1] An emergency motion was tabled in the Johor legislative assembly to discuss the mural, with Johor Jaya's assemblywoman Liow Cai Tung deploring the action taken by the state authorities as 'self-deceiving'.[2] On the internet, thousands of netizens posted comments on the artist's Facebook page, expressing support and gratitude for his artwork as it embodied the concerns of the community in JB. In addition, on a radical level, memes of the mural started spreading online. While retaining the original idea of two Lego characters, netizens found different ways to remember the mural by inserting their own stories of Johor/Malaysia – from narratives of the corrupt police force and their encounters with pickpockets, to issues relating to the newly enforced GST (Goods and Services Tax), the state government, and even scandals relating to the First Lady's jewellery. Each meme generated by netizens and the debate it produced were unique, often presenting new (or altered) connections between spaces, places and people; suddenly every space became a possible Jalan Molek, such as walls, vehicles and t-shirts throughout the country, thus forming new communities online and offline, much to the dismay of local authorities.

The practice of street art/murals in Malaysia has suffered a bad reputation since the days of the country's economic crisis in the 1980s, as graffiti is often linked to delinquency and vandalism among gangsters or drug addicts (it was often found in alleyways and under bridges). It was later stereotyped as a subculture that was popular among students who played truant. While graffiti may also serve as an art form for 'young people to feel independent, empowered, creative, and heard' (Ensminger, 2011: 68), it could also be interpreted as a way for youth to defend themselves against the rise of consumer culture. Rather than a matter of 'social struggles for power', Ensminger (2011: 70) understands it as 'a form of resilient, outsider assertiveness'. Several scholars, including Schacter (2014), have also argued that graffiti is performed by political activists and is used as propaganda both for and against dominant power all over the world, positing that it is akin to healthy public debate rather than a hate crime. Indeed, the use of public space is seen as an alternative to mass media, and street art has become a mode of expression in various societies. The trend re-emerged in George Town and Malacca in 2011 as part of city council efforts to gentrify those cities and preserve/promote cultural heritage (both George Town and Malacca are UNESCO World Heritage Sites). In recent years, various other street arts have emerged in numerous parts of the country (many painted by Zacharevic) and become tourist attractions and conversation pieces among the locals. However, several of these artworks have also attracted criticism and controversy.

The attempt to (re)construct a so-called 'Malaysian identity'[3] has often been the emphasis of both the state and society amidst pressures to conform to globalizing forces. In this context the challenge for those interested in designing interventions may be to recognize and effectively manage these interactions in ways that positively influence the emergent flow of events that constitute the cultural activities of certain groups or communities. However, the desire to protect and preserve a 'national culture' has led to the imposition of state laws and cultural policies that seem to be more limiting than liberating. In many respects, as is evident in governmental efforts concerning the local culture industry in Malaysia (Rahim and Pawanteh, 2010), public policy towards culture struggles to respond simultaneously to contrasting national and new global demands (Craik et al., 2003). This raises questions about the significance of intervention by the state and others in the cultural sphere as a means of delivering personal or societal goals.[4] Arguably a hegemonic tool, the national cultural policy is also an identity policy, which may be geared towards strengthening or weakening different groups or individuals representing different cultural identities, and can be identified as an effort to sustain cultural hegemony or promote cultural diversity.[5] However, more pertinent to the discussion of shared identities is the importance placed on culture in establishing nationhood. While the cultural polemic preceding and immediately following the country's independence was strongly linked to the kind of 'culture' to be accepted, developed and promoted at a national level – whether this be Malaysian, Western and progressive or protected 'high' forms of regional cultural heritage – the debate never questioned the basically accepted premise of the educative value of culture itself as a civilizing agent of human behaviour and, as such, a source of pride and a sense of identity. While participatory art in Malaysia is encouraged and recognized as a tool for promoting positive interaction between groups representing different cultural identities, only a selected range of activities and artists is legitimized (or approved by the state). Nevertheless, independent social participatory (art) groups such as ArtsEd, TACKit! and Greenpeace Malaysia have led various participatory efforts, though seldom with the support of the authorities, perhaps due to fear of links to overly liberal ideas of free speech and expression. Furthermore, graffiti is open to all and is an accessible subculture that anyone can enter to serve their own agenda; hence being viewed as a threat to the state.

Freedom of speech and expression are controlled and monitored because a protectionist state regards these concepts as 'Westernizing' and thus as threats to the purity and harmony of the nation. The state's attitude is reflected in two recent pieces of legislation – the National Harmony Act and the Peaceful Assembly Act (an adapted version of the repealed Internal Security Act). With these laws in place, the preservation of culture and heritage has become highly problematic, especially with the proliferation of religious and racial struggles in the country's urban areas. The question of legitimized spaces for cultural expression and the restrictive control of such physical (and, to some extent, virtual) locations have further impinged on society's sense of belonging and identity. Increasingly, activities that aim to promote social inclusivity and cultural expression in cities like George Town in Penang, Ipoh, Malacca and Johor Bahru through spatial experimentation (i.e. architecture, art installations and street performances) have started to attract civic interest and participation, notwithstanding the tensions arising between creative practitioners and policy-makers due to the ambiguity of state support towards the nurturing of creative/cultural practices.[6]

This chapter discusses the politics behind these aesthetic forms alongside the work of Jacques Rancière (2004), which sees politics as an intervention to the visible, and recognizes aesthetics as fundamental to the constitution of the political. First, by drawing upon examples of how creative/cultural networks are structured and mobilized (in both cyber and urban spaces), particularly within the Malaysian context, I argue that the dialectical struggle between cultural policies and creative practices may signal the advent of a 'creative turn' in Malaysia's socio-political history. In juxtaposing the case studies[7] with Paulo Freire's work on the 'pedagogy of the oppressed', it is argued that the (vandalized) murals embody responses, reactions and resistances towards prevailing governance structures set up to 'protect' so-called public spaces from cultural contamination and 'non-Asian values'. Such fragmented conditions pertaining to the construction of cultural cities in Malaysia allow for negotiations to take place, resulting in new ways of thinking, as well as the production of new urban spatial orders. Finally, I explore the intersections of 'creativity' between different cities in Malaysia within a larger narrative of a postcolonial nation.

Cultural policy and the struggle of creative networks

As inhabitants of complex cultural spaces, urban city dwellers in Malaysia seek to define themselves in different spaces both individually and collectively, while also facing the complex task of dealing with global and local forms of cultural expression, which can be contradictory. As this cultural space grows even more complex and fragmented, the urban society's capacity to participate fully in both social and economic settings is becoming ever more closely linked to the ability to participate in cultural activities. For this reason, policy-makers are confronted with the task of facilitating and supporting diverse means for cultural expression. Yet, formal narratives concerning policy-making and planned interventions in relation to culture are fraught with a range of tensions that reflect the state's difficulties in dealing with concepts and practices such as those relating to the cultural sphere. Amidst concerns to establish clearly defined policy objectives, state power relations often seek to legitimize rather than legalize their actions, resulting in contradictory and seemingly makeshift responses (and reactions) to new or alternative cultural expressions. Whereas the authorities in Johor were quick to condemn the murals, Ipoh City Council Licensing and Enforcement Assistant Director Ahmad Zaiyadi Sudin said Zacharevic's murals were always welcome: 'The city council, Datuk Bandar Datuk Harun Rawi included, have no objections toward these artworks. These can bring in more tourists to the city and we welcome that.'[8] Penang Chief Minister Lim Guan Eng had similarly declared, 'We are not that autocratic. We are not like Johor' (Looi, 2013).

This draws attention to the significance of events during the creative process and following the completion of the wall art at the intersection of those implementing cultural projects – be they independent or state-commissioned artists

– and other equally knowledgeable actors, such as, in this case, the society with whom they engage. Local authorities reacted to these aesthetic forms, mimicking the original artist perhaps in a less sophisticated way – the murals in Johor were whitewashed and walls repainted on two separate occasions by the local authorities, who read the murals as a means to destroy the city's image and deter tourists.[9] 'The picture stirred controversy by bringing attention to two things that Johor Bahru is most known for: a Legoland theme park and a high crime rate,'[10] thus generating a negative image of the town. Nonetheless, local residents and the general public viewed that as a cowardly response from the authorities (see Table 9.1, below). The act of 'covering up' the wall reflects what Rancière calls the 'distribution of the sensible' – a set of consequential laws that condition what one may see and hear, say and think, do and make. In desperately trying to hide their inadequacies and constantly striving to avoid confrontations that intend

Table 9.1 Netizens' repsonses to the whitewashing of the Lego mural(s) in JB

Comment by James1067[a]
The truth is the truth and you can rewrite, erase or even put a lid on it. It will rise up to remind and prick your conscience of what is wrong and what needs to be put right. So stop trying to close or wipe it out but face the reality that crime is still not under control and the public is sending you a message.

Comment by mufc1978[b]
The whole JB town is full of posters, signages by loansharks, and yet MBJB did not bother to clean them up for years . . . and when someone drew something that is very reflective of what is happening in JB, especially Taman Molek area (where the drawing was), MBJB very 'effectively' and 'efficiently' cleaned it up. UBAH for a better Malaysia come PRU 14!!!!

Comment by Bigjoe[c]
It's not that they don't know the lesson. It's a matter they don't want to. It's not their brain that is dead. It's their soul. You can't teach addicts of abuse of power lessons without consequences and there is only one consequence that will teach – losing power.

Comment by taktahan[d]
. . . going after Zacharevic's mural will only prove the arrogance of the authority to admit one's incompetence and failure to tackle crimes. Go after the real criminal, Mr Authority!

Comment by Godfather[e]
Yes folks, I have resolved not to pay the unreasonable hike in assessment rates by Bandaraya. I am willing to fight them in court. Now who wants to join me? I am hoping for a 25 pct population support which will bring Bandaraya to sanity.

Notes
a https://weehingthong.wordpress.com/2013/11/12/the-lego-mural-that-launched-a-thousand-angry-words/.
b http://www.niamah.com/2013/11/some-juicy-bits-you-might-have-missed.html.
c http://blog.limkitsiang.com/2013/11/21/the-zacharevic-lesson-all-those-in-authority-must-learn-the-greater-the-unreasonable-pressure-by-those-in-power-the-greater-the-righteous-reaction-by-the-public/.
d Ibid.
e Ibid.

to shame or question state decisions, the 'sensible' reflects delimiting forms of inclusion and exclusion in society.

Thus, the distribution of the sensible becomes displaced in this very struggle with the politicization of art and aesthetics. The political plays on a multiplicity of levels that go beyond state law enforcement, activism and public interventions. On the contrary, the events that have played out in relation to street art (art being the *raison d'être*) suggest a dismantling of representational hierarchies. The paradox of art's singularity and freedom from hierarchy becomes evident in the legal–legitimate dichotomy reflected in the ambiguous position taken by the authorities in relation to art and aesthetics. In Penang, for example, Chief Minister Lim Guan Eng expressed his support for Zacharevic's artwork 'to frame up a small uncovered pothole' in order 'to allow for art to grow'. However, he was not as receptive towards paintings of Minions and Superman along Lebuh Ah Quee and Lebuh Bishop, respectively, and this inevitably raised questions among the public about what constitutes art and how it is being defined by the state. Lim justified his reactions by saying, 'We have received complaints, even from the media, that some public artworks do not complement the outstanding universal values of the heritage city.' A special panel was then set up to 'manage public art works and prevent George Town from being overwhelmed with graffiti'. The panel – comprising members 'with expertise' who conduct daily inspections and review all unauthorized work – has the power to decide whether an artwork is 'appropriate', whether permission should be granted for new artworks, and whether murals should be recommended for removal.[11] What becomes apparent is the entanglement of what is now 'legally legitimized', along with the revolutionary quest for new art forms, and perhaps new modes of expression and life.

In response to the whitewashing and erasure of Zacharevic's paintings in JB, a mural of a man wearing a *songkok* (Muslim headgear) and holding up a sign which read 'Keep Johor Bahru Clean' had phrases such as 'Make Wall a Threat Again', 'City of Hell' and 'This is Fuckin Johor Bahru' spray-painted over the top of it. Members of the public were also reported to have defaced several Malacca street artworks that had been painted by local artists. This was particularly evident in:

- a mural of eight running horses titled 'Towards a New Journey' painted along the walls of Jalan Hang Kasturi in Malacca by renowned artists Chong Chen Chuan and Quake Kah Ann;
- the Calligraphy Wall in Lorong Hang Jebat, next to the Malacca River; and
- several other walls in Jalan Hang Lekiu and Jalan Kota Laksamana.

These murals, which were part of a project to paint fifty-seven walls around Ipoh in conjunction with Malaysia's fifty-seventh Independence Day, were 'defaced' with words such as 'Failed Loyal', 'Secret Society' and 'Erase the Law'.[12] Local councils and mainstream media unanimously labelled these as 'delinquent acts' of 'vandalism'. In response, online forums immediately started to question why this was deemed vandalism while the authorities' whitewashing of murals was considered 'legitimate'.

Although seemingly vandalistic in nature, the 'delinquent acts' may instead be regarded as extensions of existing conversations or political expressions inspired by the original artworks. The original artists had subsequently invited local residents to add to their artworks. Within the aesthetic regime, such visualized debates embody the struggle between autonomy and heteronomy, between art becoming life and life becoming art. Evidently, there are no criteria for relating art and politics. Themed 'The Eternal Flame of Cultural Traditions Live on through the Hill and River, Its Glory Illuminating the Past and Present', the intention of the paintings was to portray the 'diligence of our ancestors in nation-building'.[13] Far from reducing the significance of art, Rancière's 'distribution of the sensible' challenges us to rethink the functionality of art. What also becomes pressing is an investigation into the conditions that allow and encourage such artistic choices to be made. In terms of its functionality, the 'modified' murals may be read as allegorical of the struggles and resistance of the community of people within a shared space. It becomes apparent that the first layer of painting depicts a rather clean and idealized image of the city whereas the second layer offers emotions that have been evoked by the original images. Here, the public is seen to use everyday elements and spaces to subvert the rituals and representations that institutions (namely, the state) seek to impose. Such becomes the ideal condition for what Freire (1970/1993) suggests is the liberation of oppression through the transformation of humans into self-actualized, *creative* and empowered beings. Here, the 'oppressed' creatively and consciously work to shape and reshape their world.

Production of creative practices

In contrast to what traditional instrumental approaches to cultural policy suggest, planned cultural interventions – in the case of wall art or murals – do not operate in a vacuum; instead, they involve negotiations between actors and the space(s) they inhabit, with very different knowledge interests and understandings that shape their responses in unpredictable and sometimes contradictory ways. Whether deemed a discovery of new aspects of 'talent' or a powerful cultural weapon in the service of a real class struggle, public reaction to the murals seems to be in contrast to actions taken by the authorities in response to Zacharevic's murals. Herein lies the possibility of a 'creative turn' for the nation. Often, these paintings encourage onlookers to 'be part of the artwork' rather than merely appreciate the artwork from afar (as would be the case when viewing conventional paintings in a museum or gallery, for example). The movement of art from the offline space to the virtual space is initiated through the attempt to be photographed with the street art; in desiring an image of themselves with the street art and to have it posted and/or 'liked' on Facebook or other social media platforms.

Again drawing upon Rancière's work, it is possible to understand art as a medium that effectively makes communities, and that artworks, not unlike knowledge and political statements, can produce 'regimes of sensible intensity' (Rancière, 2004: 39). Rather than a mere collection of Facebook images, it is the social relationship between people that is mediated by these images. Without privileging a particular scale, the murals develop over time as a collective event that rejects participant–spectator distinctions through its own fundamentally anarchic structure and open-access spaces, which imagines everyone present as participants and allows them to engage at will and at random (Roberts 2003: 59). In doing so, participants are empowered to create and modify the new 'illusions' that identify and support the movement's conceptual identity as a unique socio-political phenomenon. Produced through outpourings of both individual and group creativity, and engrained in the experience of a collective (virtual) art form, the resulting images have been subsequently recorded, distributed and consumed in the form of a visual spectacle made possible by bridging the collective and the cultural. Thus, the conversations are perpetuated while encouraging a different level of participation among members of the public. Unlike the rigid multicultural elements frequently found in state-funded cultural activities, these new or reconstructed art forms are deemed 'real' stories and expressions that are not spared from emotions of anger, frustration and envy. Prompting active engagement with the original artwork, the artwork is extended online (as memes) and (re)produced in other physical locations (on vehicles, sidewalks, shopfronts and office buildings). As one local said, 'You can cover a painting but you can't cover an idea' (Woon, 2013), while a shop-owner stated, 'The authorities should spend more time fighting crime instead of focusing on the mural' (Hon, 2013).

Thus, in understanding the promise of new modes of art and new forms of life and community, Rancière's system of heterologies, which ties art to non-art, is crucial in understanding the interchange between material space to virtual space and back again. The complexity of this system extends beyond critiques of modernism and artistic activism. Working in a dialectical manner, the public (re)produces the offline artwork and photographs it in order to post it online. The (re)productions of the Lego woman and robber at various physical locations throughout Malaysia were then photographed and shared online to spur further mobilization of and support for the 'JB Lego' movement. In this context, the conversations begin offline while the online platform becomes the main tool to generate public interest in the issue(s). By looking at the wider notions of culture, we observe how culture and cultural spaces are produced, and how the everyday cultural processes within them may signal forms of resistance.

Contesting the wall: the 'city' online and in the everyday

By engaging in a co-creative relationship, prosumers (see Luers, 2007; Bruns, 2008) come together to produce various forms of cultural content, including videos and inter-textual images (which are often satirical due to the draconian state monitoring of online spaces), commonly known as memes.[14] Among over thirty memes of the Lego mural that went viral online were:

- Thor looking dandy carrying a Chanel handbag in one hand and his Mjölnir in the other;
- the wife of Malaysian Prime Minister Najib, Rosmah Mansor, superimposed on to the Lego woman along with her RM77 million diamond ring; and
- a GST-knife-wielding Lego man waiting for a recipient of BR1M (a government scheme established to offer assistance to low-income households).

By considering these memetic texts alongside the eruption of events offline, it may be conceived that whenever art appeals to the memory of society, it may in fact be appealing to something else ('fabulation' – a term Deleuze (1991) borrowed from Bergson), and whenever they think they are producing memories they are, in fact, engaged in 'becomings'. Thus, the production of memory and conversations does not necessarily begin or end online. These artistic constructions may be read as the embodiment of such memories, and/or creative attempts to reconstruct past memories by drawing upon the present.

The examples discussed here enable us to consider how societies are being compelled to create new sites for exploration, to present new connections between spaces, places and people, and to recompose the variety of issues and experiences into an alternative art form. These new sites allow for individual/ group experiences to develop, drawing together 'remembered' associations with (new) communities, thus creating contemporary forms of collective memory. Memory, here, is seen as active and constantly on the lookout for opportunities to 'alter space' (see de Certeau, 1984). The 'memory site', then, is one that encourages prosumers to develop their own experiences through offline engagement with various issues, and online participation in these cultural forms. As one netizen said:

> The mayor's order can of course have the graffiti removed but it will not remove the sadness of local people, as well as the people's *memory* about the graffiti and the message it brought . . . instead of the graffiti depicting a snatch-theft crime, it is crimes that have ruined the image of Johor Bahru!
>
> (Soong, 2013)

In response to this, the people of Johor Bahru and throughout Malaysia were warned via the mainstream media that the Johor Bahru City Council (MBJB) had given tenants and landowners one week to remove the paper cut-outs of Zacharevic's street mural that had been pasted on the walls of their buildings or risk a fine of RM500, allegedly for committing acts of vandalism themselves.[15] On Facebook, at least 16,700 users accessed links that enabled them to download and print the Lego characters.

The overall understanding of aestheticization warrants the question: what can we learn from aesthetics mobilized by this street art/graffiti? How does the use of strong visual imagery (of crime, for example) help us understand the politics and practice of everyday life in these cities/townships? Walking around in these spaces, one is mostly astonished by its spectacle, a spectacle of resistance, built not only to be experienced, but above all to be mediated. In this visual spectacle, it is the surface that matters, more so than the content – and, following Rancière, 'contrary to the modernist thesis, the surface has not been a boundary, isolating the purity of an art, but, rather, a place of slippage between various spaces' (Carnevale and Kelsey, 2007: 256). These surfaces or spaces (both offline and online) allow for different sensory experiences. In general we witness what Rancière (2004) would call a redistribution of the sensible as seen through a flashmob (organized online) that took place near the said wall after a call to 'protect the Taman Molek graffiti'.

The politics of street art enters the field of aesthetics when it pushes at the boundaries of, for example, the visible and the invisible, the online and the offline. It is thus premised upon the regime of the sensible, rather than operating outside of it. This encourages a deeper sense of attachment to the artwork, which is evident in netizens' emotional responses (see Table 9.1). In addition, numerous people who had painted the 'Lego' graffiti on their walls and vehicles in other parts of the country had not seen the actual mural in JB but had felt a connection with it, particularly due to the controversy it had generated, labelling it a most honest piece of work.

Conclusion

The obvious issue concerning street art lies in the authorities' obsession with labelling it vandalism and then whitewashing over or removing this form of creative expression. However, where other means of communicating with the authorities have failed, these murals or graffiti may in fact serve as gap-bridging platforms. In the case of JB, Zacharevic's mural conveys the need for greater effectiveness in reducing crime in the township and eradicating its reputation as Malaysia's crime capital. Here, creating a most affecting piece of participatory art challenges the authorities to adopt a co-productive policy-making process whereby participatory art must build on the interests and assets of the community, and cannot be successful if the ends, means and skills needed have been already decided before it is carried out – that is, entailing city council approvals and permits whereby decisions are made on the basis of either an ambiguous or too rigid set of rules. This asset-based approach is important in political discourse as well, as there is an intention to change the elite structure of 'helping society' within our social and cultural policies.

Juxtaposed with Rancière's understanding of street demonstrations as an exemplary instance of producing dissensus, controversial street art becomes a collective performance that transforms space – that is, it transforms the walls along the streets from 'ordinary' and mundane to a disruptive spectacle of so-called 'vandalism' that occasions the participation of the public to engage with the art. This chapter has considered various examples depicting the struggle between policies and practices in constructing cultural cities in Malaysia. Through the discourse of street art/graffiti and the online platform, it becomes evident that political conflict arises when there is an intervention to the system of organizing modes in society (also referred to as dissensus), such as modes of doing, being, making and communicating within a common existence. Participatory art, and in this case street art, then, requires both the artistic (artists and the public as participants) and political spheres to listen to how people already engage and allow this to form new routes in order to co-produce both art and policy. The failure of participatory art lies in placing too much emphasis on policing and politicizing the act of participation when the focus should be held within the message conveyed by the art created, just as the focus of political participation should be social change. Hence, the contents of each mural or street art are inputs which should be valued and embraced more meaningfully in order for creative environments to thrive as diverse, open and inclusive spaces.

Often the mismatch of cultural value concerns between the ordinary citizen and the state is highly problematic – where the intrinsic, institutional and instrumental values of culture and creativity differ within a state. In observing the nature of societal engagement with (new) art forms, there is a need to examine whether support in the form of planned interventions related to cultural activities can help (creative) collectives/individuals meet these challenges. On the one hand, the case of street art in Malaysia shows how the lack of policy coordination and local political competition as well as inappropriate micro-cultural management have culminated in a failure of cultural development to connect sufficiently with the felt needs and experiences of the cultural producers and participants in the local community. However, amidst efforts by the state to encourage national economic growth, a new problem has arisen where gentrification and cultural homogeneity have occurred. What is highly arguable then is the purpose of cultural policies. Such policies are seen to be attempts to establish the image of an idealized Malaysian identity rather than to serve or to meet the needs of the community. Instead of nurturing culture, the ultimate aim is to attract foreign investment through Malaysia's struggling tourism industry. It becomes apparent that the discourse of Malaysian identity takes on a more prominent role in rendering a city 'attractive' to tourists. In short, the focus on economy supersedes the intention to develop culture, whereby the process of globalization has resulted in a crisis of cultural values that are indispensable components of the production, consumption and experience of culture. In a context in which the skills necessary to participate fully in cultural life are increasingly similar to the skills that are necessary to participate in the modern economy, questions concerning what these skills are and whether there is a role for planned intervention in supporting their development are of increasing importance. Within a larger narrative of a postcolonial nation, the intersections of 'creativity' embodied in street art become visible, particularly in the dialectical struggle between the oppressor and the oppressed (Freire (1970/1993), as discussed earlier) and in the alienation of the 'non-creative class' through labels such as 'gangsters', 'delinquents' and 'vandals'.

This chapter has established the scaling up of an art form on two separate dimensions – from street art as individual work to participatory art as collective work (contributed in various ways by locals and tourists alike). In addition, the work moves from material space to virtual space, and ultimately back to material space that has been expanded geographically, reproduced in various spaces within the country. This makes it difficult and perhaps even superfluous to determine or locate art's singularity, or to identify a distinction between street art and other means of expression. Indeed, these movements and (re)constructions of art revolve around an interplay between issues of open, playful and participatory *socio-cultural* politics, on the one hand, and overtly *political* mobilization on the other. While not without its critics, participatory (street) art offers an opportunity to create and manage interactions between actors who inhabit separate, equally valid cultural spaces and use this as the basis for generating positive social and cultural outcomes. Regardless of its macro-political or micro-oriented implications, there must to be a shared interest in exploring the potential of culture and creativity within the everyday lives of people for the expression of alternative social, political and economic forms of production, consumption and resistance.

Notes

1 Zacharevic's street mural had dominated not only Johor but national headlines for almost a week, and attracted international coverage before it was whitewashed by the municipal council.
2 See   www.freemalaysiatoday.com/category/nation/2013/11/13/jb-lego-mural-removed/ (accessed 12 January 2015).
3 Depending on the object of bonding and identification, cultural identity may be associated with a linguistic, ethnic, religious, ideological, political, sexual, global, national, regional and social domain or symbolic hierarchy. Identity also involves strong value structures.
4 It is also useful to note that the defacing of murals in Ipoh and Malacca took place only after authorities had whitewashed the JB Lego artwork.
5 In Malaysia, the first full agency for culture at ministerial level was established in 1964, seven years after independence. Nevertheless, its government culture portfolio has never been part of the Ministry of Education. In Indonesia, where the debate about cultural heritage and national identity had been raging long before independence, the government department for culture was established as soon as that was achieved in 1945. The Philippines established a culture department within the Department of Education in 1947, one year after independence. In Thailand, the government agency for culture (the Department of Fine Arts) was established in 1933 as part of the state's new independence under a constitutional monarchy, the year after the absolute monarchy was overthrown, with an emphasis not on creation of something new in terms of fashioning national identity, but rather on making the cultural heritage that had been attached to the institution of monarchy public property. In 1942, this department became the Bureau for Culture.
6 Malaysian artists do not usually apply independently for grants for their own projects; instead, they are appointed to projects devised by the state cultural office (or centre) at national or regional level. A lucky few may also receive awards in recognition of their work.
7 An archive comprising photographs taken of the various creative expressions in Penang, Ipoh, Malacca and Johor has been collated between 2012 and 2014, along with 400 related memes downloaded from the internet and over 800 comments from online forums and message boards. Interviews were conducted with cultural practitioners and personnel from the Ministry of Unity, Culture, Arts and Heritage.
8 See   www.thestar.com.my/News/Community/2014/06/30/Coffeecommissioned-murals-Artist-splashes-the-walls-around-Ipoh-Old-Town-with-his-renowned-artwork/ (accessed 8 April 2015).

9 Views expressed by Johor Domestic Trade, Consumerism and Tourism Executive Committee Datuk Tee Siew Kiong and JB City Mayor Ismail Karim.

10 See http://thediplomat.com/2013/11/malaysian-authorities-whitewash-street-artists-lego-mural/ (accessed 10 March 2015).

11 According to the general manager of George Town World Heritage Incorporated (GTWHI), Lim Chooi Ping, only twelve public art projects, including Zacharevic's murals, were done with permission and authorization. The panel had identified forty-six illegal public artworks at the time of writing (www.themalaysianinsider.com/malaysia/article/review-panels-to-monitor-public-artwork-in-george-town#sthash.JDO4w2V0.dpuf) (accessed 3 January 2015).

12 See www.thestar.com.my/News/Nation/2014/07/27/Malacca-murals-defaced-Vandals-spraypaint-heritage-zone-walls-with-gangster-slogans/ (accessed 3 January 2015).

13 See www.thestar.com.my/News/Nation/2012/10/28/Mural-themed-Towards-a-New-Journey-to-usher-in-Chinese-festival/ (accessed 3 January 2015).

14 The term 'meme' was coined by Richard Dawkins in his book *The Selfish Gene* (1976/2006) to refer to small cultural units of transmission, analogous to genes, which are spread by copying or imitation. Like genes, memes undergo variation, selection and retention. At any given moment, many memes are competing for the attention of hosts. However, only memes suited to their socio-cultural environment will spread successfully; the others will become extinct. Memes can be ideas, symbols or practices formed in diverse incarnations, such as a melodies, catchphrases, fashion, or architectural styles. While some memes are global, others are more culture-specific, shaping collective actions and mindsets (Lankshear and Knobel, 2007).

15 According to a news report, several angry users took it to the next level, creating T-shirts with slogans on both the front and the back. The white shirts, selling at RM20 each, aimed to remind the government to tackle crime rather than cover up the facts and issue propaganda that JB is a safe place. The front of the T-shirt read, 'Art doesn't damage a city's image' while the back said, 'Crime does'.

References

Anheier, H.K. and Isar, Y.R. (eds) (2008). *Cultures and Globalization: The Cultural Economy*. London: Sage.

Azzam, A.M. (2009). Why creativity now? A conversation with Sir Ken Robinson. *Educational Leadership*, 67(1): 22–26.

Bruns, A. (2008). *Blogs, Wikipedia, Second Life, and beyond: From Production to Produsage*. New York: Peter Lang.

Carnevale, F. and Kelsey, J. (2007). Art of the possible: Fulvia Carnevale and John Kelsey in conversation with Jacques Rancière. *Artforum International*, 45(7): 256–267.

Cherbo, J.M. and Wyszomirski, M.J. (eds) (2000). *The Public Life of the Arts in America*. New Brunswick, NJ: Rutgers University Press.

Craik, J., McAllister, L. and Davis, G. (2003). Paradoxes and contradictions in government approaches to contemporary cultural policy: an Australian perspective. *International Journal of Cultural Policy*, 9(1): 17–33.

Dawkins, R. (1976/2006). *The Selfish Gene*. Oxford: Oxford University Press.

de Certeau, M. (1984). *The Practice of Everyday Life*. Berkeley: University of California Press.

Deleuze, G. (1991). *Bergsonism*. Trans. Hugh Tomlinson and Barbara Habberjam. London: Continuum.

Ensminger, D.A. (2011). *Visual Vitriol: The Street Art and Subcultures of the Punk and Hardcore*. Jackson: University Press of Mississippi.

Florida, R. (2002). *The Rise of the Creative Class: And How It's transforming Work, Leisure, Community and Everyday Life*. New York: Perseus Book Group.

Freire, P. (1970/1993). *Pedagogy of the Oppressed*. New York: Continuum.

Gibson, L. (2004). *Cultural Planning and the Creative Tropical City*. Darwin: Charles Darwin University.

Hebdige, D. (1979). *Subculture: The Meaning of Style*. London: Methuen.

Holden, J. (2006). *Cultural Value and the Crisis of Legitimacy: Why Culture Needs a Democratic Mandate*. London: Demos.

Hon, C. (2013) Johor mural cut-outs being plastered in KL too. *The Star*, 21 November, www.thestar.com.my/News/Nation/2013/11/21/Johor-mural-cutouts-being-plastered-in-KL-too/ (accessed 10 March 2015).

Hubbert, J. 2010. Spectacular productions: community and commodity in the Beijing Olympics. *City and Society*, 22(1): 119–142.

Jenkins, H. (2006). *Convergence Culture: Where Old and New Media Collide*. New York: New York University Press.

Kubo, A.E. (2013) Malaysian authorities whitewash street artists lego mural. *The Diplomat*, 18 November, http://thediplomat.com/2013/11/malaysian-authorities-whitewash-street-artists-lego-mural/ (accessed 16 January 2015).

Landry, C. and Bianchini, F. (1995). *The Creative City*. London: Demos.

Lankshear, C. and Knobel, M. (2007). Sampling 'the new' in new literacies. In C. Lankshear and M. Knobel (eds), *A New Literacies Sampler*. New York: Peter Lang.

Leadbeater, C. (2008). *We-Think: Mass Innovation Not Mass Production: The Power of Mass Creativity*. London: Profile Books.

Looi, S-C. (2013). To Penang's chagrin, Lithuanian makes art out of unfilled George Town pothole. *Malaysian Insider*, 16 December, www.themalaysianinsider.com/malaysia/article/to-penangs-chagrin-lithuanian-makes-art-out-of-unfilled-george-town-pothole #sthash.UP9OblHw.dpuf (accessed 10 July 2015).

Lovink, G. (2002). *Dark Fiber: Tracking Critical Internet Culture*. Cambridge, MA: Massachusetts Institute of Technology.

Luers, W. (2007). Cinema without show business: a poetics of vlogging. *Post Identity*, 5(1), http://quod.lib.umich.edu/p/postid/pid9999.0005.105/--cinema-without-show-business-a-poetics-of-vlogging?rgn=main;view=fulltext (accessed 17 May 2015).

Pratt, A.C. (2008). Locating the cultural economy. In H.K. Anheier and Y.R. Isar, *Cultures and Globalization: The Cultural Economy*. London: Sage.

Rahim, S.A. and Pawanteh, L. (2010). The local content industry and cultural identity in Malaysia. *Journal of Media and Communication Studies*, 2(10): 215–220.

Rancière, J. (2004). Who is the subject of *The Rights of Man*? *South Atlantic Quarterly*, 103(2): 297–310.

Roberts, D. (2003). Towards a genealogy and typology of spectacle: some comments on Debord. *Thesis Eleven*, 75(1): 54–68.

Roslani, A. (2013) Ernest Zacharevic's controversial Lego Thief mural in Johor. *Venusbuzz*, 12 November, www.venusbuzz.com/archives/58176/ernest-zacharevics-controversial-lego-thief-mural-johor/ (accessed 27 April 2015).

Schacter, R. (2014). *Ornament and Order: Graffiti, Street Art and the Parergon*. Aldershot: Ashgate.

Soong, P. (2013) Remove crimes, not the graffiti. *Sin Chew Daily*, 13 November, www.mysinchew.com/node/93728 (accessed 5 August 2015).

Woon, L. (2013) JB's 'woman, mugger (and police)' mural removed. *Free Malaysia Today*, 13 November, www.freemalaysiatoday.com/category/nation/2013/11/13/jb-lego-mural-removed/ (accessed 12 May 2015).

10 Global knowledge and local practices

Reinventing cultural policy in Busan, South Korea

Se Hoon Park

Urban knowledge as global–local interplay

Today, knowledge about cities is produced and circulated on a global scale. In a competitive economic environment, urban policy-makers are hard pressed to learn the most updated urban theories and 'best practices' from around the world and quickly adopt, convert and adjust these into their local contexts to solve local problems. According to recent literature, cities are 'assembling' and 'worlding' by this global–local interplay of knowledge production (Roy and Ong 2011; McCann and Ward, 2011; MaCann, Roy and Ward, 2013). The process of knowledge production and consumption is beyond simple policy transfer. Rather, it indicates that cities can evolve based on knowledge and policy-making which are locally produced and globally relational.

Perhaps, for a city like Busan, the second-largest city in South Korea, troubled with population loss and economic decline, global knowledge of new urban theories and best practices was expected to provide a way out of the dead-end of urban development. In the past twenty years, Busan has been an arena of conflict and competition between traditional developmentalist ideology and emerging cultural and/or creative city discourse. While the former was a deep-rooted practice based on the city's own experience of modernization and industrialization, the latter was relatively new and built on a concept adopted from Western urban theories and practices. Of course, there is no clearly marked battle line between these two policy stances. Instead, they have often intermingled, influenced and transformed each other.

Generally speaking, Busan's developmental strategies have focused on infrastructure and industrial development. Despite the rise of a new cultural economy and the success of the Busan International Film Festival (BIFF), the city considered only a couple of development projects as its growth engines. In fact, developmentalism has been a dominating characteristic in local politics in Korea since the introduction of the local autonomy system in 1995 (Cho, 2003). Large-scale development projects in Korean cities are mostly linked to the national government's subsidy programmes, which aim to promote balanced national development. Thus, it is common for local governments to compete against each other to secure national government funds. This competition has become even more fierce since cities started to face the intensified neoliberal environment in the 2000s (Choi, 2012).

The adoption and transformation of culture as an urban policy in Korea can be discussed in this developmentalist policy context. In some ways, the notion of culture was translated into developmentalist language, and soon functioned as a tool for development projects. Or cultural practices by local actors such as artists and residents challenged mainstream conceptualizations of culture and created a new cultural vision of the city. The notion of a cultural city – or creative city – as a model has been imported, contested and reshaped by this global–local interplay of knowledge production.

This chapter will deal with these contested policy discourses in the formation of the cultural vision for Busan with special emphasis on two critical cultural projects and their impact on urban knowledge: the BIFF and the Totatoga Project. While the former is a typical large-scale, top-down, tourist-targeted project, the latter is a small-budget, bottom-up, community-oriented one. In these cultural projects, the developmentalist and cultural and/or creative city discourses have contested, and become integrated with, each other and, as a result, reinvented a cultural vision of the city. Following the exploration of the cultural policies, I will examine how the concept of the cultural/creative city is adopted and transformed in the developmentalist policy tradition, and how it was countered and reinvented by local actors in the context of Busan.

Culture as a tool for development: the Busan International Film Festival and its urban impact

Unexpected success of the BIFF

'Big and strong Busan.' This phrase was offered as the city vision by Huh Nam Shik, former mayor of Busan, in his third-term inauguration speech of 2010. He explained,

> Busan should be big enough to be on a par with other global cities . . . As the centre of the southeastern region of the nation, and a gateway linking the Pacific Ocean to Eurasia, Busan should become one of the world's top ten city-regions.
> (*Buvi News*, 11 September 2010)

However, the reality of Busan is somewhat different from his ambitious vision. Since the early 1990s, the city has been troubled with population loss and industrial decline. The population in Busan reached a peak of 3.9 million in 1995, but by 2013 it had decreased to 3.6 million. The number of businesses and jobs in the city has also been decreasing since the 1990s, as Busan has failed to advance its industrial structure. The elderly population ratio was 14 per cent in 2014, the highest among Korea's large cities.

Despite all of these figures indicating the city's shrinkage, Busan's urban strategies have remained strikingly developmental. The city has launched a number of iconic, large-scale development projects over the past fifteen years. These include: the Busan Jinhae Free Economic Zone, a mega-sized (104-square-kilometre) industrial complex development; the Centum City, a residential and commercial town development; the Munhyeon Innovation City, a state-sponsored urban development to promote financial industries; and the North Port Redevelopment Project, a multi-use commercial development in the former port area. These projects were effective tools for attracting national government funds for the cash-strapped local government.

The introduction of the local autonomy system in 1995 brought significant changes to the policy environment of local governments.[1] Since then, the concept of 'urban entrepreneurialism' (Harvey, 1989; Jessop and Sum, 2000), emphasizing the role of city government as a business actor, has gained substantial meaning in Korea. Newly elected mayors and governors have competitively pursued development projects and strategies to boost their cities' economies and images. Culture has been easily incorporated into this process. Hundreds of festivals and sports events have been launched, and cultural assets developed as tourist destinations.

The BIFF was one of these initiatives. When the new mayor and a group of film professionals in Busan began discussing the possibility of hosting an international film festival, few expected the event to be as successful as it has become. Busan did not have the budget, experts or experience to hold such an international event. Given that all the resources and infrastructure related to the film industry were concentrated in Seoul, such an event seemed nothing more than an empty mayoral election campaign pledge. Ironically, some now claim that the BIFF has proved such a success because it was held in Busan rather than Seoul (Kim, 2013). Although the capital obviously had the infrastructure that the event needed, it also had many different interest groups that would have made it difficult to build effective governance for the festival. By contrast, Busan had no vested interest groups involved in the film industry, so the city was well positioned for film professionals to take the initiative and focus on the event itself with no need to worry about local political interference.

The first BIFF was an unexpected success. A total of 170 films from 27 countries were screened, attracting more than 180,000 visitors to Busan. The US$2.04 million budget was raised by the city government and corporations (see Table 10.1). After the third BIFF in 1998, the festival secured stable status for further development. Despite the extremely harsh fiscal environment following the Asian financial crisis, the numbers of screened films and visitors both grew. Since then, the BIFF has consolidated its position as the most renowned film festival in Asia, while many rival film festivals in Korea have faltered and disappeared (Lee, 2007).

A couple of factors are generally thought to have contributed to the success of the BIFF (Kim, 2013). First, the unwavering support of Mayor Mun Jeong Su has been crucial since he came into office. He provided the initial financial and administrative support and enabled the city's film professionals to launch the event without the interference of administrative and political interests. Second,

Table 10.1 Key numbers of the BIFF in the first three years, 1996–1998

	1st BIFF	2nd BIFF	3rd BIFF
	13–21 September 1996	10–18 October 1997	24 September– 1 October 1998
Number of screened films (from number of countries)	170 (27)	163 (33)	211 (41)
Number of invited guests	224	450	659
Budget (US$ million)	2.04	2.30	2.32
Number of visitors	184,071	170,206	192,547
Total revenue (US$ million)	0.44	0.53	0.70

Source: Lee, 2007.

Busan's film professionals played a pivotal role in launching the festival. In the early 1990s, the idea for the BIFF came from a group of young cultural activists involved in film-making; this group became the core of the event's implementation. In particular, Kim Dong Ho, the chairperson of the BIFF Steering Committee and a former vice-minister in the Ministry of Culture, played a critical role. His extensive network of connections and personal commitment contributed greatly to gaining cooperation from both the national government and overseas film experts.

Towards the Cine Culture City

After the successful launch of the BIFF, the festival soon became a valued cultural asset for the city. Busan has long pursued new industrial strategies to replace declining traditional urban industries with financial and logistics industries. Given the weak cultural tradition and assets in the city, culture could not be seriously considered as one of its new growth engines. However, powered by the success of the BIFF, Busan quickly repositioned itself and sought an alternative path of development as a cultural city.

Since the inauguration of the new mayor in 1999, culture has been actively incorporated into the city's official development strategies. For example, a report, *Promotion Strategies of the Film Industry in Busan*, released by the city government in 2000, declared the new city vision of becoming 'the Hub City of the Film Industry in Asia' (BMG, 2000). It suggested the strategy of building a communication and film-making hub for the Asian film industry in Busan. Another report, *Busan Cultural Vision 21: Busan's Cultural Vision and Strategies in the 21st Century* (BMG, 2000), went beyond promotion of the film industry and provided comprehensive cultural strategies for urban development. The report set up Busan's vision of becoming the 'New Millennium Cultural Capital' and suggested seven strategies and twenty-one projects to achieve this vision.

The year 2004 was highly significant in Busan's journey to becoming a cultural city. As part of the national cultural policies to promote local culture as a new

Table 10.2 Key strategies of the Cine Culture City

Categories	Contents
Building film-related facilities and organizations	Busan Cinema Centre, Busan Cultural Content Complex, Cinematheque Busan, AZworks, Busan Film Experience Museum
Holding events and fairs	Busan International Film Commission and Industry Showcase, Asia Film Market, Asia Film Academy, Asia Cinema Fund, Asia Film Committee Net
Relocating film-related government agencies to Busan	Korean Film Council, Korea Media Rating Board, Game Rating and Administration Committee

Source: Busan Metropolitan Government, 2005.

growth engine, the Culture and Tourism Ministry designated Busan as the 'Cine Culture City'. This designation meant that, compared to other cities with similar ambitions, the national government acknowledged Busan's pre-eminent role in the film industry and film festival domain. Thus, the city secured stable financial support from the national government in pursuit of becoming the Cine Culture City. The national government and the Busan Metropolitan Government jointly launched new projects to enhance the city's position as the Cine Culture City.

According to the plan endorsed by the national government (BMG, 2005), the strategies for the Cine Culture City were organized into three areas. The first was to develop the BIFF by providing it with supporting infrastructure, such as the Busan Cinema Centre and the Busan Cultural Content Complex. The second was to enhance the city's position as a film-oriented cultural city by relocating public agencies to Busan from the Seoul metropolitan area, which formed part of the national government's Balanced Regional Development Policy. The third strategy was to boost the film-making industries and related industries in Busan (see Table 10.2).

The first and second strategies were carried out with few problems because the BIFF was already on track and the public agencies were relocated according to the plan of the national government. However, the third strategy, which was the most highly anticipated in terms of boosting the local economy, failed to produce any tangible results. In a situation where the foundation of film-related industries was weak, the BIFF's impact on those industries and other economic sectors in the city proved limited, even though it attracted a large number of visitors during the festival period itself.

The cultural city under developmentalism

The notion of the cultural city, when it was first introduced to Busan in the mid-1990s, was nothing more than another area of economic development. Cultural city policy often narrowed down to various construction projects to provide culture-related facilities, such as a museum, convention hall, theme park, opera house and so on.[2] In this approach, the idea of culture as a way of life, community participation and art promotion was almost entirely unrecognized. In this context, by taking advantage of the success of the BIFF, the urban cultural policy of Busan began to focus on infrastructure development, among many other issues. Film-related facilities that have been built in the city include the Busan Cinema Centre (a main BIFF venue), the Busan Cultural Content Complex (an institute for the development of cultural content in Busan), Cinematheque Busan (an art movie theatre) and AZworks (a film processing and editing facility).

In particular, the construction of the Busan Cinema Centre (BCC), which finally opened in 2011, had been a key issue since the Cine Culture City was first conceived. Because the BIFF did not have its own facility, the organizing committee had to rent commercial theatres in the city for the duration of the festival. This caused several problems, including difficulties in fixing the festival schedule. The controversy over the location of the BCC showed how the facility was conceived in the urban cultural policies in Busan. The issue with the construction of the BCC was not the role the facility would play in the BIFF and Busan's film industry in general, but its funding, location and symbolic meaning as a city landmark. At first, film professionals and the BIFF organizers favoured a coastal location, which could enhance the meaning and atmosphere of the festival, as expressed in the slogan 'Come to the Ocean of Film'. However, in 2004, the city government decided to build the BCC at Centum City, a newly developed upmarket area (see Figure 10.1). The city government claimed that the area was chosen because it already benefited from film-related facilities, but the real reason was a desire to

Figure 10.1 The Busan Cinema Centre

Source: *Seoul Economy Daily*, 14 October 2014, authorized for reuse.

expedite the development of the new town and promote the area's image by locating a landmark facility there (Kim, 2009). In addition, voices from the film-making circle, focusing on the BCC's role in Busan's film industry, were largely ignored in the decision-making process. As a result, the issues of how best to use the facility during the non-festival period and who pays the operating costs remain unsolved.

Under the influence of the national policy of the Cine Culture City, the Busan Metropolitan Government released a new comprehensive cultural plan entitled *Busan Cultural Vision 2020* in 2007 (BMG, 2007). The plan contained extensive policy items but clearly featured infrastructure development, especially in relation to film-related facilities (Cha, 2014). In line with the city government's strategy, an astronomical budget was allocated to construct museums, art galleries, opera houses and film-related facilities. However, the plan lacked community-level cultural strategies and facilities. Small-scale cultural facilities such as libraries and cultural centers were burdened with budget constraints and were too few in number to meet local demand. In addition, the plan did not offer any strategies for providing artists' spaces or cultural spaces at the community level, concerns that were already at the forefront of cultural policies in other Korean cities.

In short, the success of the BIFF offered a great opportunity to a city that has been looking for an alternative development path. However, as the urban cultural policy in Busan has focused too much on the festival itself and related projects, other aspects of culture, particularly community-level cultural strategies, have been largely ignored. The city budget has been lopsidedly allocated to making the Cine Culture City, leaving few resources for other areas of cultural policy.

Creative city, local practice and the formation of new cultural policy

Creative city discourse and policy-making in Busan

The notion of the creative city arrived in Busan in the mid-2000s, first as a topic for academic discussion and later as a concept for policy implementation. The works of Charles Landry (2000) and Richard Florida (2002) were translated into Korean in 2005 and 2002, respectively. Urban scholars in Busan started to pay attention to their books and discuss their implications for Busan's future. A critical moment came in 2007 when Landry visited Busan to present a keynote speech to a seminar organized by Busan National University. During a visit to Mayor Heo Nam Sik, Landry reportedly said, 'Instead of constructing roads, invest in young people and encourage them to launch start-ups' (*Busan Daily*, 24 December 2007).

The discourse of the creative city resonated throughout academic and policy circles in Busan. As Landry mentioned, in Busan the concept was understood as the new paradigm of urban development focusing on culture-driven and people-oriented strategies, differentiated from the previous strategies that focused on manufacturing industries and real estate development. Some progressive academics and journalists in Busan quickly adopted the notion as the antithesis of the conventional developmentalist approach.[3] Armed with the new concept, articles and policy reports commonly pointed out that Busan should depart from its previous developmentalist inertia and adopt a creative city concept which emphasized cultural creativity and community-based neighbourhood re-vitalization (Oh et al., 2011). Researchers and activists/artists in Busan launched the 'Cultural City Forum' in 2010 with a view to creating a platform to learn creative city discourses and discuss ways to transform the city into a creative city (*Kukje Daily*, 19 February 2010). Emphasizing the significance of the creative city concept, one local newspaper pointed out that 'We should change our mindset from a hardware oriented one to software oriented. We should build a creative network to discuss the city's strength and weakness' (*Kukje Daily*, 9 January 2009).

The notion of the creative city rapidly penetrated civil society and policy circles largely due to its global character. In circumstances in which many local govern-ments, including Seoul, had already adopted the concept as a development model, officials in Busan tried to jump to the forefront of the new trend. At first, since the notion was rather abstract, it seemed to have no specific meaning in actual policy practices. However, once the term 'creative city' was institutionalized in organi-zational structures in 2010, a specific connotation was immediately created at the policy level. Interestingly, the Creative City Executive Office in Busan was launched in 2010 as an agency in charge of urban regeneration, urban design and landscape, *not* cultural policies (press release from the Busan Metropolitan Government, 3 March 2010). Regenerating the distressed neighbourhoods in the city's hilly areas, the so-called *Sanbokdoro*, has long been a major headache for Busan. Against this backdrop, the notion of the creative city was applied as a way of humanizing urban regeneration strategies, placing much more emphasis on building community and preserving the existing environment and local culture. Establishing the Creative City Office was broadly in line with what academics and journalists were suggesting because the newly adopted urban regeneration policies provided an alternative development path to conventional clearance and redevelopment strategies.

The city government did not adopt the new approach so swiftly merely because it viewed it as a good concept. Rather, it is fair to say that it did not have many alternatives, given a sluggish real estate market. With a prolonged economic downturn since 2007, the conventional redevelopment strategies based on capital gain created by real estate development were clearly redundant, and the city government was pressed to find novel solutions for Busan's dilapidated areas. In addition, the national government and Seoul's metropolitan government alike have tried to devise new urban regeneration strategies based on community and cultural assets ever since the early 2000s. Busan's move reflected these nationwide urban policy transformations. Until 2010, however, the creative city discourse mostly remained within the urban regeneration policy domain; it did not spread into the area of cultural policy.

The Totatoga Project: local innovation of the creative city

In this area of urban cultural policy, a new opportunity for community-oriented and culture-based approaches came with an innovative artists' residency programme named Totatoga in 2009. The project was launched without much fanfare from either the city government or civil society, but it became a huge success, transforming the whole landscape of cultural policies in Busan.

In 2009, the Culture and Art Division of the Busan Metropolitan Government was looking for an appropriate cultural project that could benefit from the remainder of the annual budget earmarked for cultural purposes (approximately US$300,000). A veteran cultural planner who worked for the Busan Cultural Foundation and had connections with an extensive network of local artists, suggested a new type of artists' residency programme in the central district that has been plagued by declining population and failing businesses since the 1990s. After approving the project, the city government helped a group of selected artists to set up studios in vacant office space for a three-year period. In return, the artists were required to engage in community activities, such as running education programmes and holding cultural festivals geared towards the local citizens. After three years of government support the artists were required to be self-supporting (although they could remain in their workspaces), and the government would then select new artists for the next three-year term.

Crucially, Totatoga did not seek to increase economic value or bring instant development to the declining central district. Detaching itself from the city's developmentalist policy tradition, it focused instead on promoting the intangible social and cultural values of the district. The Totatoga Project aims to *minimize* physical renovation, unlike many other – more conventional – cultural strategies in Busan. The man who planned the project, Mr Cha, was well aware of the potential negative impact of physical renovation, that is, the fact that arts and culture programmes often led to rapid gentrification. For this reason, he placed an emphasis on artists' engagement in local society rather than physical improvement (Cha, 2014).

Hence there were few changes in the physical appearance of the neighborhood, yet the project still had an impressive social and cultural impact on the district. First, local artists, regardless of whether they had been selected for government support, started to open studios and linger in the area with their colleagues. They were committed to and skilled at bringing people together through various activities, such as educational projects and street festivals. As a result of these events and projects, the streets are regaining their former vitality (see Figure 10.2). In addition, thanks to increased awareness of the local culture and history of central Busan, residents have started to re-evaluate the historical and cultural value of the district. Increasingly, people are viewing it not as a shabby downtown precinct but as an important historic/cultural zone.

As the Totatoga Project began to generate unexpectedly positive results with a small budget, it soon attracted nationwide public attention as an alternative

Figure 10.2 Scene from the annual Totatoga Festival
Source: Totatoga homepage (www.tttg.kr), authorized for reuse.

strategy for urban regeneration. Since the 2000s, many Korean local governments have come up with culture-led regeneration policies at various scales, but mostly focusing on developing physical facilities, such as art centres and museums. Although these have all demanded significant budgets, they have often failed to bring the expected results in terms of urban regeneration. Hence, the 'cost-effectiveness' of the Totatoga Project attracted the attention of a number of government officials, who were soon heralding it as an ideal model to mobilize artists for urban revitalization. The local and national press touted it as the model of a new urban regeneration strategy. Its focus on the community's cultural promotion rather than on physical improvements, as well as its piecemeal approach with a small budget for urban revitalization, was well appreciated. Other city and national government officials, as well as overseas scholars, have visited the district to learn the principles and implementation processes of the project (Kim, 2013).

In its inception stage, Totatoga was not a major concern of the city government. As mentioned above, Busan's cultural policy was focused on boosting the film festival and providing related infrastructure. With such a small budget allocated to the project management team, the city government remained largely uninterested in what happened thereafter. However, given the unexpected attention from national and other local governments after the project's success, the city government began to appreciate its value as a model of urban cultural policies. Consequently, it decided to increase its support for Totatoga from 2013 onwards, and more artists have now set up studios in the district as a result.

Emerging 'soft power' and reinventing the cultural policy

The Totatoga Project had a large impact on cultural policies in Busan. Officials and cultural planners started to understand that small-budget, community-oriented strategies can produce impressive results not only in promoting citizens' cultural participation but also in revitalizing troubled communities. The city government began to appreciate the value of community-oriented culture, which had been marginalized in Busan's cultural policies, and introduced this value into its mainstream policies. In addition, many other ward offices in Busan tried to copy the Totatoga Project to produce a similar impact.

Busan's latest cultural plan, released in March 2013 and entitled *Happy and Shared Cultural City through Enhancing Soft Power*, illustrated the recent transformation of cultural policies in the city. The plan epitomized a paradigm shift in cultural policies from infrastructure-oriented to community-initiated, and from government-controlled to artists- and residents-initiated. The plan suggested three policy agendas: laying the groundwork for the cultural city; increasing citizens' cultural participation; and supporting artists' working environments. Under these policy agendas, the plan identified various supporting measures for community-level cultural activities. Examples included nurturing civil cultural communities, social inclusion through culture, expanding opportunities for cultural education, developing local cultural content, and creating jobs for artists. The plan has not erased all of the city's developmentalist cultural policies, but it seems that the city government is starting to appreciate the other aspect of urban cultural policies.

The plan also provides a strategy to expand the Totatoga model throughout the rest of the city by creating five more artists' spaces in each corner of Busan. The policy intends for these places to be centres of cultural activity in these communities as well as tourist destinations through the hosting of colourful festivals and other events. For instance, the Gamman Creative Community Project, following the Totatoga model, is aiming for urban revitalization through art and cultural activities in the Gamman-dong area, one of the most deprived sectors of old downtown Busan. Using a former elementary school as its base, it provides space for cultural activities and education for both artists and citizens. The Busan Cultural Foundation, the city's central organization for cultural planning, was relocated to this space in order to maximize the policy effect.

It is difficult to claim that the Totatoga Project alone brought about this paradigm shift. It was only a small part of the city's cultural policy, and it was a coincidental product of the combined efforts of the cultural planner and a group of committed artists. As mentioned above, the creative city discourse was circulated and adopted as an alternative to the conventional developmentalist ideology in Busan. Powered by its globalness – supported by internationally renowned scholars such as Landry, Florida and Sasaki Masayuki – the concept spread into academic and policy circles with ease, although it did face some opposition from existing interests and policy stances. Meanwhile, the local practice of the Totatoga Project, showcasing the significance of alternative cultural practices, emerged as vivid evidence of a localized version of the creative city. As the project gained recognition from policy-makers nationwide, 'Totatoga as a model' became sufficiently powerful to transform the entire landscape of urban cultural policy in Busan. Under this combined influence of global knowledge and local practice, the soft power plan came into existence. A city official in Busan's cultural division echoed this point by saying, 'This is quite an impressive change. I think the Totatoga Project had an influence [on the policy shift]. As Totatoga gained attention nationwide, community-oriented cultural practices could come to the fore of mainstream cultural policies in Busan' (interviewed 5 December 2013).

Conclusion

This chapter has described how the notion of the cultural/creative city arrived in Busan and how the concept, together with local practices, reinvented the city's urban cultural policy which had long been rooted in a developmentalist tradition. The mobile urban knowledge of the cultural/creative city has been practised in several ways, and reinterpreted in local policy-making processes.

Urban cultural policy, like other policy fields, can be an arena where different social and political ideologies and interests are contested. In Korea, with urban development policies tightly linked to the national government's subsidy politics, the cultural city discourses are easily distorted to serve existing policy interests and the inertia of local developmentalism. Busan City Government drove the ambitious plan for the Cine Culture City, based on the successful launch of the BIFF and adopted the cultural city concept in an existing developmentalist policy framework, placing the policy emphasis on a couple of infrastructure development projects. In this framework, the other side of culture – the residents' cultural practices and needs in daily life – was largely sidelined.

The creative city discourse could have many different versions in its policy implementation in local context from providing upmarket commercial development to boosting cultural industries. In Busan the discourse coincidentally produced an innovative consequence. First, the notion of the creative city was adopted as an alternative to the conventional developmentalist ideology and soon gained substance in the form of community-oriented cultural strategies in the wake of the successful operation of the Totatoga Project. As a result, global knowledge about the creative city powered by local practice of Totatoga reshaped and reinvented urban cultural policy in Busan.

The recent policy change does not mean that Busan's cultural policies are totally free from the developmentalist tradition. In fact, many development projects are still high on the agenda for the city. The new cultural policies, however, are replete with such phrases as 'cultural democracy', 'community space', 'building an ecosystem of production and consumption of culture' and 'citizen-oriented approaches'. This signifies that the city government understands the various aspects of culture and the people's need for culture, which is a solid starting point for the city's own version of the cultural city.

Notes

1 The local autonomy system in South Korea dates back to 1949, when the Local Autonomy Law was first enacted. However, the law was suspended in 1961 under the country's military regime, and resumed only after 1988. The local election of mayors and governors resumed in 1995, signalling the advent of an era of local government. Under the neoliberal policy environment after the 1990s, competition among local governments for national government funding and private capital intensified (Jeong, 2015).
2 Representative was the city's vision plan, *Dynamic Busan 2020 Road Map*, published in 2001. This plan offered the cultural city project as one of seven major projects for Busan's future. It comprised eleven cultural facilities construction projects, with no regard of local and community culture or residents' cultural participation.
3 The discourse on the creative city has many different and sometimes conflicting connotations in urban policies. Basically, the argument stresses the role of creative classes such as knowledge workers and artists in urban development. At a policy level, however, the discourse is often translated into policies that provide upmarket residential facilities and/or organize cultural events to attract the creative classes and artists. The discourse itself does not have any fixed policy implications, and thus can produce many variations depending on local context.

References

Busan Metropolitan Government (BMG) (2000) *Busan Gwangyeoksi Yeongsang San-eob Baljeon Jeonryak* [Promotion Strategies of the Film Industry in Busan], Busan: Busan Metropolitan Government.

Busan Metropolitan Government (BMG) (2000) *Busan Munwha Bijeon 21* [Busan Cultural Vision 21], Busan: Busan Metropolitan Government.

Busan Metropolitan Government (BMG) (2001) *Dynamic Busan 2020 Road Map*, Busan: Busan Metropolitan Government.

Busan Metropolitan Government (BMG) (2005) *Busan Yeongsang Munwha Dosi Yukseong-eul Uihan Jonghab Kyewhek* [The Comprehensive Plan for Making the Cine Culture City Busan], Busan: Busan Metropolitan Government.

Busan Metropolitan Government (BMG) (2007) *Busan Munwha Bijeon 2020* [Busan Cultural Vision 2020], Busan: Busan Metropolitan Government.

Busan Metropolitan Government (BMG) (2013) *Hamkeheaseo Hengbokhan Munwhadosi* [Shared Cultural City by Enhancing Soft Power], Busan: Busan Metropolitan Government.

Cha, J.G. (2014) 'Busansi toshi munwha jeongchek-eui seonggwa-wa gwaje' [The achievements and tasks of the urban cultural policy in Busan], in S.H. Park et al., *Changjo Dosiruel Neon-eo-seo* [Beyond Creative Cities], Kyeonggi: Nanam.

Cho, Myeongrae (2003) 'Hanguk gaebalju-eui-eui yeoksawa hyeunjuso' [History and current status of developmentalism in Korea], *Whangyeongkwa Sengmyeong* [Environment and Life], 37: 31–53.

Choi, Byung-Doo (2012) 'Developmental neoliberalism and hybridity of the urban policy of South Korea', in B.G Park, R. Child Hill and A. Saito (eds), *Locating Neoliberalism in East Asia: Neoliberalizing Spaces in Developmental States*, West Sussex: Wiley-Blackwell.

Florida, R. (2002) *The Rise of the Creative Class*, New York: Basic Books.

Harvey, D. (1989) 'From managerialism to entrepreneurialism: the transformation in urban governance in late capitalism', *Geografiska Annaler, Series B: Human Geography*, 71(1): 3–17.

Jeong, I.S. (2015) *Hanguk Jibang Jachiron* [Local Autonomy in Korea], Seoul: Daeyoung Co.

Jessop, B. and Sum, N.L. (2000) 'An entrepreneurial city in action: Hong Kong's emerging strategies in and for (inter-)urban competition', *Urban Studies*, 37(12): 2287–2313.

Kim, H.G. (2013) 'Totatoga Ichasaup Sunhang' [The Totatoga project enters the second phase smoothly], *Kukje Daily*, 28 August.

Kim, H.I. (2009) *Busan Kukje Yeongwhaje* [Busan International Film Festival], Seoul: Jayeon-gwa Inmun.

Kim, J.Y. (2013) 'Busan yeongsang munwha dosi hyeongsong-e kwanhan yeongu' [A study on making Cine Culture City Busan], unpublished dissertation, Busan National University.

Landry, C. (2000) *The Creative City: A Toolkit for Urban Innovators*, London: Comedia.

Lee, J.H. (2007) 'Busan yeongsang munwha dosi: seonggwa, gwaje, dae-an' (Busan Cine Culture City: achievements, tasks, and alternatives], *Jiyeok Sahui Yeongu* [Studies on Regional Society], 15(1): 29–41.

McCann, E. and Ward, K. (eds) (2011) *Mobile Urbanism: Cities and Policymaking in the Global Age*, Minneapolis: University of Minnesota Press.

McCann, E., Roy, A. and Ward, K. (2013) 'Urban pulse: assembling/worlding cities', *Urban Geography*, 34(5): 581–589.

Oh, Jae Hwan et al. (2011) *Changjo dosi Busan: jeonryakkwa kwaje* [Creative City Busan: strategies and tasks], Busan: Busan Development Institute.

Oh, S.J. (2012) 'Chukje Munwhaeo Ilsangwha' [Making festival and culture everyday routines], *Kukje Daily*, 18 March.

Roy, A. and Ong, A. (eds) (2011) *Worlding Cities: Asian Experiments and the Art of Being Global*, West Sussex: Blackwell.

11 'Creative class' subversions

Art spaces in Beijing and Berlin

Julie Ren

Hackneyed cliché

What is the purpose of studying creativity-driven urban policy, if it has been reduced to a 'hackneyed cliché of contemporary policy making' (Peck 2011: 41)? The ubiquity of variously named 'creative class', 'creative industry', and 'creative city' policies often reflects an inconsistent set of ideas, values, and even concrete tactics. Yet, rather than receding into the policy wastelands, it continues to gain traction. This chapter seeks to investigate some of the externalities of this creativity imperative, to examine how the ubiquity of creativity-led policies generates a financially and politically formidable form of creative capital. Among those standing to gain from this are artists able to trade on their creative capital in their place-making activities, thus appropriating and subverting 'creative class' ideas and reshaping the competitive urban landscape along the way.

Creative class theory is most often attributed to Florida (2002; 2005), whose aim is to offer a normative argument about urban development policy focused on knowledge-based economies. Positing that 'creativity has become the principal driving force in the growth and development of cities', he introduces the idea of the creative class (Florida 2005: 1). Creative class critics have taken issue with the theory's causal argument (Marcuse 2003), its failure to address equity (Krätke 2010; Peck 2005), and its conflation of professional categories, often resulting from an unclear definition of 'creative' (Reese et al. 2010; Markusen et al. 2008; Storper and Manville 2006; Rausch and Negrey 2006). These issues only begin to reflect the general academic scepticism about the utility of the concept (see, e.g., Shearmur 2007; Montgomery 2005; Glaeser 2005; Hall 2004; Musterd and Ostendorf 2004). One pair of scholars writes that 'if vague concepts are vaguely understood, then their meaning will always be in doubt. If there is no agreement on how to define and measure the creative class, there is little prospect that it will provide useful public policy guidance' (Reese and Sands 2008).

Despite the academic scepticism about the efficacy, normative implications and/or scientific cogency of creativity-led urban policy, policy-makers in cities around the world have latched on to the concept of 'creative class' spurring economic growth in urban development strategies. Recent volumes on the creative city in 'global' and 'peripheral' places (Mellander et al. 2013; Gibson 2012) only begin to document the proliferation of its influence around the world. The elevated influence of creativity renders it not only a 'cliché' but an urban imperative for economic development strategies. This creativity imperative has indeed empowered new actors in the realm of inter-urban competition (Peck 2005).

Lacking in conceptual coherence yet rich in influence, the creativity imperative lends itself to co-option by a diversity of interests and actors. These actors may extend well beyond the creative industries like IT or media that mayors' creativity policies may have intended to address. The newly empowered actors are able to appropriate the various creative class policies, norms, or ideas that are influential in the city for their own interests. These interests may have nothing to do with the economic development goals intended by the creativity imperative. This area of unforeseen impacts of appropriation and subversion remains relatively unexplored.

Therefore, rather than contributing to the extensive literature critiquing the concept or investigating its possible applications, this chapter assumes that, regardless of its efficacy, the ubiquity of the creative policy discourse has empowered new constellations of actors in the competitive urban arena through the valorization of creative capital. Among these new subjects are artists who are able to leverage creative for financial and political capital in their place-making activities. Learning about their strategies across different contexts can be a means to improve understanding of the mechanisms of appropriation and subversion, the unforeseen externalities of 'making cultural cities'. Through this focus, the significance of making cultural cities extends beyond the usual suspects, and presumed barriers to engage with comparative research, especially for Asian cities, begin to dissipate.

Approach

Investigating artists' place-making activities is a means to measure the tangible exchange value of creative capital. It underscores artists' various subversive strategies and delineates the spatial consequences of the creativity imperative. The artists' activities represent the changing constellations of agency shaping the urban landscape, reflecting how 'articulations of social relations', which do not have particular fixed meanings, are being renegotiated (Massey 1995: 119). These place-making activities consist of initiating and sustaining art spaces often in conflict with other interests, rendering them full of cultural meaning (Schneekloth and Shibley 1995). Indeed, these activities suggest that the 'power to claim' these urban spaces is being co-opted from policy-makers seeking to implement 'creative cities' by those who are effectually asserting alternative visions of creative spaces.[1]

Though Bourdieusian ideas of cultural capital (see Bourdieu 1983) are instructive in understanding how capital can take different forms, the creative capital of artists in the city is not just embodied, objectified or institutionalized. Rather, the value of creative capital can be gauged in its exchange value, as manifested in artists' various place-making strategies. Krätke (2012: 3) defines the 'creative capital of cities' as the 'ability of urban economic actors to produce

... innovations on the basis of relational assets that are socially produced within a city'. As will be evident, the creative capital of artists can be similarly defined in terms of their ability to enact their interests – in their place-making activities.

The examples presented below will define creative capital in terms of its exchange value in leveraging financial and political capital. Doing so, this analysis of the value of creative capital borrows from Schumpeterian ideas of 'exchange value' as social value-in-use (Schumpeter 1909). It adopts an understanding of the value of capital as something that is socially determined and encompasses a value-creation process. In Schumpeter's discussions of 'money', he differentiates between money price and commodities; whereas the price of the latter can be measured by the traditional supply-and-demand apparatus, the former is measured in its exchange value (Schumpeter 1939: 547). This malleable understanding of capital valuation establishes the foundation for understanding the utility of creative capital in the following examples. Creative capital is not like an object of art in its valuation, which is determined on the basis of a supply-and-demand market; the value of creative capital is determined by its exchange.

The examples cited in this chapter are sourced from a larger comparative study of artists' spaces in Beijing and Berlin involving site visits and interviews conducted in 2012.[2] Artists' spaces were defined as spaces of artistic production, so exhibition venues like museums and most commercial galleries were excluded. A semi-public component was also one of the selection criteria, eliminating spaces that served exclusively as artists' personal living and studio spaces. Hence the examples are largely artist-run spaces that do not have a commercial gallery structure. The primary source of revenue for running the space is not from selling art objects. The artists are not vendors of art, but employ a variety of funding strategies through mixed uses of their spaces, applications for public or project-based grants, direct resource transfers and negotiations for lowered rents and other costs. Indeed, artist-run spaces may have a greater need for inventive survival strategies.

Place-making

Enabling conditions and agential possibilities

The ubiquity of the creativity discourse creates an enabling condition, increasing the value of creative capital in which artists are able to trade on their place-making activities, and establishing the agential possibilities of being an artist in the city. To understand the place-making activities behind art spaces in Beijing and Berlin, it is important first to lay out the context of intra-urban competition for space and the awareness that artists have about their position in this struggle. This establishes both the need for trading in creative capital and the artists' awareness enabling them to take advantage of their situation, ultimately allowing for an interpretation of their activities as subversive.

The intra-urban competition is evidenced through the feeling artists have that they are under constant threat of losing their art spaces. They feel they are in perpetual competition with more financially powerful actors who threaten to displace them. This persistent threat is exacerbated by uncertain, often complicated relationships with property owners or landlords. For the art space Nali Nali (Where Where), located in Caochangdi, an urban village outside of Beijing's Fifth Ring Road, this relationship is interpreted as an entrenched, imbalanced power dynamic. One of the founders of the space describes this perception:

> China is a place where relationships between the landlord and the tenant are almost feudal. It's a system that continues a longstanding power dynamic where there's very little recourse for a tenant in terms of receiving proper services, or compensation, or challenging things. It's a very interesting thing to look at – how that dynamic, the lack of autonomy, the lack of control that the artists have over the spaces where they work, affects the development and changes for the art community. Because *many* art districts have been torn down for new developments, condominiums, and stuff because they serve the financial interests of the landlords, even though they break long-term agreements and leases in doing so … And it gives many of the art communities and spaces a tentative feel.
>
> (OBJ19)

These comments allude to the contested land-use issues in urban China. One of the main reasons why the governance of land-use in urban China is so contentious is because it serves as a key source of revenue for local governments (Hsing 2010; Wu 2011). Whereas the real estate ownership structures in Berlin are highly diverse (state, corporate, private, and cooperative ownership structures abound), in Beijing ownership contracts are limited in time, and the control resides ultimately with the local government.[3] Local governments have strong incentives to convert land use to maximize the most lucrative opportunity. Liu and Lin (2014: 119) argue that the system that drives these conversions is a result of the 1994 tax-sharing reform that burdened local governments on multiple fronts: the reform simultaneously decentralized responsibility while recentralizing tax revenue collection, and it also eliminated other sources of tax revenue that had been available to local governments. Land conveyance thus became their primary source of income. The conversion of land use is seen as a key problem of land use governance, because local governments tend to want to convert regardless of 'legal procedures and their responsibility for people's livelihood' (Liu, Fang, and Li 2014: 7). The impetus towards these changes to increase land use revenue regardless of legality is even more pronounced in peripheral areas (Ren and Sun 2012) such as Caochangdi, where infrastructure remains rudimentary and housing is primarily in the form of low-rise buildings.

Although the artists in Berlin benefit from more dependable contract-based relationships with their landlords, these contracts often include clauses allowing the owners to ask the artists to vacate on short notice. This again reinforces the feeling that the artists are in competition with more financially powerful renters, who could displace them at any time. Several art spaces in 'Kolonie Wedding', a cluster of small store-front spaces in Berlin's Wedding district, have these kinds of contracts. The landlord, DeGeWo, is a real estate corporation that is the largest residential property-holder in Berlin. The artists in Kolonie Wedding are the ground-floor tenants of apartment buildings, and the spaces may otherwise be used for commercial purposes. The founder of the art space OKK Raum29 comments on their relationship with the landlord:

> Well, the contract economically for us is very good, because of the low rental costs. But on the other hand, obviously, we have a clause in this contract, if there's somebody coming in or looking for the room and they can pay the *full* rent, the economic rent, which is more than twice the price we are paying now, a little bit more than twice, if somebody like this comes along, DeGeWo, this consortium, has the possibility to get you out in very short time. I'm not sure, but I think our minimum time to be out is within the month. So, two or three weeks before, you get notice that it's over.
>
> (OBL16)

In other words, the artists are able to rent the space for below-market price because of lack of interest. They are also aware, however, that demand for the space could change at any time.

Both examples of landlord–tenant relationships reflect the predominance of financial interests on the part of the landlords, and the resulting precarious position the artists inhabit. Art spaces seem, in both cases, to function for property-holders as stop-gaps before better, more lucrative renters can be found. The artists feel that their spaces are constantly under threat, meaning they feel the need to gain leverage in their relationships with the landlords.

Artists' awareness of their position vis-à-vis the creativity discourse as well as this inter-urban competition for space is explicit, and a necessary prerequisite towards understanding their behaviour as subversive. For instance, one of the cultural managers of the Platoon Kunsthalle in Berlin describes their longevity as a function of their awareness of the urban landscape, and the artists' assumed functions within it:

> If you give space to creatives, they make something amazing out of it. It's just that if they're instrumentalized just because of profit motivations from real estate people or even the city itself, then you can get lost. *But* Berlin is different because people are aware of it, and also the creatives are aware that even though they are against these processes, they are the ones that make it happen, you know.
>
> (OBL18)

In other words, artists are aware that creativity signifies profit for 'real estate people'. Although artists do not seek to participate in increasing property values, they know that urban development precepts assume that they perform that function. The awareness of others' assumptions about creativity directly influences their strategies in claiming and sustaining their art spaces, as evidenced in the following examples.

From creative to financial capital

As alluded to with regards to their function as transient tenants, artists are seen by real estate holders to be at the forefront of creativity-led property development. This can be an especially useful assumption for artists in their negotiation of favourable rental terms. Based in Berlin-Mitte, Platoon is part PR branding and consulting, connecting artists and designers with corporate clients, part art residency and performance or event space. Their building, which they call a *Kunsthalle* (art hall), consists of portable shipping containers. In 2012, they moved into their third location in Berlin's Mitte district. The space they need is essentially an empty lot with enough room for several of the shipping containers. Their cultural manager describes their negotiation approach:

> We create a cultural value for the space, which translates also into a real estate value, which, because it becomes an address in the head of people, it's not just an abandoned lot . . . Something happens there, and obviously the value goes up, everyone wants to go there. Everywhere where we were before, there is either a design hotel or something more in that direction. So, that's how we can create a deal with the owners where we basically add this value, pay a really minimum rent, just cover some costs and help to raise the profile of the lot really. Which is obviously not our aim; it's just a consequence of what we do.
>
> (OBL18)

So, Platoon makes a value proposition for a temporary rental contract at very favourable terms to use an empty lot for an art space. They are able to take advantage of the assumptions made about art spaces increasing property values in order to access spaces at very little cost. Over the years, these assumptions have proved justified as Platoon's residency has invariably led to the arrival of commercial ventures that are willing to pay premium market rents because Platoon has helped to establish what was previously an empty lot as a desirable destination.

In terms of creating a destination, Beijing's 798 art district has become a major tourist attraction since it was designated an official cultural site and infrastructural investment was made prior to the flood of foreign visitors for the Olympic Games in 2008.[4] The 798 art district, which forms part of the Dashanzi district, is a large industrial site that was formerly dominated by the manufacturing sector. It now houses numerous artists' studios, international art galleries, museums, bookstores and restaurants. During a 2012 meeting of artists whose studios and art spaces are located in the district, they hoped to form an association with a view to publicizing the value that artists added to the area.[5] Since 798 had become a major tourist destination, businesses had moved in, infrastructure had been improved (roads were paved and streetlights installed), and property values had increased sharply. Throughout the meeting, artists argued that the area's main attraction was still the art, not the cafés and businesses that came after. One suggested that they should organize a kind of strike, closing all of the galleries' doors, to emphasize the crucial role that they continued to play in the area.

Still, in numerous interviews with artists whose art spaces are located elsewhere in Beijing, they voiced a common belief that the commercialization of 798 was, and will continue to be, inevitable. Just as Platoon organizes their contract agreements for a limited number of years, there are limits to the exchange of creative to financial capital. When the financial interest reaches a certain level, the symbolic value of creativity cannot complete. The symbolic value of creativity seemed to function on a speculative basis, so the exchange rate for creative capital was vulnerable, depending on the other currencies available. When renting spaces in Berlin-Wedding to artists for below market rates, the landlord assumes that creativity will eventually lead to higher forms of capital. Thus, although it is exchangeable, the exchange rate of creative capital to financial capital will always favour finance. However, as an alternative or supplement to exchanging creative for financial capital, art spaces can also turn to political capital.

From creative to political capital

Indeed, the history of 798 is a powerful illustration of exchanging creative for political capital. Before it became a desirable destination, in 2004 it was under threat of demolition. Artists who had moved into spaces in the district sought to retain them, and they secured support from the artist Huang Rui, who argued for the need to re-infuse culture into cities, and the French curator Berenice Angremy, who admitted that, 'at the beginning, I played with the SoHo words' in order to increase 798's cachet, inviting staff from foreign embassies to attend an international art festival she helped to organize (Currier 2008: 206). These tactics helped to make 798 a landmark case, given the experience of several art villages that had previously been demolished. The campaign's success was secured when Sun Jiazheng, the Chinese Minister of Culture, apologized for the destruction of 'traditional' Beijing in the process of modernization – the first time any high-level minister had issued such a public apology (Currier 2008).[6]

Compared with the ability of financial interests to determine access to and rental costs of spaces, political capital can powerfully serve artists in fundamental, existential ways. When creative capital is leveraged for political capital, even the seemingly intractable 'growth machine' (Zhang 2008) or 'growth first' (He and Wu 2009) characterizations of cities like Beijing seem malleable. Recalling the experience in Caochangdi, the founder of Nali Nali describes how political leverage helped to preserve the area where his art space is located:

> The power brokers, the landlords or the government officials who work as the municipal advisers for the village, saw this as fabulous. But at a certain point

... now that we have that establishment, now what we can do is take over your space, tear down your buildings, do condominiums ... They actually sent out notices to Platform China, to 3 Shadows, to Ai Wei Wei's art archive space down the road. Well, thank you very much, we've decided your buildings have all been constructed illegally, without proper leasing, so we're going to be tearing them down. But the thing that's a little bit different with Caochangdi is that a large number of these were set up by major public galleries from other parts [of the world] – from Europe and North America. And they would sign contracts, legal contracts with lawyers that sort of vetted them ... Then these places went to their embassies, and they go to their cultural attachés, or to their political or legal advisers within their embassies, and the embassies phone central planning in Beijing, or their counterparts that have a certain degree of *guanxi* [i.e. good connections]. And they say, well, what [do the authorities] think they're doing? These people have put hundreds of thousands of dollars into these buildings. You can't just take them down, because they make more money.' Then Beijing's kind of saying, 'OK, this is looking like a bit of a hassle, this is embarrassing. This is not going well.' So a phone call is made ... because these galleries are known internationally. And they're run by Europeans.

(OBJ19)

The source of the political leverage was in trading on their creative capital in tandem with their social capital as foreigners. The international character of the art spaces was an important factor in influencing key decision-makers in Beijing. This story highlights the confluence of multiple factors: the nature of these spaces as art spaces that have attracted large amounts of foreign financial investment and have generated significant revenues, but also the international backgrounds of the artists themselves, which provide unique leverage with politically influential institutions like embassies. This is perhaps most evident when contrasted to the many art villages in Beijing that have been torn down (Ren 2011). It can also be contrasted to the standard tactic of exercising municipal power to drive out renters, as Nali Nali's founder describes:

The way it works is that you say no, and they say yes, and then you say, 'We're not leaving,' and then they turn off your electricity, and then, if you still don't go, they get thugs and they beat the shit out of you and they pull you out of your space. Some of the landlords here – basically corrupt officials that run Caochangdi – were made to understand that they can't do this to European galleries. They can't. They would have to have to find another way. But then it kind of evolved. That was three years ago, that major crisis. And I think since then they have found other ways to think about building and developing a community ... in the same way as 798 did, which people saw as very valuable. Now I think that some of the city people in the village see it as very valuable too. So they're supportive at this point.

(OBJ19)

In this case, the political influence was a necessary prerequisite for speculating on the financial capital that these art spaces may help to generate. The people in decision-making positions in Caochangdi shifted their positions on the legality of the art spaces once more powerful political actors started to exert their influence.[7] Though landlords remain motivated by financial interests, their appreciation of the value of art spaces developed only through the chain of events that began with foreign artists exploiting their unique position and political access.

While merely being foreign in Berlin may not lead to the same degree of influence, artists there are also active in political lobbying and activism. Organizing for their common interests, groups like the Koalition der Freien Szene (Coalition of the Free Scene) and Projektnetzwerk Berlin (Project Network Berlin) have effectively lobbied the Berlin Senate for more recognition and policies to support art spaces that fall outside the major publicly funded artistic institutions like museums, theatres and opera houses. The Koalition argues that visitors are attracted by the artistic initiatives of the 'free scene', with five out of every seven tourists drawn to the city by Berlin's artistic events.[8] Jan Eder, the managing director of Berlin's Chamber of Commerce, agrees, arguing that, unlike Munich or Hamburg, Berlin defines itself culturally, yet the 'free scene' receives only 5 per cent of the public funding for the arts, about half of which is from the federal government (rather than the city of Berlin) ('Aufbruch oder Abbruch?' 2012). Moreover, the Koalition argues that the decision-making behind the Liegenschaftsfond (public real estate holdings) must give consideration to maintaining the 'creative authenticity' of Berlin and not just distribute property to the highest bidder (OBL14).

The leveraging of creative for political capital functions in this example in two ways. First, the artists are seeking out public funds for their art spaces – either by way of a greater proportion of the existing city budget, or through additional revenue streams, such as a new tourist tax. Second, and similar to the Caochangdi experience in Beijing, the Koalition is attempting to shape the way that property is distributed through the Liegenschaftsfond.

Taken in tandem, the exchange of creative capital for financial and political capital is crucial in initiating and sustaining art spaces. This exchange also reflects how the elevation of creativity to an urban imperative has allowed artists to exercise tangible influence on the urban landscape of cities like Beijing and Berlin. The exchange value of creative capital reflects the context in which creativity enjoys this inflated status. Trading in creative capital can also imply at times conflicting tendencies: properties are sometimes valorized and neighbourhoods commercialized; at other times, entire districts avert condominium takeover and powerful market influences are subverted by the power of 'cultural heritage' or 'creative authenticity'.

These examples also show that while Berlin and Beijing are extremely different places politically, economically, socially, and culturally, some of the basic behaviours and mechanisms of leveraging and trading in creative capital for their place-making are very similar.[9] This points to potential lessons for how studies of policy mobility (McCann and Ward 2011) must also consider the changing actor constellations that encompass ubiquitous policy norms. The proliferation of creativity in urban policy has enabled artists with no interest in economic development to take advantage of the speculative assumptions made about them to negotiate lower rents and impact political decisions about urban space relating to conservation and the distribution of public funding. Since these processes are sourced in a small study, the final section considers the possible lessons of this experience for comparative analysis.

Comparative lessons

The examples of artists' place-making activities show how the ubiquity of creativity-led urban policies empowers changing constellations of actors who have actively shaped both Beijing and Berlin. The congruency of these basic mechanisms across dramatically different contexts also challenges assumptions about incommensurability with regards to comparative research. As I have argued previously, methodologies for studying the 'Asian city'

> require balancing contextual work with tendencies to isolate research in this region into a new parochial frame. This also implies bringing down the 'Asian City' from its mythical pedestal, the imagined place of hyper-skylines and sleek postmodernity, and rejecting the exceptionalism of the 'Asian City', which renders it incommensurate as a site for comparison.
>
> (Ren and Luger 2014: 154)

Context remains important in comparative research, but it is also important to find a balance for integrating the local without idolizing the particular. This is particularly evident in considering the land use and rental contract issues in Beijing and Berlin. Although the legal structures and actors are very different, the art spaces have shared an experience of precariousness across different contexts.

In linking these experiences, common mechanisms of urban place-making become more evident. Moreover, it undermines the justifications that make the 'Asian city' incommensurate with other cities. Perhaps the two most influential justifications underpinning the lack of comparative research with cities in Asia are developmentalism and exceptionalism. Robinson (2011: 3) has argued that the fear of falling into developmentalist fallacies has often prevented researchers from selecting comparative sites across economic difference, creating 'a landscape in which assumptions about the incommensurability of wealthier and poorer cities are taken for granted, and reproduced through separate literatures that find few grounds for careful and mutual comparative reflection'. Theorizations about 'Asian cities' have suffered as a consequence, because urban theory sourced in wealthier cities continues to serve as universal knowledge about all cities (Robinson 2011; Ong 2011). And the fallacy that the 'Asian city' has to catch up in order to be compared fails to account for the circulations and inter-referencing of urban experience (Roy and Ong 2011).

Second, and perhaps especially relevant for cities in China, there is a persistent spectre of exceptionalism that serves too easily as an umbrella explanation. Developing theoretical frameworks for comparative research with Chinese sites is a challenge, as evidenced in Logan and Fainstein's (2008) and Kong and O'Connor's (2009) comparative volumes. 'To what do we compare China?' they plead – alluding to its numerous exceptional qualities (Logan and Fainstein 2008: 1). In addition to the dominant area-specific nature of research about cities in Asia, Chinese exceptionalism is itself a subject of investigation (see, e.g., Pow 2012). Researchers can certainly point to a rich diversity of factors to highlight China's exceptionalism, ranging from the role of the state (from the Chinese Communist Party to municipal-level actors), to its ruptured history of transformation (politically, culturally, and economically), to the structures that shape everyday life, like the *danwei* or *hukou* systems. As an explanatory instrument, however, the concept of Chinese exceptionalism restricts the greater potential to develop urban theory from its experiences of urbanism.

Indeed, both justifications threaten to isolate the research on cities in China, constraining its cities to the urban shadows of theory-building (McFarlane 2008). If comparative research is forever rooted in categories or 'wealthy' and 'poor' or 'East' and 'West', how will urban research contribute to understandings of urban transformation and transnational mobility, like the kind of policy mobility underpinning the cultural policies evidenced in this volume? If urban China remains the exceptional case, will the experiences of its vast urban landscape be forever relegated to case studies? Critiques of the pervasive Western bias in urban theory stand to benefit from more constructive contributions from comparative research across difference.

Given the international mobility of ideas, the global exchange of capital, the transnational mobility of people, and the disciplinary shortcomings of parochialism in urban theory, a more relational comparative approach is both useful and necessary. Following Massey's ideas about the relationality of space, cities do not exist in isolation but in constant interaction with other places. The experiences of the art spaces described here reflect the circulating, inter-referencing nature of cities elevating the influence of creative capital (Roy and Ong 2011). They also show that making cultural cities in Asia implies a more holistic accounting of not only the creativity-driven ideas but the various agencies to which the ubiquity of these ideas gives rise. Whether in urban villages outside of Beijing's Fifth Ring Road or in Berlin-Wedding's store-fronts, art spaces demonstrate the power of creative capital to shape the urban landscape.

Notes

1 Zukin (1995: 279) has argued, 'historically, those with power over a space enforce the vision of that space; yet the power to impose a coherent vision of a space can actually grant the power to claim that space'.
2 The interviewees' anonymity is maintained and the coded references reflect a system devised for the larger study. 'O' represents an artist who also owns/manages/curates/runs the art space, while 'BJ' represents Beijing and 'BL' Berlin, indicating where the interview took place, followed by a unique identifying number.

3 For a more differentiated analysis of local governance structures, see Ren and Sun (2012).
4 As a district, 798 obviously does not fit into the description of 'art space' set for the study. The meeting described included several spaces covered in the study, however, and pertained to the area where they were located. Therefore, I feel it merits inclusion in this discussion.
5 The meeting included several renowned artists, gallery owners and shop owners based in 798 and was convened after one artist was locked out of their space by the 7 Star Corporation, which manages the enclosed district. Following the meeting, a demonstration marched from the meeting place to the local offices of that corporation.
6 While protected under the guise of 'Chinese cultural heritage', the buildings in 798 were constructed with the aid of East German architects in the Bauhaus style, and many of the art spaces were built and managed by foreigners. The conservation pledge was thus clearly a political decision.
7 As mentioned above, land-use governance is highly contested. In the experience of artists, this is reflected in the constant renegotiation of what is 'legal'.
8 The mutually supportive positions of the Koalition and the Chamber were established in a public podium discussion about the meaning of the independent art scene in Berlin ('Aufbruch oder Abbruch?' 2012).
9 This is, of course, specific to the activities of place-making around art spaces. Other studies of artists have shown them to resist neoliberal policies directly (e.g., Novy and Colomb 2013).

References

'Aufbruch oder Abbruch? Podiumsdiskussion zur Bedeutung der Freien Künste für die Zukunft der Stadt – neue Ideen zwischen Eigenverantwortung und politischen Weichenstellungen', public discussion with Jan Eder, Burkhard Kieker, Christophe Knoch and Andreas Krueger, 15 May.
Bourdieu, P. (1983). 'Economic capital, cultural capital, social capital', *Soziale-Welt*, Supplement, 2: 183–198.
Currier, J. (2008) 'Art and power in the new China: An exploration of Beijing's 798 district and its implications for contemporary urbanism', *Town Planning Review*, 79(2/3): 237–265.
Florida, R. (2002) *The rise of the creative class: And how it's transforming work, leisure, community and everyday life*, New York: Basic Books.
Florida, R. (2005) *Cities and the creative class*, London and New York: Routledge.
Gibson, C. (ed.) (2012) *Creativity in peripheral places: Redefining the creative industries*, London: Routledge.
Glaeser, E. (2005) 'Review of Richard Florida's *The rise of the creative class*', *Regional Science and Urban Economics*, 35(5): 593–596.
Hall, P. (2004) 'Creativity, culture, knowledge and the city', *Built Environment (1978-)*, 30(3): 256–258.
He, S. and Wu, F. (2009) 'China's emerging neoliberal urbanism: Perspectives from urban redevelopment', *Antipode*, 41(2): 282–304.
Hsing, Y.-T. (2010) *The great urban transformation: Politics of land and property in China*, Oxford: Oxford University Press
Kong, L. and O'Connor, J. (eds) (2009) *Creative economies, creative cities: Asian–European perspectives*, New York: Springer.
Krätke, S. (2010) '"Creative cities" and the rise of the dealer class: A critique of Richard Florida's approach to urban theory', *International Journal of Urban and Regional Research*, 34(4): 835–853.

Krätke, S. (2012) *The creative capital of cities: Interactive knowledge creation and the urbanization economies of Innovation*, New York: John Wiley & Sons.

Liu, T. and Lin, G.C.S. (2014) 'New geography of land commodification in Chinese cities: Uneven landscape of urban land development under market reforms and globalization', *Applied Geography*, 41: 118–130.

Liu, Y., Fang, F., and Li, Y. (2014) 'Key issues of land use in China and implications for policy making', *Land Use Policy*, 40: 6–12.

Logan, J. and Fainstein, S. (2008) 'Introduction: Urban China in comparative perspective', in J. Logan (ed.), *Urban China in transition*, Malden, MA: Blackwell: 1–23.

Marcuse, P. (2003) 'Review of *The rise of the creative class* by Richard Florida', *Urban Land*, 62: 40–41.

Markusen, A., Wassall, G., DeNatale, D. and Cohen, R. (2008) 'Defining the creative economy: Industry and occupational approaches', *Economic Development Quarterly*, 22(1): 24–45.

Massey, D. (1995) *Space, place and gender*, Minneapolis: University of Minnesota Press.

McCann, E. and Ward, K. (2011) *Mobile urbanism: Cities and policymaking in the global age*, Minneapolis: University of Minnesota Press.

McFarlane, C. (2008) 'Urban shadows: Materiality, the "southern city" and urban theory', *Geography Compass*, 2(2): 340–358.

Mellander, C., Florida, R., Asheim, B. T., and Gertler, M. (eds) (2013) *The creative class goes global*, London: Routledge.

Montgomery, J. (2005) 'Beware "the creative class": Creativity and wealth creation revisited', *Local Economy*, 20(4): 337–343.

Musterd, S. and Ostendorf, W. (2004) 'Creative cultural knowledge cities: Perspectives and planning strategies', *Built Environment*, 30(3): 189–193.

Novy, J. and Colomb, C. (2013) 'Struggling for the right to the (creative) city in Berlin and Hamburg: New urban social movements, new "spaces of hope"?', *International Journal of Urban and Regional Research*, 37(5): 1816–1838.

Ong, A. (2011) 'Introduction: Worlding cities, or the art of being global', in A. Roy and A. Ong (eds), *Worlding cities: Asian experiments and the art of being global*, Malden, MA: Wiley-Blackwell: 1–25.

Peck, J. (2005) 'Struggling with the creative class', *International Journal of Urban and Regional Research*, 29(4): 740–770.

Peck, J. (2011) 'Geographies of policy: From transfer-diffusion to mobility-mutation', *Progress in Human Geography*, 35(6): 773–797.

Pow, C.P. (2012) 'China exceptionalism? Unbounding narratives on urban China', in T. Edensor and M. Jayne (eds), *Urban theory beyond the West: A world of cities*, London and New York: Routledge: 47–64.

Rausch, S.E. and Negrey, C. (2006) 'Does the creative engine run? A consideration of the effect of creative class on economic strength and growth', *Journal of Urban Affairs*, 28(5): 473–489.

Reese, L.A. and Sands, G. (2008) 'Creative class and economic prosperity: Old nostrums, better packaging?', *Economic Development Quarterly*, 22(1): 3–7.

Reese, L.A., Faist, J.M. and Sands, G. (2010) 'Measuring the creative class: Do we know it when we see it?', *Journal of Urban Affairs*, 32(3): 345–366.

Ren, J. and Luger, J. (2014) 'Comparative urbanism and the "Asian City": Implications for research and theory', *International Journal of Urban and Regional Research*, 39(1): 145–156.

Ren, X. (2011) *Building globalization: Transnational architectural production in urban China*, Chicago: University of Chicago Press.

Ren, X. and Sun, M. (2012) 'Artistic urbanization: Creative industries and creative control in Beijing', *International Journal of Urban and Regional Research*, 36(3): 504–521.

Robinson, J. (2011) 'Cities in a world of cities: The comparative gesture', *International Journal of Urban and Regional Research*, 35(1): 1–23.

Roy, A. and Ong, A. (eds) (2011) *Worlding cities: Asian experiments and the art of being global*, Malden, MA: Wiley-Blackwell.

Schneekloth, L. and Shibley, R. (1995) *Placemaking: The art and practice of building communities*, New York: John Wiley & Sons.

Schumpeter, J.A. (1909). 'On the concept of social value', *Quarterly Journal of Economics*, 23(2): 213–232.

Schumpeter, J.A. (1939) *Business cycles: A theoretical, historical and statistical analysis of the capitalist process*, New York: McGraw-Hill.

Shearmur, R. (2007) 'The new knowledge aristocracy: A few thoughts on the creative class, mobility and urban growth', *Work Labour and Globalization*, 1(1): 31–47.

Storper, M. and Manville, M. (2006) 'Behaviour, preferences and cities: Urban theory and urban resurgence', *Urban Studies*, 43(8): 1247–1274.

Visser, R. (2008) 'Diagnosing Beijing 2020: Mapping the ungovernable city', *Footprint*, Spring: 15–29.

Wu, F. (2011) 'Urbanization', in W.S. Tay and A.Y. So (eds), *Handbook of contemporary China*, Singapore: World Scientific: 237–262.

Zhang, Y. (2008) 'Steering towards growth: Symbolic urban preservation in Beijing, 1990–2005', *Town Planning Review*, 79(2–3): 187–208.

Zhang, Y. (2014) 'Governing art districts: State control and cultural production in contemporary China', *China Quarterly*, 219: 827–848.

Zukin, S. (1995) *The cultures of cities*, Cambridge, MA: Blackwell.

12 Making cultures and places from below

New urban activism in Hong Kong

Agnes Shuk-mei Ku

In Hong Kong, a new wave of preservation movements has emerged since the start of the twenty-first century. The government's launch of massive redevelopment and reclamation plans in Central and Wanchai has provided the backdrop for the rise of a new breed of urban activism among architects, urban planners, community workers and preservation groups. The chain of pro-preservation protests bespeaks deep-seated conflict between two divergent approaches to urban space among the government and the preservation movement. The former promotes an ideology of developmentalism in narrow economic terms, often at the expense of local cultures and lived space. Since the late 1990s, following the trend of cultural globalization worldwide (Crane 2002), the government has started to put cultural activities at the forefront of a policy of urban entrepreneurialism (Ku and Tsui 2008; Jessop and Sum 2000). The West Kowloon Cultural District Project, the promotion of heritage tourism and the proposals for creative industries are all examples of such initiatives. Culture is incorporated into the economy through a new discourse of cultural economy that defines culture as the principal means for adding economic value. While the government's discourse appears to allow more room for the development of culture and heritage than in the past, it is in effect a product of the deepening of the market principle as well as a worldwide expansion of the tourism industry (Ku 2010). The new breed of urban activism, however, has raised a host of new claims regarding living space, community, history and local identity, which calls forth a very different approach to urban space. Western scholars have coined the term 'new social movements' to characterize such culture- or identity-based actions, as differentiated from conventional class-based and economically oriented protests (Melucci 1985; Offe 1985; Touraine 1985).

This chapter will present two cases of urban activism to illuminate the interplay between discursive and spatial practices in the process of remaking cultures and places from below. The two cases pertain to the Central Police Station compound in Central and two piers at the Victoria Harbour, namely the Star Ferry and the Queen's piers, between 2003 and 2008 (Ku 2010 and 2012). The juxtaposition of these two cases will show not only a common thread of anti-commercialism underlying the emergent movement but also tensions, differences and multiple possibilities unfolding in the process.

Remaking heritage: implications for space, culture and history

In Central, beside the business district is an upscale 'Soho' area that has evolved out of a different facet of commercialism: consumption and entertainment. Around 1997, a new discourse of cultural economy began to emerge by which the government sought to expand the area and link it to the Central Police Station compound and other nearby heritage sites for tourism purposes (such as Man Mo Temple and various places bearing Sun Yat-sen's footprints in Hong Kong). Tourism is not a new feature in Hong Kong but the notion of cultural or heritage tourism brings a new idea of realizing the commercial potential of historic sites. The gist of the discourse is to turn culture, arts and heritage into profitable business while passing the economic burden of restoration, maintenance and development from the government to the private sector (see Boyer 1994 and Zukin 1995). This new discourse has been spearheaded by the newly established Tourism Bureau, founded amidst an economic downturn as a result of the Asian financial crisis.

In 2001, in an attempt to restructure the economy, Chief Executive Tung Chee-hwa unveiled a HK$18 billion (US$2.3 billion) plan to boost tourism. One of the main projects listed in the plan was the adaptation of the area around Lan Kwai Fong and Hollywood Road in Central into a cultural and historical district. The government initially envisaged turning the whole area into a retail and entertainment complex, with a slice of the project reserved for cultural and community use. Under a commercial framework, the project was placed under the Economic Development and Labour Bureau – championed by the Tourism Commission within that bureau – rather than the Home Affairs Bureau, which was supposed to be in charge of heritage.

Civil society: confronting commercialism

The Central Police Station (CPS) compound consists of the Victoria Prison, the Central Police Station itself and the former Central Magistracy, which has a long history dating back to the mid-nineteenth century. It was officially listed as a historic monument in 1995, but uncertainties remained as to how – and how far – it would be preserved and developed in the future. In April 2003, conflicts began to emerge when the government earmarked the CPS compound for tourism-related restoration and development and prepared to schedule for a private tender. At stake was possible commercial encroachment upon a public heritage site, the uses of which had yet to be defined. The struggle was initiated by a wealthy family group, the Hotung Group, which drafted a counter-proposal with an emphasis on arts, culture and the principle of non-profitability, and backed this up with the promise of HK$500 million (about US$64 million). This quickly generated an opposition movement spearheaded by an alliance of architects, preservationists and politicians, including the Hong Kong Institute of Architects, the Conservancy Association and members of the Central and Western District Board. The opposition discourse asserted itself primarily as a challenge against commercialism – or against the government playing into the hands of the business sector – with regard to four interrelated sets of issues: non-profit versus profit-driven operation; public space versus privatized use; open process versus behind-closed-doors dealing; and historic value versus ahistorical/anti-historical development. The government subsequently agreed to postpone the tender without putting in place further plans. This created a period of uncertainty and indeterminacy.

In the meantime, another debate arose regarding the breadth and depth of preservation, which also manifested itself as conflicts over preservation versus commercialism and over proper (i.e. democratic) versus improper procedures. In October 2004, a paper prepared by the Tourism Commission and the Economic Development and Labour Bureau for discussion at the Legislative Council stated that seventeen of the eighteen buildings were likely to be preserved at the site. The list nonetheless did not include a building on the grounds that it was modified in the 1950s after the original structure had been dismantled, and that it did not match the architectural style of the surrounding environment. Clearing that building would mean that a new high-rise block with lucrative commercial opportunities could be built on the site. This raised a new round of debates and concerns and moved the conflict forward from showing a general anti-commercial stance to confronting issues of history, memory and lived space.

Heritage, socio-cultural values and collective remembering

The compound formed the oldest and the largest architectural complex under colonial rule and displayed the classical style of its time. From the perspective of architectural aesthetics, rarity added to the historical value of the site, as most of the colonial buildings of this kind of design had been demolished. This perspective, moreover, was intermingled with other discourses and narratives that celebrated the site as an icon of Hong Kong with immeasurable value regarding its historical origin, symbolic meanings and geographical location. A neutral idea of history was used as a primary framework for collective memory, which stripped the colonial past of any ideological baggage: 'It is just a matter of history and culture, and one need not think politically in terms of honour and disgrace associated with the nation' (*Hong Kong Economic Times*, 30 April 2003; author's translation). A flurry of history talks appeared in the public sphere as a counterweight to commercialism. Detailed knowledge of the history of the place nonetheless was unavailable, leaving a void of historical meanings yet to be filled. As it developed, representations of the place became endowed with specific spatial, historic and symbolic meanings at the core of the definition of a Hong Kong identity. Most conspicuously, a benign state-centred framework that equated colonial rule with the rule of law began to prevail in public discourse.

The compound, which concentrated law enforcement, courts and correctional services in one place, laid the early foundation for legal development in the territory. As stated on the Antiquities and Monuments Office's website, the compound formed 'a group of historical architecture representing law and order in Hong

Kong'.[1] Public discourse was mostly pitched at an abstract symbolic level around the idea of law as the basis for remembering, historicizing and narrating, or for a claim to collective memory. The prevalent view that the compound was a historical icon associated with the development of 'law and order' or 'rule of law' in fact constituted a familiar Hong Kong story. Spatially, Central was the base of the British political and military establishment and was once dubbed the 'Victorian City'. It also quickly grew into an economic base for commerce and trading activities, making itself the centre of an ever-expanding urban region, differentiated from the rural and the less developed areas in the periphery. Over the years, it remained the political, economic and cultural hub of Hong Kong.

On a narrative level, the compound was considered as marking a process of development from a more desolate past to modern civilization. The narrative carried a subtext with a benign reading of the colonial government, which was looked upon as an agent of development. Why did the rule of law discourse prevail? A critical look at the discrepancy between local historiography and the general public discourses is instructive. In the former, scholars have shown the rather complex, multiple relations between the state and society ranging from repression/resistance to collaboration. Legal reforms in the direction of equality were, according to Munn (1999: 67), only 'recent achievements' in the past few decades. The notion of collective memory, however, underpins an approach to the past that is different from local historiography. Collective memory is the active past informed by the present, yet it is not entirely free-floating or autonomous from the past but is sedimented in existing discourses (Schwartz 1996) and undergoes an ongoing process of negotiation over time (Olick and Levy 1997). From a quasi-presentist perspective, the rule of law was not only a legacy from the past but also carried much relevance and significance for contemporary Hong Kong, especially for a generation that had gone through a profound political transition during the 1980s and 1990s. In a more political reading, the rule of law tradition in Hong Kong was juxtaposed against the rule by law system on the mainland, underscoring a sense of difference under the 'one country, two systems' framework. The repeated reference to the salient idea of the rule of law in the debate over the CPS compound was largely shaped by a discursive framework that had been deposited in the public sphere over more than two decades.

While this familiar, hegemonic framework was key to the success of the benign statist reading, alternative narratives that could compete were not quite readily available. For instance, when the mode of remembering shifted from the state to the people, there were no ready narratives or discursive space that either related their stories to the development of Hong Kong or challenged the hegemonic narrative with these stories, which were largely fragmentary accounts from personal memories relating to police officers, prisoners or detainees. Such accounts neither evoked fond feelings from the public nor built up a coherent narrative about Hong Kong. As such, they failed to be tied to a Hong Kong story with an equal symbolic significance to the state-centred account.

Creating new spatial experiences

To an average citizen, the compound was indeed a place bearing little personal memory or immediate experience. The sense of lived space was too thin for the majority to be able to conjure up deep sentiments. Viewed from another angle, however, it was precisely because of its relative lack of public accessibility and the people's sense of unfamiliarity with it that the compound was like a forbidden place suddenly opened up for public visits. The sense of strangeness and mystery about the place aroused much curiosity or 'a morbid fascination with prison life' (*South China Morning Post*, 6 January 2007). Thus, apart from the abstract discourse of the rule of law, the civil groups also launched a series of activities that turned the place into a relived space to create a sense of intimacy with the past and cultivate a space of creativity for the present. These activities included not only guided tours and public lectures that focused on the site's histories but exhibitions that showcased contemporary artworks. The discourses arising out of these activities were in part subsumed in a benign statist framework and in part impregnated with other possibilities. For example, in early 2008, an exhibition on 'The Hong Kong Shenzhen Bi-City Biennale of Urbanism/Architecture' was organized by local architects, planners and designers together with the Shenzhen Planning Bureau. While many of the artworks focused on the theme of freedom versus imprisonment, the main purpose of the exhibition was to explore the spatial possibilities of the place in an artistic fashion. For instance, one exhibit allowed visitors to imprison themselves for one minute and read what previous 'prisoners' had written on the walls. The exhibition blended with the physical and spatial layout of the compound and extended the creative possibilities of the site into a living cultural space. Through such activities, the uses of the site remained open to new definitions.

Outcomes of the struggle

Was the campaign successful? The idea of non-commercialism as a parameter for developing the future uses of the site remained a cornerstone of the opposition throughout the struggle. In October 2007, after three years, it was suddenly announced in the press that a well-established non-profit organization, the Hong Kong Jockey Club, would run the project to restore the CPS compound into a vibrant, iconic, cultural landmark comprising a mix of cultural, heritage and commercial elements. To the extent that the project would be turned over to a non-profit organization, the struggle against commercialism ended in a victory. Nevertheless, preservationists and local residents remained apprehensive over two issues: first, more than half of the venues would be adapted for commercial use; second, a tower with a 160-metre viewing deck would be built on the existing upper courtyard. The new catchword was 'revitalization'. While the public generally supported a non-profit approach, they were against the tower, which appeared to be completely out of proportion with the heritage compound and exceeded the maximum height set by the Antiquities Advisory Board. After another six months of public consultation, the government, while approving the

Jockey Club's proposal, finally conceded that an observation tower would not be in sight in the future design. This was another major concession to the public's wishes. Nevertheless, a number of issues remain undecided and unresolved, including the future uses of the compound.

Reclaiming the people's space

During 2006 and 2007, in the midst of the struggle over the CPS compound, new conflicts arose over the demolition of two piers in Central. To many Hong Kong people, Victoria Harbour is the heart of the city's identity both locally and globally. By the mid-1990s, however, more than half of the harbour's original 6,500 hectares had been lost to reclamation. Governments past and present have primarily pursued a reclamation-led urban development strategy for land supply (Ng and Cook 1997). In particular, with the vision of a global city, the focus has been on expanding the central business district in Central. A first Territorial Development Strategy was formulated in 1984, then reviewed and updated in 1989. This laid the foundation for subsequent developments to improve transport infrastructure facilities and enhance the role of Hong Kong as a regional financial centre. The idea has translated into a set of spatial practices including massive reclamation, land rezoning for commercial use, the constant building and rebuilding of super-high-rise commercial buildings, and the expansion of roads and transportation. By 2006, the first two phases of the reclamation project that had started in 1999 were complete, and the third phase, which concerned the area where the two piers were situated, was about to start. The plan was to demolish the Star Ferry and Queen's piers to make way for a massive shopping centre and a road linking Sheung Wan and Wan Chai, respectively.[2]

Prior to 2006, the Conservation Association and Society for the Protection of the Harbour had already initiated action to try to protect the harbour, which bore fruit with the legislation of the Harbour Protection Ordinance. Despite this, the government continued with the reclamation projects that were already under way, including one in Central to relieve traffic congestion. While previous demands had been framed generally in terms of anti-reclamation and protection of the harbour on a macro-policy level, the campaigns of 2006 and 2007, led by a new group of activists, specifically aimed to conserve the Star Ferry and Queen's piers in situ. However, these two piers, unlike the CPS compound, were not heritage listed, and the government finally demolished the former and relocated the latter.

Although the campaigners ultimately failed to save the piers in material terms, the symbolic effects of their protests were by no means insignificant. Not only were certain place-specific qualities of the piers highlighted, but a new opposition discourse of people's space began to take shape in the course of the conflict. The struggle increasingly focused on commemorating and protecting the piers as particular places of value and forging a new understanding of urban space more generally.

Interplay among discourse, memory and spatiality

Throughout the struggle, a folk perspective stressing the people's relations with the piers in their everyday-life context came to prominence. The campaign over the Star Ferry pier was launched by a few cultural workers in 2006, around the ideas of heritage, affection and memory. In particular, the Star Ferry clock tower caught the public's imagination as a focal icon – an endearing landmark for the Hong Kong people. The clock tower – a gift from Jardine Matheson in 1957 – contained the city's sole remaining antique mechanical clock and it was widely viewed as Hong Kong's version of Big Ben in London. Artists and art students began to gather at the square adjacent to the pier every Sunday, using participatory arts as a means to draw further attention to the campaign. They turned the place into a space of gathering, creativity and performance for and by the people. Preservation groups also organized coastal walks, harbour cruises and a carnival. The mass media quickly picked up on the growing affective mood and propagated a discourse of collective memory with a sentimentalized appeal to nostalgia.

As a verbal code, the idea of collective memory nonetheless was like an empty signifier capable of holding different meanings. Secretary for Housing, Planning and Lands Michael Suen, for instance, appropriated the notion of collective memory to suggest that the tower was merely a symbol of memory with little architectural value, while the symbol of memory itself could be relocated, recreated or even replicated. The government was appropriating the notion with a de-spatialized and de-materialized twist. As it happened, the new pier, built on some nearby reclaimed land, mimicked the old-fashioned style but was fitted with a new clock that chimed electronically.

In the meantime, the multivocality of the idea of collective memory also gave rise to new interpretations among the preservation movement's participants, which helped push the campaign in some new directions. On the one hand, it served to buttress the claim that the clock tower, as well as the pier, should be preserved on its original site. The idea was that the collective memory should be inscribed in a form of spatiality that honoured history and respected people's living environment. In this regard, spatiality was being reclaimed through a discourse that stressed historical and living connection. The new agenda of architecture, history and space, different from the earlier appeals to heritage, memory and affection, began to gain greater prominence. Beyond the pier itself, ever more people began to perceive the entire area as integral to the spatial history, structure and experience of Hong Kong society and its people, with the Star Ferry pier, the Queen's pier and the City Hall forming a trinity within an open area: the Edinburgh Place. In spite of the colonial character of the architecture, public discourse focused on its local, everyday relationships with the city as well as the people. Apparently, the issue was not just about memory but also about space, culture and identity embodied in the idea of a landmark. Hence the movement's participants demanded that the historical and social values of the place should be preserved in situ.

On the other hand, in the midst of the campaign a discursive shift took place within the movement. The activists kept a critical distance from the popular notion of collective memory yet retained a folk perspective in interpreting the relations between the past and the present. One banner read: 'Our Hong Kong story landmark is vanishing; we don't want a clock in a museum, we just want living history'. The idea of living history marked a departure from the better-known understanding of collective memory and its popular usage. It underlined the importance of grounding the symbol of memory in everyday life, and – in this case – in a place that was part of the Hong Kong people's everyday life.

At the same time, as public discourse continued to dig into the past, the threads of historical memories appeared to look pluralistic rather than singular. In the campaign over the Star Ferry pier, the idea of collective memory unwittingly opened up a discursive space for looking to the past for more stories, which provided cultural resources for a more critical mode of remembering. One past incident in particular was recalled. On 4 April 1966, twenty-five-year-old So Sau-chong launched a hunger strike outside the Star Ferry concourse to protest against a five-cent fare increase. He was arrested the next day, prompting thousands of young people to riot on the streets. This was the first time that many young Hong Kong residents had protested over a local issue, and it led to a host of social reforms by the colonial government. Consequently, at the time of the campaign four decades later to save the Star Ferry pier, one popular newspaper described it as the 'seedbed of social activism' (*Apply Daily*, 12 November 2006).

So was the Star Ferry pier a place of social affection, a seedbed of social activism or nothing but an old landing stage? While histories were embedded in the place, it was the acts of reading, remembering and interpreting that defined and redefined its meaning in the present context. That is, the same space could be read and remembered in numerous ways. The 1966 riot was an almost forgotten event in popular memory, but, as we shall see in the second campaign to save the Queen's pier, it was summoned up again to define the site as a place that was tied to a tradition of local activism. The mode of remembering was more critical than nostalgic (or arguably both critical and nostalgic). This reading in turn gave rise to different spatial practices. In analytical terms, such changes were mediated through the rise of a new form of political agency that constituted a different articulation of discourse and spatiality.

Fashioning a counter-discourse of people's space

In a few months, the movement took a radical turn when the government barricaded the pier and surrounded it with scaffolding. New actors then joined the protest and assumed more active roles. Tensions accelerated after it was disclosed that the government had covered up some discussions within the Antiquities Advisory Board, which placed the credibility of the government's final decision in serious doubt. In haste, the government sent in a crew to remove the clock and tear down the tower, which was smashed to pieces and then dumped in landfill despite on-site opposition from several dozen protesters. The movement was radicalized by this confrontation, giving birth to a loose alliance of participants known as Local Action.³ A new form of political agency emerged in the process of protest that began to turn the place from a mere icon of affection and memory to a site of citizenship and resistance. This inadvertent activism, which entailed such spatial forms as encroachment and transgression, prefigured some changes in the discursive-cum-spatial strategy in the next campaign over the Queen's pier.

Using the conventional definition of heritage, the Secretary for Home Affairs reiterated that the second pier did not possess the requisite historical, archaeological or palaeontological significance to be declared a monument, so it could be relocated. The activists challenged the government's decision by engaging in a politics of meaning reconstruction about the site. As with the Star Ferry pier, Local Action's goal was to conserve the Queen's pier in situ. Unlike the previous campaign, however, the struggle now had to grapple with ways of negotiating the colonial history as the site had royal and political significance associated with the ex-colonial state. Drawing on and extending the notions that had evolved in the earlier campaign, the movement's participants redefined the meaning of the Queen's pier from the perspective of the people. Through varied symbolic, verbal and spatial practices, they articulated and enacted a discourse of people's space in the dual sense of common folk and autonomous citizens. The mechanisms underlying these varied practices included: reconstructing meanings about the place from a society-centred perspective; grounding the role of the specific place in a larger social narrative that addressed the people as the subject; and acting or performing in the site in a capacity that (re)defined the subject or agent of the narrative.

The history of a place could be seen as embodying divergent meanings depending on perspective. Under a statist framework, the pier merited heritage status as the symbolic landing place for six former colonial governors after their arrival at the airport, and also the first port of call for a host of British royals, including Queen Elizabeth II, over the previous half century. Reporters and politicians tended to define the historical value of the pier from this perspective. Under a nationalistic framework, however, this could cause some embarrassment for the preservationist cause as pro-Beijing forces ridiculed the pier as an incongruous remnant of colonialism. Resorting neither to a statist nor to a nationalistic framework, Local Action rendered a new interpretation of the site by shifting to the perspective of society. From this perspective, the users of the place were not so much state officials as common folk and citizens. Apparently, Local Action was seeking to reclaim the site from the state and give it to the people.

To buttress this perspective, Local Action drew on an existing narrative of Hong Kong identity and yet rearticulated its meanings pertinent to the spatial context of the new struggle. It encapsulated the history of a local place in the history of the city, beginning the narrative in the 1960s, which marked the birth of local consciousness among a new, local-born generation who viewed Hong Kong as their home, witnessed a fast-growing economy, and grew up with a sense of citizenship (Ku and Pun 2004). Within this narrative, the events of 1966 was recalled with renewed significance, as were other protests. Immediately after the campaign over the Star Ferry pier, Local Action staged a hunger strike that clearly echoed that of So Sau-chung in 1966, which was touted as a symbol of the birth of local activism.

The activists recalled the historical episode in the colonial era and cast themselves in an ironic light by lodging their protest against a post-colonial government that was failing to listen to local voices. Moreover, they recalled that the Queen's pier was historically a popular site for protests in the 1960s and 1970s. In the words of one Local Action member, Chow Sze Chung, the place had witnessed the development of a 'self-strengthening civic personality' among the Hong Kong people since the 1950s (*Ming Daily*, 22 August 2007). To drum up public concern and galvanize activism, Local Action organized a series of seminars and forums at the Queen's pier to debate the history of local social movements. From the activists' perspective, the movement that had aimed to achieve institutional or representative democracy had ended up chipping away at participatory politics and giving in to compromise. The campaigners were keeping a critical distance from institutional politics and seeking to revive a radical tradition through autonomous and confrontational actions. This formed the basis for a more politicized meaning of people's space.

Enacting agency and identity

Following the narrative of identity, the movement's participants further expressed a renewed relationship with the place as the subject of the narrative – the people – through an assortment of discourses, actions and performances. They claimed that the place belonged to the people. On one level, this meant the place was a free space filled with everyday meanings by the people, including familiar leisure activities and fresh experiences newly explored. The idea of free space was prominent in the account. Indeed, when the place was designed, it was intended for free use by the people. According to the original architect, Ron Phillips, the whole design – including the Queen's pier and the public space around it – was unified in providing a setting for the arrival of visiting dignitaries as well as open space and public access to City Hall for pedestrians. In addition to seminars and forums, Local Action organized cultural performances and musical events to convey the idea of free use of the space. This was place-making through the creation of 'affordances' – that is, the perception of values and meanings as activated through people's sensory experiences of their everyday environment (Urry 1995).

On another level, the claim also meant that people could be agents of participation in a more proactive sense. Local Action performed certain symbolic practices to act out such meaning. On 20 January 2007, they staged a ceremony to symbolize public landing at the pier, which marked a shift from a framework of history and memory to the *here and now*, and from state power to *citizenship*. About a hundred people participated in the public landing, originating from a broad spectrum including residents affected by redevelopment, preservation groups, legislators, workers, migrant workers, right-of-abode seekers, students,

Local Action activists, artists, academics and architects. As one newspaper report stated, 'This is no longer collective memory, but collective action' (*Economic Journal*, 20 January 2007).

In a more theatrical way, since the closure of the pier, Local Action campaigners had occupied the site day and night, setting up tents, building a home base and sleeping there. This was done to assert, through spatiality, that the place belonged to the people and therefore they would make it their home. The activists turned the place into an open stage to perform the meanings of home through such props as hanging beds, pyjamas and cooking utensils. The physical occupation of the site was also an act of civil disobedience against the government's plan for demolition. The dual role of the people as common folk and resilient citizens was played out in this single drama. The protesters stayed at the pier for more than three months – with some starting hunger strikes in the final days – until the police evicted them on 1 August 2007.

Concluding remarks

Culturally, much of Hong Kong's new urban activism has been place-bound. Rather than predetermined, the significance of places often entails a process of social construction of meanings (Harvey 1996). According to Lefebvre (1991), diversion or reappropriation of space opens up the possibility of the production of new spaces. As the case studies in this chapter have shown, while a common thread of anti-commericialism drove the struggles, discourse and space interacted to create divergent meanings for places. The protests, one after another, became vehicles for the articulation of hegemonic and contestatory ideas and practices. In the case of the CPS compound, its future development aroused concern and conflict even though it was listed as a historic monument. The campaign subsequently raised the issues of history and culture through a narrative of modernization framed within hegemonic terms. The struggle ended with at least partial victory for the campaigners. In contrast, in the cases of the Star Ferry and Queen's piers, the main goal of conserving the piers in situ was not achieved. The divergent outcomes between the two cases not only reflect a narrow and conventional view of conservation in government thinking that denigrated folk meanings and values but also testify to the relative power of hegemonic discourses in lending force to the successful campaign over the CPS compound.

Despite the ultimate failure of the campaigns to save the two piers, a new opposition discourse of people's space was developed, which, outgrowing its initial claims, challenged the hegemonic ideology of developmentalism with noticeable symbolic effects. A dual process of discursive re-formation and spatial reappropriation unfolded (Ku 2012). The process resulted in some significant shifts in perspective: from the government to the people; from collective memory to public space; from one stream of history to another; and from the past to the present. The ongoing civic movement was in part a new struggle over preservation issues and in part a conscious effort to re-enact a tradition of local activism inherited from the past. It rearticulated a local identity in relation to democracy and everyday space. Public critics increased the significance of the event by placing it in the larger context of the people seeking a cultural identity in post-handover Hong Kong. A meta-discourse that linked the movement to a process of identity re-search in the context of unrelenting development in the city was emerging. Apparently, the movement was broadening its significance from a struggle over history, memory and space to a struggle over local identity and political agency. In retrospect, what took place in 2006 and 2007 might have laid the foundations for subsequent social activism that employed novel and increasingly confrontational action around the idea of people's space, epitomized most vividly in the Occupy movement of 2014.

Notes

1 http://www.amo.gov.hk/textmode/en/monuments_53.php (accessed 4 March 2014).
2 According to Chu Hoi Dick, a citizen reporter and activist, the future Central waterfront would comprise four symbolic landmarks: the International Financial Centre, the huge shopping mall, the new government headquarters and the People's Liberation Army berth (*Ming Pao Daily*, 29 April 2007).
3 Local Action consisted mostly of youngsters in their late twenties or early thirties, many of whom were affiliated with minor NGOs or were variously involved in the pro-democracy and other social movements. The new actors were mobilized into the movement at different stages through an organic, flexible network via the internet and cellular phones.

References

Boyer, C. (1994) *The City of Collective Memory: Its Historical Imagery and Architectural Entertainments*, Cambridge, MA: MIT Press.
Crane, D. (2002) 'Culture and Globalization: Theoretical Models and Emerging Trends', in D. Crane, N. Kawashima, and K. Kawasaki (eds), *Global Culture: Media, Arts, Policy and Globalization* (pp. 1–25), New York: Routledge.
Harvey, D. (1996) *Justice, Nature and the Geography of Difference*, Oxford: Blackwell.
Jessop, B. and N. Sum. (2000) 'An Entrepreneurial City in Action: Hong Kong's Emerging Strategies in and for (Inter-) Urban Competition', *Urban Studies*, 37: 2287–2313.
Ku, A.S. (2010) 'Making Heritage in Hong Kong: A Case Study of the Central Police Station Compound', *China Quarterly*, 202: 381–399.
Ku, A.S. (2012) 'Re-making Places and Fashioning an Opposition Discourse–Struggle over the Star Ferry Pier and the Queen's Pier in Hong Kong', *Environment and Planning D: Space and Society*, 30: 5–22.
Ku, A.S. and N. Pun (eds) (2004) *Remaking Citizenship in Hong Kong: Community, Nation and the Global City*, London: Routledge Curzon.
Ku, A.S. and C.H. Tsui (2008) 'The "Global City" as a Cultural Project: The Case of the West Kowloon Cultural District', in H.F. Siu and A.S. Ku (eds), *Hong Kong Mobile: Making a Global Population* (pp. 343–365), Hong Kong: Hong Kong University Press.
Lefebvre, H. (1991) *The Production of Space*, Oxford: Blackwell.
Melucci, A. (1985) 'The Symbolic Challenge of Contemporary Movements', *Social Research*, 52(4): 789–816.
Melucci, A. (1988) 'Social Movements and the Democratization of Everyday life', in J. Keane (ed.), *Civil Society and the State* (pp. 245–260), London: Verso.

Munn, C. (1999) 'The Criminal Trial under Early Colonial Rule', in T.W. Ngo (ed.), *Hong Kong's History: State and Society under Colonial Rule* (pp. 46–73), London: Routledge.

Ng, M. and A. Cook (1997) 'Reclamation: An Urban Development Strategy under Fire', *Land Use Policy*, 14(1): 5–23.

Offe, C. (1985) 'New Social Movements: Challenging the Boundaries of Institutional Politics', *Social Research*, 52(4): 817–868.

Olick, J.K. and D. Levy (1997) 'Collective Memory and Cultural Constraints: Holocaust Myth and Rationality in German Politics', *American Sociological Review*, 62: 921–936.

Schwartz, B. (1996) 'Memory as a Cultural System: Abraham Lincoln in World War II', *American Sociological Review*, 61: 908–927.

Touraine, A. (1985) 'An Introduction to the Study of Social Movements', *Social Research*, 52(4): 749–787.

Urry, J. (1995) *Consuming Places*, London: Routledge.

Zukin, S. (1995) *The Cultures of Cities*, Cambridge, MA: Blackwell.

13 The cultural grassroots and the authoritarian city

Spaces of contestation in Singapore

Jason Luger

Introduction

From the top of the monumental Marina Bay Sands Hotel, fifty-seven floors above Singapore's glistening financial district, the city-state spreads away into the tropical haze in a sea of towers. The street, far below, looks very small. Yet, ensconced in the city's nooks and crannies, an increasingly vocal cultural grassroots has emerged. Singapore's quest to be a 'Global City for the Arts' has been well documented (Chang, 2000; Chang and Lee, 2003; and Chapter 6, this volume; Yue, 2007; Yun, 2008; Kong, 2012; Goh, 2014) as it has positioned itself among the world's elite club of global cultural cities. Yet only recently have researchers begun the task of exploring the Singaporean grassroots, and how cultural activism manifests and engenders various encounters on the ground. How to locate politics in Singapore's cultural context and how to conceptualise the ways in which cultural and political encounters shape each other are now compelling questions.

It is possible to look back, and reflect, upon the decades of cultural policy in cities, as Bell and Oakley (2015) have done. However, while cultural policy may be well explored, the nexus of art, politics and activism within the cultural city is very much in vogue. 'Cultural activism' (Buser et al., 2013), 'creative resistance' (Colomb and Novy, 2012) and 'artivism' (Krischer, 2012) are terms used interchangeably to refer to that segment of the creative community seeking new 'spaces of hope' (Harvey, 2002). Such activism also uses creative methods such as visual and performance art, music and sculpture to remake and reconceptualise urban space (Buser et al., 2013). More broadly, authors are using recent cases (in the post-'Occupy Wall Street' era) to question what it means to be an activist and perform activism: can simply showing up be included? What are the contemporary forms of micro-resistance that may look quite different from traditional conceptions of activism and protest (see Solnit, 2005; Chatterton and Pickerill, 2010)? How do cultural spaces shape political encounters, and how do such encounters shape spaces?

Furthermore, locating and mapping the contextual contours of emergent cultural activism across various spatial typologies and scales, and the ways in which complicated networks, coalitions and alliances overlap (and sometimes contradict) in these places are other important, difficult tasks. Andy Merrifield (2013) speaks of 'wormholes' and 'nodes' within the urban fabric, while Harvey (2012) suggests that cultural groups are critical to forming spaces of contestation, opening up new possibilities. What these wormholes look like, or how a 'space of hope' might differ in context and fabric from Paris to Singapore, therefore invites exploration: do cities remain privileged sites for political struggle as Lees (2014: 235) proposes? And within and across cities, how do privileged sites – squares, parks, the home, the café, online social networks – define new cultural–political movements, and how are they shaped and defined by these movements?

Asian cities have recently gained more prominence as case studies, as a call for new modes of comparison and 'worlding' theory (Robinson, 2011; Roy and Ong, 2011) has coincided with an upswing in resistance and contestation in Asian cities (and everywhere else). Asian cities such as Singapore have also become increasingly influential in global policy circuits, envisioned not only as policy recipients but also as policy generators (Ren and Luger, 2015). This volume therefore represents an important and timely attempt to bring to light the geographies of the Asian cultural city.

If Merrifield (2013) seeks to 'scale up' to the 'planetary' level in developing a new urban ontology, then this chapter seeks to 'scale down': it will offer a cursory tour of three interconnected spatial scales and contexts of the Singaporean cultural-activist 'encounter': the critical theatre space (the Substation); the central public square; (Speakers' Corner, also known as Hong Lim Park); and the Singaporean 'digital agora' of social media and blogs, which Habermas (1989) called the 'public sphere' and which Merrifield (2013) points to as indicative of the 'planetary' reach of the urban encounter (in this case, transcending the physical boundaries of the island city-state). Groups and networks overlap across these spaces, using art and culture in complex ways to probe and challenge the social and political landscape and the built/digital environments.

What these examples show is both the destabilising potential of art-led activism in Singapore to form 'spaces of hope' within the authoritarian fabric and, simultaneously, the ways that the built and digital environments are engineered in ways to control and *stabilise* the arts. This dichotomy is present in many contexts, but particularly in Singapore. In negotiating the networks of encounter and the encountering of networks in and across the city-state, we can continue the task of mapping the contours of the planetary city, the transformative potential of cultural activism, and the contextual geographies of contemporary socio-political movements while also probing the located complexity and contradictions of one version of authoritarian governance (at the island city-state scale).

Singapore-focused authors have begun to probe, critically, how cultural/ creative spaces are used (Ho, 2009; Chang, 2014 and Chapter 6, this volume) but, as yet, the connection between artists, arts spaces and broader activism has not been fully explored. It is here that this chapter aims to fill a gap, and probe the question of how Singapore's art, cultural and activist networks interweave, overlap and encounter one another in urban space.

Globalising (and questioning) the spaces of cultural activism

Urban space is being reconceptualised within the new reality of a hyper-networked world, and, thus, the shifting spaces/places of activism and lateral activist networks are likewise being re-examined. The longstanding material/immaterial dichotomy of socio-spatial relations and interactions remains a prescient (and unresolved) discussion, as cyberspace and social media mean that the revolution is being 'tweeted' and is simultaneously occurring in situ on the urban street (see Gerbaudo, 2012). Authors are reintroducing and reincorporating 'place' and 'space' into the lexicon of networked geographies, arguing that the daily practices of activists in 'place' remain a critical concern in the study of social activism (Amin, 2005; Soja, 2010; Harvey, 2012). Specific, material sites remain key to explore, and to be part of the efforts within urban studies to connect the study of local sites to the networked and transnational relationships that make up social activism (Cumbers et al., 2008; Featherstone, 2008). Merrifield (2013) calls upon Castells's conception of a 'space of flows' to describe the global landscape of emerging resistance and activism:

> The space of flows is not placeless: it is made of nodes and networks; that is, of places connected by electronically powered communication networks through which flows of information . . . circulate and interact . . . [T]he space of the network society is made up of an articulation between three elements: the places where activities are located; the material communication networks linking these activities; and the content and geometry of the flows of information that perform the activities in terms of function and meaning.
>
> (Castells 2009: 34)

Within the space of flows, 'nodes' emerge that can be material and central (such as Zuccotti Park near Wall Street, or Tahrir Square in Cairo), but these nodes can also be immaterial and highly moveable, lacking clear delineations of fixities. Buser et al. (2013) stress the importance of particular sites and urban 'places' that are infused with meaning by cultural activism, and are crucial to *shaping* such activism. They use the Stokes-Croft neighbourhood in Bristol, UK, to demonstrate how 'place' can 'play a critical role in the fostering of political collectivity'. They also argue that taking 'place' seriously within critical activism necessitates 'analysis of how neighbourhoods, streets, sites, structures (and so on) may serve as flexible referents for radical politics, cultural sensibilities or the potentials of cultural activism more generally' (Buser et al., 2013: 2). Exploring the new geographies of cultural activism therefore requires a journey through various spatial scales and urban places, as different socio-spatial relations and networks interact, encounter and form one another differently, within and across these scales. That is not to say that material sites of activism are discounted, but rather that they are understood to be extended by (and into) cyberspace, and vice versa.

A new strand of literature has emerged which focuses less on the policy implications of the urban cultural turn and more the relationship between the arts, urban space and broader activist and resistance movements. These movements are portrayed as a collection of coalitions and alliances, with varying levels of cohesion and tenacity, differing in form, style, aims and agenda. Colomb and Novy (2012) explore the (sometimes contradictory) cultural coalitions and alliances that seek 'spaces of hope' in (and against) what is portrayed as Berlin and Hamburg's neoliberal appropriation of arts and culture, while Buser et al. (2013) look at the ways in which disparate networks come together to form a cohesive 'aesthetics of protest' (as Rancière envisioned) in Bristol. One shortcoming of both studies is their European focus. Perhaps the broadest recent survey of 'socially engaged art' is Nato Thompson's (2012) exploration of various forms of cultural activism (ranging from theatre to street art), as this at least ventures into the Global South (citing cases in South America, for example).

Despite the lingering problem of urban research sometimes handling Asian cities with kid gloves due to perceived 'otherness' (see Ren and Luger, 2015), more explorations of what art-led activism looks like across Asia's contours and textures are emerging. This is particularly true as recent activist earthquakes have shaken Hong Kong, Bangkok, Taipei, a number of Chinese cities and, albeit less sensationally, Singapore. The arts play a central role in this new geography of Asian activism, partially due to the arts' relative space for expression within the confines of (varying degrees of) authoritarianism.

In Thailand, 'red shirts' became a pop-culture fashion symbol of anti-government protest (see Thammaboosadee, 2014); and in Hong Kong, Sonia Lam (2014) has explored how performance art (the Post-80s movement) has linked up with traditional street demonstrations over a variety of issues – most recently efforts to resist Beijing's increasing control over the territory (known as the 'Umbrella Revolution'). Krischer (2012) journeys through Tokyo, Seoul and Hong Kong to explore the ways in which artists use a variety of methods to confront social, cultural and political issues and challenge both state and corporate power. On the ground conditions vary across Asia: an activist activity that might be tolerated in one place (such as still relatively open Hong Kong) might land an artist in detention somewhere else (such as mainland China). Still, this Asian 'artivism' is connected laterally, Krischer suggests, by bilateral learning processes and by common, overarching issues of concern such as housing costs, poverty and the neoliberal appropriation of urban space.

A number of authors have traced the growth and evolution of 'creative city' policies in Asia (see Kong et al., forthcoming), as well as the self-conscious ways in which artists have positioned themselves as agents of change (such as gentrification) within Asian cities (see Chapter 11, this volume). Thus far, however, Singapore – a particularly complex and hybridised Asian city due to its blend of 'Eastern' and 'Western' approaches, progressive and conservative cultural factions, and democratic and authoritarian political characteristics – has been largely absent from the discussion on the nexus of art, activism and urban space. As mentioned above, it is here that this chapter attempts to fill a gap. Findings are based on the first comprehensive study to explore the crossroads of the arts, activism, space and place in Singapore. The research incorporated semi-structured interviews with thirty artist–activists, as well as participant and site observations (including digital ethnography), and was carried out between 2012 and 2014. With this in mind, I will now turn to Singapore's current climate of socio-cultural upheaval, and the related spaces of contestation.

Cultural contestation in the city-state

Political, cultural and social activism have grown in Singapore as the city-state has embraced – and been impacted by – global currents and ideas (Tan, 2003, 2008; Goh, 2014). Singapore's status as an (economically and ideologically) open global city is also a leading cause of societal discontent: local wages have stagnated as manual labourers have arrived from places like Sri Lanka and Bangladesh, while housing costs have skyrocketed as wealthy expatriates have moved into gated villas and luxury private condos. Singapore has remained the world's most expensive city for several years.[1] Government censorship of media, public discourse and the arts has generated a loud national debate, particularly following the recent prosecution – and conviction – of a number of political bloggers. LGBT rights continue to be divisive, as slow liberalisation of colonial-era anti-gay laws have generated a conservative backlash (such as 2014's 'wear white' campaign). Films and visual and performance art that cross certain limits (which Ooi (2009) explains can be political, cultural or moral) face the Censorship Review Committee (CRC) and may be banned (as the play *Stoma* was in 2014).

The arts and cultural realm is crucial in Singapore's wider landscape of contestation because more direct political action is largely out of the question. It is impossible to 'Occupy' in Singapore: political protests are highly sanitized and come with many caveats and restrictions (including rather vague rules on threats to ethnic, racial or religious harmony). At the same time, the arts-scape becomes a contested, destabilising force with anti-state and anti-globalisation factions: arts and culture (and related spaces and networks) therefore become staging grounds for wider political movements, given relatively more space and room to breathe within authoritarian confines. Arts spaces and places, both material and digital, take on a decidedly political identity by proxy; the encounters in and across these spaces, which occur concurrently at various scales, are, by default, *political* encounters. Herein arises the central paradox of 'cultural Singapore': while the government rarely tolerates direct protest, it accepts 'artistic' protest (to a degree, at least) as a necessary (and forgivable) externality of the Singaporean cultural turn within its new global positioning (Chang, 2000; Chang and Lee, 2003; Ooi, 2008, 2009, 2010a; Kong, 2012).

In conceptualising the socio-spatial forms of the Singaporean cultural-activist-scape (what Hartley (1992: 29–30) calls the 'place of citizenry'), we can summarise here the typologies of space through which this chapter will journey: a smaller, indoor space (the Substation Theatre); a larger, outdoor park, (Hong Lim Park/Speakers' Corner); and finally, the digital place of cultural activism, which Merrifield (2013) suggests is 'planetary' in scale and therefore transcends the boundaries of the city-state. Howell (1993: 313) conceptualises spaces such as these, which function as small openings within a repressive power structure, as 'islands of freedom' surrounded by Foucault's 'carceral archipelago'. In these 'hidden islands' (or 'wormholes' or 'nodes'), groups and networks interact with one another, and with the political sphere, in different ways – formed, emancipated and limited by the possibilities and restrictions each place allows, within the broader context of Singapore's particular form, scale and politics.

Indoor cultural activism: The Substation Theatre

The Substation is located on Armenian Street at the base of Fort Canning Park and very much in the centre of Singapore's 'Arts and Civic District'. It is a theatre as well as a rehearsal, meeting and gallery space. Founded a generation ago by the pioneering playwright Kuo Pau Kun, it is one of the primary material spaces where disparate groups (from theatre and dance companies to activist groups) can hire out spaces at low (subsidised) rates in a safe environment where they will be able to express themselves (relatively) freely, critically or not. It must be noted, however, that like any other organisation or space in Singapore that receives part of its funding from the state (in this case, the National Arts Council), users must not step (too far) over the 'out of bounds' markers. Therefore, anti-government activities or any event, display, discussion or forum that might upset Singapore's delicate political, racial, cultural and religious order is generally restricted. Examples of recent events that have faced censorship or even an outright ban include a public forum on the death penalty and a play that probed sexual abuse in the Catholic Church.

Nevertheless, for Singapore, this is a radical space. It allows a wide range of fringe (and mainstream) groups to use a variety of micro-spaces: a large black box theatre, a gallery space, and upstairs rehearsal spaces/studios, all located in a refurbished 'shop-house'[2] which has a characteristic vibe and atmosphere. The Substation's versatility is deliberate: it is a space for other spaces, a space for all users, or, in the words of the creative director, a 'renaissance space'. On any given day (including during my visit), a punk-band may be rehearsing in one room, an art exhibition may be in the gallery, and a public activist forum or debate may be under way in the black box theatre, all at the same time (see Figure 13.1). All of the disparate groups are united through their use of the space, if not by any cause, mission or social relationship. The Substation's creative director appreciates the delicate role that the building plays as a space of critical possibility within the confines of the state. Above all, he explains that it is a sort of all-encompassing home for both the arts and other critical dialogues to take place: 'We are a space first and foremost in the sense that we facilitate, we provide . . . spaces for incuba-tion, for process, for creation, for dialogue, for learning. And I think of late maybe it's also a space for "unlearning"' (interview, Substation creative director, November 2012).

As such, The Substation's role in fostering activist encounters is far more important than might be the case with a theatre space in another city. It is a

Figure 13.1 Posters for upcoming events on the wall of The Substation
Source: the author.

conventional theatre space in the sense that it has a regular programme of events (plays, recitals, exhibitions), but it is also a focal point for all, or at least most, of the cultural-activism encounters that occur in Singapore, making it an anchoring 'node' in the city-state's activist/artistic fabric. The Substation was mentioned in many research interviews as perhaps the only building with the scale, scope and freedom to facilitate the mixing and interaction of artistic, activist and political groups under one roof. During my conversation with one activist painter, for example, I asked where artists, activists and the broader community could come together indoors in Singapore. After a pause, he responded, 'Yeah, the Substation, because . . . sometimes you see . . . theatre plays, punk music next door, art in the gallery, and activists outside' (interview, painter, January 2013).

There is tension in the diverse use of the space, both when the state's 'out of bounds' markers are crossed and within and among the various users, but this tension is one of the stated aims of the creative director. He believes that cultural possibilities – and radical new directions – that are unique in Singapore emerge out it and from the flexible occupation of interior space:

> Within that diversity [there are] opposites – many opposites – that coexist, and we welcome that tension, we nurture that tension, in the hope that there will be . . . cross-dialogue, cross-cultural dialogue . . . And it's not a

top-down thing, it's a bottom-up . . . phenomenon. We encourage a kind of confrontationist approach. So our role is really to ensure that this tension can continue to exist in Singapore.

(Interview, Substation creative director, November 2012)

The spatial tension therefore unites in situ groups that may not normally encounter one another. The Substation serves as a sort of reference point capable of instigating new discussions and linkages. Several interviewees viewed it as a 'meeting place' where a certain idea was generated, a connection was made, or a friendship was formed.

That is not to say that The Substation's possibilities are limitless. Though it enjoys a large degree of autonomy, it must operate within state boundaries, which continuously expand and contract, resulting in a permanent sense of precariousness. The Substation might be described, at best, as a partially opened 'wormhole' in that it fosters a unique type of encounter but is limited by its own roof and walls and by the inflexibility of Singapore's political–cultural arena. Neither its independence nor its ability to cross certain boundaries as an 'island of freedom' is guaranteed.

The next example demonstrates how these limits and possibilities are extended to the realm of outdoor public space. Hong Lim Park is larger and far more visible than the Substation and, as such, it has a centrality and resonance as a node of the cultural-activist encounter.

Outdoor cultural activism: Speakers' Corner/Hong Lim Park

Speakers' Corner, a state-designated place for free expression, can be found in Hong Lim Park, a two-acre grassy square near the financial district. The park is unique in Singapore as a site where large groups (sometimes numbering in the thousands) can assemble (peacefully) to voice critical opinions – albeit with certain restrictions. Thereby, it has become a focal point for cultural activism in the authoritarian built environment. Comparisons with 'pop-up' revolutionary areas, such as Manhattan's Zuccotti Park or Cairo's Tahrir Square, are difficult to make because Hong Lim Park is officially designated (by the authorities) as a protest space; it did not assume its identity through bottom-up social upheaval. It is also strictly demarcated (and monitored), making it something of a Foucauldian 'panopticon' (Foucault, 1980). On most days, its landscaped lawn is devoid of people (at least that was the case whenever I walked through it), and large gatherings must be pre-approved and abide by a number of rules. Several signposts around the park denote what is and what is not permitted: any activity that is seen to be against 'racial or religious harmony' (a grey area that is constantly evolving in Singapore's ongoing moral and cultural conversation) is forbidden.

Nevertheless, due to its size, centrality, symbolic meaning and historical significance, Hong Lim Park is unique as a public space in Singapore that provides a stage for thousands of diverse voices. Despite the rules and regulations, it is a place where activists, artists and indeed any other groups can and do gather for a variety of causes and in sufficiently large numbers to garner national and even international attention. Merrifield (2013: 66) notes that such squares have crucial importance as physical meeting places:

> Squares like Zucotti Park or Tahrir are urban public spaces not for reason of their pure concrete physicality but because they are meeting places between virtual and physical worlds . . . that is why they are public – because they enable public discourses and public conversations to talk to each other, to meet each other, quite literally.

On 'International Human Rights Day' in December 2012, I came across the 'Really, Really Free Market' in Hong Lim Park (Figure 13.2). This event was sponsored by an arts group (anonymised here due to political sensitivity), who were present along with a wide variety of unrelated activists: for instance, migrant workers' groups shared the space with an anti-rape organisation. There were opportunities to trade books, clothes and other items. On one blanket sat relatives of some of Singapore's long-term political detainees. Krischer (2012) describes a similar 'free market' in Tokyo, and the movement has its origins in the cooperatives of the United States (several US cities have 'free markets', including my home

Figure 13.2 The 'Really, Really Free Market' at Hong Lim Park
Source: the author.

town of Durham, North Carolina). This therefore represents an example of cross-cultural influence and co-learning of 'artivist' techniques and tactics applied in a Singaporean setting (within site-specific authoritarian confines that do not exist in the United States or Tokyo). So the event is both comparable and incommensurable.

The Really, Really Free Market – with its ambiguous mission and seemingly unrelated, disparate participants – is the type of grassroots activity that can take place in Hong Lim Park without fear of censorship from the authorities. Viewed as a strategy, such an event allows decidedly political activism (human rights campaigners; those seeking the release of political detainees and the return of exiled dissidents) to mingle with more banal art displays and enjoy the non-monetary exchange of goods, foodstuffs, clothes and crafts. Viewed from above, perhaps, this is not a political event – it poses no threat to state. Picked apart, and closer to the ground, however, it contains pointed political messages, all curated by artists who revealed in interviews that they were acutely aware of the potential for such events to promote activism and the exchange of (radical) ideas. Part of the Really, Really Free Market's success, and ability to force a cross-cultural conversation, is this ambiguity and lack of overtly political over-tones. It is therefore a rather dressed-down, sanitised version of political activism, rendered acceptable to Singapore's 'moral majority' and to the authorities. Naturally, this leads to the question: is this really activism at all? And if it is, can it be truly transformative, radical or political?

As such, there are mixed opinions on the sort of emancipatory 'spaces of hope' that Hong Lim Park may or may not enable to emerge out of the cultural-activist landscape and whether such a controlled, demarcated activist site has the potential to host transformative urban encounters. Some activists I interviewed genuinely seemed to appreciate the possibilities afforded by Hong Lim Park and the simple fact that it was a designated space for expression, but most agreed that the space alone was not enough and should be utilised alongside other openings, nodes and wormholes:

> I'm always looking for spaces. I mean, it's great that we have Hong Lim Park, to some extent – it's a public gathering space. But you need to complement public work with private work as well. And that's when we need more closed spaces, more safe spaces, where smaller groups of people can come together. And it would be slightly more intimate, I guess.
>
> (Interview, activist, February 2013)

Other voices were more sceptical of Speakers' Corner as a legitimate space for free expression, envisioning it more as a gestural space, emasculated of its radical potential by authoritarian restrictions. An architect who has designed many of Singapore's recent buildings commented: 'They tried to make it a park but there are too many restrictions. It's a public space, but it is not really utilised the way it could be utilised. Historically it was quite a big gathering place' (interview, architect, March 2013).

Hong Lim Park does have many limitations, but it allows a scale and visibility for activism that are impossible elsewhere in Singapore and thus represents an opening: it has the capability to induce a nationwide discussion and for that reason it is powerful. Moreover, 'rare alliances'[3] that are simply impossible in a theatre like The Substation have the potential to form in the park. The 'free market' allows activists, artists and those who are merely interested onlookers to come together and thus expand the reach and capabilities of Singaporean activism.

An even larger, and potentially more destabilising, space is the cyber-city of digital activism that stretches far beyond Singapore's borders. Though material activism cannot occur online, cyberspace provides a different, novel type of platform. This enables new possibilities for socio-cultural interaction and for spaces like The Substation and Hong Lim Park to become much larger and more significant than their physical forms allow by extending into cyberspace.

Singapore's digital 'artivists'

#FreeAmosYee. 7 people like this.

(Singaporean artist's Facebook page, 2015)

In contrast to Singapore's modest physical scale and rigid authoritarian restrictions, cyberspace, or what Habermas (1989) called the aspatial/normative 'public sphere', is notably large and loud in the City-State. Cyber-Singapore remains relatively open, with blogs and social media serving as numerous digital speakers' corners. This space contains a wide cross-section of voices and opinions, reflecting society at large – from conservative groups to radical organisations, with coalitions and alliances that sometimes intersect and overlap in ways that are unique to cyberspace. Artists, in digital form, play a crucial role as online instigators and curators of digital activist movements.

Though Habermas (1989) and Don Mitchell (1995, 2014) remain sceptical, and Malcolm Gladwell (2010) suggests that the 'revolution will *not* be tweeted', theorists such as Merrifield (2013) and Gerbaudo (2012) assign a crucial place (and a high potential) to the digital street in today's complicated global web of urban networks. Digital activism may not supplant the city street as a primary site of encounter, but in a context such as Singapore's (where use of the street and the material commons comes with so many restrictions), it forms an important addition, helping to 'scale up' and amplify the activities occurring in material form.

The digital city is no panacea. Cyber-Singapore is subject to surveillance and censorship by the authorities, as well as varying degrees of self-censorship. The government's sporadic prosecution of bloggers for posting critical comments indicates the increasing reach of authoritarianism into cyberspace. For instance, in 2014, the blogger Alex Au of yawningbread.wordpress (which frequently airs critical views on any number of topics) was convicted of defamation for comments he posted that were critical of the way in which Singapore's high court had handled gay rights cases. The following year, a sixteen-year-old named Amos Yee was found guilty of libel over comments he made on YouTube about the recently deceased Lee Kuan Yew (Singapore's prime minister for more than thirty years). Still, the cloak of anonymity and the difficulties of policing the internet's many highways and tributaries give bloggers a degree of power and freedom: physical space is not needed to express opinions and there is room for almost everyone. Just as a material arts spaces such as The Substation allow for some (relative) breathing room and free expression, so too do cyber arts spaces, as is evidenced by the highly charged (and often overtly political) posts, comments and discussions that have appeared on the social media pages of several Singaporean artists over recent years. People act differently online, frequently saying and doing things that they would never dream of doing on the street or at a party.

One arts group (anonymised here due to political sensitivity) that frequently organises events in Singapore has an extremely vocal online presence, forming new types of encounters that are often more directly political and critical than when observed in places like The Substation and Hong Lim Park. While semi-structured interviews conducted with one member of this group about the nature of their work did not garner any overtly political comments, digitally shadowing the same artist on Facebook revealed a very different tenor and tone. The themes, aims and missions of the public events that the artist curates seem to be about raising awareness and using art to induce reflexivity, introspection and self-questioning. Rather than championing any specific political cause or topical protest, the artist organises events around broader themes of social and grassroots values:

> We set up in spaces and we attempt to change the economic laws. We demand that everything inside here be free. And we talk about the values, the qualities, of having to share. That is the only value that we argue for.
>
> (Interview, artist, 2013)

Online, however, the same artist is ardently political, posting angry opinions about Singapore's and other nations' ruling elites. Their Facebook page – which is open to the public, not private – covers a wide range of artistic and political themes. These posts have generated a cross-cutting discussion, and a new space for art–activist encounter not found on the Singaporean streets or in any Singaporean building. For instance, Amos Yee's arrest prompted the artist to instigate a critical discussion. The artist crossed into the activist space to spearhead a digital campaign to 'free Amos Yee' and fund his legal defence: 'Anyone who would like to lend their support to this photo campaign, please do so today!' (Artist's Facebook page, 1 May 2015). The artist allied with the Community Action Network (CAN) – a Singapore-based grassroots advocacy group – to release a (digital) statement that protested both the public's condemnation of Yee and the official charges that had been laid against him. One of the comments on this posting encapsulated the digital art–activist space's generative potential: 'Thank God for the Internet. There is a God.' It received four 'likes'.

Conclusion: cultural revolution Singapore-style

As Lefebvre surmised (and Merrifield paraphrased), 'human beings make space just by encountering other human beings' (Merrifield 2013: 36). In Singapore these encounters occur digitally and materially and thus 'the urban consolidates, creates its own definition, its own coming-together'. In Singapore, centrality is moveable, relative, not fixed and (as Merrifield might propose) always in a state of constant mobilisation and negotiation (sometimes decentring itself). It resembles a spider's web rather than a fixed square, in contrast to Zucotti Park or Tahrir Square. Lefebvre (1968) wrote that there can be no city without centrality. Yet, in Singapore, 'centrality' has a peculiar meaning: it may lie closer to Merrifield's interpretation of a place (or space) where

> People encounter one another because of certain situations, because of certain collisions in time and space, because of certain attributes . . . people discover interpellated group commonality because bodies and minds take hold in a space that is at once territorial and deterritorial, in a time that isn't clock or calendar time but eternal time.
>
> (Merrifield 2013: 35)

Singapore's multitude of 'minor spaces' – including The Substation Theatre, Hong Lim Park and innumerable websites – may be combining to form 'major spaces' (as Merrifield calls them), enabling new possibilities to emerge, remaking the cultural city-state and sending it forward in new directions.

Notes

1 Economist Intelligence Unit, 2014.
2 A type of vernacular, colonial-era architecture common in Singapore and Malaysia.
3 http://blogs.wsj.com/indonesiarealtime/2014/06/28/rare-alliance-forms-in-singapore-to-challenge-gay-rights-rally/ (accessed 10/06/15).

References

Amin, A. (2005) 'Local community on trial', *Economy and society*, 34(4): 612–633.
Bell, D. and Oakley, K. (2015) *Cultural Policy*, London: Routledge.
Buser, M., Bonura, C., Fanin, M. and Boyer, K. (2013) 'Cultural activism and the politics of placemaking', *City*, 17(5): 606–627.
Castells, M. (2009) *Communication Power*, Oxford: Oxford University Press.
Chang, T.C. (2000) 'Renaissance revisited: Singapore as a global city for the arts', *International Journal of Urban and Regional Research*, 24(4): 818–831.
Chang, T.C. (2014) '"New uses need old buildings": gentrification aesthetics and the arts in Singapore', *Urban Studies*, http://usj.sagepub.com/content/early/2014/03/17/004209 8014527482.full.pdf+html (accessed 29/07/15).
Chang, T.C. and Lee, W.K. (2003) 'Renaissance City Singapore: a study of arts spaces', *Area*, 35(2): 128–141.

Chatterton, P. and Pickerill, J. (2010) 'Everyday activism and transitions towards post-capitalist worlds', *Transactions of the Institute of British Geographers*, NS35: 475–490.

Chua, B. (2011) 'Singapore as model: planning innovation, knowledge experts', in A. Ong A. and A. Roy (eds), *Worlding Cities: Asian Experiments and the Art of Being Global*, London: Blackwell.

Colomb, C. and Novy, J. (2012) 'Struggling for the right to the (creative) city in Berlin and Hamburg: new urban social movements, new "spaces of hope"?', *International Journal of Urban and Regional Research*, 37(5): 1816–1838.

Cumbers, A., Routledge, P. and Nativel, C. (2008) 'Labour agency and union positionalities in global production networks', *Journal of Economic Geography*, 8: 369–387.

Davis, M. (1990) *City of Quarts: Excavating the Future in Los Angeles*, London: Verso.

Featherstone, D.J. (2008) *Resistance, Space and Political Identities: The Making of Counter-Global Networks*, Chichester: Wiley-Blackwell.

Foucault, M. (1980) *Power/Knowledge*, London: Harvester.

Fraser, N. (1990) 'Rethinking the public sphere: a contribution to actually existing democracy', *Social Text*, 25/26: 56–79.

Gerbaudo, P. (2012) *Tweets and the Streets: Social Media and Contemporary Activism*, London: Pluto Press.

Gladwell, M. (2010) 'Small change: why the revolution will not be tweeted', *New Yorker*, 28 September.

Goh, D. (2014) 'Walking in the global city: the politics of rhythm and memory in Singapore', *Space and Culture*, 17(1): 16–28

Habermas, J. (1989) *The Structural Transformation of the Public Sphere: An Inquiry into a Category*, trans. T. Burger with F. Lawrence, Cambridge, MA: MIT Press.

Hartley, J. (1992) *The Politics of Pictures: The Creation of the Public in the Age of Popular Media*, Perth: Psychology Press.

Harvey, D. (2002) *Spaces of Hope*, Berkeley: University of California Press.

Harvey, D. (2012) *Rebel Cities: From the Right to the City to the Urban Revolution*, London: Verso.

Ho, K.C. (2009) 'The neighbourhood in the creative economy: policy, practice and place in Singapore', *Urban Studies*, 46: 1187–1201.

Howell, P. (1993) 'Public space and the public sphere: political theory and the historical geography of modernity,', *Environment and Planning A*, 11(3): 303–322.

Kong, L. (2012) 'Ambitions of a global city: arts, culture and creative economy in "post-crisis" Singapore', *International Journal of Cultural Policy*, 18(3): 279–294.

Kong, L., Ching, C.-H. and Chou, T.-L. (forthcoming) *Arts, Culture and the Making of Global Cities: Creating New Urban Landscapes in Asia*, Cheltenham: Edward Elgar.

Krischer, O. (2012) 'Lateral thinking: artivist networks', *Art Asia Pacific*, 77: 96–105.

Lam, S. (2014) 'Re-examining political expression in Hong Kong: Post-80s youths and performance art', paper presented at the American Association of Geographers' Annual Meeting, Tampa, FL, April.

Lees, L. (2014) 'Re-encountering Andy Merrifield and the *Politics of the Encounter: Urban Theory and Protest under Planetary Urbanisation*', *Progress in Human Geography*, 4(2): 233–235.

Lefebvre, H. (1968) *Le Droit de la Ville* (2nd edn), Paris: Anthropos.

Lefebvre, H. (1991) *The Production of Space*, trans. D. Nicholson-Smith, Oxford: Basil Blackwell.

Merrifield, A. (2013) *The Politics of the Encounter: Urban Theory and Protest under Planetary Urbanization*, Athens: University of Georgia Press.

Mitchell, D. (1995) 'The end of public space? People's park, definitions of the public, and democracy', *Annals of the Association of American Geographers*, 85(1): 108–133.

Mitchell, D. (2014) 'Reviewing Andy Merrifield's *The Politics of the Encounter: Urban Theory and Protest under Planetary Urbanism*', *Dialogues in Human Geography*, 4: 235–238.

Ooi, C. (2008) 'Reimagining Singapore as a creative nation: the politics of place branding', *Place Branding and Public Diplomacy*, 4: 287–302.

Ooi, C. (2009) 'Government and creativity: arts city Singapore', *Creative Industries*, 3: 44–47 (in Chinese).

Ooi, C. (2010a) 'Political pragmatism and the creative economy: Singapore as a city for the arts', *International Journal of Cultural Policy*, 16(4): 403–417.

Ooi, C. (2010b) *Singapore's Cultural Policy: Authenticity, Regulation and Stratification*, report on IPS Seminar, Faculty of Law, National University of Singapore, 11 August.

Ren, J. and Luger, J. (2015) 'Comparative urbanism and the "Asian City": implications for research and theory', *International Journal of Urban and Regional Research*, 39: 145–156.

Robinson, J. (2011) 'Cities in a world of cities: the comparative gesture', *International Journal of Urban and Regional Research*, 35(1): 1–23.

Roy, A. and Ong, A. (2011) *Worlding Cities: Asian Experiments and the Art of Being Global*, London: Wiley-Blackwell.

Soja, E. (2010) *Seeking Spatial Justice*, Minneapolis: University of Minnesota Press.

Solnit, R. (2005) *Hope in the Dark: The Never Surrender Guide to the Changing World*, Edinburgh: Canongate.

Tan, K.P. (2003) 'Sexing up Singapore', *International Journal of Cultural Studies*, 6(4): 403–423.

Tan, K.P. (2008) 'Meritocracy and elitism in a global city: ideological shifts in Singapore', *International Political Science Review*, 29(1): 7–27.

Thammaboosadee, R. (2014) 'Urban cultures that affect performance identity of PDRC protester in Thailand', paper presented at Performance Place Possibility: Performance in Urban Contexts, 31 March–6 April, University of Leeds, UK.

Thompson, N. (ed.) (2012) *Living as Form: Socially Engaged Art from 1991–2011*, Cambridge, MA: MIT Press.

Yue, A. (2007) 'Hawking in the creative city: rice rhapsody, sexuality and the cultural politics of New Asia in Singapore', *Feminist Media Studies*, 7(4): 365–380.

Yun, H.A. (2008) 'Singapore, the evolving creative city', in P. Cooke and L. Lazzaretti (eds), *Creative Cities, Cultural Clusters, and Local Economic Development*, Cheltenham: Edward Elgar.

14 Gentrification in the mill lands of Mumbai

Changing spatial practices and everyday life in working-class chawls

Dwiparna Chatterjee and
Devanathan Parthasarathy

Introduction

A process of deindustrialisation followed by a prolonged textile mill strike lasting for two years (1982–1983) led to the eventual and gradual closure of Mumbai's textile mills (Chandavarkar, 1994, 2009; Kidambi, 2007). Currently these areas are witnessing massive redevelopment and regeneration of the built environment. The emergence of a new landscape of service-sector firms, IT industries, creative-sector industries, shopping malls, high-end restaurants, pubs, nightclubs, fashion houses and gated communities existing cheek by jowl with long rows of working-class chawls[1] has produced a landscape of contrast, contestation and aspiration (see Figure 14.1). The existence of creative spaces in the form of art galleries along with an agglomeration of small-scale industries, big and small eateries with *vada pav* snack stalls, and printing presses run by former textile-mill workers in the erstwhile textile mill compounds brings uniqueness to this place. The arrival of the upwardly mobile middle class (Fernandes, 2004) and the spill-over effects of bourgeois culture have deeply disturbed the older urban rhythms related to space, place, work and life in these localities for the working-class population. The gradual disappearance of the chawls from the neighbourhood and their replacement with low-cost residential high-rise towers for chawl dwellers and adjacent high-end luxury apartments for the rich (as part of the government's redevelopment strategy) complicates the situation even more. Different classes mix in the same area without complete displacement of one by the other. The remaining working-class chawls are being increasingly ghettoised and entrapped by the high walls of the emerging gated communities on the mill lands, not only creating a sense of discontent but igniting a process of negotiation and bargaining for some and entrapment for many.

This chapter focuses on the intricate relationship between the chawls and the surrounding working-class neighbourhoods. Chawls, with their indigenous social and urban practices, are in a most vulnerable position at present (Pendse et al., 2011; Adarkar, 2011). Based on an ethnographic study carried out through

Figure 14.1 City space of contrast, Parel, Mumbai
Source: the author.

non-participant observation and in-depth interviews with former mill workers and trade union leaders, we consider chawls as sites of 'spatial practice' (Lefebvre, 1991: 38), bringing out the nuances of everyday practices and interactions in chawls and their social reproduction across time vis-à-vis the production of new city spaces. While reference to Lefebvre's concept of spatial practice may suggest a framing around his well-known triad of spatial practice, representations of space and spaces of representation, here we draw only on spatial practice as a heuristic analytical device to help bring out the nuances of our description of transformations in Mumbai's mill lands. As summarised by Schmid (2008: 36), spatial practice 'designates the material dimension of social activity and inter-action. The classification *spatial* means focusing on the aspect of simultaneity of activities.' Thus, we pay particular attention to the simultaneity of activities that condition the transformation of spatial practice in the chawls. Viewing the chawl as a socially constructed space, we take into account the sense of confinement and exclusion within the contrasts, contestations, rising aspirations and negotiations in the everyday life of the working-class chawl communities. The chapter argues that the process of mill land redevelopment transforms the spatial practices and everyday life of the working class, producing a new space of gentrification where conflict, contestation, negotiation and aspirations evolve and are played out.

The contemporary space of the mill land areas

The contemporary space of the mill lands of Mumbai appears like a historical collage, with remnants of a number of old mill gates rusting forlornly, cold, functionless chimneys jutting up to the sky alongside rugged brick and stone buildings and typical working-class chawl residences. Presently it is a space of juxtaposition. It is difficult to escape the gaze of the residential high-rises and corporate offices with modern architecture standing alongside eroding mill buildings. The agglomeration of large and small mill structures (see Ghag, 2006: 74–75), small-scale industries and hundred-year-old chawls juxtaposed with recently emerging gated communities, high-end restaurants, nightclubs, sprawling slums and slum redevelopment buildings makes this area heterogeneous and unique. What was once exclusively mill land is now a space of plurality and contrast. The dark ten-by-twelve-square-foot chawl rooms, the old inhabitants (mostly working class), the busy office workers and the idle unemployed all seem to have their own narratives. The informal daily market at one end of the road contrasts dramatically with the high-end shopping malls at the other end.

Figure 14.2 A chawl in the neighbourhood of Sitaram Yadav Marg, Lower Parel, Mumbai

Source: the author.

With such contrasts as a backdrop, this chapter will first describe the spatial structure of a chawl in contemporary times, and will then turn to the 'spatial practices' (Lefebvre, 1991: 38) of chawl dwellers.

Chawls as spaces of spatial practice

The neighbourhood around Sitaram Yadav Marg in Lower Parel has rows of chawls (see Figure 14.2). They are mostly two-storey buildings, all leaning against each other. Most of the chawls are ninety to one hundred years old. Almost all of them have a gate at the entrance where the name of the chawl, the name of the building society and the year of construction are engraved. There is a cemented sitting arrangement on both sides of the entrance that remains dark and cool during the day. There is also a small religious space in every chawl just after entering through the main gate, where mostly idols of Shirdi Sai Baba and Hanuman are to be found. Often people rest in these areas during the day. In larger chawls the religious spaces are located in the courtyards. Every floor has a long, dark corridor filled with colourful clothes hanging from the ceiling and rooms with open doors facing each other. Four to five toilets are arranged separately at one corner of the corridor on each floor, and there is a separate washing area. In some of the chawls the toilets are located outside. Chawl rooms are usually very small, typically 225 to 375 square feet, although some can be as large as 450 square feet. Each room has a loft reached by a wooden staircase and a half-enclosed area with a three-to-four-foot wall on one side. Called a *mori*, this is used for bathing, changing clothes and washing utensils.

In one such chawl – the Amoledina Building in Sitaram Yadav Marg – we interviewed Binayak Dhamapurkar. His chawl was constructed in 1924 and consists of 35 rooms in total: 11 on the ground floor, 12 on the first floor and 12 on the second floor. He lives in No. 17, an unusually large room at around 450 square feet. At present two generations of the Dhamapurkar family live in this tenement, or *kholi*. Two rooms – one small kitchen and a very small attached washroom – seemed to be a much bigger space compared to many other chawls. When Dhamapurkar's father migrated to the city to work in the mill, he moved into this chawl along with his brothers. They paid rent of Rs.5; now it is Rs.150. The larger outer room is the hall, the middle room is the bedroom, and the inner smaller room is the kitchen. As there are three families staying in this *kholi*, the concept of hall and bedroom no longer exists. The outer room is used by Dhamapurkar and his elder brother's family. Leaving a small space as a passageway to the kitchen, the rest of the bedroom is separated by curtains made of sarees. This room is used by the extended family, who have been living there since the time of the mills.

During our first visit, the chawl was undergoing renovation. The *mori*, or bathing place, was being fully enclosed. The floors and the kitchen space were also getting a makeover. The room was messy and household goods of all kinds had been piled on to shelves. A very slender man of about sixty was sleeping on a cot near the door. The door of the room was always open. On the other side of the room a woman was making *chapatti* on a gas oven. A number of people repeatedly entered then left the room, sometimes talking to Dhamapurkar. None of these visitors seemed to be members of the family, yet no one – including those who were resting – seemed concerned by this apparent invasion of privacy. There were no obvious demarcations between inside and outside, between the private and public spheres of daily life. Chandavarkar (2009) mentions that the shortage of space in the chawls from the early days of the mills meant there was no distinction between the streets and the chawls. Large numbers of migrants slept in corridors, up staircases, on footpaths and on the platforms of the local railway stations.

Every corner of Dhamapurkar's chawl had multiple uses, and the residents' lives seemed harmonious, even though they occupied a very small space. The renovation work had been completed by the time of our second and third visits. Two gas ovens were now in the small kitchen space, one for Dhamapurkar's family and one for his brother's family. A small kitchen sink had been fitted and the wall had been tiled. A water tank in the loft provided adequate water for the whole day.

In the everyday lives of the chawl's inhabitants and in their spatial practices there was always a strong attachment towards each other, a feeling of brotherhood, or *bhaichara*. People from the same village would move to Mumbai for work and reside together in the same chawl, then continue to live there. This kind of bonding still prevails among the older generation. Workers who left their families in the villages would live together in a single room and work in shifts. Often family members would engage in small business activities, such as making lunch boxes, or *dabbas*, for other workers in order to earn some extra income (Pendse et al., 2011; Adarkar, 2011; Shetty, 2011; Chandavarkar, 2009; Kidambi, 2007). The mills operated three shifts – morning, noon and night. The workers, each with a *dabba* in hand, would leave their chawls and walk to the mill gates. The roads were filled with people at every hour of the day. A number of vegetable sellers would do business on the neighbourhood streets till late at night, and the small hotels and workers' eateries would typically stay open until midnight. Sundays were rest days for the workers. Those who lived with their families would look forward to spending time together, whereas those who lived with other workers in a single room faced problems because of the lack of space. Therefore, many of them would go elsewhere on Sundays and holidays. Janardan Deshmukh (a former mill worker) described his childhood in the chawl:

> The tenth of every month, *dus tareek*, was like Diwali for us . . . People would get their salary on the tenth, so there was happiness and celebration all around . . . The date was engraved in our minds . . . We used to enjoy it a lot. My father used to bring food for us. We used to wait for that. Then he would give us five or ten rupees . . . that was a moment of happiness. The workers would drink . . . the business of alcohol would run in the chawl.
>
> (Janardan Deshmukh, interview, May 2011)

According to the respondents, when the mills were operating, the chawls were occupied by mill workers at a nominal rent of Rs.3 or Rs.4 (about 5 or 6 US cents), and they moved frequently from one chawl to another. Dhamapurkar recalled that his father had plenty of options when he arrived in the city as there were many empty chawls in those days. Therefore, whenever the owner of a chawl was due to arrive to collect the rent at the start of the month, the workers would simply shift to a vacant chawl. Rooms were rented without the workers having to present any legal documents. If someone resided in a chawl for a long time and paid the rent regularly, he eventually automatically became the 'owner', although he still had to pay rent to the original owner.

The Rent Control Act and tenancy law resulted in the stagnation of rent and encouraged unauthorised and illegal tenancy activities, producing a black market for housing. If a tenant wished to become the legal owner of their room or wanted to sell it to others, they had to give a percentage of money to the original owner in order to transfer the property to their name. Various kinds of subterfuge were endemic in these transactions and in the negotiations between the tenants themselves and between tenants and owners.

Owners' lack of interest in their properties, due to the Rent Control Act, resulted in many of the chawls becoming increasingly dilapidated (Chandavarkar, 2009; Shetty, 2011; Kidambi, 2007). Soon whole neighbourhoods would become run-down. As Smith (1996) has noted, when an area deteriorates, rental income declines, creating a wide gap between current and optimum rent. This gap attracts real estate developers who are looking for investment opportunities. We argue that although Smith's theory and the process of 'revanchism' was based on a North American perspective, something similar happened in Mumbai. As the gap between the 'capitalised ground rent' and the 'potential ground rent' widens, the land becomes much dearer. It turns into a matter of higher speculation and leads to redevelopment in the neighbourhood. This entire process of redevelopment has been initiated by the closure of the mills since 1984 and has become a point of entry for the city's real estate developers. Smith's process of 'revanchism' was also known as a 'back to the city movement' for elites and capital. The relevance of his theory for Mumbai will be discussed later, but first we would like to describe the refurbishment of the chawls.

Some of the rooms in old chawls undergo minor repairs and renovations, as we witnessed in Dhamapurkar's *kholi*. But a neighbourhood might equally be subject to wholesale redevelopment, which necessitates eviction of all of the chawl dwellers. Here we have categorised three processes that a chawl may undergo: repair, renewal and redevelopment. The repairing process is settled through the funds given by a local representative of the Legislative Assembly after estimates are made. There is generally a nominal increase in rent after each repair. If the tenants want more extensive improvements to be made they might renovate, which we prefer to call a 'renewal process', since the chawl can be considered a neighbourhood in itself. During this renewal process the tenants are not evicted, and it is their decision to improve the room. The process of renewal is based on the tenants' own financial capacity, suggesting class differentiation within the chawl. This will be explored further in subsequent sections.

Redevelopment of the mill lands and redevelopment of chawls

The redevelopment of both the mill lands and the chawls has been occurring simultaneously. Mill lands accounted for almost 600 acres (243 hectares) of Mumbai, of which 270 acres belonged to the National Textile Corporation (NTC) and 315 acres to private mills. The creation of 600 acres of vacant land at the heart of the city following the closure of the mills became a matter of speculation for real estate developers, mill owners and the government. With the establishment of Development Control (DC) Rule 58 in 1991, the mill owners were allowed to develop the land by either demolishing or retaining the mill structures. If they chose the former option, they were required to relinquish 33 per cent of the total land to Brihanmumbai Municipal Corporation (BMC) and 27 per cent to the Maharashtra Housing Area Development Authority (MHADA). That left 40 per cent, which they were allowed to sell on the open market with an increased Floor Space Index (FSI) of 0.89.[2] However, retention of only 40 per cent of their land was unappealing to the mill owners, so some of them started the process of restoring the mill buildings and redeveloping them in a haphazard manner. Sometimes they also leased out parcels of land for various commercial purposes. This meant that they no longer had to surrender any land to the BMC or the MHADA. After a year several changes were made to the DC regulations. It was decided that the increased FSI would be given to the owner in the form of Transferable Development Rights (TDR) that could be used in the suburbs, not on the actual sites, for surrendering land for civic amenities and affordable housing. Second, mill owners were permitted to sell up to 15 per cent of their land without having to surrender any to the state. This amendment soon proved counterproductive as many mill owners did not surrender any land or sold only 15 per cent of their land. Some sold their mill buildings to others without surrendering any land. Under a 2001 amendment it was decided that only vacant spaces on mill lands could be shared between the BMC, the MHADA and the mill owners. Since this vacant land was a very small percentage of the total, the mill owners had to surrender almost nothing for public amenities. The available land for BMC and MHADA was reduced to 60 per cent. Through the DC Regulation Act of 2001, the mill owners were no longer required to surrender any land if they demolished mill structures for redevelopment (Adarkar et al., 2005; D'Monte, 2002; Correa, 2006).

Therefore, as a result of this modified DC regulation, the owners' share of the property effectively increased (D'Monte, 2002). Almost immediately, the entire area of the Kamla Mill was transformed into corporate offices, with no land allocated for open spaces or low-cost housing. The Phoenix Mill was developed into the High Street Phoenix Mall (see Figure 14.3), along with two high-rises and a discotheque. Once again, the redevelopment featured no low-cost housing or open spaces. After the new DC rules came into effect, the owner of the Piramal Mill was able to redevelop 32,712 square metres rather than the 14,200 square metres that had been available to him before 2001, while the area earmarked for recreational purposes decreased from 11,715 square metres to 1,533 square metres. The

Figure 14.3 High-end shopping mall on the Phoenix Mill compound, Lower Parel,
Mumbai

Source: the author.

area designated for public housing also decreased – from 9,585 square metres to
just 1,255 square metres (*Times of India*, 19 December 2004). Casa Grande – 'two
ultra-luxury 23-storey buildings' – has been constructed on the Matulya Mill compound (see Figure 14.4). The luxurious Ashoka Tower was erected on Morarjee
Mill Unit 1, while the Peninsula Tower was constructed after the demolition of
Gokuldas Morarjee Mill No. 2. The latter is now a world-class office complex on
400 acres of land – about six times the size of Nariman Points[3] (Choudhury and
Mehta, 2005a).Therefore, the redevelopment process soon expanded beyond the
boundaries of the mill lands to encompass the neighbourhood chawls, too.

The chawls have been transformed in recent years along with the transformation of the city as a whole. A number of them are already undergoing redevelopment, and several more are slated to follow. Approximately 15,000 chawls under
Rent Control were deemed to be in a state of dilapidation due to overcrowding
and the age of the buildings, so it was decided to demolish and replace them.

Figure 14.4 Gated community on the Matulya Mill compound, Lower Parel, Mumbai
Source: the author.

By 1990, real estate developers were exerting immense pressure for the redevelopment of the chawls. In response, the government came up with new regulations stipulating that all redeveloped buildings must re-house the original tenants in a better state than before but also provide extra floor space which may be sold on the open market at much higher rates to compensate for the cost of redevelopment (Shetty, 2011). Interviews revealed that the owner has first say on whether and when a chawl is to be redeveloped, followed by the tenants. If neither owners nor tenants initiate redevelopment, real estate developers may step in to begin the process. In order to persuade an owner to vacate a single room in one of the chawls surrounding the mill land developers will typically pay 50 to 60 lakh rupees (US$80,000–96,000). After acquiring the property, the developer is obliged to construct a new building for the tenants of the demolished chawl. This must meet all of the statutory requirements, but most of the remaining land may then be used to construct tall residential towers. Apartments in these are sold at extremely high prices, resulting in huge profits.

In the first phase after the demolition of a chawl, the tenants move to temporary accommodation. Sometimes the developers give them a lump sum based on current market rents, in which case most of the tenants will usually invest some of the money and then find somewhere cheaper to live. One interviewee, Ravi Dass, said that the builders provided no cash for rent when his chawl was redeveloped. Instead, all of the tenants were shifted to the Pratiksha Nagar transit camp. Some of Dass's fellow tenants have sold their rooms in the new building at very high rates and have moved to houses in the suburbs. Therefore, this whole process of chawl redevelopment generates certain aspirations in the mind of the inhabitants, and displacement of the original working-class residents becomes inevitable.

Debraj Balakrishna Ambaokar was a former mill worker who sold his two rooms at Prabhadevi for five lakh rupees (US$8,0000) each in the 1990s, and purchased two rooms in Worli Koliwada. By 2015, the value of the Prabhadevi rooms had increased to more than one crore (US$160,000) each. When asked about the redevelopment process, he replied candidly, 'Redevelopment is good because we get good amount of money and good price. Now, if I had stayed in Prabhadevi, the builder would have given us more than a crore, for the same chawl, the same building.' He now hopes that his Worli Koliwada rooms will be redeveloped. He also said,

> As per the government rules, the builders give us 350 square feet of space. But they incorporate the maintenance charges. In the initial period the maintenance charges are low. After one or two years the builders charge 3,500–4,000 rupees [US$56–64]. The building remains under the control of the residents for ten years. But after ten years a society is formed and the maintenance charges increase. The residents cannot afford to pay those charges, so they have to sell their rooms and move to the suburbs.
>
> (Debraj Balakrishna Ambaokar, interview, July 2011)

The prime intention of the builders is to evict the chawls' residents by offering cash incentives, occupy the whole area and redevelop with a focus on high-end residential towers, gated communities and a minimum number of redevelopment buildings. They would always much rather build a forty-storey building than a seven-storey building. In order to procure the entire chawl, the builders make an estimate of its value and then offer a certain amount of cash to the residents. Those with less bargaining power tend to leave the chawl, while the rest negotiate for more money.

With the redevelopment of the mill lands and the chawls, the city space is becoming a post-industrial area. Many former mill workers have left Mumbai altogether and moved back to their villages. 'Textile mill workers are a disappearing concept at present,' explained the trade union leader Datta Ishwalkar. Those chawls that remain are now occupied by the next generation of mill workers and people who work in other sectors. Ishwalkar further explained that

> The city is no more for the mill workers. They have to leave the city by any means. The mill workers want to stay in this city but how can they stay? A 225 square-foot room in a slum costs 25–30 lakh rupees [US$39,000–47,000]. People are selling their rooms and moving to the suburbs. This is not forced eviction – it happens according to their own will.
>
> (Datta Ishwalkar, interview, 2012)

Although Ishwalkar's comments highlight the vulnerable positions of those former mill workers who feel they have no option but to sell off to developers and move out, they also suggest rising aspirations among some other working-class dwellers, who prefer to wait and struggle on in the hope of securing much higher prices for their rooms. The construction of residential towers and rising land prices have proved extremely lucrative for many residents, so even in their utter despair they may look forward to windfalls through redevelopment. One interviewee who had spent her entire life struggling to make ends meet hoped for the redevelopment of her chawl so that she could live a better life. However, two others – Sunanda and her daughter Geeta – were extremely apprehensive about the possibility of eviction from their neighbourhood if their chawl was redeveloped.

The transition from industrial to post-industrial is reflected not only in the number of newcomers to the area but in the older residents who are trying to find a balance between the space where they have lived for decades and the new, globalised world. Through the process of redevelopment and the increasing availability and visibility of all kinds of electronic items, such as laptops, mobile phones and refrigerators, there is a further class contradiction and spatial contraction in the chawls. The contradictions of the outside world have entered the chawls in the form of 'commodity fetishism'. Some chawl rooms are filled with so many consumer goods that the residents scarcely have room to move. Datta Ishwalkar expressed concern about the city of Mumbai, as he felt that the changes in the spatial practices among the chawl dwellers reflected a wider transformation of the built environment. His discomfort over this transformation was related to diminishing space for members of the middle class and lower middle class.

Production of space

The eviction of tenants from their neighbourhoods and their gradual replacement with a more affluent class of people is an ongoing process but not yet complete. In addition to giving the city space an irregular skyline, it has also resulted in a complicated class structure. The contemporary redeveloped towers that have replaced demolished chawls stand cheek by jowl with high-end buildings and the remaining chawls, and they provide housing to former chawl dwellers but do not change their class status. Some former chawl dwellers experience an initial sense of pride and contentment when they move into a tower, but many of them ultimately leave the city. A standard 350-square-foot room in a tower, a box-like space, lacks many of the natural comforts and spatial practices of life in a chawl, which many old mill workers subsequently miss. In a melancholic frame of mind, Janardan Deshmukh explained that three generations of his family had spent their whole lives in his chawl, so he would miss it when it was demolished. He said, 'The chawl is strong enough to provide shelter to all the generations but the wages are not strong enough to let us stay in the chawls.'

The process of transformation has produced a new space – a space of class conflict, of dichotomy – new spatial practices and gentrification. There is a gradual effacing of the old and a creation of new space. The simultaneous disappearance of small restaurants, old grocery shops and *paan* (betel leaf) stalls and their replacement with fancy stores and innumerable fast-food stands are manifestations of Mumbai's gentrification, due to the decline of the textile mills and arrival of small-scale service firms and corporate offices. The business of *'khanaval'*[4] (Shetty, 2011: 60) and the *dabba* system are in decline. *Paan* shops that once catered to the working-class residents now sell costly cigarettes. The local trains that once carried the mill workers to and from work now carry office workers to their small-scale businesses. During one interview, looking out of his chawl window, Ramdas Panduram Harke pointed to the twenty-eight-storey building that was being constructed on the Piramal Mill compound:

> The road used to be very narrow here. People would walk all the time . . . there were fewer cars. Now people don't walk. With the construction of residential towers the number of cars has increased. More traffic signals have been installed. The place looks nice, no doubt, but people have suffered. There are very few mill workers now.
>
> (Ramdas Panduram Harke, interview, 2013)

Discussion

As a new spatial production, the former textile mill lands of Mumbai represent a gentrified landscape with new spatial practices. Gentrification is a widely used and well-travelled concept. When the term was first coined by Ruth Glass in 1964 it referred to the gradual displacement of London's working class from their traditional neighbourhoods, the arrival of the middle classes in those areas, and the consequent change in these boroughs' character as the new arrivals started to renovate the old dilapidated buildings (Lees et al., 2008). In New York, gentrification came to be associated with the 'back to the city movement', in which the middle classes returned to the central city area from the suburbs. Zukin (1987) characterised gentrification as the renovation of condominiums and the preservation of architecture and heritage in the construction of middle-class housing. For her, it also involved the conversion of lofts into studio apartments for artists' groups.

In Mumbai gentrification seems to be an amalgamation of various complex processes. The decline of the textile mills has had a profound effect on the surrounding area and especially on the neighbourhood chawls, turning it initially into a blighted landscape. This had been termed a 'donut effect' (Pendse et al., 2011: 6) in which a 'rent gap' (Smith, 1996) is generated. Real estate speculation over the vacant mill land leads to astronomical increases in its value and eventually to redevelopment. Once that process begins there is continuous displacement of the working class and changing spatial practices. This entire redevelopment process, based on the rent gap, is similar to Smith's (1996) concept of gentrification, whereas the process of working-class displacement and the former residents' replacement by members of the upwardly mobile middle class is more akin to what he terms 'revanchism'. Mumbai has not undergone a process of suburbanisation, which led to revanchism in the West; nor does its city planning follow the Western concentric-circle model. Here we argue that in the process of gentrification there is no *wholesale* replacement of the working class by the affluent middle class. The mill workers' chawls are not being taken over directly by the middle classes; rather, they are undergoing structural redevelopment. The simultaneous growth of high-end apartment towers for the affluent juxtaposed with the redeveloped chawls has meant a large proportion of the land is no longer occupied by the working class. Rising rents, rising land values and a shortage of space, along with the juxtaposition of rich and poor, have resulted in the displacement of many working-class families. Those who remain in the city are engaged in a process of continuous negotiation and/or contestation with the developers.

This has produced a uniquely heterogeneous city space instead of the homogenisation that has occurred as a result of most Western gentrification processes. Instead of complete class displacement, there has been an alteration in the built environment and simultaneous cohabitation of different classes, resulting in a transformation of everyday interactions. While this appears to be a case of classes intermingling, a strict segregation has arisen in the form of gated communities. Those working-class families who refuse to leave and cannot afford redevelopment are increasingly trapped. An invisible wall has been constructed between the rich and the poor, producing a relationship of power, segregation and confinement. Moreover, in their continuous negotiations with the developers in order to acquire better housing, the chawl dwellers indirectly initiate gentrification or become part of it.

Gentrification in the mill lands of Mumbai has resulted in the arrival of workers employed in small-scale manufacturing industries, service-based industries, a managerial class, an executive class and creatives. It has also generated a widespread informal sector. High-end restaurants, art galleries, micro-breweries and nightclubs are juxtaposed with small manufacturing firms within the old mill compounds, producing fragmentation and heterogeneity as well as a new form of economy and a new form of gentrification. This new economy has generated new jobs in the form of security guards, drivers and restaurant and nightclub waiters, attracting people from adjacent neighbourhoods as well as from the distant suburbs. There seems to be cohabitation and even a symbiotic relationship between the two economies, but a continuous process of merger and appropriation is taking place as well. Small eateries are taken over by big restaurants, residents are displaced from the mill compounds by more affluent workers, and high-end stores replace family-run shops. Gentrification from within has also occurred where some of the mill structures have not been demolished; instead, the interiors have been restructured into nightclubs or restaurants. New spaces are thereby created in old structures. For instance, the Phoenix Mill became a high-end shopping mall but retained the original chimney as a symbolic representation of the original building's heritage.

Conclusion

Mumbai has always (re)produced itself as a city of transformation. It has evolved from a cluster of fishing villages, to a trading centre, to an industrial city, and finally to a post-industrial metropolis (Chandavarkar, 1994, 2009). Therefore, the city has its own concept of growth which has always occurred along the line of class. According to Chandavarkar (1994, 2009), in the settlement pattern of Mumbai the rich traditionally occupied the southern part of the city while the poor lived in the central marshy lands. However, in the post-industrial period, Mumbai has expanded northwards, with the poor and marginalised pushed ever further in that direction. Hence, the central part of the city is now a space of contradiction and contrast.

This chapter has attempted to sort through this complex evolution from the point of view of the chawls. The chawl is the protagonist here. It is through the transformation of spatial practices within the chawl that we have attempted to explore the production of a new space both within and outside the chawl. We have pointed out that class contradiction is not only visible externally, in the juxtaposition of high and low structures, but can also be seen within the chawl itself. Several issues – such as the redevelopment of mill lands and chawls, changes in spatial practices and the displacement of mill workers from the chawls, the formation of a new middle class, contrast, contestation and negotiation of chawl dwellers with developers, the birth of new aspirations and the development of new working-class areas through the creation of new jobs are all highlights of this transformation.

Acknowledgements

This research work is part of Dwiparna Chatterjee's ongoing PhD dissertaion. Here we would like to express our deep sense of gratitude to Professor Kushal Deb for his constant support and guidance. We would also like to thank our fellow researchers Aneetha Rao Kasuganti and Aswathi Jerome for their comments on the previous drafts of the chapter and would also like to show our gratitude to all the reviewers for their constant reviews and valuable comments.

Notes

1 Chawls are the arrangement of linear tenements for the working class of Mumbai. During the operation of the cotton textile mills these tenements were specially constructed for the textile mill workers.
2 Floor Space Index determines how high a building may be built and it is directly proportional to the size of the plot. For example, an FSI of 1.0 on a 1000-square-metre plot means that the total floor space constructed in the building should not exceed 1000 square metres. In current building regulations there is a restriction on the floor space that can be constructed on any plot. The amount of floor space translates into the number of occupants. This has some relation to the carrying capacity of the locality in terms of water supply, sewerage, transport infrastructure and so on.
3 Nariman Points is the first Central Business District of Mumbai.
4 This refers to the system whereby a family (or even a single woman) would cook meals for most of the residents of their chawl.

References

Adarkar, N. (2011). Salaries and Wages: Girangoan, in N. Adarkar (ed.), *The Chawls of Mumbai: Galleries of Life*, Haryana: Gurgaon, 15–25.

Adarkar, N., Srinivasan, S. and Pradhan, A. (2005). *600 Acres of Mill Lands: For the Public or the Privileged*, Mumbai: Girni Kamgar Sangharsh Samity.

Chandavarkar, R. (1994). *The Origins of Industrial Capitalism in India: Business Strategies and the Working Classes in Bombay 1900–1940*, Cambridge: Cambridge University Press.

Chandavarkar, R. (2009). *History, Culture and the Indian City*, Cambridge: Cambridge University Press.

Choudhury, C. and Mehta, R. (2005a) I Am No Fat Cat . . . This Land is Mine, *Indian Express*, 27 February.

Choudhury, C. and Mehta, R. (2005b) Why Mill Body is a Hot Potato, *Indian Express*, 3 February.

Correa, C. (2006). Recycling Urban Land, in D. D'Monte (ed.), *Mills for Sale: The Way Ahead*, Mumbai: Marg, 16–27.

D'Monte, D. (2002). *Ripping the Fabric: The Decline of Mumbai and its Mills*, New Delhi: Oxford University Press, 187–231.

Fernandes, L. (2004). The Politics of Forgetting: Class Politics, State Power and the Restructuring of Urban Space in India, *Urban Studies*, 4(12): 2415–2430.

Ghag, P. (2006). List of 58 Cotton Textile Mills' Status as of September 2006, in D. D'Monte (ed.), *Mills for Sale: The Way Ahead*, Mumbai: Marg, 73–75.

Kidambi, P. (2007). *The Making of an Indian Metropolis: Colonial Governance and Public Culture in Bombay, 1890–1920*. Aldershot: Ashgate.

Lees, L., Slater, T. and Wyly, E. (2008). *Gentrification*, New York: Routledge.

Lefebvre, H. (1991). *The Production of Space*, Oxford and Cambridge, MA: Blackwell.

Pendse, S., Adarkar, N. and Finkelstein, M. (2011). Overview, in N. Adarkar (ed.), *The Chawls of Mumbai: Galleries of Life*, Haryana: Gurgaon, 1–11.

Schmid, C. (2008). Henri Lefebvre's Theory of the Production of Space: Towards a Three Dimensional Dialectic, in K. Goonewardena, S. Kipfer, R. Milgrom and C. Schmid (eds), *Space, Difference, Everyday Life: Reading Henri Lefebvre*, New York and London: Routledge, 27–45.

Shetty, P. (2011). Ganga Building Chronicles, in N. Adarkar (ed.), *The Chawls of Mumbai: Galleries of Life*, Haryana: Gurgaon, 58–66.

Smith, N. (1996). *The New Urban Frontier Gentrification and the Revanchist City*, London: Routledge, 28–45.

Zukin, S. (1987). Gentrification: Culture and Capital in the Urban Core, *Annual Review of Socioliology*, 13: 129–147.

15 Afterword

Creative city policy and social resistance

Margit Mayer

This chapter deals with the relations between neoliberal urbanism, cultural/ creative city policies, and movements engaging these policies. These relations have come into view in several of the chapters of Part II of this book. In this concluding reflection, the Asian experiences are put in conversation with global trends in neoliberal urban restructuring and the role of the 'cultural/creative city' as a global practice of neoliberal governing. As creative workers and artists have played such increasingly important roles in these processes in cities across the globe, this chapter explores some of the paradoxical ways in which cultural workers and other creatives have been implicated in these models of urban development. It first highlights some ways in which urban policy-makers around the world have sought to cope with the tensions entailed by neoliberalization, which have contributed to shaping various contemporary urban conflicts and contestations. The second section discusses creative/cultural city policies in terms of their ambiguous impacts on the urban movement terrain, exploring in particular movements driven by (sub)cultural insurgent groups. Finally, the chapter recontextualizes these findings within the larger interrelations between resistance movements and the local state and scans this restructured urban terrain for its specific potentials and difficulties.

Today, after several rounds of neoliberalization – roll-back, followed by roll-out, followed by a post-crisis round of austerity urbanism[1] – urban conditions have become fundamentally different from those of the Keynesian or socialist city, or of whatever model preceded it. Where there used to be welfare infrastructures, these have been replaced by workfare, and urban policy-making hinges ever more on business, real estate, and developer interests (all of them increasingly global) and less and less on the institutions of an (elected) state and its bureaucrats.

The latest round of neoliberalization in countries affected by the financial crisis of 2008 has been characterized by a devolved form of extreme fiscal constraint, which in still-stable countries (such as those of North America and northern Europe) is projected largely on to sub-national state scales, while in southern Europe it manifests at the national level as well, thanks to the politics of the International Monetary Fund and the European Union. Everywhere, though, municipalities have been adversely affected (except in flourishing wealthy cities), and many of these municipalities have developed an advanced form of austerity politics, which not only dismantles Fordist social welfare infrastructures (as during the first roll-back phase), but grinds away at whatever has survived repeated cutbacks and neoliberal restructuring. Four features of the resulting neoliberal urbanism have direct effects on urban social movements.

1   As in the early phases of neoliberalizing urbanism, the overarching political strategy continues to be growth first – that is, urban managers do whatever they can to accelerate investment flows into the city and to improve their position in the inter-urban rivalry. But they now increasingly engage in forms of locational politics that make more use of symbolic (and, where austerity rules, less costly) signature events and projects, and look for low-cost ways of attracting 'creative classes' to help culturally upgrade their brand. While many Asian cities (often with help from central government) have been able to pour huge investments into rebranding themselves as, for example, an 'ecologically resilient cultural city' (see Chapter 5, this volume), cities in the Global North have been seeking lower-budget ways of achieving analogous results. These have included simple measures such as facilitating the establishment of internet cafes and trendy coffee shops. And policy-makers are always on the lookout for innovative, and especially culture-led, efforts to mobilize city space for unfettered growth. These cultural branding strategies often benefit and incorporate some artist scenes and also subcultural or alternative movements as elements of such 'creative city' upgrading, particularly when these movements can be fitted easily into creative city projects, while further displacing or marginalizing groups that lack symbolic cultural resources, thus frequently triggering their protest.

2   In terms of governance, cities have been expanding the use of entrepreneurial forms of governance to ever more policy areas: they adopt presumably efficient business models and privatized forms of governance, and complement them with an increase in bidding for (speculative) investments (see Peck 2012: 649). This has entailed more out-contracting and a shift towards task- and project-driven initiatives such as developing a particular part of town, or competing for mega-events such as the Olympic Games or the Football World Cup. In these endeavours mayors and their partners from the business sector (often bypassing council chambers) set up special agencies to deliver target-driven initiatives that focus on specific, concrete objectives. To the extent that this type of governance entails the production of hegemony, this occurs via small-scale involvement: instead of the traditional modes of regulation designed in tripartistic, corporate and long-term ways, now flexible, small, and constantly changing concessions are made to shifting particular groups. In this ad hoc and informalized political process, *global* developers and *international* investors have come to play ever more leading roles: increasingly, it is they who shape the urban environment rather than local actors. These strategies and their lack of public transparency have given rise to many struggles over (the erosion of) representative democracy, as ever more residents who

do not conform to the standards of the global developers are excluded from 'the right to the city', yet continue to demand it in greater numbers and with louder voices (see Brenner et al. 2012; see also Chapter 12, this volume).

3   A third characteristic of the neoliberal city is how the intensified privatization of public infrastructures and services has transformed the relationship between the public and the private. Public infrastructures and services have been privatized so that socially oriented institutions of the public sector, public transport and utilities, and social housing are all now exposed to the market. Public coffers have been raided, often by government-sponsored private companies, which have turned public infrastructures and services into options for expanded capital accumulation by dispossession. Privatization has morphed into financialization as urban resources and assets have been turned into speculative stocks. This intensification of privatization has equally pertained to land: the extortion of maximal land rent works best through dedicating ever more private space to elite consumption, while the privatization of other (semi-public) areas, such as shopping malls and train stations, has meant limiting access to collective infrastructures and/or making their use more expensive. Whole urban centres – from Paris, Manhattan and London to Singapore and Hong Kong – are becoming, in the words of a *Financial Times* article, 'exclusive citadels of the elites . . . [T]he middle classes and small companies are falling victim to class-cleansing. Global cities are becoming patrician ghettos' (Kuper 2013). These enclosure strategies have triggered a variety of contestations, from protests against rent increases and occupation of social centres to guerrilla actions in the semi-public privatized spaces of surveillance and consumption (see Eick and Briken 2014). More recently, massive counter-movements have enjoyed notable successes through popular referenda that have forced municipalities to recommunalize water and/or energy utilities (see Becker et. al. 2015).

4   Finally, the neoliberal toolkit for dealing with intensifying social polarization has also evolved. During the roll-out phase of neoliberalism this toolkit consisted of area-based programmes (that is, some combination of neighbourhood, revitalization, and activation programmes) that were designed to stop the presumed downward spirals in 'blighted' neighbourhoods. Such programmes have now been severely curtailed and superseded by a novel two-pronged policy. On the one hand, attrition and displacement policies are pushing the poor to the outskirts or into invisible interstices of blight within the urban perimeter. Such coercive policies restrict both protest movements and vulnerable urban residents who now find themselves more aggressively policed or pushed to the margins. On the other hand, a plethora of more benign programmes seek to incorporate impoverished areas as well as social groups into upgrading processes, thereby to undergird efforts to attract growth, investors, creative professionals, and tourists. For example, large (development) projects and urban spectacles, such as garden shows and international building exhibits, are increasingly held in (ex-)industrial or social housing districts (such as Hamburg's Wilhelmsburg), while upscale hotels

can be found in the Bronx, New York City. All of these are designed as vehi-
cles to upgrade those neighbourhoods and induce a gradual residential shift.
However, they can be controversial (see, for example, the dispute between
Saskia Sassen and an activist organization in Wilhelmsburg[2]).

The interplay and repercussions among these currently popular policies have
reshaped the urban terrain by producing growing precariousness and impoverish-
ment even among social groups that used to be protected from downward trends,
at the same time as they have upgraded and revalorized not just central urban
districts but also a variety of 'up-and-coming' neighbourhoods. Some of these
policies trigger resistance directly, while others affect urban protest through the
way they shape the political opportunity structures. Particularly the policies
geared to attracting cultural producers and the so-called 'creatives', as well as the
policies designed to enhance the 'creative potential' of cities, impact directly on
critical segments of urban social movements. They have often induced a dynamic
interaction between policy-makers and the various institutions involved in
developing and implementing creative city policies, on the one hand, and urban
movement groups that have benefited from, sought to (re)shape, or resisted those
policies, on the other. It is on these interactions that the next section will focus.

Creative city policies: urban valorization through the cultural capital of creative producers

In looking at the creative/cultural policies installed to use art and culture as ways
to promote urban development and enhance the 'vibrancy' of the city, I am
particularly interested in exploring their effects on urban movements. But in order
to appreciate the ambiguous effects these policies have generated in this realm,
first a look at the development and goals of creative city policies may help to cut
through their apparent inchoateness.

Creativity has become a key concept globally signalling urban competitiveness, and a broad array of measures – from attracting knowledge-intensive
services to subsidizing cultural and creative economies – has been designed to
foster a concentration of firms and activities in the areas of new media, new technologies, fashion, advertising, tourism, and cultural industries. In cities within the
so-called first world, whose manufacturing sectors have relocated to regions
with cheaper labour and laxer working and environmental standards, it has
become the prevailing assumption that only these types of creative industries will
generate growth. But as this book has documented, cities across Asia are equally
seeking to harness the power of local culture and creativity to foster economic
growth and prevail in inter-city rivalries. Thus, Singapore has used state-led cultural planning to develop a 'creative sector' including art galleries, museums, the
performing arts, film production, entertainment centres, and theme parks with
the aim of 'enhancing Singapore as a tourist destination; improving the quality
of life and helping Singaporeans become more productive' (see Chapter 6, this
volume). Meanwhile, the declining South Korean city of Busan has sought to

forge a path to a brighter future as a cultural city through a top-down launching of an international film festival involving large-scale development projects, but also by 'nurturing and promoting the intangible social and cultural values' of the Totatoga district, where minimal funds (e.g., to provide artists with studio space), much to the surprise of city leaders, garnered maximum attention (see Chapter 10, this volume). Finally, Beijing's local decision-makers support the 798 art district because they understand it attracts considerable foreign investment and generates significant revenue, which in turn allows the artists to leverage and trade on their creative capital for their place–making (see Chapter 11, this volume).

However, the multiple and contradictory effects of these policies on communities, cultural actors, and activists have not yet been thoroughly researched, which is why an account of such interactions as they have unfolded over the last couple decades in Western cities might prove useful in spite of the structural and positional differences between Asian cities and those of the Global North.

Ever since the 'SoHo model' of the late 1970s[3] proved that the transformation of old warehouses and decaying tenement districts into valuable real estate could be accomplished merely by allowing artists to live and work in them, city governments have recognized the particular role such people might play in upgrading their cities. However, as not every city can rival New York as a natural magnet for the arts,[4] a new breed of urbanists soon identified an opportunity to develop – and sell – a new policy toolkit to city managers confronted with the problems of economically ailing cities. In 2000 Charles Landry emphasized 'the value of cultural industries which, as an interconnected sector, are perhaps the fastest growing in modern urban economies' (Landry 2000: 6). He focused on the creative talents of indigenous, existing populations, which, if appropriately supported, could revitalize a city's public and social life. Richard Florida (2002) also promised that, with the right tools, any city could become a creative city. In contrast to Landry's model, though, Florida's creative class was to be attracted from elsewhere, and for that to happen, he argued, a city must be vibrant, diverse, and have an attractive cultural infrastructure – then jobs would follow.

Both of these theorists have made impressive consulting careers out of selling their 'advisory services' to cities around the world.[5] Even though their methodology and categories have come under severe criticism (see Peck 2005; Krätke 2010; Pratt 2011), city governments across the globe nowadays define the construction of a 'creative economy' as a policy goal and have come to invest in 'soft infrastructure' such as galleries, cafés, juice bars, and bike lanes as well as in programmes which aim to keep artists and cultural workers in high-cost inner cities either by subsidizing their work spaces or by allowing them to 'squat' for limited periods in areas of transition, thus helping to prepare such sites for more lucrative uses in later years. Since most of these investments are far cheaper and promise better results more easily and earlier than investing in hard infrastructure such as luxury apartment blocks, office buildings or freeways, the concept of the creative city came to be seen as a quick fix for tackling problems of urban disinvestment. Apparently, all city managers had to do was make their cities culturally vibrant and cosmopolitan – aside from paying some hefty fees to the globe-trotting consultants who advised them on how best to mobilize their local creative economic potential.

Thus, local leaders everywhere are now preoccupied with culture: both culture as a productive force bringing in those economy-rescuing 'creatives' and culture as a critical component of the 'soft infrastructure' that is today's 'must-have' requirement in order to compete for mobile capital, jobs, the upwardly mobile middle classes, and tourist spending, and thus as guarantor of regeneration. Obviously, there is a broad variety of local cultural potential and treasures to be put to such productive use: cities have identified all kinds of unique aspects of the material and symbolic landscapes within their boundaries that might be seen as radiating sufficient 'indigenous authenticity' to attract tourists, investors, and upwardly mobile groups – and they have seized and built upon them. Most well known and publicized is the use – to great effect – of local art scenes that play big roles in city place-marketing campaigns (see Shaw 2013; see also Chapters 6 and 10, this volume); similarly, urban underground cultures and interim uses have been promoted and officially institutionalized into urban growth strategies (see Colomb 2012a: 140; see also Chapters 6, 10, and 13, this volume). Amsterdam's municipal authorities were among the first to acknowledge that the many artists' workspaces created in squatted buildings contributed to the favourable climate for the arts in the city. In setting up a bureau dedicated to the preservation and creation of 'breeding grounds' to ensure the continuous supply of affordable space for artists, they drew on the experience of former squatters (Pruitt 2013: 37).

Strategies that make use of cultural heritage and immigrant traditions are just as relevant in this context, as Ku has shown with respect to two contested cases of Hong Kong's culture and heritage development, and Bowen has shown in his study of the Cheonggyechon street vendors who have been integrated into Seoul's Folk Flea Market (Chapters 12 and 5, this volume). The instrumentalization of cultural heritage for valorization purposes has become very obvious in North American cities as they have highlighted artefacts and cultural legacies of their black and brown history in order to polish their brand – often at the risk of packaging ethnicity for consumption by tourists and gentrifiers (Hackworth and Rekers 2005). Exhibits and museums nowadays identify and celebrate local assets of African-American history (see, for example, Tarleton's (2014) description of the 'Black Radical Brooklyn' exhibition). Chicago's Bronzeville has seized on a (reconstructed) version of the area's black history (see Boyd 2005, 2008), while Los Angeles's Boyle Heights – along with Latino neighbourhoods in other US cities such as East Harlem in New York, Pilsen in Chicago, and the Barrio in Philadelphia – have used everything from Latin American and Mexican food to arts and murals in order to improve the image of formerly neglected neighbourhoods. Frequently, this has occurred by creating an exotic and adventurous – and apparently authentic – image (see Davila 2004; Wherry 2011), while at the same time opening up ethnicity for consumption and spectacle. What initially appears as a positive recodification of race attracts developers who exploit the momentum generated within the community and 'utilize nostalgic or popular conceptions of ethnicity to [re]invent neighbourhoods they seek to revalorize' (Mele 2013: 599).

It is the 'cultural capital' of creative producers and artists that city officials and developers most covet when they seek to increase the cachet of an area. For this purpose, developers will deliberately engineer the movement of artists into an area – at least until rents rise and the artists themselves are priced out, along with the original lower-income residents. Even when the process is not premeditated, developers are quick to spot areas where artistic energy and revitalization are flourishing, and target them for speculation and luxury development. Critics have labelled this process as 'artwashing' (O'Sullivan 2014):

> By highlighting the new creative uses for inner-city areas, [artwashing] presents regeneration not through its long-term effects – the transfer of residency from poor to rich – but as a much shorter journey from neglect to creativity. The process can happen by design, such as at the Balfron Tower or in East London's Hackney Wick, where landlords rented warehouses cheaply to artists as a preliminary step to residential conversion. It often happens organically, however, when developers spot areas that have attracted residents from creative industries, then earmark them as ripe for investment and remarketing to a new kind of customer . . . These artist communities are not long-lasting but liminal. In a rising property market like London's, artists can live and work in such situations only in the brief period between low-income occupancy (or vacancy) and an area's ultimate remarketing to wealthier incomers or absentee investors.

As a result, artists' arrival in previously marginal and often oppositional neighbourhoods is now perceived as a harbinger of rising property prices, displacement of existing communities, and a taming and upgrading of the landscape (see Bolton 2013). Holm (2010) distinguished four ideal–typical phases in this journey towards gentrification, in all but the last of which artists may be deployed as tools by the real estate business. In the first ('pioneering') phase artists form a sub-group who move into still de-valorized neighbourhoods, squat in lofts, and engage in non-commercial projects, such as self-organized artists' cooperatives, galleries, and performance spaces. Their precarious living conditions and bohemian lifestyles correspond to an urban area that is still cheap and has the allure of the 'grid and grime' of the long-neglected. During the second ('imagineering') phase a 'symbolic valorization' of a still economically de-valorized area takes place: arts-related spaces and shops plus an official media campaign change the image of the neighbourhood into an exceptional place that becomes marketed by realtors and city marketing officials. Sometimes the pioneering artists will deploy these new marketing images for their own self-promotion. At other times, they may resist the upgrading and 'touristification' of the neighbourhood, for instance by spraying graffiti (see Chapter 9, this volume). Alternatively, in settings such as Berlin, where anarchists and subcultural groups have spruced up dilapidated areas that are then marketed as 'hip' to investors and tourists, the activist–artists will deface or destroy their own murals and graffiti to make the area less attractive to potential newcomers (see, e.g., Henke 2014). In the third ('gentrifying') phase artists have decreasing value as a tool as rising ground rents facilitate infrastructure improvements and upscale shops multiply, while 'symbolic' cultural capital is replaced by 'real' cultural capital. Affluent gentrifiers start to move in, and poor residents start to be displaced. In the fourth ('completed' or 'supergentrification') phase, artists have no value as tools. The second 'economic valorization' that takes place during this final phase implies a closing of the rent gap, which means that formerly anticipated ground rent is exceeded by a far higher monopoly rent, with wealthy buyers and high-earning tenants paying an additional 'exceptional' rent for the now famous 'exceptional' place. All of the pioneering artists have been displaced, and the formerly bohemian, alternative, or genuinely innovative (creative) arts scenes have been replaced by arts institutions that cater exclusively to the gentry or by expensive shops and restaurants that extinguish the artistic atmosphere of the previous phases.

Not all places may complete this ideal–typical model. However, since different areas are undergoing different phases at any point in time, we can observe widespread participation by artists in 'staged' or policy-led regeneration initiatives as 'shock troops of gentrification' while others challenge the neoliberalization of their cities. Even when artists resist, though, they often find themselves paradoxically implicated in neoliberal development models. In order to explore the roles artists and cultural/creative workers have played or can play within existing frameworks – that is, within the constant evolution of neoliberalizing cities – the final section takes a closer look at these actors.

Creative/cultural workers between instrumentalization and resistance

In Florida's 'shell game' (Rosler 2012), 'creatives are defined under one shell as people whose mental engagement is at the heart of their work and under another as people who know how to live nicely, decoratively, and cheaply, and under yet another as primarily a high-earning, tax-paying economic grouping'. Obviously, all of these types exist in the neoliberal city, but it is important to beware of one becoming the face of the other – a move encouraged by Florida's messy definition of 'the creative class'. The previous sections have shown how the features characterizing aspiring competitive cities today not only attract high-income creative professionals into their centres, but also contribute to the elimination of affordable inner-city workspaces for creative professionals. As traditional subsidy programmes and support structures for artists have been slashed in the wake of municipal budget crises, ever more cultural workers have entered the ranks of the precarious. At the same time, city managers in both East and West, as shown above, have begun to respond to polarization and blight problems with 'benign' and novel policies that include a 'productive' role for (precarious) creatives, by making vacant space available and employing their skills to help transform blighted neighbourhoods into vibrant and fashionable sectors.

Dovetailing with these trends described in the previous section is a development within art and design schools, which, besides preparing their students for entry into the art market, have added departments of 'social practice' that teach new forms of activism and community practice to prepare the students for engagement with civic issues and articulation of their voices in the public realm (Rosler 2012: fn26). Thus, young creative arts and design graduates are now trained to take advantage of interim-use programmes as offered by city governments, foundations[6] and new agencies and networks[7] that identify, coordinate and mediate vacant office space or derelict buildings to enable legally sanctioned uses until investors can be found to develop them (see Colomb (2012a: 135–136) on Berlin). A similar process was observed in Busan (see Chapter 10, this volume), where city officials and cultural planners realized that artists could be mobilized for urban revitalization through small-budget, community-oriented strategies with impressive results.

In Britain, temporary artist-run spaces have been set up by local public institutions, supported by national agencies such as Arts Council England (Arts Council England 2009) as well as professional arts organizations. Ferreri and Graziano (2014) have studied recent art school graduates who submitted applications to work in such spaces. The successful applicants were aided by a 'creative development agency' for young artists called Emerge, which coordinates advisory support by borough arts officers on empty properties and legal issues so as to enable the artists to organize exhibitions and other projects 'in dialogue with local communities' (i.e., deprived communities) within limited time frames (ArtQuest 2012). Since the funding is meagre and the young creative arts and design graduates are mobilizing their own professional networks and 'know-how', the self-organized, non-profit, temporary art spaces they create are bargains for the city, but often leave the artists themselves frustrated. Ferreri and Graziano found that, while the applicants wanted to explore cooperative models and insert political principles of solidarity into their collective practice and art production, the commissioning bodies wanted fast, visible results, so they pressured the artists 'just [to] produce something', forgoing artistic integrity and nurturing, if anything, an emphasis on self-promotion and branding, while simultaneously wrapping this entrepreneurial art production in a narrative of charitable intervention or service provision to a community in need. 'The practical need to draw on the place marketing logic in justifying an art project through the value it may bring to an area in the form of real estate property value increase elicited strong and passionate reactions' (Ferreri and Graziano 2014: para. 38). What the artists had intended to be 'art activism' in the provided context turned into art-based place marketing that would benefit real estate developers and property owners.

Such hijacking of art activism is far from unusual, as is evidenced by the recent craze for pop-up temporary galleries and shops in recession-hit town centres (see http://emptyshops.wordpress.com). These venues, which are often legitimated as community projects with the goal of engaging local constituencies, tend to be short-lived due to their precarious arrangements with landlords and despite their objectives of engaging local constituencies. Though shaped by a more dominant role of the state, the arts spaces discussed in Chang's study of Singapore (Chapter 6, this volume) reveal similar problems in the form of a 'competitive rat race' which deprives artists of the time and space they need to engage with each other or the community.

Since these new cultural policies end up threatening (and frequently displacing), rather than effectively supporting, the cultural workers on whom they rely, the latter have spoken out and, in various places, have begun to organize and resist. In Berlin, for example, a manifesto signed by 2,420 cultural producers, curators and representatives of the local artistic, cultural and educational institutions was published in 2011 (Haben und Brauchen 2012). It demanded a public debate on the politics of urban development 'within the context of the current transformation process of privatization and commercialization of public space' and about 'how the production and presentation conditions of contemporary art in Berlin can be sustainably supported and developed away from media beacons' (Jakob 2012: 178). The manifesto contends that culture-makers' engagement in neighbourhood cultural work should not be itemized in city budgets as a trade-off for the anomie and disruptions of a shrinking social state (Haben und Brauchen 2012: 4). Like similar organizations in other cities, Haben und Brauchen champions, through its ongoing events and actions, the needs and interests of artistic producers in Berlin (see www.habenundbrauchen.de/en). On an international level, ArtLeaks is engaged in a similar struggle against the abuse of artists' and curators' professional integrity and the infraction of their labour rights by organizing workshops and assemblies and providing the artistic community with online tools (available at http://art-leaks.org/).

Going beyond organizing around their material and professional interests as cultural workers, artistically creative workers have also become strong voices in contestations over the neoliberalization of their cities, taking issue with the growth-oriented entrepreneurial policy agendas that city managers are pursuing as well as with the appropriation of culture and creativity that such agendas entail (Novy and Colomb 2013: 1820). For instance, cultural producers have played prominent roles in local struggles over Berlin's waterfront in the Mediaspree area and Hamburg's Gängeviertel. In the early 2000s the redevelopment of the Mediaspree (a 3.7-kilometre section of the eastern bank of the River Spree) encountered massive resistance from small-scale cultural enterprises and alternative temporary uses that had set up over the previous decade on various disused sites in the area. Some had become successful commercial enterprises while others maintained a more socio-cultural outlook or a radical political character (Colomb 2012a: 145–46; Colomb 2012b: 292–295). Protests against the plans for the site were launched as soon as a coalition of landowners, large media corporations and the Berlin Senate began to promote the redevelopment of the area into a large-scale office and entertainment complex for the media and music industries, with particular emphasis on the enormous scale of the project and the predicted privatization of access to the riverside. Alternative and leftist groups joined forces with 'subcultural actors (in particular from the club scene), creative entrepreneurs, parts of the alternative middle class (often coming from previous movements) and the marginalized' (Scharenberg and Bader 2009: 332) and succeeded in persuading the investors and the local state to reconsider some of their plans. The artists, cultural entrepreneurs, club owners, and activists who had initiated the temporary uses, and whom the Berlin Senate labelled 'young creatives' or 'urban pioneers', played a prominent role in this protest movement, fighting in particular against the eviction of all of the temporary users (Novy and Colomb 2012). From 2008 onwards, the movement was renamed Megaspree and expanded its agenda to address Berlin-wide issues of increasing rent, the displacement of low-income residents, gentrification and the eviction of alternative, subcultural projects (Holm 2010; Holm and Kuhn 2011; Novy and Colomb 2012).

The 2009 struggle to save a cluster of historic buildings in Hamburg's central business district, the Gängeviertel,[8] highlights cultural workers' rejection of creative city policies even more forcefully. The activists who planned the 'artistic occupation' – a weekend-long festival of performances, exhibitions, and music – had already endured a history of temporary, interim and precarious workspace arrangements (Twickel 2010). In publicizing this event, they drew attention to the planned demolitions and advertised the 'occupation' broadly, with the result that more than 3,000 people turned up to register their support. Rather than evicting the squatters (and their art), the municipal government entered into negotiations with the activists, which eventually resulted in a contract allowing for their self-management while the buildings were renovated rather than demolished (Twickel 2010; Füllner and Templin 2011). The artist–activists had deliberately invoked the city's discourse about Hamburg as a centre of culture and the arts, and their own role and importance as part of the 'creative class' within such a policy, rendering it impossible for the authorities to respond with the kind of repressive force they routinely deployed against squatters.[9] Going beyond their own interests, the activists also used their powerful position within Hamburg's city politics to criticize the functionalization of art in urban upgrading processes (e.g. Gängeviertel n.d.).

A couple of months after the squatting of the Gängeviertel buildings, a group of musicians, producers, actors, performers, and journalists (the city's so-called 'creatives') published a manifesto – 'Not in Our Name, Brand Hamburg' – which also explicitly criticized the instrumentalization of the arts and 'funky' artists as creative forces for an entrepreneurial city based on 'creative' economies such as media, fashion, design, software industries, and the arts (NION 2009). The press conference that launched the manifesto to the public was staged in the Gängeviertel. In the document, the signatories criticized how the working conditions of 'off-culture', the free scene, and alternative music clubs had deteriorated, while politicians continued to promote the city on the basis of its cultural vibrancy:

> The brand Hamburg is flooding the republic with brochures that turn Hamburg into a consistent, socially pacified Phantasialand with Elbe Philharmonic and ... gay parades, alternative art spectacles ... Reeperbahn festivals, fan miles

and Cruise Days. Hardly a week goes by without some tourist mega-event carrying out its 'brand-strengthening function'.

(NION 2009; see also Rinn 2014: 184–185)

Thus, while the Hamburg struggle was initially about the demolition of a cluster of heritage buildings and saving creatives' (precarious) workspaces, the politicization of the arts scene and its embeddedness in the local 'right to the city' network expanded the campaign into broad criticism of contemporary neoliberal urban politics for its oversupply of office space, residential developments for the (super) rich, rent increases for everyone else, shrinking social housing stock, the sale of public buildings and open spaces to the highest bidder, and the displacement of the poor and immigrants to the peripheries. The artists explicitly rejected the exploitation of their milieus and subcultures for the purposes of growth-oriented urban policies, stating in no uncertain terms their firm opposition to policies formulated in their name as well as the market-based urban development agendas that they camouflaged (Novy and Colomb 2013: 1832–1834).

These two German struggles highlight a pattern we see at work in the production of creative cultural infrastructures in Asia, too: whether in Seoul's Dongdaemun History and Culture Park, which 'incorporated' some of the previously resisting illegal street vendors of Cheonggye Street 'within the matrix of the same creative city development project that initially sought to exclude them' (Chapter 5, this volume); or in Busan's Totatoga project, in which the informal creativity of people who had been previously ignored or even victimized by the authorities was eventually recognized as a valuable asset in the city's cultural development strategies (Chapter 10, this volume). Thus, these groups have ended up participating in and lending legitimacy to their city governments' strategies. Yet the Hamburg struggle demonstrates that it is also sometimes possible to maintain and defend *self-managed* spaces for art, cultural production, and community activism within the restricted frame of the neoliberal city. Such success in achieving and defending autonomous space is certainly predicated on the fact that cities seeking to bolster their economies via 'creative city' and cultural policies *need* creatives and artists, and even grassroots (sub)cultural activism, which gives this 'creative class' at least a degree of bargaining power (see Birke 2011).

Many Asian cities still benefit from manufacturing-based growth, so they are not as reliant on their creative sectors as are post-industrial cities of the Global North. Also, the legacy of the developmental state is stronger. Thus, the activist–artscape in these countries is often more harshly regulated than is the case in Western cities. Still, what Luger describes as a 'uniquely Singaporean paradox' (Chapter 13, this volume) – that authoritarianism has facilitated arts-led activism by easing restrictions, providing space, and even encouraging critical art – is not quite as unique as he makes out. The same paradox is at play in the 'free West', where local governments also seek to limit and control artistic activism, even using similar 'divide and conquer' strategies that differentiate and filter out more 'useful' creative types from potentially disruptive ones.

However, the very asset that grants creatives leverage and bargaining power in their negotiations with city governments also demarcates its limitations: while the provision of cheap accommodation for artistic uses has become a widely shared and celebrated policy, 'non-creative' labour is becoming ever more marginalized and downgraded. Groups with space-making practices that are of little or no interest to municipalities have no legitimate claim to the right to the city and become increasingly stigmatized (see Atkinson and Easthope 2009: 71). As a key indicator of 'successful' creative city strategies consists in decreasing vacancy rates and increasing land values, it is intrinsic to these strategies that they trigger the displacement of low-income residents – including members of the creative class. Thus, when creative city strategies 'work' (i.e., when land prices increase), they result in the displacement of the very creative people they were supposed to foster (see Grodach 2013), but an even more rapid displacement of the many vulnerable groups that are immediately affected by the austerity side of neoliberal urbanism: precarious and undocumented workers; the unemployed and homeless; and other groups whose 'non-creative' behaviour is unwelcome in aspiring 'vibrant' cultural cities. Such groups are directly targeted by policies of attrition and austerity, which restrict and suffocate the spaces where they live as they are more aggressively policed, stigmatized, and even criminalized.

Thus, the dynamic that is set in motion by the new urban creative/cultural policies globally reveals the conditions for achievement in our increasingly unequal, polarized cities adopting the neoliberal creed. It is up to social movements and urban activists – including the comparatively privileged cultural insurgents for whom these policies have opened up some new spaces and new resources – to link up with the 'urban outcasts' (Wacquant 2007) whom the neoliberal city strives to exclude and push ever further to the periphery (see Mayer 2012, 2015).

Notes

1 The phases of roll-back of the 1980s (reacting to the limits of the Keynesian city), roll-out of the 1990s (addressing some of the problems created by the rolling back and austerity measures of the first phase), and, starting with the dot.com crash of 2001, a third round, in which urbanization became a global phenomenon thanks to the integration of financial markets to debt-finance urban development around the world in order to rekindle new growth, are well described in Peck et al. (2009). Austerity urbanism is covered by Peck (2012).

2 The controversial effects become manifest in a debate between the local community organization AKU Wilhelmsburg and Sassen, triggered by her interview as a member of the board of curators of the International Building Exhibit IBA. See 'Wir haben die Leute geschützt in tageszeitung', 5/28/2013: www.taz.de/!116970/; 'Open Letter to Saskia Sassen', 7/22/2013: http://akuwilhelmsburg.blogsport.eu/2013-07-offener-brief-an-saskia-sassen/; Sassen's reply: http://saskiasassen.com/to-aku.php or http://akuwilhelmsburg.blogsport.eu/2013-07-antwort-von-saskia-sassen-auf-offenen-brief/; and AKU's reply and invitation to Sassen: http://akuwilhelmsburg.blogsport.eu/2013-09-antwort-und-einladung-an-saskia-sassen/#more-2063 (all accessed 12 April 2014).

3 In the 1970s, galleries and studios flooded into Lower East Side and SoHo warehouses and lofts left empty by New York City's industrial decline. Sharon Zukin (1982) first

explored the correspondence between the appearance of art studios and galleries, and the upgrading of New York districts such as SoHo in the 1970s.
4 Meanwhile, however, the New York art scene, as well as that of San Francisco, has been smothered so severely by mega-gentrification that some authors fear it is doomed (e.g., Davis 2015).
5 See the website of Florida's Creative Class Group: www.creativeclass.com/about_ccg/who_we_are (accessed 2 November 2014).
6 An array of foundations and public–private institutions seek to foster the nexus of art and cultural creativity in the context of social and community-based activism, and have adopted the creativity meme connecting imagination, design, and advocacy. One of the place-making foundations that has been globally active in this sphere is the BMW Guggenheim Lab, which created 'a mobile laboratory travelling around the world to inspire innovative ideas for urban life' (Dover 2012).
7 For examples of such agencies and networks see, for example, www.artistsandmakers.com/staticpages/index.php/emptyshops or www.3space.org (both assessed 13 November 2014).
8 The city had sold the buildings to investors in 2003, and in 2008 the authorities negotiated a deal which lifted historical heritage preservation and planned for office and residential use. The buildings were still partially lived in and housed several galleries at the time (Gängeviertel e.V. 2012)
9

> The squatters and supporters of Gängeviertel come from the very bohemian milieu, for which, according to Richard Florida, metropoles nowadays have to compete if they want to play in the upper economic league. That is why politicians are using velvet gloves in dealing with the new Hamburg squatters. The eviction of Gängeviertel would do damage to the image of a city that pitches itself in glossy magazines as a 'vibrant metropolis' for 'cultural producers of all kinds'.
>
> (Twickel 2010: 79)

References

ArtQuest (2012) *How to Set up an Artist-Led Space: Empty Shops*, www.artquest.org.ul/articles/view/empty–shops, last accessed 12 December 2014.

Arts Council England (2009) *Art in Empty Spaces: Turning Empty Spaces into Creative Spaces*, http://press.artscouncil.org.uk/Content/Detail.aspx?ReleaseID=800&NewsAreaID=2, last accessed 12 December 2014.

Atkinson, R. and H. Easthope (2009) 'The Consequences of the Creative Class: The Pursuit of Creativity Strategies in Australia's Cities', *International Journal of Urban and Regional Research*, 33(1): 64–79.

Becker, S., R. Beveridge, and M. Naumann (2015) 'Remunicipalization in German Cities: Contesting Neo-liberalism and Reimagining Urban Governance?', *Space and Polity*, 19(1): 76–90.

Birke, P. (2011) 'Zurück zur Sozialkritik. Von der "urbanen sozialen Bewegung" zum "Recht auf Stadt"', in A. Holm, K. Lederer, and M. Naumann (eds), *Linke Metropolenpolitik. Erfahrungen und Perspektiven am Beispiel Berlin*, Münster: Verlag Westfälisches Dampfboot, 34–49.

Bolton, M. (2013) 'Is Art Really to Blame for Gentrification?', *Open Democracy*, 29 August, www.opendemocracy.net/ourkingdom/matt-bolton/is-art-really-to-blame-for-gentrification last, accessed 23 November 2014.

Boyd, M. (2005) 'The Downside of Racial Uplift: The Meaning of Gentrification in an Afro-American Neighborhood', *City and Society*, 17(2): 265–288.

Boyd, M. (2008) *Jim Crow Nostalgia: Reconstructing Race in Bronzeville*, Minneapolis: University of Minnesota Press.

Brenner, N., P. Marcuse, and M. Mayer (eds) (2012) *Cities for People, Not for Profit: Critical Urban Theory and the Right to the City*, London and New York: Routledge.

Colomb, C. (2012a) 'Pushing the Urban Frontier: Temporary Uses of Space, City Marketing, and the Creative City Discourse in 2000s Berlin', *Journal of Urban Affairs*, 34(2): 131–152.

Colomb, C. (2012b) *Staging the New Berlin: Place Marketing and the Politics of Urban Reinvention Post-1989*, London: Routledge.

Davila, A. (2004) *Barrio Dreams: Puerto Ricans, Latinos, and the Neoliberal City*, Berkeley: University of California Press.

Davis, B. (2015) 'Why I Believe New York's Art Scene is Doomed,' *Art Net News*, 12 January, http://news.artnet.com/art-world/why-i-believe-new-yorks-art-scene-is-doomed-214970, last accessed 12 February 2015.

Dover, C. (2012) 'Making the City: A Look back at the Berlin Lab', http://blog.bmwguggenheimlab.org/tag/berlin/page/4/, last accessed 15 December 2014.

Eick, V. and K. Briken (eds) (2014) *Urban (In)Security: Policing in the Neoliberal Crisis*, Ottawa: Red Quill.

Ferreri, M. and V. Graziano (2014) 'Passion without Objects: Young Graduates and the Politics of Temporary Art Spaces', *Recherches Sociologiques et Anthropologiques*, 45(2): 85–101, http://rsa.revues.org/1271, last accessed 22 January 2015.

Florida, R. (2002) *The Rise of the Creative Class: And How It's Transforming Work, Leisure, Community and Everyday Life*, New York: Basic Books.

Füllner, J. and D. Templin (2011) 'Stadtplanung von unten. Die "Recht auf Stadt"-Bewegung in Hamburg'. in A. Holm and D.Gebhardt (eds), *Initiativen für ein Recht auf Stadt. Theorie und Praxis städtischer Aneignungen.* Hamburg: VSA, 79–104.

Gängeviertel (n.d.) *Das Gängeviertel Info*, http://das-gaengeviertel.info, last accessed 2 November 2014.

Gängeviertel e.V. (ed.) (2012) *Mehr als ein Viertel. Ansichten und Absichten aus dem Hamburger Gangeviertel*, Hamburg and Berlin: Assoziation A.

Grodach, C. (2013) 'Cultural Economy Planning in Creative Cities: Discourse and Practice', *International Journal of Urban and Regional Research*, 37(5): 1747–1765.

Haben und Brauchen (2012) http://www.habenundbrauchen.de and http://www.habenundbrauchen.de/en/2012/01/haben-und-brauchen-manifest-2/, last accessed 12 December 2015.

Hackworth, J. and J. Rekers (2005) 'Ethnic Packaging and Gentrification: The Case of Four Neighborhoods in Toronto', *Urban Affairs Review*, 41(2): 211–236.

Harvey, D. (2001) *Spaces of Capital*, London and New York: Routledge.

Henke, L. (2014) 'Why We Painted over Berlin's Most Famous Fraffiti', *Guardian*, 19 December, www.theguardian.com/commentisfree/2014/dec/19/why-we-painted-over-berlin-graffiti-kreuzberg-murals, last accessed 15 March 2015.

Hodkinson, S. (2012) 'The New *Urban* Enclosures', *City*, 16(5): 500–518.

Holm, A. (2010) 'Gentrifizierung und Kultur: Zur Logik kulturell vermittelter Aufwertungsprozesse', in C. Hannemann, H. Glasauer, J. Pohlan, A. Pott, and V. Kirchberg (eds), *Jahrbuch Stadtregion. Stadtkultur und Kreativität*, Opladen: Budrich, 29–39.

Holm, A. and A. Kuhn (2011) 'Squatting and Urban Renewal: The Interaction of Squatter Movements and Strategies of Urban Restructuring in Berlin', *International Journal of Urban and Regional Research*, 35(3): 644–658.

Jakob, D. (2012) '"To Have and to Need": Reorganizing Cultural Policy as Panacea for Berlin's Urban and Economic Woes', in C. Grodach and D. Silver (eds), *The Politics of Urban Cultural Policy: Global Perspectives*, London: Routledge, 176–194.

Krätke, S. (2010) '"Creative Cities" and the Rise of the Dealer Class: A Critique of R. Florida's Approach to Urban Theory', *International Journal of Urban and Regional Research*, 34(4): 835–853.

Kuper, S. (2013) 'International Cities Are Turning into "Elite Citadels"', *Financial Times*, 17 June, www.businessinsider.com/global-cities-too-expensive-paris-2013-6, last accessed 19 November 2014.

Landry, Ch. (2000) *The Creative City: A Toolkit for Urban Innovators*, London: Earthscan.

Mayer, M. (1993) 'The Career of Urban Social Movements in West Germany,' in R. Fisher and J. Kling (eds), *Mobilizing the Community: Local Politics in the Era of the Global City*, London: Sage, 149–170.

Mayer, M. (2012) 'The "Right to the City" in Urban Social Movements', in N.Brenner, P. Marcuse, and M. Mayer (eds), *Cities for People, Not for Profit*, New York: Routledge, 63–85.

Mayer, M. (2013) 'Urbane soziale Bewegungen in der neoliberalisierenden Stadt', *Sub\ urban: Zeitschrift für Kritische Stadtforschung*, 1: 155–168, www.zeitschrift-suburban. de/sys/index.php/suburban/article/view/13, last accessed 31 July 2015.

Mayer, M. (2015) 'Das Recht auf Stadt ohne Armut', in ÖGFA (ed.), *Das Geschäft mit der Stadt. Zum Verhältnis von Ökonomie, Architektur und Stadtplanung, UmBau 28*, Vienna: Birkhäuser, 14–17.

Mele, C. (2013) 'Neoliberalism, Race and the Redefining of Urban Redevelopment', *International Journal of Urban and Regional Research*, 37(2): 598–617.

Not in Our Name (NION) (2009) *Not in Our Name! Jamming the Gentrification Machine: A Manifesto*, www.signandsight.com/features/1961.html, last accessed 14 December 2014.

Novy, J. and Colomb, C. (2013) 'Struggling for the Right to the (Creative) City in Berlin and Hamburg: New Urban Social Movements, New "Spaces of Hope"?', *International Journal of Urban Studies*, 37(5): 1816–1838.

O'Sullivan, F. (2014) 'The Pernicious Realities of "Artwashing"', *CityLab*, 24 June, www.citylab.com/housing/2014/06/the-pernicious-realities-of-artwashing/373289/, last accessed 17 January 2015.

Peck, J. (2005) 'Struggling with the Creative Class', *International Journal of Urban and Regional Research*, 29(4): 740–770.

Peck, J. (2012) 'Austerity Urbanism: American Cities under Extreme Economy', *City*, 16(6): 626–655.

Peck, J., N. Theodore, and N. Brenner (2009) 'Neoliberal Urbanism: Models, Moments, Mutations', *SAIS Review of International Affairs*, 29(1): 49–66.

Pratt, A.C. (2011) 'The Cultural Contradictions of the Creative City', *City, Culture and Society*, 2(3): 123–130.

Priemus, H. (2011) 'Squatters and Municipal Policies to Reduce Vacancy: Evidence from the Netherlands', paper presented at the Enhr Conference, Toulouse, July, www. enhr2011.com/sites/default/files/Paper-H.Priemus-WS21.pdf, last accessed 4 November 2014.

Pruitt, H. (2013) 'Squatting in Europe', in Squatting Europe Kollektive (eds), *Squatting in Europe: Radical Spaces, Urban Struggles*, Brooklyn: Autonomedia, 17–60.

Rinn, M. (2014) 'Konflikte um Stadtentwicklungspolitik in Hamburg. Eine Analyse von Akteur_innen, Praktiken und Dynamiken', PhD dissertation, Universität Düsseldorf.

Rodatz, M. (2012) 'Produktive "Parallelgesellschaften". Migration und Ordnung in der (neoliberalen) "Stadt der Vielfalt",' *Behemoth: A Journal on Civilization*, 5(1): 70–103.

Rosler, M. (2012) 'The Artistic Mode of Revolution: From Gentrification to Occupation', *e-flux*, 33, www.e-flux.com/journal/the-artistic-mode-of-revolution-from-gentrification-to-occupation/, last accessed 17 November 2014.

Scharenberg, A. and I. Bader (2009) 'Berlin's Waterfront Site Struggle', *City*, 13(2–3): 325–335.

Schnier, D. and O. Hasemann (2014) 'Bremen weckt schlafende Häuser. Zwischennutzung von leerstehenden Immobilien und Brachflächen', *Alternative Kommunalpolitik*, 5: 22–23.

Shaw, K. (2013) 'Independent Creative Subcultures and Why They Matter', *International Journal of Cultural Policy*, 19(3): 333–352.

Smith, N. (2002) 'New Globalism, New Urbanism: Gentrification as Global Urban Strategy', *Antipode*, 34(3): 427–450.

Tarleton, J. (2014) 'Black Radical Weeksville', *Urban Omnibus: The Culture of CityMaking*, 24 September, http://urbanomnibus.net/2014/09/black-radical-weeksville/, last accessed 31 July 2015.

Twickel, C. (2010) *Gentrifidingsbums oder eine Stadt für alle*, Hamburg: Edition Nautilus.

Wacquant, L. (2007) *Urban Outcasts: A Comparative Sociology of Advanced Marginality*, New York: Polity.

Wherry, F. (2011) *The Philadelphia Barrio: The Arts, Branding, and Neighborhood Transformation*, Chicago: University of Chicago Press.

Ziehl, M., S. Osswald, O. Hasemann, and D. Schnier (eds) (2012) *Second Hand Spaces: Über das Recyceln von Orten im städtischen Wandel*, Berlin: Jovis.

Zukin, S. (1982) *Loft Living. Culture and Capital in Urban Change*, Baltimore, MD: Johns Hopkins University Press.

Index

For Product Safety Concerns and Information please contact our EU
representative GPSR@taylorandfrancis.com
Taylor & Francis Verlag GmbH, Kaufingerstraße 24, 80331 München, Germany